שמירת שבת כהלכתה

SHEMIRATH SHABBATH

a guide to the practical observance of the Sabbath

Volume III

Rav Yehoshua Y. Neuwirth

SHEMIRATH SHABBATH

a guide to the practical observance of the Sabbath

the English edition of
שמירת שבת כהלכתה
Sh^emirath Shabbath K^ehilchathah

prepared by
W. GRANGEWOOD
in close collaboration with the author

III

from the second edition of the Hebrew
Volume II, Chapters 42-68

FELDHEIM
Jerusalem / New York

Typeset by Astronel

Feldheim Publishers Ltd.
POB 35002 / Jerusalem, Israel

Philipp Feldheim Inc.
200 Airport Executive Park
Nanuet, NY 10954

Library of Congress Cataloging-in-Publication Data

Neuwirth, Yehoshua.
Shemirath Shabbath.

Translation of: Shemirath Shabbath Kehilchathah.
"The English edition of Shemirat Shabat ke-hilkhatah,
Shemirath shabbath kehilchathah, prepared by W.
Grangewood in close collaboration with the author."
1. Sabbath (Jewish law) 2. Judaism—Customs and practices.
I.Grangewood, W. II. Title.
[BM685.N6513 1989] 296.4'1 88-33448
ISBN 0-87306-298-1 (U.S. : v. 1)
ISBN 0-87306-375-9 (U.S. : pbk. : v. 1)
ISBN 0-87306-477-1 (U.S. : v. 2)
ISBN 0-87306-478-X (U.S. : pbk. : v. 2)
ISBN 0-87306-820-3 (U.S. : v. 3)
ISBN 0-87306-821-1 (U.S. : pbk. : v. 3)

10 9 8 7 6 5 4 3 2 1

Printed in Israel

הקדשת המחבר

מצבת זכרון עולמים

לחותני, הר"ר **יעקב** ב"ר **חיים הלוי** זצ"ל **זון**
נלב"ע ט' כסלו תשל"ג
ולחותנתי, מרת **צירלה** בת החבר ר' **נתן** ע"ה **שילר**
נלב"ע ט"ז אייר תשנ"ג

אשר היו מוקירי תורה כל ימי חייהם
וגדלו את יוצאי חלציהם לתורה וליראת שמים.
יהא זכרם ברוך
ת. נ. צ. ב. ה.

ויה"ר שזכותם הגדולה תעמוד לנו ולזרענו
שלא תמוש תוה"ק מפינו ומפי זרענו עבג"צ בב"א.

מוקדש

על ידי המתרגם והעורך לאנגלית

ר׳ קלמן וואלף גרנג׳וּוד נ״י

לעי״נ הוריו

ר׳ **שלמה ברוך** ב״ר **ישעי׳** ז״ל **גרינוואלד**

נלב״ע ח״י אדר א׳ תשל״ח

ואשתו מרת **יוטא רויזא** בת ר׳ **זאב** ז״ל

נלב״ע כ״ג חשון תשכ״ה

ולעי״נ

חותנו הרופא החבר ר׳ **אברהם** ב״ר **יששכר** ז״ל **אדלר**

נלב״ע ט״ז מנחם אב תש״ח

וחותנתו מרת **טויבא** בת ר׳ **יוסף בן-ציון הלוי** ז״ל

נלב״ע י״ד אלול תשמ״ח

* * *

על ידי ר׳ יוסף נ״י בן החבר יהודה

לעי״נ הוריו

החבר **יהודה** בן החבר **יחיאל** ז״ל

נלב״ע ז׳ שבט תשל״ט

ואשתו מרת **חנה** בת ר׳ **שמואל** ז״ל

נלב״ע ב׳ שבט תשכ״ז

* * *

על ידי ר׳ **דניאל גריר** נ״י

לעי״נ הוריו

ר׳ **משה** ב״ר **שלום** ז״ל

נלב״ע י״ג אייר תשמ״ג

ואשתו מרת **מזל-טוב** בת ר׳ **משה** ז״ל

נלב״ע כ״ד אדר תשמ״ג

*

על ידי ר׳ **זאב הכהן שטרן** נ״י

לעי״נ אביו

מוה״ר **חיים** ב״ר **משה אליהו** ז״ל

נלב״ע י״ז טבת תשל״ז

היטיבה ה׳ לטובים ולישרים בלבותם

תהלים קכ״ה

PUBLISHER'S FOREWORD

The Hebrew edition of Rabbi Yehoshua Y. Neuwirth's *Shemirath Shabbath Kehilchathah*, first published by Feldheim in 1965, revolutionized the world of religious publishing. For the first time, an essential work of Halachah was presented in a format that rendered the body of detailed laws accessible to scholar and layman alike, to students, educators, and even those unfamiliar with the traditional source books of Jewish Law.

So well received was this work that it opened the door to the production of many other similarly formatted halachic texts, texts which had previously been relegated to the exclusive domain of learned rabbis and those well-versed in Torah study. At long last, Jews of every stripe who had not enjoyed the benefits of a yeshiva education, became aware of the intricacies of Jewish Laws and began to observe them meticulously. Even the more capable of navigating their way through traditional works, acclaimed the advent of the conveniently organized editions, and demand has continued to grow each year.

Rabbi Neuwirth's most notable achievement, however, was his application of Halachah to contemporary Jewish living, wherein electrical and electronic devices, manmade fabrics, modern medical developments, and a vast array of other innovations play an ever-increasing role. This salient feature generated boundless interest in his work.

The next natural step for Feldheim was to produce *Shemirath Shabbath Kehilchathah* in English translation, to answer the burgeoning needs of the English-speaking Torah world. The very nature of the material mandated an inordinate level of dedication in addition to a thorough command of language and style and a firm grasp of the Halachah. To our great fortune, Mr. W. Grangewood undertook this formidable task, and the result speaks for itself.

The first volume of *Shemirath Shabbath*, the English edition of Rabbi Neuwirth's groundbreaking work, appeared in 1984, and the second in 1989. That this third and final volume has been in preparation for eight years is not only an indication of the large quantity of material covered herein, but also of the care taken by Mr. Grangewood and the editorial staff at Feldheim to insure its accuracy.

Volumes I and II of *Shemirath Shabbath* each contained extensive indices, in addition to very detailed Tables of Contents. While the present volume does contain an extensive Table of Contents, the sheer bulk of a comprehensive index covering all three volumes rendered its inclusion here impractical. The intention, therefore, is to produce the full index in a separate volume of its own, enabling the user to identify a particular entry and then select the appropriate volume of text.

May Hashem grant that this work serve to bring His People closer to Torah and help them bear the joyous burden of His mitzvos with love and understanding.

CONTENTS

44: Kindling the Yom Tov and Yom Kippur lights: special laws

45: Kindling the Shabbath and Yom Tov lights when not at home

---

46: Receiving Shabbath and Yom Tov

47: Kiddush on Shabbath and Yom Tov: the cup, the wine and the order

---

50: The morning kiddush

51: Making kiddush for others

52: Prohibition upon eating before kiddush

53: Kiddush with or without wine

pages 863-870

54: The rule that kiddush must be followed by a meal — the Shabbath and Yom Tov meals in general

pages 871-890

57: Mentioning special days during birkath ha-mazon

58: The time when Shabbath and Yom Tov end, and the principles of the mitzva of Havdalah

59: Performing prohibited activities, eating and drinking before Havdalah

pages 935-947

60: Havdalah with wine and the order of Havdalah

pages 948-968

61: The spices and the light at Havdalah

62: Havdalah on special days

65: Laws of mourning on Shabbath and Yom Tov in general

66: Chol ha-mo'ed: its sanctity, the needs of the Festival, body care and laundering

---

67: Chol ha-mo'ed: avoiding a loss, commerce and activities in furtherance of a mitzva

---

68: Chol ha-mo'ed: public needs, impoverished workmen, a miscellany including activities involving trouble, and using the services of a non-Jew

Comprehensive index to Volumes I, II, and III appear in a separate volume.

The Contents of Volume I

The Contents of Volume 2

שמירת שבת כהלכתה

SHEMIRATH SHABBATH

a guide to the practical observance of the Sabbath

Volume III

Chapter 42

Preparing for Shabbath and Yom Tov

GENERAL APPROACH

awe of the Shabbath

1. *a.* God commands us in the Torah (Leviticus 26:2), "My Sabbaths shall you observe and My Sanctuary shall you hold in awe."

b. The author of the *Sefer Yere'im* (paragraph 410) explains the juxtaposition of the Shabbath and the Sanctuary (the Temple) in the following way:

1) Just as the Almighty commanded us to hold in awe and honor the Sanctuary, so did He command in regard to the Shabbath.

2) How does awe of the Shabbath manifest itself? By a deeply felt concern for its honor and observance.

3) Of course, the fear experienced is not of the Shabbath itself, but of He who admonished us to observe it.

looking forward to Shabbath

2. *a.* 1) An interesting terminological comparison is made by the Or Hachaim:

a) in Exodus 31:16 appears the exhortation, "The Children of Israel shall **keep** the Shabbath";

b) in Genesis 37:11 we are told of Jacob's reaction on hearing his son Joseph's dreams, "and his father **kept** the matter (in mind)."

2) Rashi explains the latter verse as meaning that Jacob waited with anticipation for the time when the dreams would be fulfilled.

3) Similarly, a person should keep the Shabbath in mind and look forward to it with eager anticipation.

b. 1) The verse in Exodus continues (literally translated), "to make the Shabbath...."

2) How can one make the Shabbath? One makes and prepares in advance whatever one needs, so that

it will be worthy to honor the Shabbath (Rabbeinu Bachaye).

remembering Shabbath during the week

3. *a.* "Remember the Shabbath day to keep it holy" (Exodus 20:8).

b. The Mechilta, as explained by Nachmanides and other commentators, sees in this an exhortation to remember Shabbath throughout the week.

c. 1) Thus, whenever one comes across anything particularly tasty, one should keep it for Shabbath.

2) Moreover, Hebrew does not give special names to the days of the week, like other languages, but refers to them as "the first day (after Shabbath)," "the second day (after Shabbath)" and so on.

leaving the best for Shabbath

4. *a.* 1) It is said of Shamai the Elder that every day of his life he ate in honor of Shabbath.

2) If a suitable animal came his way, he would say, "This is for eating on Shabbath."

3) If he found a better one, he would eat the first and leave the second one for Shabbath.

b. 1) Hillel the Elder took a different approach.

2) He had absolute trust in God to provide him day by day with his needs, including an appropriately superior animal to slaughter for Shabbath.

c. However, since not everybody has sufficiently strong faith to prevent him worrying about the future, even Hillel would agree that the ordinary person should act as Shamai did.

washing clothes

5. *a.* 1) Ezra the Scribe laid down the rule that the people were to wash their clothes on Thursday in honor of Shabbath.

2) They were not to wait until Friday, so that they should be free to busy themselves then with the other preparations for Shabbath.

b. If the Fast of the Ninth of Av falls on a Thursday, one must not do one's washing during that day, but

1) should do it at the end of the Fast, on Thursday night, and
2) need not wait until the morning after the Fast (Friday morning), as one would usually have to do.

6. *a.* 1) It is better to buy what one requires for Shabbath on Friday, rather than on Thursday. *buying for Shabbath*
2) In this way, it is more apparent that one is making the purchase in honor of Shabbath.

b. 1) This applies to provisions which do not need a great deal of preparation, such as drinks.
2) Provisions which do require a great deal of preparation, such as meat and fish, should preferably be bought on Thursday.
3) If one buys them on Thursday, one will have longer to prepare them and make all one's other Shabbath arrangements on Friday.

c. When buying, one ought to say that one is doing so in honor of Shabbath.

7. *a.* The Children of Israel in the desert prepared the manna for Shabbath immediately after collecting it on Friday morning (Talmud Bavli, *Shabbath* 117b, on Exodus 16:5). *starting early on Friday*

b. Likewise, one should make an early start with one's Shabbath preparations immediately after prayers on Friday morning.

c. Nonetheless, Torah-study sessions which regularly follow prayers should be completed first.

SEPARATION OF *CHALLA*

8. *a.* Since ancient times, it has been the custom for the Jewish woman to make a special effort, on Friday or on the day before Yom Tov, to do her own baking. *why bake for Shabbath?*

b. This is yet another way of honoring Shabbath or Yom Tov.

c. A further reason for the custom is that it enables the woman to fulfill the mitzva of taking *challa*,* so that, all in all, it is a custom well worth preserving.

quantities for taking challa

9. *a.* *Challa* need not be taken unless the dough is made from a minimum amount of flour.

b. The minimum amount is a *kav* and a quarter, equivalent in volume to forty-three and one fifth eggs.

c. In practice, *challa* is taken,

1) without reciting a blessing, when the amount of flour is 1,200 grams (about 2 2/3 lb.) or more, but less than 1,660 grams (about 3 2/3 lb.), and,

2) after reciting the blessing appearing in paragraph 12 below, when the amount of flour is 1,660 grams or more.

d. Some have the custom not to recite the blessing unless the amount of flour is 2,250 grams (nearly 5 lb.) or more.

e. Although the average housewife does not usually bake such quantities, except when preparing for Shabbath or Yom Tov, she should not forget to take *challa* in the event that she does bake enough in the middle of the week.

combining doughs to take challa

10. *a.* 1) One takes *challa* from two doughs together, even though neither by itself contains the minimum quantity of flour, if

a) both doughs belong to the same person,

b) both are made from the same type of flour (for instance both wheat or both barley),

c) one would not be disturbed if they became intermingled and

d) the total amount of flour contained in both together is at least 1,660 grams (or 2,250 grams in accordance with the second custom mentioned in paragraph 9 above).**

---

* She should, of course, take *challa* only if the dough contains the requisite quantities of flour. (See paragraphs 9 to 11 below.)

** If the total amount of flour is less, but there are at least 1,200 grams, then *challa* should be taken without reciting a blessing.

2) One should recite the appropriate blessing and take *challa* in the manner which will be described.

3) Before reciting the blessing, both doughs should be put either

a) into one container and (if any dough protrudes above the sides of the container) covered with a cloth or vessel or

b) onto a cloth which should be folded over to cover them both.

4) One should see to it that the doughs are touching.

5) All of the above applies not only in the case of doughs, but also in the case of already baked products (from which *challa* was not taken earlier).

b. 1) A dough intended for bread and a dough intended for cake cannot be taken into account cumulatively to make up the minimum amount required for separating *challa*, because one is in fact particular to keep them from intermingling.

2) This is so even if one puts them both into the same container, or covers them both with the same cloth.

3) a) The same applies when one puts together baked products made from separate doughs, each of which was too small for *challa* to be taken.

b) One cannot take the cumulative quantity into account, if the differences between them are such that one is particular to keep them from intermingling.

challa from dough one intends to divide

11. *a.* 1) Sometimes, one makes a dough with the intention of dividing the resulting **baked products** into two separate portions.

2) For example, out of one dough, one may intend to make several cakes, some of which will be eaten on the following day and some of which will be put away for a subsequent Shabbath.

3) One should take *challa* from the dough and recite the blessing in the usual way (when the conditions set out in paragraph 9 above are fulfilled), even if

each portion, when separated, will contain less than 1,200 grams of flour.

b. 1) *Challa* should similarly be taken when

a) one intends to divide **the dough itself** into two portions, so as to keep one portion (unbaked) for use on a subsequent occasion, but

b) the portions will not be of different kinds, which one is particular to keep separate (as in paragraph 10*b* above).

2) In this case, however, the blessing should not be recited if no individual portion will contain 1,660 grams of flour (or 2,250 grams in accordance with the custom mentioned in paragraph 9*d* above).

c. 1) On the other hand, *challa* is not taken if

a) **the unbaked dough** is to be divided into two (or more) portions,

b) no portion by itself will contain as much as 1,200 grams of flour, and

c) one is particular to keep each portion separate.

2) This might occur where

a) one portion is to be used for making bread and the other for making cake or

b) each portion is to be used for making a different type of cake.

d. 1) There are manufacturers of food and baked products who knead a large quantity at a time and then divide it into small portions for sale as ready-to-bake doughs.

2) *Challa* should be taken from the dough before any of it leaves the factory.

3) The blessing should be recited even if each of the subdivided portions contains less than 1,200 grams of flour.

4) a) The division in this case does not affect the obligation to take *challa* and recite a blessing, since it is made, not for any substantive reason, but purely as a means of facilitating sales.

b) That this is so can be seen from the fact that,

were the subdivided doughs to remain unsold, the manufacturer would not hesitate to combine them again and use them to make whatever other product was commercially expedient.

12. *a.* 1) The practice when taking *challa* is to remove a quantity of dough (or of the baked product) having a minimum volume of 19.2 cubic centimeters (1.14 cubic inches). *how to take challa*

2) The blessing to be recited on separating *challa* is as follows:

בָּרוּךְ אַתָּה יהוה אֱלֹהֵינוּ מֶלֶךְ הָעוֹלָם, אֲשֶׁר קִדְּשָׁנוּ בְּמִצְוֹתָיו, וְצִוָּנוּ לְהַפְרִישׁ חַלָּה.

"Blessed art Thou, O Lord our God, King of the universe, Who has sanctified us with His commandments and has commanded us to separate *challa*."

3) After the blessing, what one has separated should be explicitly designated as *challa*.

b. 1) *Challa* may be eaten *what to do with challa*

a) only by a *kohen* who is in a state of purity (as defined by the Halacha) **and**

b) only if the *challa* itself is undefiled (as defined by the Halacha).

2) Nowadays, for practical purposes, all *kohanim* are in a state of impurity, and all *challa* is defiled.

3) a) Consequently, the *challa* removed cannot be eaten, and is burned.*

b) A person who is not a *kohen* may not derive any benefit from the heat produced when *challa* is burned, but

c) one may give *challa* to a *kohen* to burn, and it is permissible for the *kohen* to enjoy such benefit as he can derive from its heat.

* If burning the *challa* presents a difficulty, one may wrap it in two layers of paper, or put it into a plastic bag, and then deposit it in the garbage.

taking challa after baking

13. While *challa* should be removed from the dough, if one has forgotten to do so, one should separate it after baking.

omission in taking challa

14. *a.* As a general rule, if one forgot to take *challa* before Shabbath or Yom Tov began, one cannot separate it on Shabbath or Yom Tov. (See Chapter 11, paragraph 16.)

b. For exceptions to this rule, see Chapter 11, paragraphs 18 and 19 and 21 to 28.

c. If one forgets to take *challa* from dough kneaded outside what the Halacha regards as the Land of Israel, then, since the obligation to separate *challa* there has always been only a Rabbinical one,

1) one is permitted to eat the bread or cake in question, **but**

2) one must leave over a piece from which one will separate the *challa* at the end of Shabbath or Yom Tov.

(See Chapter 31, paragraph 41.)

ACQUIRING FOOD

spending for Shabbath and Yom Tov

15. *a.* One honors Shabbath and Yom Tov by the zeal with which one prepares for them.

b. One should expend every effort in making the necessary preparations to the best of one's ability, remembering that what one receives from Heaven for this purpose is over and above what one receives for one's day-to-day budget.

c. 1) a) That is to say, in general, the amount one receives during the year towards satisfaction of one's material needs is fixed in Heaven from one Rosh Hashana to the next.

b) Indeed, one should be careful not to overspend, in case one spends more than one has been allotted.

2) With regard to Shabbath and Yom Tov, however, we are promised that, if we spend more, so leaving

ourselves less for the rest of the week, we will be granted more from Heaven.*

meat, wine and fish

16. *a.* While there is no actual obligation to eat meat and drink wine on Shabbath, the Torah Sages recommended that one ought to be as liberal with meat, wine and other delicacies as one's circumstances permit.

b. 1) It is a good thing to make a point of having not less than two dishes, and of eating fish, at each of the three Shabbath meals.

2) Of course, one need not eat fish if one does not like it, since Shabbath is meant to be enjoyed.

giving to the poor

17. *a.* Those who are in charge of the distribution of charity should try to ensure that each poor person has the wherewithal to enjoy Shabbath (or Yom Tov) in the manner to which he has been accustomed.

b. At all events, they should not give each person less than is sufficient for three Shabbath meals (or two Yom Tov meals for every day of Yom Tov).

those with enough for only two Shabbath meals

18. *a.* Someone who has food, but only enough for two (instead of the required three) Shabbath meals, can fulfill the mitzva of enjoying Shabbath with that.

b. Such a person should not beg to obtain more food for Shabbath.

c. To these particular circumstances, the Rabbis applied the maxim, "Make your Shabbath like a weekday, rather than have resort to other people."

d. Still, it is only right that a person in this position should do whatever else he can to keep the additional mitzva of eating a third Shabbath meal.

e. 1) The rules set out in the two preceding paragraphs, and in the ensuing paragraph, apply also on Yom Tov, but

---

* The same applies to the amount one spends on teaching one's children Torah.

2) there is no special mitzva obligating us to eat a third meal on Yom Tov (as explained in Chapter 54, paragraph 27).

borrowing for Shabbath

19. *a.* If one has no ready cash, one should borrow so that one should be able to perform the mitzva of enjoying Shabbath.

b. In this case, one can rely on the Almighty to provide one with the means of discharging the debt.

c. The Talmud Bavli (*Beitza* 15b) records God's promise, "My children, borrow on My account to sanctify the day; trust in Me and I shall pay."

d. One may even borrow money at interest (in a way that does not contravene the general prohibition against paying interest).

KASHRUTH

roasting and baking in same oven

20. *a.* 1) One's preparations for Shabbath or Yom Tov must not be at the expense of one's diligent observance of the usual rules of Kashruth.

2) Some common situations in which care must be taken appear in this and the following paragraphs.

b. 1) One should not roast meat, and bake food containing dairy products, inside the same oven compartment, unless either the meat or the food being baked is kept covered.

2) The same applies if the food to be baked is *parve*, but is intended to be eaten with dairy products.

3) Covering may be either with a lid or by means of wrapping, for instance in aluminum foil.

4) The prohibition is not confined to roasting the meat and baking the food in one oven compartment at the same time, but extends to baking dairy food in the same oven compartment even a considerable time after the meat has been roasted in it (and vice versa).

cooking in same oven

21. *a.* Similarly, one should not cook two pots, one containing meat products, or *parve* food intended to be eaten with meat products, and the other dairy food, inside the same, closed oven compartment, unless one of them is covered.
b. The same applies if one of the pots contains *parve* food intended to be eaten with dairy products, and the other contains meat products.
c. Here too the prohibition is not confined to cooking both pots in one oven compartment at the same time.
d. It extends to cooking the second pot (uncovered) in the same compartment, even a considerable time after the compartment has been used for cooking meat or dairy products (uncovered), as the case may be.

baking parve food in oven previously used for meat

22. If an oven compartment has been used for roasting uncovered meat, then, although it may not be used for baking dairy food uncovered, there is room for permitting its use to bake uncovered *parve* food intended to be eaten with dairy products, but only if
a. one has no other suitable oven available,
b. there is no practicable way of covering the *parve* food while it is baking and
c. at least twenty-four hours have elapsed since the uncovered meat was roasted.*

broiling unkashered meat or liver

23. *a.* An oven compartment that one uses for roasting meat may also be used for broiling meat or liver which has not been kashered (by extracting the blood in accordance with the Halacha).
b. One should take care not to broil the meat or liver at too high a temperature (because this would result in its being burnt on the outside, but not properly broiled inside, so that the meat or liver would remain unkashered).
c. The tray or other receptacle into which the blood drips

---

* The same applies to baking uncovered *parve* food intended to be eaten with meat products, in an oven compartment used for baking uncovered dairy products.

becomes *taref* and must not be used in contact with Kosher food.

d. 1) Liver must not be roasted in a microwave oven.

2) This is because the blood is cooked inside the liver by the radiation and does not come out.

TRAVELING ON FRIDAY OR THE DAY BEFORE YOM TOV

general rule

24. *a.* 1) As a general rule, a person may not walk more than three *parsaoth* after daybreak on Friday or the day before Yom Tov.

2) This is the distance which the average man would traverse if he walked until one third of the day had elapsed.

application of rule

b. 1) The object of the rule is to ensure that the traveler arrives at his destination in good time to have his Shabbath or Yom Tov meals prepared for him.

2) Consequently, the restriction is applicable only if he fails to announce his arrival in advance.

3) If he does give notice in time, he can walk much farther, since the necessary preparations can be made at his destination, while he is still under way.

4) a) Similar considerations apply when he knows that generous quantities of food are customarily prepared for the Shabbath and Yom Tov meals at his destination.

b) In those circumstances, it is not the practice to adhere strictly to the limitation in distance, since his unexpected arrival will not necessitate any special preparations.

travel by vehicle

c. According to some authorities, parallel restrictions apply to traveling in a vehicle on Friday or on the day before Yom Tov (making allowance for the greater distance a vehicle traverses in a third of the day).

what to do in practice

d. 1) Given the availability of modern methods of communication, the above restrictions will not often be applicable, but, in any event,

a) one must plan one's journey carefully to be certain of reaching one's destination in good time, before Shabbath or Yom Tov,
b) one must make allowances for the possibility of unforeseen delays and
c) one must avoid placing oneself in a situation where one might risk violating Shabbath or Yom Tov.

2) See also Chapter 30, paragraph 55.

EATING ON FRIDAY OR THE DAY BEFORE YOM TOV

25. *a.* Part of the honor due to Shabbath and Yom Tov is to enter upon them with a longing to partake of the Shabbath or Yom Tov meal. *purpose of restrictions*

b. The prior care which this necessitates finds expression in a number of different situations, as explained in the following paragraphs.

c. See also Chapter 47, paragraph 21.

26. *a.* Subject to the exceptions mentioned in paragraph 27 below, it is forbidden, throughout Friday or the day before Yom Tov, to have a meal which is not one's customary weekday meal. *special meals: general rule*

b. One should not, therefore, invite friends to a luncheon.

c. Even a meal which is a mitzva is also prohibited, if the proper time for it is not actually on that day.

d. Thus, one should not arrange a full-scale meal to celebrate the completion of a tractate of the Talmud, unless its study has been completed that day.

27. *a.* 1) A meal which is a mitzva may be arranged for Friday or for the day before Yom Tov, if that is the proper time for it. (For examples, see *b* below.) *meals which are a mitzva*

2) One ought to arrange the meal for the morning, if this is not too difficult.

3) If, for any reason, one has does not have the meal in the morning, one may have it after midday.*
4) In that event, if the meal takes place before the last quarter of the day,** one may eat as much as it is usual to serve at such a meal.***
5) However, should the last quarter of the day already have begun, one must be careful not to eat too much and, in particular, may not eat a large quantity of bread, so that one will be able to eat the Shabbath or Yom Tov meal in the evening with appetite.

b. The following are examples of meals which are affected by these rules:
1) the third Shabbath meal on a Shabbath which is the day preceding Yom Tov;
2) the daytime meal on a Yom Tov which falls on Friday, if one has not managed to eat it before midday;
3) the celebration meal eaten after a circumcision which takes place on a Friday or on the day before Yom Tov (whether on the eighth day from birth or subsequently);
4) the celebration meal eaten when a firstborn son is redeemed, if the ceremony takes place on a Friday or on the day before Yom Tov (whether on the thirty-first day from birth or subsequently);
5) the Purim banquet, when Purim falls on a Friday;
6) a meal eaten in honor of a bar mitzva, on the actual day of the celebrant's thirteenth birthday, when it falls on a Friday or on the day before Yom Tov.

avoiding a late meal

28. *a.* It is proper, during the last quarter of the day*** on Friday or on the day before Yom Tov, to refrain from partaking even of one's customary weekday meal.

---

* A "day," for these purposes, means the hours between sunrise and sunset.

** If the meal is likely to take a long time, as in the case of a meal to celebrate a circumcision, one should recite the afternoon prayer before washing one's hands to eat.

*** A "day," for these purposes, means the hours between sunrise and sunset.

b. During the short winter days, it is proper to refrain from such earlier time as will enable one to eat the Shabbath or Yom Tov meal in the evening with appetite.

29. *a.* One may have light snacks, that is to say without sitting down to a regular meal, throughout the day, up to the beginning of Shabbath or Yom Tov. *snacks*

b. Nonetheless, one must not eat or drink anything from the moment one has received Shabbath, or the public has done so (until after *kiddush*), as explained in Chapter 43, paragraphs 45 to 47, and Chapter 52, paragraphs 1 to 4.

30. *a.* During the last quarter of the day* on the day preceding Pesach, it is forbidden to eat a proper meal, *the day before Pesach*

1) not even one's customary weekday meal,
2) even if neither *chametz* nor matza will form part of that meal.

b. 1) However, one may eat a little fruit and vegetables, or small quantities of meat or fish, but
2) one must not eat one's fill of them.

c. The same rules apply on the day preceding Sukkoth.

d. See Chapter 56, paragraph 12, for how to eat the third Shabbath meal when the day before Pesach occurs on Shabbath.

31. *a.* It is the custom for neighbors or friends to bring relatives of a deceased their first meal after the burial. *the first meal for mourners*

b. Since this practice is not obligatory, it is as well not to provide the meal close to the commencement of Shabbath or Yom Tov, as the mourners too have a duty to honor the day by enjoying their Shabbath or Yom Tov meal.

c. For further details, see Chapter 65, paragraph 2.

---

* See previous note.

BUSYING ONESELF WITH WORKADAY ACTIVITIES ON THE DAY BEFORE SHABBATH OR YOM TOV

general rule

32. *a.* The general rule is that one should cease busying oneself with workaday activities some time before Shabbath or Yom Tov commences.

b. Numerous exceptions to the rule are mentioned in the succeeding paragraphs.

c. 1) The length of the period which should be free of activity depends on the length of the day (from sunrise to sunset).

2) The day (from sunrise to sunset) is divided into twelve equal parts ("variable hours").

3) Workaday activity should cease two and a half "variable hours" before sunset.

d. 1) The Talmud states (*Pesachim* 50b) that a person who engages in a workaday activity during this period will not profit by it.

2) Maimonides (*Mishneh Torah, Hilchoth Yom Tov*, Chapter 8, Halacha 17) says one should rebuke him and make him desist.

e. 1) The prohibition was imposed in honor of Shabbath and Yom Tov.

2) a) Its object is to leave one free to prepare what one needs for the coming day.

b) This explains most of the exceptions to the rule, which are detailed in the paragraphs below.

f. There is no difference in the application of the rule between the day before Shabbath and the day before Yom Tov (except in the case of the day before Pesach, which is discussed in paragraph 41 below).

employees

33. *a.* An employee should try to make it a condition of his employment that he should be allowed to stop work two and a half "variable hours" before sunset on Friday and on the day before Yom Tov (unless he or his work fall within one of the exceptional categories set out in the paragraphs which follow below).

b. If he has omitted, or is unable, to make such a stipulation, then he should come home early enough to complete all essential preparations in good time before Shabbath or Yom Tov commences.

34. *a.* Special considerations apply to someone who is so poor that he cannot afford to buy meat or fish with which to enjoy Shabbath or Yom Tov. *the very poor*

b. He may work until just before Shabbath or Yom Tov begins, so that he can earn enough to buy meat and fish.

35. One may work until just before Shabbath or Yom Tov starts, if failure to do so will result in a loss.* *avoiding loss*

36. *a.* Where it is apparent, from the activity itself, that one is performing it for Shabbath or Yom Tov, one may engage in it during the whole day, right up to the beginning of Shabbath or Yom Tov. *activities obviously performed for Shabbath*

b. One may do so even if one is undertaking it for others in return for remuneration.

c. An example is a barber who cuts the hair of a fellow-Jew on Friday or on the day before Yom Tov.

d. At all events, one must stop in good time to avoid any risk of a violation of Shabbath or Yom Tov.

37. *a.* Where it is **not** apparent from the activity itself that one is performing it for Shabbath or Yom Tov, one may engage in it right up to the beginning of Shabbath or Yom Tov **only if** *activities performed for Shabbath, but not obviously so*

1) one is indeed performing it for Shabbath or Yom Tov **and**
2) one is doing it for oneself, or, if one is doing it for another person, one is not being paid for the work done during the two and a half "variable hours" before sunset.

---

* Loss of payment one would receive for hours worked is not regarded as a loss for this purpose.

b. One may, by way of example, sew or repair a garment for Shabbath or Yom Tov,
1) even just before Shabbath or Yom Tov starts and
2) even for another person, if no payment is received.

c. One must of course take care to stop in good time, so that one should not come to violate Shabbath or Yom Tov.

activities requiring only casual attention

38. *a.* An activity which only requires casual attention may be undertaken during the course of the whole day,
1) even if it is not being done for Shabbath or Yom Tov and
2) even if one is being paid to do it.

b. Instances of this type of activity could be
1) watering the garden, if it is only done superficially,
2) sewing on a button or
3) writing a letter to a friend.

c. One must of course take care to stop in good time, so that one should not come to violate Shabbath or Yom Tov.

activities requiring closer attention

39. *a.* An activity which requires one's fuller attention should not be performed in the last two and a half "variable hours" before sunset on Friday or the day preceding Yom Tov, if it is not being done for Shabbath or Yom Tov.

b. This is so even
1) when one would not be receiving payment or
2) when one desires to perform the activity for oneself.

c. An instance of this type of activity could be more serious gardening work which can take several hours to complete.

trading

40. *a.* Trade or business is not included within those activities which are restricted on Friday or on the day before Yom Tov.

b. While the practice is for shops to be closed a short while before Shabbath or Yom Tov commences, it is proper to shut them somewhat earlier, namely, an hour prior to sunset.

the day before Passover

41. *a.* Additional restrictions forbid the performance of certain activities after midday on the day before Passover.

b. Generally speaking, the activities in question are of a kind which one has to take trouble to perform, but this must not be taken as a definition.

c. These activities must not be performed
1) even when they are needed for the purposes of the Festival and
2) even if one receives no remuneration for them.

d. By way of example, one may not, after midday,
1) sew new clothes,
2) wash clothes or
3) cut one's hair.

e. 1) One may request a non-Jew, on the day before Passover, to perform an activity which one is not allowed to perform that day oneself.
2) Thus, one may have one's hair cut by a non-Jewish barber even after midday.
3) One may ask a non-Jew to perform even activities which are not required for the purposes of the Festival and involve a great deal of trouble.

f. 1) Fingernails should be cut before midday, but,
2) if one forgets, one may cut them afterwards.

g. One is allowed, even after midday,
1) to do what is necessary to prepare food for the Festival,
2) to perform activities whose omission would entail a loss and
3) to sew up a small tear in a garment one wishes to wear on the Festival,

even if one does so in an expert manner.

h. Paid* work must not be done by a Jew after midday on the day before Passover (unless he is so poor that he does not have enough to eat for the Festival),

---

* A qualified halachic authority should be consulted if one requires something to be done for the Festival, or to avoid a loss, and cannot find anyone to do it other than a Jew who demands payment.

1) even if it is required for the Festival
2) even if it can be performed without any trouble.

ordering work from a non-Jew

42. Regarding the ordering, on Friday or the day before Yom Tov, of work or services to be performed by a non-Jew for a Jew on Shabbath or Yom Tov, see Chapter 30, paragraphs 25 to 27, and Chapter 31, paragraphs 20 and 23 to 25.

INITIATING ACTIVITIES WHICH WILL BE COMPLETED ON SHABBATH OR YOM TOV

activities automatically completed

43. *a.* 1) Sometimes, an activity which would be forbidden on Shabbath or Yom Tov can be set in motion,
a) even just before Shabbath or Yom Tov commences,
b) with the object that it should continue or complete itself automatically on Shabbath or Yom Tov.

2) The practice, however, is to permit this only in one of the following situations:
a) if a loss would otherwise be incurred;
b) if the process does not cause a commotion which is liable to derogate from the sanctity of the Shabbath or Yom Tov or arouse a suspicion that one is actually performing a forbidden activity on Shabbath or Yom Tov;
c) if it is a matter of universal knowledge that the process in question is commonly activated before Shabbath or Yom Tov begins and is left to complete itself.

leaving pots on the flame

b. The following examples illustrate the operation of the rule.

1) One may leave a pot on the flame before Shabbath, to continue cooking on Shabbath (but see Chapter 1, paragraph 63).

irrigation sprinklers

2) One is allowed to turn on irrigation sprinklers before Shabbath or Yom Tov commences and leave them on over Shabbath or Yom Tov. (See further Chapter 26, paragraph 8.)

3) a) It is permitted to insert eggs into an electric incubator before Shabbath or Yom Tov starts, but *incubators*
b) one should consult the opinion of an expert in the Halacha regarding the attention they must be given during the course of the Shabbath or the Festival.

4) a) On the other hand, it is forbidden to activate a washing machine (or a clothes drying machine) before Shabbath or Yom Tov, with the intention that it should continue to operate after their commencement. *washing machines*
b) This is because the noise and the vibration emitted may create a disturbance in the vicinity and detract from the sanctity of the Shabbath or the Festival.

5) a) It is prohibited to leave a radio receiver on, so that one will be able to listen to broadcasts during the course of Shabbath or Yom Tov. *radio receivers*
b) One should not do this even if the broadcasts one wishes to hear are transmitted from a station operated by non-Jews.
c) If it is operated by Jews in violation of Shabbath or Yom Tov, listening by means of this subterfuge is not only wholly unjustifiable, but brings into contempt the name of the God whose Shabbath or Yom Tov one is purporting to observe.
d) It is equally forbidden to set a timer before the start of Shabbath or Yom Tov, so that it will switch on a radio receiver on Shabbath or Yom Tov.

6) a) One may set a timer before Shabbath or Yom Tov to disconnect or connect the electric current at predetermined hours. (See Chapter 1, paragraph 26, and Chapter 13, paragraph 23.) *timers*
b) Nevertheless, one must not do so with the object of

activating a dishwashing machine on Shabbath, as explained in Chapter 12, paragraph 35.

c. 1) See Chapter 29, paragraph 28, in connection with automatic vending machines.

2) See Chapter 28, paragraph 29, in connection with the winding up of an alarm clock before Shabbath or Yom Tov, so that it should ring on the following day.

pouring concrete or plaster

44. *a.* One ought not to pour concrete or plaster shortly before Shabbath or Yom Tov.

b. One will thus avoid the temptation to violate Shabbath or Yom Tov by watering the freshly poured concrete or plaster.

c. See also Chapter 23, paragraph 43, and Chapter 30, paragraph 13.

WASHING ONESELF AND CUTTING ONE'S HAIR AND NAILS

washing oneself: general rule

45. *a.* One ought, on Friday or on the day before Yom Tov, to wash the whole of one's body in hot water in honor of Shabbath or Yom Tov.

b. If one is unable to do so, one should at least wash one's face, hands and feet in hot water.

c. One ought to wash one's hair, too.

d. There is, in addition, a custom to immerse oneself in a *mikveh* on Friday or the day before Yom Tov.

cutting hair and nails: general rule

46. *a.* On Friday or the day before Yom Tov, one ought also to cut one's hair* (if it is too long), shave** (if one is in the habit of doing so) and trim one's nails.***

b. There are certain customs relating to the cutting of nails, namely

---

* This includes one's beard, where one is accustomed to trimming it regularly.

** It goes without saying that shaving must be carried out in a manner which is sanctioned by the Halacha.

*** After a haircut or shave, or after cutting one's nails, one should wash one's hands.

1) not to cut fingernails and toenails on the same day* and
2) not to cut the nails of consecutive fingers, but,
   a) on the left hand, to begin with the ring finger and then go on to the index finger, the little finger, the middle finger and the thumb, in that order (D, B, E, C, A, where the thumb is A), and,
   b) on the right hand, to begin with the index finger and then go on to the ring finger, the thumb, the middle finger and the little finger, in that order (B, D, A, C, E, where the thumb is A).

c. One must not throw the nails on the floor, but should
1) burn them,
2) bury them or
3) cut them into the sink.

when to wash, cut hair and trim nails

47. *a.* 1) Washing oneself, cutting one's hair and trimming one's nails on Friday, or on the day before Yom Tov, is best done after midday.
2) This makes it more obvious that what one is doing is in honor of Shabbath or Yom Tov.

b. 1) Sometimes,
   a) one is unable to wash oneself, cut one's hair or trim one's nails after midday, or,
   b) if one does so, one will not be left with enough time to complete one's preparations for Shabbath or Yom Tov before they commence.
2) This is particularly likely to occur during the short winter days.
3) a) In such an eventuality, one may wash oneself, cut one's hair or trim one's nails before midday, or even on Thursday (or two days before Yom Tov), but
   b) if one does wash early, it is as well quickly to rinse

* This does not apply to women when they cut their nails preparatory to immersion in the *mikveh*.

one's face, hands and feet again in hot water just prior to the beginning of Shabbath or Yom Tov.

c. 1) One should be very careful not to delay washing until just before Shabbath or Yom Tov starts, so that one should not run the risk of violating Shabbath or Yom Tov.

2) Particular attention has to be paid to this during the short winter days.

3) It is better not to wash at all rather than to violate Shabbath or Yom Tov in so doing.

women

48. Women, as well as men, ought to
a. wash themselves in hot water,
b. cut their hair and
c. trim their nails
in honor of Shabbath or Yom Tov, as set out in paragraphs 45 to 47 above and 49 to 53 below.

rosh chodesh

49. Some have the custom not to cut their hair or trim their nails on *rosh chodesh*, even if it occurs on a Friday.

chol ha-mo'ed

50. *a.* 1) It is forbidden to cut one's hair on *chol ha-mo'ed*,
a) even if one wishes to do so in honor of Shabbath or the last day of Yom Tov and
b) even if, through no fault of one's own, one was unable to cut one's hair before the Festival.

2) a) The same prohibition applies also to shaving.
b) One may not shave on *chol ha-mo'ed*, even if one was not neglectful and did shave on the day before Yom Tov.

3) For full details, and exceptions to the rule, see Chapter 66, paragraphs 22 to 32.

b. 1) The custom is also not to cut one's nails on *chol ha-mo'ed*.

2) For details and exceptions, see Chapter 66, paragraph 33.

51. *a.* 1) On the day before Pesach one may cut one's hair and shave only up to midday. *the day before Pesach*

2) One should not cut one's hair or shave after midday, even if one forgot, or was too busy, to do so earlier, but

3) haircutting or shaving by means of a non-Jew is permitted even after midday.

b. 1) One should also take care to cut one's nails before midday.

2) Nonetheless, if one forgot or was unable to do so, one may cut them after midday.

c. See also paragraph 41 above.

52. *a.* The Fasts of the Seventeenth of Tamuz and the Ninth of Av, and the three weeks between them, are observed as days of mourning for the destruction of the Temple. *between the Seventeenth of Tamuz and the Ninth of Av*

b. The custom is not to cut one's hair (or shave) during this period, even if one would wish to do so in honor of Shabbath.

c. From the first to the Ninth of Av, washing oneself is permitted only to a limited extent.

d. 1) However, when the first of Av occurs on a Friday, a special exception is made in the combined honor of Shabbath and *rosh chodesh*, namely

2) to permit a person who is used to washing the whole of his body in hot water every Friday to do so on this Friday too.

e. 1) More restricted exceptions are made to the rule on the last Friday before the Ninth of Av.

2) A person who is used to washing his face, hands and feet in hot water every Friday is allowed to do so on this Friday too, but

3) he should not use soap, unless it is required to remove dirt or sweat.

4) He should not wash the whole of his body, even in cold water.

5) Somebody who washes his hair in hot water every Friday may do so also on this Friday, but not with

shampoo or soap.

6) Someone who customarily immerses himself in a *mikveh* every Friday should immerse himself as usual on this Friday also, but not in hot water.

7) When the following day (Shabbath) is the Ninth of Av, so that the Fast is postponed to Sunday, one should be particular to wash on Friday before midday, if one possibly can (subject to the limitations mentioned above).

f. Although the usual custom is not to have one's hair cut after the Fast of Av until midday on the following day, the tenth, if

1) the Ninth of Av falls on Thursday and
2) one will not have time to have one's hair cut on Friday,

one may have it cut on Thursday evening after the Fast.

g. 1) The custom is not to cut one's nails in the week during which the Ninth of Av occurs (that is to say, during that part of the week which precedes the Ninth of Av).

2) Yet, when the Ninth of Av is on Shabbath, one may cut one's nails on the previous day, Friday.

the days of the omer

53. *a.* 1) a) It is also the custom not to cut one's hair (or shave) during the days when the *omer* is counted.

b) There are local variations in custom as to exactly on which days during this period one does not cut one's hair.

2) When, however, *Lag Ba-omer* falls on Sunday, the custom is to cut one's hair on the previous Friday, in honor of Shabbath.

3) Similarly, when the first day of Iyar falls on Shabbath, one can, in the combined honor of Shabbath and *rosh chodesh*, permit haircutting on the preceding Friday for those whose custom would otherwise forbid it.

4) The same applies when the first of Sivan falls on Sunday, for those whose custom would otherwise

forbid them to cut their hair before that date.

b. 1) Regarding washing by a mourner on Friday during his seven days of deep mourning, see Chapter 65, paragraph 7. *mourners*

2) For the law concerning washing on Friday during the thirty-day period of mourning see Chapter 65, paragraph 42.

3) For washing on the day before Yom Tov during the seven days of deep mourning, see Chapter 65, paragraph 45.

4) For the law regarding washing by a mourner on Friday when the following day, Shabbath, is the thirtieth day of mourning, see Chapter 65, paragraph 43.

5) For the law regarding washing on the day before Yom Tov during the thirty-day mourning period, see paragraphs 47 and 48 there.

6) For details regarding haircutting during mourning, see Chapter 65, paragraphs 42, 43 and 46 to 48.

7) Regarding cutting of nails during the thirty-day period of mourning, see Chapter 65, paragraph 44.

FINAL PREPARATIONS

54. *a.* 1) In Exodus 16:5, God tells Moses, concerning the manna gathered on Friday, "they shall prepare what they bring and it shall be twice as much." *Biblical source*

2) The Sages saw in this an indication that one should prepare twice for Shabbath,

a) once on Friday morning, as stated in paragraph 7 above, and

b) again, if one can, close to the commencement of Shabbath.

b. 1) Indeed, the more one does to prepare for the Shabbath the better. *personal participation*

2) The mitzva is to busy oneself personally with preparations for Shabbath.

3) One should personally attend to as many of the Shabbath preparations as one can, even if one has domestic servants who can do it for one.

4) a) No person, however exalted his status, should regard this mitzva as beneath his dignity.

b) On the contrary, the dignity of a Jew manifests itself in the way he honors Shabbath.

c. 1) In these laws, there is no distinction between Shabbath and Yom Tov and

2) whatever one has to do in honor of Shabbath one should also do in honor of Yom Tov.

tidying the house

55. *a.* One should honor Shabbath and Yom Tov by sweeping and tidying the house before they start.

spreading tablecloths

b. 1) Likewise, one ought to have a cloth spread on the table at which one eats,

a) from the beginning of Shabbath or Yom Tov until after *havdala* and,

b) after Shabbath, at the time of the *mᵉlaveh malka* meal.

2) Moreover, it is proper to spread cloths on all the tables in the house for Shabbath.

Shabbath and Yom Tov clothes

56. *a.* 1) a) The Prophet Isaiah (Chapter 58, verse 13) enjoins us to respect the Shabbath.

b) The Rabbis expounded this as including an injunction not to wear the same clothes on Shabbath and Yom Tov as on another day of the week.

2) One should put one's Shabbath or Yom Tov clothes on as soon as one has finished washing in honor of Shabbath or Yom Tov.*

3) It is as well not to wear any article of clothing one has worn during the week.

---

* a. When one changes one's *arba kanfoth* for Shabbath, one should repeat the appropriate blessing (if the *arba kanfoth* is of the requisite size).
b. If one takes off one's *arba kanfoth* in order to bathe, and afterwards puts back on the selfsame *arba kanfoth*, one should not recite the blessing, since there is a doubt as to whether, in these circumstances, a blessing is required.

4) One should wear one's Shabbath or Yom Tov clothes,
   a) after Shabbath, until one has eaten the *m^elaveh malka* meal, and,
   b) on Yom Tov, until after *havdala*.

b. 1) Even somebody who is alone in the house or away from home should change his clothes.
   2) This is because the clothes are worn not in honor of the people who see them, but in honor of Shabbath and Yom Tov.

c. 1) There is a difference of opinion among the authorities as to whether one may wear Shabbath clothes on the last Shabbath before the Fast of Av.
   2) a) The widespread practice is to follow the view of the Vilna Gaon, who permitted it.
      b) However, one should not put one's Shabbath clothes on until shortly before Shabbath begins.
      c) Furthermore, one should change out of them immediately after *havdala*.

d. 1) The accepted custom is that even a mourner within the seven days of deep mourning changes his clothes in honor of Shabbath.
   2) For particulars, see Chapter 65, paragraphs 7 and 33.

READING THE WEEKLY PORTION
OF THE TORAH WITH ITS TARGUM

57. *a.* 1) Each week, every individual is required to complete his own reading of the portion of the Torah which the congregation is reading that week. *the mitzva*
   2) He should read the Hebrew text twice and the Aramaic translation of Onkelos (*Targum*) once.
   3) The God-fearing person should also study Rashi's commentary on the weekly portion.

b. Even someone who studies Torah all day should not omit to read the weekly portion and its *Targum* as detailed in this and the following paragraphs.

when to do it

58. *a.* A person can begin his reading for the coming week immediately following the Shabbath afternoon service, that is to say, after the congregation has begun the reading of the ensuing week's portion.

b. The best way to perform the mitzva is

1) to read the whole of the Hebrew text and the *Targum* on Friday or

2) to read part each day and complete the reading on Friday.

c. 1) If one has not finished the reading on Friday, it is best to complete it before eating one's Shabbath morning meal.

2) Nonetheless, one should not on this account delay one's Shabbath meal beyond midday, but should instead complete any remaining reading after the meal.

3) If one has not managed to do so, one should read what is left on the first three days of the following week.

4) a) A person who omits to read the Hebrew text and *Targum* one week can catch up during the course of the next week.

b) He should read first the portion that he has missed and afterwards the portion of the current week.

5) According to some authorities, one can, as a last resort, complete one's reading of the weekly portions and *Targum* up to Simchath Torah.

how to do it

59. *a.* 1) a) The correct procedure is to read the Hebrew text of each verse, or of each paragraph (depending on one's practice), twice, followed by its *Targum* once, before going on to the next verse or paragraph.

b) The beginning and end of each paragraph is indicated in the *Chumash* by the Hebrew letters *pei* or *samech*.

2) a) One should not read the *Targum* after only one

reading of the Hebrew text, but,

b) if one has erroneously done so, one is permitted to complete the mitzva by reading the Hebrew another once.

3) a) If one really has no other opportunity, one may read in a whisper together with the Reader, while the latter is reading the Torah in the synagogue.

b) One is then considered to have read the Hebrew text once.

c) Should one adopt this expedient, however, one should be careful, at the same time, to listen attentively to what the Reader is reading from the *sefer Torah*.

b. A person who knows how to do so would be well advised to perform the mitzva in a particularly fine manner by reading with the proper cantillation from a *sefer Torah* which is fit to be read from in the synagogue.

60. *a.* There is an obligation to read only the regular weekly portion which will be read to the congregation on Shabbath, as distinct from the specially selected extracts which are read to the congregation on Yom Tov. *Yom Tov*

b. While women are exempt from the obligation to read the text twice and the *Targum* once, they would do well to listen to the reading of the Torah that takes place in the synagogue. *women*

c. Even a mourner during his seven days of deep mourning should perform the mitzva of reading the Hebrew text twice and the *Targum* once, as explained in Chapter 65, paragraph 11. *mourners*

d. The Talmud Bavli, in reference to this mitzva, says, "Whoever completes [the reading of] his portions with the congregation [that is to say, during the period of time defined in paragraph 58 above] shall have his days and years prolonged" (*Berachoth* 8b). *the reward*

e. There is a custom, after one has completed one's reading of the Torah text twice and the *Targum* once, to read also the weekly portion from the Prophets. *the portion from the Prophets*

CHECKING SHABBATH PREPARATIONS

tasting the food

61. *a.* One ought to taste every dish on Friday, before Shabbath, to make sure it is tasty and needs no improvement.

b. 1) The custom is not to eat meat during the nine days beginning with *Rosh Chodesh* Av, except on Shabbath.

2) Consequently, when tasting a dish cooked with meat on the last Friday before the Fast of Av, one should not swallow any of the food.*

c. Similarly, when the Fast of the Tenth of Teveth falls on Friday,

1) one may taste the food prepared for Shabbath, but

2) one should not swallow any of it.**

d. 1) Somebody who has a private fast day on Friday should do likewise.

2) This could occur, for example, if a person has the custom of fasting on a *yahrzeit*.

enquiring if everything is ready

62. *a.* Just before the commencement of Shabbath, a person should politely ask the members of his household whether they have removed *t^e^rumoth* and *ma'asroth* and separated *challa*.

b. He should also ask them whether they have attended to all the things which cannot be seen to on Shabbath, such as the removal or disconnection of the internal light in the refrigerator.

c. Then he should tell them to light the Shabbath candles and cease all activities which are forbidden on Shabbath.

MISCELLANEOUS LAWS

keeping food hot

63. *a.* 1) One may, before the commencement of Shabbath, place a porous cloth bag, containing rice or similar food, in soup which is standing on the fire.

---

* No blessing should be recited.

** See previous note.

2) This is not included in the prohibition against keeping food warm by wrapping.

b. 1) On the other hand, sealing *kugel* in aluminum foil and burying it below the surface of *cholent* which is standing on the fire is included in the prohibition.

2) One should not do this, even prior to the commencement of Shabbath.

3) What one may do, and that only before Shabbath begins, is

a) to put the *kugel* into the *cholent* in such a way that it is not entirely below the surface or

b) to perforate the aluminum foil, so that the food in the pot is in contact with the *kugel*.

c. Compare Chapter 1, paragraph 72.

d. For rules with regard to wrapping pots in a cloth before Shabbath to keep them warm, see Chapter 1, paragraph 65.

e. For rules with regard to leaving pots on the fire before Shabbath, see Chapter 1, paragraph 63.

turning off the water heater

64. *a.* One should take care to shut off the heating apparatus of one's water heater before Shabbath.

b. See further Chapter 1, paragraph 39.

eiruv tavshilin

65. When Yom Tov occurs on Friday, or on Thursday and Friday, one should make an *eiruv tavshilin* on the day before Yom Tov, as explained in Chapter 2, paragraphs 10 to 15.

preparing candles to fit holes in candlesticks

66. *a.* When

1) Yom Tov occurs immediately before or after Shabbath, or

2) two days of Yom Tov, whether the two days of Rosh Hashana or of *yom tov sheini shel galuyoth*, follow each other,

one should prepare one's candles for both (or all three) days, to make them fit the holes in one's candlesticks, before the commencement of the first day, since to do so on Shabbath or Yom Tov is prohibited.

b. See further Chapter 13, paragraphs 42 and 43.

opening cans and bottles

67. As explained in Chapter 9, the preferable and proper course is to open cans of preserves, bottles with reusable tops that break open when removed for the first time and all similar, sealed containers before Shabbath or Yom Tov starts.

terumoth, ma'asroth and challa

68. Regarding the stipulations which may be made before Shabbath or Yom Tov, so that *t^erumoth, ma'asroth* and *challa* may be separated on Shabbath or Yom Tov, see Chapter 11, paragraphs 18 to 27.

checking pockets

69. *a.* Just before the commencement of Shabbath, one ought to check one's clothes (especially one's pockets), to see that one is not carrying anything which one might come to take out into *r^eshuth ha-rabbim.*

b. Similarly, just before the commencement of Shabbath or Yom Tov, one ought to check one's clothes to see that one is not carrying anything which is *muktzeh* and must not be moved on Shabbath or Yom Tov.

c. See Chapter 18, paragraph 46.

mourning

70. *a.* Mourners observe the laws of mourning until just before the beginning of Shabbath or the Festival.

b. These laws are explained in Chapter 65, paragraphs 7 and 45.

patient preparing for the Day of Atonement

71. It is desirable that an ill person who has to eat in *shi'urim* on the Day of Atonement should, before the Day of Atonement begins, measure and ascertain the amounts he may eat (as explained in Chapter 39, paragraphs 19 and 20).

advertisements for publication on Shabbath or Yom Tov

72. It is forbidden to deliver an advertisement before Shabbath or Yom Tov for publication in a newspaper that is to appear on Shabbath or Yom Tov, even if it is owned and managed by non-Jews.*

---

* See also Chapter 31, paragraph 25.

73. Concerning the mailing of letters on Friday, or on the day before Yom Tov, in a place where the post office employees are not Jewish, see Chapter 31, paragraph 20. *posting letters*

74. *a.* When arranging the date for an operation which is not urgent, one should do one's best not to fix it for Wednesday or a subsequent day of the week. *non-urgent operations*

b. The object is to obviate the necessity which may arise for Shabbath to be violated in the course of postoperative treatment.

c. See further Chapter 32, paragraph 33.

75. *a.* A circumcision may be performed on Thursday or Friday, or during the two days before Yom Tov, and one need not fear that, as a result, one may have to violate Shabbath or Yom Tov in order to treat the baby. *circumcision on Friday or day before Yom Tov*

b. This is so even when the eighth day has passed, as, for example, in a case where the baby was ill on the eighth day, so that the circumcision could not then take place.

c. Regarding the celebration meal to be eaten on the same day, after the circumcision, see paragraph 27 above.

76. *a.* A *mohel* who has been asked to carry out a circumcision at some distant place on Shabbath or Yom Tov should spend Shabbath or Yom Tov there, in order that he should be able to circumcise the baby at the proper time, namely on the eighth day after birth. *mohel staying over Shabbath or Yom Tov*

b. If indeed

1) he finds it extremely difficult to be cut off from his family for the whole of Shabbath or Yom Tov or
2) he will be unable to perform other mitzvoth, such as hearing the *shofar* or praying with a congregation, in the place where the circumcision is to be performed,

he should consult the opinion of a halachic authority as to what he should do.

Chapter 43

Kindling the Shabbath and Yom Tov Lights: General Laws

THE MITZVA AND HOW TO PERFORM IT

importance of the mitzva

1. *a.* The kindling of Shabbath and Yom Tov lights is obligatory.

b. The Rabbis ordained that one should kindle lights as part of the mitzva of enjoying Shabbath and Yom Tov, so that one will be able to eat one's meal by their glow. (See Chapter 54, paragraph 34.)

c. 1) The importance of the obligation is such that even a person who is so poor that he has nothing of his own to eat is bound by it.

2) He should, if necessary, beg for money to buy oil or candles.

3) If one cannot afford to buy both oil or candles for Shabbath or Yom Tov lights and wine for *kiddush*, one should give precedence to the lights.]*

minimum number of lights

2. *a.* The obligation can be discharged by kindling just one light.

b. However, the mitzva is better performed by lighting more,** and the custom is to kindle a minimum of two, representing the twin precepts,

1) to remember Shabbath (by carrying out its positive mitzvoth) and

2) to observe Shabbath (by not doing what is forbidden).

---

* On the other hand, if the choice is between bread to eat and lights, bread has precedence.

** One should not use a candelabrum similar to that in the Temple, that is to say, made of metal and having seven branches,

a. even if it differs, in having its lights arranged, not in a straight row, but, for example, in a circle, and

b. even if one lights with candles, and not with oil.

3. *a.* 1) a) A woman who habitually kindles a particular number of lights for Shabbath should not kindle less. *lighting more than the minimum*

b) The adoption of the habit is viewed as being in the nature of a vow to kindle that specific number of lights.

2) a) Consequently, if circumstances make it difficult for her to kindle so many lights, she should obtain a release from her "vow."

b) An instance of such difficulty is where, due to poverty, she could afford to kindle her regular number of lights only if she made a reduction in her other Shabbath expenses.

3) The same considerations apply to a woman who habitually kindles specially large lights.

b. 1) The above "vow" is binding only when a woman kindles her lights at home.

2) If she is spending Shabbath away from home,

a) the custom is for her to kindle only two lights, and

b) they need not be specially large, even though she is accustomed to kindling large lights when she is at home.

c. A woman who wishes to kindle more lights than the number to which she has been accustomed until now should not do so against her husband's will.*

4. *a.* 1) The finest way of performing the mitzva is to light with olive oil. *what to light with*

2) If one has no olive oil, one should kindle with other types of oil which give a clear light.

3) One should make the wicks from absorbent cotton (cotton wool) or from some other material which maintains a good flame.

4) a) One may put water into the lamp before Shabbath

---

* She would also do well to stipulate, before kindling additional lights, that she is not thereby making a vow to do likewise on future occasions.

in order to raise the level of the oil.

b) On Shabbath itself, however, it is forbidden to do the above.

b. 1) It is also permissible to light with candles made of wax or some other substance, so long as they give a clear light.

2) They should not be stood too closely together, since, otherwise, they heat each other up, the wax drips and they go out sooner.

c. 1) There are authorities who hold that the mitzva can be satisfactorily performed by turning on electric lightbulbs.

2) A person who does this should recite the appropriate blessing in the usual way, provided he indeed switches on the lights in honor of Shabbath. (See paragraph 32 below.)

forgetting to light

5. *a.* A woman who forgot to kindle Shabbath lights, and whose husband did not turn any lights on in the house in honor of the Shabbath, should thenceforth add one light to the number she was hitherto accustomed to kindling.

b. If she forgot several times, she should add one light for each time she forgot.

c. 1) Should she be poor, it is enough for her just somewhat to increase the size of the lights she is accustomed to kindle.

2) That is to say, she can

a) add a little more oil or

b) light larger candles.

d. 1) Where her failure to kindle the lights was due, not to forgetfulness, but to the force of circumstances, she need not make any addition to the lights she kindles in the future.

2) An example would be where she was occupied with tending her sick child and, as a result, could not manage to kindle the lights.

WHO IS OBLIGED TO KINDLE THE LIGHTS?

6. *a.* Both men and women are bound by the mitzva of kindling the lights. *as between husband and wife*

b. 1) However, the greater responsibility is placed upon the women, since they spend more time at home and look after the domestic arrangements.

2) Consequently, the practice is that the wife kindles the lights for Shabbath and Yom Tov.

3) a) Even if the husband wishes to kindle the lights in order to have the privilege of performing the mitzva, his wife takes precedence, and

b) she is entitled to object to his kindling those lights over which one says the appropriate blessing, usually those at the dining table. (See paragraph 15 below.)

c. 1) Nevertheless, it is good for the husband also to take some part in the mitzva, by preparing the lights for kindling before Shabbath.

2) He should light them briefly and then extinguish them, since, if the wicks are singed, it will be easier for his wife to light them later.*

3) He should also

a) put on the other lights which are to be lit in the dining room and

b) put on the lights which are required in other rooms, where his wife is not kindling.

d. A woman who lives on her own, for instance an unmarried woman, a widow or a divorcee, is also obliged to kindle the lights.

7. *a.* Someone *where there is no wife*

1) who has no wife, or

---

* When

a. Yom Tov falls on Friday or Sunday or

b. there are two successive days of Yom Tov,

then he should prepare the lights for both (or all three) days in advance, before the first day of Yom Tov or Shabbath (as the case may be) commences.

2) whose wife is not at home, or
3) whose wife, for some reason, is not kindling the lights,
is, nonetheless, obliged to kindle the Shabbath or Yom Tov lights and make the appropriate blessing. (See paragraph 30 below.)

b. His obligation is not discharged if his daughter, being less than twelve years old, lights for him.

daughters

8. *a.* Some have the custom that, not only the woman of the house, but also all the daughters who are old enough to understand what they are doing kindle Shabbath lights.

b. 1) There are those who hold that the daughters should even recite the blessing when lighting.
2) Where this is the practice, it is better, in so far as possible, for each daughter to light in a different one of the rooms used on Shabbath. (See Chapter 45, paragraph 9.)

after childbirth

9. *a.* Even a woman who has just given birth has an obligation to kindle the Shabbath or Yom Tov lights.

b. See further Chapter 36, paragraph 16, and Chapter 45, paragraph 6.

the blind

10. *a.* If a woman is so unfortunate as to be blind, her husband should kindle the lights and recite the blessing.

b. In the event that if she lives alone, she should kindle the lights herself, if it is safe to do so, and also say the blessing.

c. 1) If she lives together with others who have an obligation to light, she should also light, but should not recite the blessing.
2) She would, however, do well to hear the blessing when it is being said by one of the others, who should intend thereby also to discharge any obligation which she may have to recite the blessing.

WHEN AND WHERE TO LIGHT

recommended time

11. *a.* The time to kindle the Shabbath lights is a little while before sunset.

b. How long before sunset one lights depends on the custom of the place where one lights.

c. Where there is no established custom, one should light at least twenty minutes, or, better still, about half an hour, before sunset, in order to try and comply with even the most strict of the differing opinions on the matter.

d. Regarding the time for kindling the Yom Tov lights, see Chapter 44, paragraph 2.

lighting early

12. *a.* 1) If one can, one should light in a way from which it is apparent that one is lighting in honor of Shabbath.

2) For this reason, one ought not to light very much earlier than is usual.

3) It is, however, perfectly in order to light earlier (within the limit mentioned below) when one takes upon oneself the observance of Shabbath as from the time of lighting. (See also paragraph 24 below.)

b. 1) At all events, one must not kindle the lights earlier than *p^elag ha-minchah*.

2) *P^elag ha-minchah* is one and a quarter hours before sunset, where one hour is defined as one twelfth of the time between sunrise and sunset on the day in question.

c. 1) If one has kindled the lights before *p^elag ha-minchah*, one has not fulfilled one's obligation.

2) In such case, one has to

a) extinguish the lights and

b) light them again, reciting the blessing.*

3) This is so even if one took upon oneself the observance of Shabbath as from the time of the first lighting, since receiving Shabbath at so early an hour is of no effect.

---

* See, however, paragraph 14 below.

d. Where, contrary to what is stated in *a* above, one
   1) has kindled lights in honor of Shabbath earlier than usual, but
   2) did **not** take upon oneself to begin observing Shabbath as from the time of lighting,

then, after the event, one has fulfilled one's duty and need not light again, provided that one kindled after *pelag ha-minchah.*

e. Whenever one does kindle lights early, as above, one should take care that the quantity of oil, or the size of the candles, is sufficient to burn until after the end of the evening meal.

avoiding late lighting

13. *a.* One should not leave the lighting until too close to sunset, in case it becomes too late to light at all. (See paragraph 14 below.)

b. If a husband
   1) sees that his wife is late in kindling the lights and
   2) is afraid that lighting any later may result in a violation of the Shabbath,

he should kindle the lights himself, even in the face of his wife's protests.

c. 1) It is a mitzva to encourage the members of one's household to finish their preparations and kindle the Shabbath lights in time.
   2) Soft-spoken persuasion is usually the best way of preventing them from being late.

what to do when it is too late

14. *a.* 1) Once the time for kindling the Shabbath lights has passed, one is no longer permitted to light them.
   2) The time is treated as having passed
      a) when the sun has set, or
      b) even when one thinks the sun may have set, but is not sure, or
      c) even if the sun has definitely not yet set, but the community has already received the Shabbath, that is to say taken upon itself to begin the observance of Shabbath.

3) The community* may receive the Shabbath by the recital of
   a) *Bo'i ve-shalom* at the end of the hymn beginning *Lecha dodi*,
   b) the psalm *Mizmor shir le-yom ha-Shabbath* (in places where the whole of *Lecha dodi* is omitted on a Friday evening which occurs during the course of, or immediately following, a Festival), or
   c) *Barechu* prior to the evening prayer (where, for some reason, neither *Lecha dodi* nor *Mizmor shir le-yom ha-Shabbath* are said).
   (See Chapter 46, paragraph 7.)

4) a) One should on no account violate Shabbath by kindling the Shabbath lights, even when there are no other lights on.
   b) It is better to sit in the dark, or even to forgo the Shabbath evening meal altogether, if one is unable to eat in the dark.

b. 1) However, although it is after sunset, one may, until just before the stars come out, tell a non-Jew to put on a light, so that one should not have to be in the dark on Friday night (in accordance with the rules set out in Chapter 46, paragraph 22).

2) One may allow the non-Jew to put on numerous lights, just as one does oneself before other Shabbathoth.

3) Furthermore, one may tell him to kindle the usual Shabbath lights,
   a) even if the electric light is on in the house,
   b) but one does not recite a blessing on lights kindled by the non-Jew.

c. From just before the stars come out, telling a non-Jew to put on a light is also forbidden, even if one will have to sit in the dark.

---

* See Chapter 46, paragraph 7.

where to light

15. *a.* 1) Essentially, the mitzva is to kindle lights in the place where one is going to eat.*

2) It is on the kindling of these lights that one says the blessing. (See further paragraph 35 below.)

b. 1) On Sukkoth, one should try to kindle the lights in the *sukka*, so that one can eat by their glow.

2) However, if

a) there is a fear that the lights will be blown out by the wind in the *sukka*, and one has not prepared a suitable protective shield for them, or

b) there is any risk whatsoever of fire,

one should light in the house.

3) In such event, one should, if one can, kindle in a window from which the light will reach the *sukka*.

4) Failing that,

a) one should kindle in the place where the preparations for the meal will be made on Shabbath, although,

b) if the women are going to eat in the house, and not in the *sukka*,** they can light where they eat.

c. 1) There should also be lights burning in all the other rooms which one uses on Friday night (and which one wants illuminated), or at least light should reach them from elsewhere.

2) The same applies to corridors and staircases.

3) Nevertheless, one should not recite a blessing when putting on these additional lights.

d. 1) A woman who kindles more than two lights for Shabbath (regarding which see paragraph 2 above) should make a point of kindling at least two in the place where the meal is to be eaten.

2) As for the other lights, she can kindle them in the other rooms which will be used on Shabbath.

---

* For cases where one should kindle lights elsewhere, see Chapter 45, paragraphs 2 to 4 and 8 to 12.

** This can happen in places where, for instance, there is only one, central *sukka*, next to the synagogue, and there is no room for women.

3) See also paragraph 35 below.

16. *a.* If the Shabbath lights go out, due to the wind or for any other reason, and the sun has not yet set, it is a mitzva to relight them, but *lights which go out*
1) they should be relit by someone who has not yet received Shabbath and,
2) where a blessing was recited at the time of the original lighting, no blessing should be said on the relighting.

(See paragraph 37 below.)

b. 1) At any rate, one should be careful to kindle the Shabbath lights in a position where the wind will not extinguish them.
2) Similarly, one should not stand them near the door, in case they go out when it is opened.

17. *a.* One must do one's best to say the blessing over lights which will burn until the end of the meal. *how long should the lights burn?*

b. They should at least burn during *kiddush* and the commencement of the meal.*

c. If a person kindles small Shabbath lights, which go out after a short while, and derives no benefit from them for the purpose of the Shabbath meal,
1) he or she has not fulfilled the mitzva of kindling the lights and
2) the blessing which he or she said at the time was recited in vain.

d. It is proper to ensure (before Shabbath) that, even after the meal, the house should not become dark on Friday night, for as long as all the members of the household are awake.

---

* See Chapter 45, paragraphs 2 to 4, and 8 to 12, for cases where one kindles lights in one place and eats in another.

RECEIVING SHABBATH WITH THE KINDLING OF THE LIGHTS

when a woman lights

18. *a.* 1) Except to the extent specified below, in this and the succeeding paragraphs, the custom is for women to receive Shabbath with the kindling of the lights.

2) Thus, all the laws of Shabbath apply to her as soon as she finishes kindling (and see paragraphs 36 and 37 below).

3) Consequently, she must be careful to complete all her preparations before kindling.

4) Nevertheless, although it is right for her to

a) wash herself in honor of Shabbath,

b) dress herself in her Shabbath clothes and

c) recite the *minchah* prayer

before kindling the lights, she must not allow this to delay her until it is so late that lighting might involve a desecration of the Shabbath.

5) If there is insufficient time, she should kindle the lights

a) without washing first,

b) without dressing for Shabbath and

c) without saying the *minchah* prayer.

6) In this last case, she should make up the *minchah* prayer which she has missed, by saying the *Amidah* of the evening prayer twice.

b. 1) Other members of the household do not receive Shabbath when the lights are kindled by the woman of the house (unless they wish to do so).

2) The rules applicable to them can be found in Chapter 46.

c. 1) A woman whose husband lights for her because he is afraid that it may become too late to light otherwise (as in paragraph 13 above), or for any other reason, is not thereby forbidden to perform activities which, on Shabbath, would be prohibited.

2) The rules applicable to her appear in Chapter 46.

d. For the kindling of Yom Tov lights, see Chapter 44, paragraph 8.

19. *a.* It may happen that a woman has kindled the Shabbath lights, so receiving Shabbath, but did not manage to complete all her preparations, or forgot to do something, before kindling. *what a woman may do afterwards*

b. In such event, there are certain things which she may do even afterwards, but only if

1) there is still a little while to go before the stars come out **and**
2) the community has not yet received the Shabbath by the recital of
   a) *Bo'i ve-shalom*,
   b) *Mizmor shir le-yom ha-Shabbath*, or
   c) *Barechu* prior to the evening prayer,

   as detailed in Chapter 46, paragraph 7.

c. In these circumstances, and subject to the above, she may

1) wrap pots, to keep them warm, as permitted before Shabbath, in accordance with the rules set out in Chapter 1, paragraph 65,
2) separate *terumoth* and *ma'asroth*,
3) separate *challa*,
4) bathe, in honor of Shabbath, in warm water (but she should not
   a) take water for this purpose out of a water heater, or boiler, except under the conditions set out in Chapter 1, paragraph 39,
   b) use a cloth or sponge,
   c) use a bar of soap, nor
   d) comb her hair,)
5) do anything which may be done during the period between sunset and the time when the stars come out on Friday night, as specified in Chapter 46, paragraphs 18 to 20, and
6) tell a non-Jew to perform activities for her which she requires to be done in honor of Shabbath, even if their performance on Shabbath is forbidden by a Torah prohibition, such as
   a) standing an urn of water on the fire or

b) putting on lights in the situation described in paragraph 14 above.

d. See also Chapter 46, paragraph 15*b*.

subsequently telling another Jew to do something

20. Moreover, if it is not yet close to sunset,

a. she may also tell a Jew who has still not received Shabbath to do for her even something which entails the infringement of a Torah prohibition, and

b. she is allowed to benefit from it.

with which lights?

21. *a.* As stated in paragraph 15 above, the lights with which one essentially fulfills the mitzva, and on which one pronounces the blessing, are those one kindles at or near the dining table.

b. It is with the kindling of these lights, and not with the putting on of additional lights in the house, that a woman receives Shabbath.

c. See also paragraph 35 below.

specifically not receiving Shabbath: general principles

22. *a.* 1) Halachic authorities disagree as to whether a woman kindling lights can effectively stipulate, verbally or by making an explicit, mental reservation, that she is not thereby receiving Shabbath.

2) Consequently, she should not rely on such a stipulation, except in case of need.

b. In any event, the stipulation can only be effective

1) until just before sunset or

2) until the time when the community receives Shabbath by saying *Bo'i v^e^-shalom*, *Mizmor shir l^e^-yom ha-Shabbath* or *Bar^e^chu* before the evening service.

c. A woman who makes the stipulation should receive Shabbath before sunset

1) by reciting *Bo'i v^e^-shalom* or *Mizmor shir l^e^-yom ha-Shabbath*, or

2) by expressly saying that she is thereupon taking upon herself the observance of Shabbath.

d. 1) It is certainly ineffective for a woman to have in mind, when lighting, merely that she will perform a specific forbidden activity afterwards.

2) a) What she should do is expressly to stipulate, verbally, or by making an explicit mental reservation, that she is not receiving Shabbath by lighting.
b) Then she will later (until the time mentioned in *b* above) be able to perform even forbidden activities which she did not originally have in mind.

effect of saying she-hecheyanu or the evening prayer

23. *a.* 1) When a woman recites the *she-hecheyanu* blessing upon kindling the Yom Tov lights (in pursuance of the custom mentioned in Chapter 44, paragraph 4), she cannot make this stipulation, even though she is lighting before sunset.
2) Accordingly, she is not permitted after lighting to perform any activity whatsoever which is forbidden on Yom Tov.

b. 1) The same applies to a woman who says the evening prayer immediately after kindling the Shabbath lights, despite the fact that the sun has still not set.
2) She too is not allowed to perform any forbidden activity, even when the community has not yet received Shabbath.

specifically not receiving Shabbath when lighting early

24. *a.* 1) It may be that a woman
a) wishes to light earlier than the usual time (within the limits set out in paragraph 12 above), but
b) does not wish to receive Shabbath immediately, because she still needs to perform activities which are forbidden on Shabbath.
2) Since she is lighting earlier than usual, she should not make this stipulation unless her husband, or some other member of the household whose obligation to kindle lights is discharged by her lighting, intends thereby to receive Shabbath immediately.
3) See further paragraph 12 above.

b. 1) This would apply, by way of example, to a woman in

Jerusalem who wishes to light early and then travel to the Western Wall before receiving Shabbath.

2) She should not postpone her reception of Shabbath in this way, unless some member of the household receives Shabbath when she lights (as above).

3) a) Failing fulfilment of this condition, she ought not to travel after kindling her lights.

b) Even where she does not have to drive, but can travel as a passenger, without paying and without herself directly performing a prohibited activity,* such conduct would reflect an insensitivity to the sanctity of the Shabbath.

4) What is more, she would do better not to travel by vehicle after kindling the Shabbath lights,

a) even if another member of the household receives Shabbath when she lights and

b) even for the purpose of a mitzva, such as praying at the Western Wall.

before going to the mikveh

25. *a.* A married woman, the time for whose immersion in the *mikveh* occurs on Friday night, should

1) first wash and comb her hair and make all her other preparations at home, then

2) kindle the Shabbath lights, thereby receiving Shabbath, then

3) walk to the *mikveh*, where she should again wash** those parts of her body which might have become dirty, and finally

4) immerse herself in the *mikveh*.

b. If she is unable to complete all her preparations at home before kindling the lights, then she should

---

* It goes without saying that, when it is actually Shabbath, traveling even in this way is forbidden.

** She should, of course, wash in a way which is allowed on Shabbath, without using a cloth or sponge, and extracting warm water from a water heater or boiler only when permitted by the Halacha, as detailed in Chapter 1, paragraph 39.

1) first kindle the Shabbath lights, stipulating that she is not thereby receiving Shabbath, as in paragraph 24 above, and
2) subsequently finish all her preparations before sunset or before the time when the community receives Shabbath, as in paragraph 22 above.

26. *a.* 1) A man who kindles the Shabbath lights (for instance, if he has no wife) does not thereby receive Shabbath, unless he specifies that he wishes to do so. *when a man lights*

2) Consequently, he may
   a) recite the *minchah* prayer and
   b) perform activities which are forbidden on Shabbath,

   even though he has kindled the lights (so long as the community has not yet received Shabbath by saying *Bo'i ve-shalom, Mizmor shir le-yom ha-Shabbath* or *Barechu* prior to the evening service).

b. 1) Nevertheless, if he wishes to perform a forbidden activity after lighting (at a time when the community has not yet received Shabbath, as mentioned above), he would do well to specify, before lighting, that he is not thereby receiving Shabbath.

2) This is because there are some authorities who hold that even a man receives the Shabbath by kindling the Shabbath lights, if he does not stipulate otherwise.

c. See also Chapter 46, paragraph 13.

d. 1) In the event that he kindles the lights early, before the usual time (as detailed in paragraph 12 above), he should receive Shabbath, and not make any stipulation to the contrary. (See paragraph 24 above.)

2) This will make it clear that he is indeed lighting in honor of Shabbath.

MISCELLANEOUS LAWS RELATING TO THE KINDLING OF THE SHABBATH LIGHTS

dressing before lighting

27. It is proper to put on one's Shabbath clothes before kindling the lights, as mentioned in paragraph 18 above.

giving charity before lighting

28. It is a good custom to give money to charity before kindling the lights.

putting Shabbath loaves on table before sunset

29. *a.* 1) It is right, before sunset, to place the Shabbath loaves on the table where the Shabbath lights will be kindled.
2) Whether this is done before or after the kindling does not matter.
3) The loaves should be left on the table together with the lights, until nightfall.
4) In this way, the table will not be turned into a *basis la-davar ha-assur*, which may not be moved on Shabbath. (See Chapter 20, paragraphs 59 to 61.)

b. Nonetheless, even if one did not put the loaves on the table, one may use it in its present position and eat from it.

order of lighting

30. *a.* Since a man does not, as a matter of course, receive Shabbath by kindling the lights (as mentioned in paragraph 26 above), he should proceed as follows:
1) He should first* strike the match (or light the candle with which he is going to kindle the Shabbath lights).
2) Next, he should recite the blessing,
בָּרוּךְ אַתָּה יהוה אֱלֹהֵינוּ מֶלֶךְ הָעוֹלָם, אֲשֶׁר קִדְּשָׁנוּ בְּמִצְוֹתָיו, וְצִוָּנוּ לְהַדְלִיק נֵר שֶׁל שַׁבָּת
"Blessed art Thou, O Lord our God, King of the universe, Who has sanctified us with His commandments and has commanded us to kindle the light of Shabbath."

---

* Doing this after saying the blessing would be an undesirable interruption between the blessing and the kindling of the lights.

3) Then he should kindle the lights.

b. 1) Since a woman, as a matter of course, does receive Shabbath by kindling the lights (as mentioned in paragraph 18 above), she should recite the blessing only after the kindling.

2) Were she to say the blessing first, she could be said to be thereby receiving Shabbath,* which would preclude her from lighting subsequently.

3) On the other hand, blessings must usually be recited immediately before the performance of the mitzva.

4) Because of this requirement, it is customary for women to abstain from enjoying the benefit of the lights which they have just lit, until they have said the blessing.

5) a) Therefore, as soon as they have kindled them, they place their hands in front of the lights or over their eyes, or they close their eyes, and recite the blessing.

b) Only then do they remove their hands, or open their eyes, and enjoy the light.

6) They should not speak between the kindling and the blessing, but should say the blessing without interruption, straight after lighting.

c. With regard to Yom Tov, see Chapter 44, paragraph 7.

31. *a.* If one kindled the Shabbath lights, but forgot to recite the blessing, one has, after the event, fulfilled one's obligation, provided that one did indeed kindle the lights in honor of Shabbath (as to which, see paragraph 32 below). *forgetting the blessing*

b. When one remembers that one forgot to say the blessing, one may, and indeed should, still say it, but **only** if

1) one did not receive Shabbath by lighting (in connection with which see paragraphs 18 and 26 above), or in any other way (as explained in Chapter 46,

---

* This is because there is a view that Shabbath is received, not so much by the actual lighting, as by the recitation of the blessing.

paragraphs 2 and 3),
2) the time for sunset has not yet arrived (as to which see Chapter 46, paragraph 7), **and**
3) the community has not yet received Shabbath by saying *Bo'i v^e-shalom*, *Mizmor shir l^e-yom ha-Shabbath* or *Bar^echu* prior to the evening service (as detailed in Chapter 46, paragraph 7).

c. With regard to Yom Tov, see Chapter 44, paragraph 6.

lighting in honor of Shabbath

32. *a.* 1) a) All lights one kindles in one's house, and which will be burning on Shabbath, should be kindled after *p^elag ha-minchah* on Friday afternoon in honor of Shabbath.
b) This applies even to those lights over which one does not pronounce the blessing.
2) Likewise, when one turns on the electric lights, which will be burning in addition to the Shabbath lights, one should be particular to turn them on in honor of Shabbath.

b. 1) In the event that one had lights prepared as usual for Shabbath, but kindled them for some other purpose, and not as Shabbath lights, one has not discharged one's obligation.
2) If it is still permissible to do so (as to which see Chapter 46, paragraphs 14 to 17), one should extinguish the lights and rekindle them, saying the blessing in the usual way.

igniting the wick

33. *a.* When kindling, one should ignite the wick until most of the protruding part is burning.

b. This is to ensure that there will be a good flame as soon as one takes one's hand away.

c. It makes no difference, in this context, whether one is lighting an oil or kerosene (paraffin) lamp or a candle.

kindling where there are other lights

34. *a.* The authorities differ as to whether one can make the blessing over the kindling of the Shabbath lights in a place which is already illuminated by another light.

b. Consequently, it is best to say the blessing in such a way that all views are satisfied.

c. Thus, the proper course is

1) a) for the woman to kindle the Shabbath lights and say the blessing and, only then,

   b) for another member of the household (who has not yet received Shabbath) to turn on the electric lights, or

2) for the timer controlling the electric lights to be set so that it will only afterwards turn them on, or

3) for the woman

   a) to turn on the electric lights in honor of Shabbath before kindling her Shabbath lights and

   b) to have the electric lights also in mind when saying the blessing over the lights.

35. *a.* 1) As mentioned in paragraph 30 above, when the lights are kindled by a man, he recites the blessing before kindling. *which lights to put on first*

2) As mentioned in paragraph 15 above, the essence of the mitzva, over which the blessing is said, is the kindling of the lights in the place where the meal is to be eaten.

3) It follows that he should kindle these lights first, immediately after the blessing, and the other lights only afterwards.

b. 1) When a woman lights, she should adopt the opposite procedure.

2) As mentioned in paragraph 21 above, she generally receives Shabbath when she kindles those lights which are at or near the dinner table.

3) It follows that she has to put on the other lights beforehand.

4) If she begins by kindling the Shabbath lights in the place where the meal is to be eaten, she may no longer put on the other lights.

c. In any event, whoever lights, whether man or woman, should, while reciting the blessing, have in mind all the lights in the house.

extinguishing the match

36. *a.* The precise moment at which, according to custom, women receive Shabbath is when they
1) have completed the kindling of the lights that are on (or near) the table, but
2) have not yet pronounced the blessing.

b. As a result, the practice is for them
1) not to extinguish the match with which they have kindled the lights, but
2) to put it down in such a way that it will go out by itself.

rekindling extinguished lights

37. *a.* 1) A woman whose lights were extinguished by the wind, or due to some other cause,
   a) after she finished kindling them, but
   b) before she recited the blessing,
   should not rekindle them herself.

2) a) What she should do is to tell another member of the household who has not yet received Shabbath* to light in her place, and
   b) that person should also say the blessing over the lights instead of her.

3) If not all of the lights over which she wishes to recite the blessing have gone out,
   a) she can say the blessing over the remaining light or lights and
   b) another member of the household (who has not received Shabbath) should rekindle the light or lights which have been extinguished.

b. 1) When the lights become extinguished after she has already said the blessing, she may also tell another member of the household who has not yet received Shabbath to rekindle them, as detailed in Chapter 46, paragraph 21, but,

2) in such event, the blessing should not be said again.

---

* See paragraph 18 above.

c. 1) The above contents of this paragraph do not apply where the lights go out because the wick has not been ignited properly.

2) A woman does not fulfill her obligation, or receive Shabbath, by an ineffectual kindling of this kind.

3) As a result, she should rekindle the lights herself.

38. *a.* 1) If the match goes out while one is in the process of kindling the lights, one must not reignite it from a Shabbath light which one has already kindled, even if one wishes to use the match for kindling another Shabbath light, but *matches going out during lighting*

2) the other Shabbath light may be kindled directly from the burning one.

b. 1) One must not heat the bottom of a candle in the flame of a previously kindled Shabbath light, so that one will be able to stand it more firmly in the hole of the candlestick. *melting bottom of candle*

2) This is the case even if the candle requiring to be stood more firmly in the candlestick has already been lit in honor of Shabbath.

39. *a.* 1) It is proper to kindle the lights over which one recites the blessing in the actual place where they are going to burn. *kindling the lights where they will stand*

2) That is to say, at the time of kindling, the lights should already be standing on (or by) the dining table, which is the place where the mitzva should primarily be performed.

b. 1) Subject to what is stated below, one must not kindle the lights in one place and afterwards move them to another place.

2) One should not do so, even if the second place is used for the purposes of the meal, so that one is obliged to light there.

c. 1) Despite the above, in time of need, one may relax the rule, so long as the place from which the lights are being moved to the dining table is also used for the purposes of eating.

2) Therefore, a woman who is unable to rise from her bed

a) should have the lights brought to her and placed on a chair or table by her bedside and,

b) after she has kindled them, should ask for them to be taken to the dining table.*

3) a) One should not, however, kindle the lights whilst the candlesticks are being held in the hand.

b) This is so, even if it is intended to put them on the dining table immediately they have been kindled.

d. 1) It can happen that a woman kindles one light and has no matches left to kindle the others.

2) She may take the light she has already kindled in honor of Shabbath and kindle with it another light in honor of Shabbath. (See also paragraph 38 above.)

e. 1) A woman who kindles the lights in a place where there is no obligation to kindle them, for instance, in a room which is not used on Shabbath,

a) has not thereby discharged her obligation and

b) is guilty of pronouncing a blessing in vain.

2) It makes no difference if the lights are subsequently transferred, by the woman or by anybody else, to a place where there is an obligation to kindle, that is to say, the dining table.

3) She has to extinguish the lights, rekindle them and recite the blessing again (but see paragraph 14 above).

moving the lights after kindling

40. *a.* Except in case of need,** once the Shabbath lights over which the blessing is recited have been kindled, one should be careful not

---

* For the situation where the lights at home are kindled by the husband, but the wife, who is in hospital, also kindles lights there, see Chapter 45, paragraph 6.

** It is, of course, absolutely forbidden to move the lights if one has already received the Shabbath, or if the time for kindling (as defined in paragraph 14 above) has passed.

1) to move them nor
2) to add oil to them.

b. This applies
1) even to somebody who has not yet received Shabbath and
2) even if the person who kindled the lights did not thereby receive Shabbath.

c. 1) The rule with regard to touching the lights is the same as that with regard to touching any *muktzeh* object. (See Chapter 22, paragraph 32.)
2) One may be lenient about touching them, provided this does not cause them to move.

41. *a.* It is permissible to make use of the illumination provided by the Shabbath lights (even those over which the blessing was pronounced), whether for the purpose of a mitzva or otherwise. *using the light*

b. 1) However, one should not do, in the glow of the lights over which the blessing was pronounced, anything which shows disrespect for the mitzva of the Shabbath lights.
2) Consequently, one should not, for example,
a) undress a child by their light or
b) put something filthy in front of them.

42. *a.* There are places where the woman says the *she-hecheyanu* blessing when she kindles Shabbath lights for the first time after she is married. *lighting for the first time*

b. 1) Where there is no such established custom, she should not pronounce this blessing, but,
2) if she so desires, she may
a) put on a new garment or
b) put on the table a fruit which she has not yet eaten that season

and she will then be able to make the *she-hecheyanu* blessing (with the garment or the fruit also in mind).

c. If a woman had the custom to kindle Shabbath lights even before she was married (as mentioned in paragraph

8 above), there are no grounds at all for her to recite the *she-hecheyanu* blessing when she kindles for the first time after the wedding.

the reward

43. *a.* Our Sages have said that a person who, as a matter of practice, makes an effort to beautify the mitzva of kindling Shabbath lights, will have sons who are great in Torah.

b. Indeed, it is fitting for a woman, after kindling, to pray that the Almighty should give her sons who will shine in Torah.

leftovers from lighting

44. *a.* 1) A Shabbath candle which went out may be used after Shabbath, even if it became extinguished within the period of time when one was obliged to have it burning.

2) The same applies to oil left in a lamp after it has gone out.

b. 1) Wax which drips from the candle is *muktzeh* on Shabbath and Yom Tov, as can be seen from Chapter 13, paragraph 38.

2) After Shabbath or Yom Tov, the candle may be thrown in the garbage, since it does not possess any sanctity.

3) Nevertheless, there are those who take a stricter view, and hold that the wax should be disposed of in a dignified manner.*

c. 1) For laws relating to Shabbath lights standing in a draft, see Chapter 13, paragraph 33.

2) For laws relating to dripping Shabbath candles, see Chapter 13, paragraph 38.

---

* One could, for example, wrap it in a plastic bag before putting it in the garbage.

EATING AND DRINKING AFTER KINDLING THE LIGHTS

45. *a.* As stated in paragraph 18 above, usually, once a woman has kindled the Shabbath lights, all the laws of Shabbath apply to her. *forbidden until kiddush*

b. These include the duty to make *kiddush*.

c. Until this obligation has been discharged, she is not allowed to eat or drink (subject to what is stated below).

46. *a.* However, if she is thirsty, she can drink water, but only until sunset. *water or tea*

b. In time of need, it is possible to permit even tea.

47. *a.* A woman who is weak, or a nursing mother, may not be able to do without food or drink. *weak women and nursing mothers*

b. She should stipulate, when kindling the lights, that she is not receiving Shabbath as a result of the kindling. (See paragraph 22 above.)

c. Then, she should eat or drink as much as she needs, until just before sunset.

Chapter 44

Kindling the Yom Tov and Yom Kippur Lights: Special Laws

THE YOM TOV LIGHTS

the obligation

1. *a.* On Yom Tov, too, there is an obligation to kindle a light in honor of that day.

b. It is proper, also on Yom Tov, to kindle a minimum of two lights, as for Shabbath.

when to light

2. *a.* The preferred course (except on the occasions mentioned in paragraph 3 below) is to kindle the Yom Tov lights a little while before sunset, as in the case of the Shabbath lights. (See Chapter 43, paragraph 11.)

b. However, there are those who have the custom to light when they come home from the synagogue, before the meal.

(*c.* From Chapter 13, paragraphs 2 and 3, it will be seen that

1) it is forbidden to light a "new" flame on Yom Tov, although

2) it is permitted to light something from a flame which is already burning, even through the intermediary of a matchstick.)

second day of Yom Tov

3. *a.* 1) The lights for

a) the second night of Rosh Hashana or

b) the night of *yom tov sheini shel galuyoth*

should be kindled only after the stars come out.

2) Furthermore, until the stars come out, these lights should not be prepared for kindling, due to the prohibition against making preparations on the first day of Yom Tov for the second.

b. 1) Nevertheless, if it is dark in the house, lights may be put on earlier* (in a manner which is permitted on Yom Tov, as explained in Chapter 13, paragraphs 1 to 3).

2) No blessing should be recited when these lights are put on, but,

3) at night, after the stars come out, the woman of the house should kindle the Yom Tov lights in the place where the meal is to be eaten and say the blessing over them in the usual way. (See Chapter 13, paragraphs 42 and 43.)

c. When Yom Tov falls on Saturday night, the woman kindling the lights should not do so until Shabbath expires and she has

1) pronounced the words, בָּרוּךְ הַמַּבְדִּיל בֵּין קֹדֶשׁ לְקֹדֶשׁ "Blessed is He Who differentiates between one sanctity and another,"

or

2) recited the evening prayer, adding in the *Amidah* the paragraph commencing *Va-todi'einu*.

4. *a.* 1) The blessing to be recited when kindling the Yom Tov lights is: *form of blessing*

בָּרוּךְ אַתָּה יהוה אֱלֹהֵינוּ מֶלֶךְ הָעוֹלָם, אֲשֶׁר קִדְּשָׁנוּ בְּמִצְוֹתָיו, וְצִוָּנוּ לְהַדְלִיק נֵר שֶׁל יוֹם טוֹב.

"Blessed art Thou, O Lord our God, King of the universe, Who has sanctified us with His commandments and has commanded us to kindle the light of Yom Tov."

2) The same blessing should be made whether it is

a) the first night of Yom Tov,

b) the second night of Rosh Hashana or

c) *yom tov sheini shel galuyoth*

3) If, however, Yom Tov falls on Shabbath, the blessing to be said is:

---

* See Chapter 13, paragraph 44.

בָּרוּךְ אַתָּה יהוה אֱלֹהֵינוּ מֶלֶךְ הָעוֹלָם, אֲשֶׁר קִדְּשָׁנוּ בְּמִצְוֹתָיו, וְצִוָּנוּ לְהַדְלִיק נֵר שֶׁל שַׁבָּת וְשֶׁל יוֹם טוֹב.

"Blessed art Thou, O Lord our God, King of the universe, Who has sanctified us with His commandments and has commanded us to kindle the light of Shabbath and of Yom Tov."

b. 1) a) It is unnecessary to pronounce the *she-hecheyanu* blessing when kindling the Yom Tov lights, but,

b) in a place where the custom is to say it, no objection should be raised.

2) a) A person who does recite the *she-hecheyanu* blessing when kindling the lights should not say it again during ***kiddush*** (unless he is making ***kiddush*** and the *she-hecheyanu* blessing for other members of his household who are listening), and

b) if he is listening to somebody else making ***kiddush*** for him, it is better for him not to answer "Amen" after the *she-hecheyanu* blessing said by the person reciting ***kiddush***.

c) This is because answering "Amen" to the *she-hecheyanu* blessing which he does not require (as opposed to the ***kiddush*** which he does require) could be considered an unjustified interruption between the blessing on the wine and his tasting it. (See also Chapter 48, paragraph 7.)

c. 1) Those who recite the *she-hecheyanu* blessing, as above, do so when kindling the lights on every Festival, except on

a) the seventh night of Pesach and

b) (outside Eretz Yisrael) the eighth night of Pesach.

2) Concerning the second night of Rosh Hashana, see Chapter 47, paragraph 44.

mistake in blessing

5. *a.* When Yom Tov falls on Shabbath, and one has kindled one's lights in honor of Shabbath and Yom Tov, as required, but has made an error with regard to the **form** in which the blessing is concluded, then,

1) if one corrects oneself within the time it would take to say "*Shalom alecha rabi*," and adds the proper form of the conclusion, the whole blessing is, after the event, considered valid and need not, indeed must not, be repeated, whereas,
2) if this time has passed, then,
   a) in a case where one concluded the blessing in the form appropriate to **Shabbath alone**, it is, after the event, regarded as valid and sufficient, but,
   b) where one ended with the form for **Yom Tov alone**, one repeats the blessing for Shabbath **and** Yom Tov, subject to the conditions in Chapter 43, paragraph 31*b* (as where one kindles Shabbath lights and forgets the blessing altogether).

b. Where one mistakenly intended to kindle **only** Shabbath lights, or **only** Yom Tov lights, and made the blessing accordingly, then,
1) if one has not yet received Shabbath, either by the lighting or in any other manner (as explained in Chapter 46, paragraphs 2 and 3), one should kindle an additional light, reciting the blessing for Shabbath **and** Yom Tov, but,
2) if one has received Shabbath,
   a) one can ask somebody who has not yet received Shabbath to kindle lights for one, and
   b) the person lighting can also recite the appropriate blessing.

6. If one forgot to say the blessing at the time one kindled the Yom Tov lights, one can say it for so long as they are still burning. *forgetting blessing*

7. *a.* A woman who follows the preferred course mentioned in paragraph 2 above and kindles Yom Tov lights before sunset (as when kindling Shabbath lights), should strike the match, recite the blessing and then kindle the lights. (Compare Chapter 43, paragraph 30.) *order of lighting*

b. Yet, a woman who adopts the same procedure on Yom Tov

as before Shabbath, and recites the blessing subsequent to kindling Yom Tov lights, also has halachic authority to support her.

c. When Yom Tov occurs on Shabbath, all the authorities agree that she should kindle first and recite the blessing afterwards.

d. A woman whose custom it is to kindle Yom Tov lights at night, before the meal, as mentioned in paragraph 2 above, should certainly recite the blessing first, and kindle the lights only afterwards.*

receiving Yom Tov

8. *a.* A woman who kindles Yom Tov lights before sunset (as mentioned in paragraph 2 above), receives Yom Tov by doing so, in the same way as she receives Shabbath by kindling the Shabbath lights.

b. 1) As a result, if she still needs to perform an activity which is forbidden on Yom Tov, she should stipulate, at the time of kindling, that she is not thereby receiving the Festival.

2) It will then be permissible for her to perform such activities, if she has to, until just before sunset, provided the community has not yet received the Festival by saying *Barechu* at the commencement of the evening service.

3) See, however, Chapter 43, paragraph 23.

extinguishing match

9. *a.* On Yom Tov too, one should be particular not to extinguish the match after kindling. (See Chapter 13, paragraph 8.)

b. It should be carefully put down and left to go out by itself.

moving lights or wax

10. *a.* One is allowed to move the lights on Yom Tov, but

b. wax which drips from a candle is *muktzeh*. (See also Chapter 13, paragraph 43.)

---

* The same applies to a woman who kindles Yom Tov lights at night because it is Saturday night or the second day of Yom Tov. (See paragraph 3 above.)

11. *a.* One may make use of the illumination radiated by the Yom Tov lights, in the same way as one may use that emanating from the Shabbath lights, whether it be for performing a mitzva, or for one's own purposes. (See further Chapter 43, paragraph 41.) *using lights*

b. 1) However, the flame itself may not be used
   a) for secular purposes, nor even
   b) for the purpose of a mitzva, if the mitzva is not done directly with the flame. (See Chapter 43, paragraph 38, which deals with Shabbath lights, where the principle pertaining to this aspect is the same.)
2) Consequently, there are those who hold that it is forbidden to use a Yom Tov light, for example,
   a) to light a cigarette or
   b) to light the gas cooker.
3) a) At all events, in time of great need, one may take a flame from a Yom Tov light, even through the agency of a matchstick.
   b) An instance would be where one has no other flame from which one can light the stove, in order to cook the food for Yom Tov.

c. One should not take into the bathroom (toilet) a light kindled in fulfillment of one's obligation to kindle Yom Tov lights.

d. For other rules relating to lighting candles on Yom Tov see Chapter 13, paragraphs 33, 38 and 42 to 44.

12. *a.* 1) When Yom Tov falls on Friday, one may not prepare any food for the next day (Shabbath), unless one prepared or put aside, on the day before Yom Tov, some cooked food and some bread (or matza) as an *eiruv tavshilin*. (For particulars, refer to Chapter 2, paragraphs 10 to 16.) *eiruv tavshilin*
2) The *eiruv tavshilin* also makes it permissible to kindle the Shabbath lights.

b. 1) Someone who is not thinking of cooking and so forth for Shabbath does not have to make an *eiruv tavshilin*.

2) Nevertheless, if he has to kindle Shabbath lights on Yom Tov, he
   a) should make an *eiruv tavshilin*, but
   b) should not recite the blessing.

c. 1) A person who forgot, or due to the force of circumstances was unable, to make an *eiruv tavshilin* on the day before Yom Tov should kindle only one Shabbath light, although,

2) if the Rabbi of the town made an *eiruv tavshilin* for the use of all the inhabitants, such a person may rely on the Rabbi's *eiruv* and kindle his usual number of Shabbath (or Shabbath and Yom Tov) lights.

3) Still, one must make one's own *eiruv tavshilin* when one can, and should not rely on the Rabbi's *eiruv* unless one has no choice.

THE YOM KIPPUR LIGHTS

the mitzva and the blessings

13. *a.* 1) It is customary to kindle lights before the commencement of Yom Kippur.

2) For Yom Kippur too, it is proper to kindle a minimum of two lights, as for Shabbath.

3) The blessing made when lighting them is:

בָּרוּךְ אַתָּה יהוה אֱלֹהֵינוּ מֶלֶךְ הָעוֹלָם, אֲשֶׁר קִדְּשָׁנוּ בְּמִצְוֹתָיו, וְצִוָּנוּ לְהַדְלִיק נֵר שֶׁל יוֹם הַכִּפּוּרִים.

"Blessed art Thou, O Lord our God, King of the universe, Who has sanctified us with His commandments and has commanded us to kindle the light of Yom Kippur."

4) The lights are kindled first, and the blessing said afterwards, as on Shabbath. (See Chapter 43, paragraph 30.)

b. 1) When Yom Kippur falls on Shabbath, the kindling of lights is obligatory, as on an ordinary Shabbath.

2) The blessing recited is:

בָּרוּךְ אַתָּה יהוה אֱלֹהֵינוּ מֶלֶךְ הָעוֹלָם, אֲשֶׁר קִדְּשָׁנוּ בְּמִצְוֹתָיו, וְצִוָּנוּ לְהַדְלִיק נֵר שֶׁל שַׁבָּת וְשֶׁל יוֹם הַכִּפּוּרִים.

"Blessed art Thou, O Lord our God, King of the universe, Who has sanctified us with His commandments and has commanded us to kindle the light of Shabbath and of Yom Kippur."

c. Whoever pronounces the *she-hecheyanu* blessing when kindling the lights (following the custom referred to in paragraph 4 above) should not repeat it at the time of the evening prayer.

14. *a.* 1) A woman who kindles Yom Kippur lights thereby subjects herself to all the laws of Yom Kippur, in the same way as she receives Shabbath by kindling the Shabbath lights. (See Chapter 43, paragraph 18.) *receiving Yom Kippur*

2) These include not only the laws relating to those activities which are forbidden on Shabbath too, but also those enjoining self-denial applicable specifically on Yom Kippur.

3) Consequently, she should remove her leather shoes prior to kindling the lights.

4) This notwithstanding, provided she did not recite the *she-hecheyanu* blessing, she may wear her leather shoes to go to the synagogue for the *Kol Nidrei* prayer.

b. 1) a) In case of need, a woman can stipulate, at the time of lighting, that she is not thereby receiving Yom Kippur.

b) She may do so either expressly or by making a mental reservation.

c) See further Chapter 43, paragraph 22.

2) She cannot make such a stipulation if she has recited the *she-hecheyanu* blessing. (See Chapter 43, paragraph 23.)

15. In the event that all the members of the household go to the synagogue for the *Kol Nidrei* prayer immediately after the kindling of the lights, one should ensure that the lights are capable of burning until the family returns home after the service. (See Chapter 43, paragraph 17.) *burning time* *moving the table*

16. *a.* The table on which the burning lights are standing at the commencement of Yom Kippur is a *basis la-davar ha-assur*, as explained in Chapter 20, paragraph 59.

b. If one will want to move the table, one must leave on it, from before the beginning of Yom Kippur, some article of importance which one will need for Yom Kippur, the loaves one would normally leave there on Shabbath not being appropriate on this occasion. (See Chapter 20, paragraph 61.)

Chapter 45

Kindling the Shabbath and Yom Tov Lights When Not at Home

1. *a.* For the purposes of the laws which are the subject of this Chapter, one must distinguish between two categories of individuals. *two categories*

1) The first category consists of
   a) members of the household and
   b) guests who are partaking of the meal at the host's table, even if they do not eat there permanently, but are invited merely for that Shabbath or Yom Tov evening.
2) The second category comprises
   a) guests who are not eating at the host's table, or even
   b) those who are, but eat their own food.

2. *a.* 1) When one kindles the Shabbath lights in the dining room, one thereby discharges also the obligation to kindle lights *family and guests who dine*

   a) of one's husband or wife, one's children and all the other members of the household, and
   b) of the guests who will be participating in the meal.

2) None of these need be present at the time of kindling or need hear the blessing.
3) Moreover, if they also kindle lights in the rooms which they will be using on Shabbath, they should kindle without pronouncing a blessing.

b. 1) However, if guests are allotted a separate room,* which is not used personally by their host or his

---

* See paragraph 5 below for how to proceed where guests (who do not belong to the same family) share a room.

family, it is preferable that they kindle lights and recite the blessing there, even if they do not use the room in any way for the purposes of eating.

2) If they do this,

a) they should light long candles (or add more oil), so that the lights will not go out before they come back to their room, or

b) one of them should stay in their room until close to nightfall, so as to enjoy the light radiated by the Shabbath lights.

3) a) In any event, they fulfill their obligation even if in this case they light where they eat, but

b) they should ensure that their room will not be completely dark when they come back to it.

family members away

3. *a.* 1) A woman* who kindles Shabbath lights in her dining room thereby discharges the obligation to kindle lights even of those permanent members of the household who do not happen to be home that Shabbath** (subject to what is stated below).

2) Instances of this are where her husband is

a) in another town,

b) away on military service or

c) in the hospital.

b. Such members of the household who are away for Shabbath, and eat in a place where Shabbath lights are kindled,

1) have no obligation at all to kindle lights themselves, and

2) need not participate in the expense of kindling,

provided that there is light in the room where they spend the night, even if it penetrates only from the corridor or from the street.

---

* For the situation where the wife is away and the husband lights at home, see paragraph 6 below.

** Regarding members of the household who are away for a more extended period of time, see paragraphs 11 to 13 below.

c. 1) If, however, there is no light at all in the room where they are to eat or spend the night, they are obliged to kindle lights there and recite the appropriate blessing.
   2) This applies also if
      a) they are invited to eat in a house where Shabbath lights are kindled in the dining room, but,
      b) after the meal, they will be returning to sleep in their room, which is completely dark, that is to say with no light coming into it even from the corridor or the street.
   3) They should kindle large lights, which will burn until they come back to their room.
   4) Of course, if leaving the lights to burn unsupervised creates any risk whatsoever of fire, it is better for them not to light and, indeed, in the circumstances, it is considered a mitzva for them not to do so.

4. The rule with regard to a guest who comes only to stay over Friday night, but does not partake of the meal at the host's table (the second category specified in paragraph 1 above), is as follows: *guests who do not dine*

a. in the event that lights are being kindled for him at his home, as mentioned in paragraph 3 above, then,
   1) if there will be light in the room he has been allotted (as in paragraph 3 above), he himself does not have to kindle lights, but,
   2) if his host has allotted him a room in which to eat or sleep, and there will be no other light there, he should
      a) kindle lights there, saying the appropriate blessing, and
      b) make provision for the lights to burn until he returns to his room after the meal (in a case where he eats elsewhere);

b. in the event that lights are not being kindled for him at his home, then
   1) the Halacha obliges him to participate with his host

in the mitzva of kindling the lights, (for instance by contributing a small amount of money towards the cost of the oil or candles, as mentioned in paragraph 5 below,) except that,

2) if his host has allotted him a separate room, he should kindle lights there, saying the appropriate blessing, and these lights should burn until he comes back to his room after the meal (if he is eating elsewhere).

c. For the rule with regard to a guest who partakes of the meal at his host's table (and falls within the first category set out in paragraph 1 above), see paragraph 2 above.

individuals together for Shabbath

5. *a.* Several individuals who are spending Shabbath together in the same place, and are liable to kindle Shabbath lights, as in some of the cases related in paragraphs 3 and 4 above, can perform the mitzva jointly.

b. The way in which they can do this is

1) a) for each of them to participate in the expense of buying the oil or the candles or

b) for one of them to buy the oil or the candles out of his own money and transfer a share in them to each of his fellows (in one of the ways specified below)

and

2) for one of them to kindle the lights and say the blessing, with the intention of discharging thereby also the obligations of his fellows.

c. The person buying the oil or the candles can transfer shares in them to the others in one of the following ways:

1) he can have the intention, at the time of purchase, to acquire the oil or the candles for the benefit of all of them;

2) after the purchase, he can let one of the others lift up the oil or the candles with the intention of thereby acquiring shares for all of them;

3) he can put the oil or the candles into lamps or into candlesticks
   a) which they bought jointly, or
   b) which they rented jointly together with the room,
   with the intention of making the oil or candles their joint property.

6. *a.* When a husband kindles lights at home and says the blessing, as mentioned in Chapter 43, paragraph 7, he also does so for his wife who is away, for example *when wife away*
1) in the hospital, or
2) in a convalescent home after a childbirth.

b. The wife is, as a result, released from her obligation to kindle lights herself, provided that
1) there is light in her room at the hospital or convalescent home or
2) light shines into it from outside

(as in the parallel situation described in paragraph 3 above).

c. Nonetheless, the custom is for every married woman to kindle lights in the place where she will be eating, and to recite the blessing. (Compare paragraph 9 below.)

d. If the wife has to eat in bed, and kindles lights at her bedside, one should be particular to leave the lights where they are and not to move them to another room after she has kindled.*

7. *a.* When parents have gone away for Shabbath, and their unmarried sons and daughters who are staying behind will be eating at home together, one of the children should kindle lights for them all, in the place where they are going to eat. *children left at home*

b. Since they usually eat together as one family, they remain such even when their parents are away.

---

* For the situation where the husband does not kindle the lights, but the wife, who is in bed, kindles them at her bedside for the family, see Chapter 43, paragraph 39.

when visiting parents

8. *a.* When a couple goes to his or her parents' house to eat the Shabbath meal on Friday night, the custom is for the wife to kindle Shabbath lights and pronounce the blessing in the parents' dining room.

b. Nevertheless, if, after the meal, they will be going home to sleep, it is preferable for her to kindle lights and pronounce the blessing in her own home, before she leaves it, but

1) she can do this only if she in fact leaves her home after *p^e^lag ha-minchah*, as explained in Chapter 43, paragraph 12, and

2) either

a) the lights must be large enough to burn until they come back home after the meal

or

b) one of them should stay at home until close to nightfall, in order to enjoy the glow of the Shabbath lights, and only then go to their parents' house.

c. 1) If she wishes to kindle lights also in their parents' dining room, she should stipulate, when lighting and saying the blessing at home prior to leaving for their parents' house, that she is not yet receiving Shabbath, as mentioned in Chapter 43, paragraph 22 (and see paragraph 24 there).

2) She will then be able to light again, without a blessing, in their parents' house.

d. 1) Similarly, if they are not going back home after the meal, but have their own private bedroom at their parents' house, the wife would do well to kindle lights* and say the blessing in their room.

2) In this case, if she wishes to light also in her parents' dining room, she should do so, without reciting a blessing, before she lights in her bedroom.

hotel guests

9. *a.* 1) When a number of guests are staying in a convales-

---

* The lights should burn until they come back to their room after the meal.

cent home or at a hotel with their wives, and eat in the common dining room, the custom is for each woman to kindle lights and pronounce the blessing in the dining room.

2) She should kindle the lights close to the table where she and her husband will be eating, and not in some far-off corner.

b. 1) Still, since each family has its own room, albeit only for sleeping, it is better if

a) one woman kindles Shabbath lights and recites the blessing in the dining room, while

b) the others kindle and say the blessing in their respective rooms.

2) Lights kindled in the bedrooms should be large enough not to go out before their occupants come back to them after the meal, as stated in the preceding paragraph.

eating at restaurant

10. *a.* 1) If one is going to eat at a restaurant on Friday night, and go back home at the end of the meal, the better course is to kindle lights and say the blessing at home (before one leaves).

2) The lights should be large enough to burn until one arrives back home.

b. 1) However, there are grounds for the view that one should kindle the lights and say the blessing in the restaurant.

2) Should one adopt this course, one should take steps to ensure that, on one's return, one's home will not be in total darkness.

c. See also paragraph 3*c* above.

at yeshiva or boarding school

11. *a.* Boys or girls who live in rooms or in a dormitory at a yeshiva, boarding school or other institution have an obligation to kindle Shabbath lights, since, for the present, the institution is their fixed abode.

b. 1) All of those who are resident at the institution are regarded as one big family.

2) Consequently, one of them should kindle lights for all of them in the dining room.

c. 1) Since Shabbath lights are kindled both in honor of Shabbath and to enhance its enjoyment, to kindle lights in just one spot in a large hall is insufficient, if not all of those eating there would be able to see them.

2) The proper thing to do, therefore, is to kindle in various places in the dining room, so that everyone can see the lights.

d. 1) It is as well for one of the boys or girls at the yeshiva, boarding school or other institution

a) to kindle all of the lights for everybody and

b) to recite the blessing when kindling at the last place.

2) If one of them recites the blessing when kindling the first lights, and the additional lights are kindled by others, they should do so without reciting a blessing.

e. 1) However, even though lights are kindled in the dining room, it is necessary, as mentioned in Chapter 43, paragraph 15, to see that every room which will be used on Friday night has a light in it.

2) There should be light in the bedrooms until bedtime.

3) At the very least, there should be light shining into the rooms from the outside, for example from the corridor.

4) This is sufficient, and there is no need to kindle actual Shabbath lights in the individual rooms, even if they are not in the same building as the dining room where the lights were kindled.

f. 1) If Shabbath lights are kindled in the bedrooms, it is better not to pronounce a blessing when lighting them, but to rely on the blessing pronounced by whoever kindles lights in the dining room.

g. 1) Nevertheless, if they so desire, the inhabitants of a room may kindle Shabbath lights and pronounce the blessing there.*

2) They can perform the mitzva jointly, as described in paragraph 5 above, one of them kindling and saying the blessing on behalf of them all.

3) See also paragraph 2. *b*. 2) above.

12. *a.* 1) Boys or girls living in a yeshiva or boarding school who *resident students eating out*

a) are invited out to eat at an acquaintance's house on Friday night and

b) will be returning to sleep at the yeshiva or school,

need not personally kindle lights where they eat, because their obligations are discharged by the kindling of the lights in their host's house.

2) Their situation, as guests who participate in their host's meal, is dealt with in paragraph 2 above (and see also paragraph 11 above).

b. 1) In any event, it is preferable that they kindle lights, and recite the blessing, in the room in which they sleep,** as mentioned in paragraph 2*b* above.

2) They should at least ensure that the room is illuminated by a light coming in from the outside, for example from the corridor.

13. *a.* A boy or girl living in a yeshiva or boarding school who goes home for Shabbath to his or her parents' house, is treated like the other members of the family, as set out in paragraph 2 above, and does not have to kindle lights. *resident students away for Shabbath*

b. 1) They are similarly free from the obligation to kindle lights if they go away to spend Shabbath

a) at the home of relatives or acquaintances, or

b) at a different yeshiva or boarding school.

2) They do not have to kindle lights

a) in the former case, because they partake of the

---

* Of course, if there is any risk of fire, it is better not to light in the bedrooms of the institution and, indeed, it is a mitzva not to do so.

** See the note to the previous paragraph.

meal at their host's table and,

b) in the latter case, because they are temporarily considered to be members of the yeshiva or school which they are visiting.

3) See, however, paragraph 2*b* above.

summer camps

14. *a.* Participants in summer camps and the like are obliged to kindle Shabbath lights.

b. If there is a family, that is to say a husband and wife, with them, the wife should kindle lights and recite the blessing in the dining room and thereby discharge the obligations of all the participants.

c. If the camp leader is unmarried and there is no other family with them, one of the participants should kindle Shabbath lights in the dining room and say the blessing for all, in joint fulfillment of their obligation to kindle.

d. 1) They should also ensure that there will be light in the bedrooms,* in accordance with the principle mentioned in Chapter 43, paragraph 15*c*.

2) There should at least be light coming in from outside, for example from the corridor in front of the room.

3) The light should stay on until they go to sleep.

(See paragraph 11 above and the note to that paragraph.)

yom tov sheini shel galuyoth

15. *a.* Someone living outside Eretz Yisrael, who,

1) on a Friday evening which is also *yom tov sheini shel galuyoth*, is the guest of someone living in Eretz Yisrael and

2) partakes of the meal at his host's table, so that he

3) falls within the same category as members of the household,

does not need to kindle lights himself. (See paragraph 2 above.)

---

* See paragraph 11 above and the note to that paragraph.

b. His obligation is discharged by the kindling of his host's lights, despite the fact that his host says the blessing appropriate to Shabbath lights alone (and not to Shabbath **and** Yom Tov lights).

on night duty

16. *a.* A person who
1) lives alone,
2) will be leaving home when Shabbath begins, or shortly thereafter, and
3) will not be coming back home that night

should not kindle Shabbath lights at home.

b. He should not do so, even if he will be unable to kindle lights in the place to which he is going and where he will be eating.

c. A situation of this kind can arise, for example, in the case of somebody on night duty.

Chapter 46

Receiving Shabbath and Yom Tov

THE MITZVA

tosefeth Shabbath

1. *a.* It is a mitzva to add time to a holy day, both at its commencement and at its conclusion, at the expense of the ordinary weekday.

b. 1) Our Sages expressed the mitzva in terms of two verses:

a) "Remember the Shabbath day to keep it holy" (Exodus 20:8).

b) "Observe the Shabbath day to keep it holy" (Deuteronomy 5:12).

2) a) Remember it at its commencement, by receiving it an appreciable time before sunset.

b) Observe it at its conclusion, by postponing its departure, like a man who does not want his friend to go, and keeps him with him for as long as he can detain him.

c. 1) The mitzva applies both to Shabbath and to Yom Tov, including Yom Kippur.

2) Consequently, a person must take their observance upon himself prior to sunset and, from the moment he does so, should desist from all forbidden activity.

d. When receiving Yom Kippur, he should take upon himself too, from the same moment, the five kinds of self-denial which are obligatory that day, namely, refraining from eating and drinking, washing, oiling the body, wearing leather footwear, and marital intercourse.

e. 1) The time which must be added to a holy day is known as *tosefeth* Shabbath, *tosefeth* Yom Tov or *tosefeth* Yom Ha-kippurim, as the case may be.

2) All three are applicable equally to men and to women.

2. *a.* 1) Receiving Shabbath or Yom Tov is not done by simply ceasing to perform prohibited activities. *intention to receive Shabbath*

2) It should be done verbally, by saying that one is taking upon oneself the observance of Shabbath (or Yom Tov).

b. Still, even if one does not bring one's intention to one's lips, but merely makes up one's mind to receive Shabbath, one is deemed to have indeed received Shabbath and should desist from all forbidden activity.

3. *a.* Even when one does not explicitly say that one is doing so, one receives Shabbath if, prior to sunset, one *saying Shabbath prayers*

1) starts reciting the blessings which precede the *Shᵉma* of the Shabbath evening prayer, or

2) says

a) *Bo'i vᵉ-shalom* (the last verse of the hymn beginning *Lᵉcha dodi*), or

b) the psalm *Mizmor shir lᵉ-yom ha-Shabbath* (on a Friday evening which occurs during the course of, or immediately following, a Festival, if one's custom then is to omit the whole of *Lᵉcha dodi*).

b. Similarly, as explained in Chapter 43, paragraph 18, the custom is for women to receive Shabbath when kindling lights. (See Chapter 44, paragraph 8, for receiving Yom Tov by kindling the lights.)

4. *a.* The latest time for beginning *tosefeth* Shabbath or *tosefeth* Yom Tov is a little while before the sun sets. *time limits*

b. It is commendable to receive Shabbath at least twenty minutes, or, better still, half an hour, before sunset, in order to satisfy all of the views on the subject.

c. 1) If one wishes to take upon oneself the observance of Shabbath from an even earlier time, from *pᵉlag ha-minchah* onwards, one is permitted to do so, and all of the laws of Shabbath would apply to one as from that time.

2) *Pᵉlag ha-minchah* is one and a quarter hours before sunset, where one hour is defined as one twelfth of

the time between sunrise and sunset on the day in question.

3) See further Chapter 43, paragraph 12.

d. To receive Shabbath before *pelag ha-minchah* is of no effect.

e. 1) Annual calendars are published, which show the times for the commencement of Shabbath and Yom Tov.

2) In places where clocks are advanced in summer, one should check whether the compiler of the calendar took this into account.

praying minchah in time

5. *a.* 1) One should try to ensure that the congregation with which one prays says the *minchah* prayer in time for the participants to receive Shabbath at least a little while before sunset.

2) a) If one sees that one's efforts are in vain, to the extent that the congregation is not going to finish the silent *Amidah* of the *minchah* prayer until sunset or even later, one should not pray with it.*

b) One should pray alone and receive Shabbath before sunset, rather than neglect the mitzva of *tosefeth* Shabbath.

c) Still, even after one has received Shabbath, one will be able to join in the responses to the *kedushah* and so forth of the *minchah* prayer.

b. 1) In the event that one has received Shabbath without having recited the *minchah* prayer, one can no longer recite it, even if there is sufficient time left before sunset.

2) One should make up for the missed prayer by saying the Friday night *Amidah* twice.

---

* When one is able to finish one's own silent *Amidah* before sunset, one can receive Shabbath by oneself, for example by saying *Mizmor shir le-yom ha-Shabbath*. (See paragraphs 2 and 3 above.)

importance of receiving Shabbath before sunset

6. *a.* A person should always come to the synagogue in good time, so that he can receive the Shabbath before sunset, and in accordance with local practice.

b. When the time for sunset approaches, the congregation should not wait, even for an important personage, but should proceed, so as not to nullify the mitzva of receiving Shabbath before sunset (quite apart from the ruling that one should not recite the *minchah* prayer after sunset).

effect of congregation's receiving Shabbath

7. *a.* 1) An individual must not perform prohibited activities after the public receives Shabbath in the synagogue.

2) Shabbath is received in the synagogue by the congregation's saying, before sunset,

a) *Barechu* prior to the evening prayer, or

b) *Bo'i ve-shalom* (the last verse of the hymn beginning *Lecha dodi*), or the psalm *Mizmor shir le-yom ha-Shabbath*.

3) A distinction must be made between

a) settlements or neighborhoods with only one synagogue and

b) localities where there are several synagogues.

b. 1) Where there is only one synagogue, the individual is bound when the congregation receives Shabbath, if most of the members of the congregation who regularly pray in the synagogue are present.

2) The reception of Shabbath by the congregation binds even those individuals who have not yet reached the synagogue, or who do not arrive at all.

3) a) Likewise, a woman is bound when Shabbath is received by the congregation with which her husband usually prays, even though she usually receives Shabbath by kindling the lights.

b) Consequently, if she has not yet kindled, she may no longer do so, and should request a non-Jew to kindle lights for her, as detailed in paragraph 22 below.

4) a) In brief, the minority of the congregation which is not in the synagogue must refrain from all

forbidden activities as from the moment when the majority receives Shabbath.

b) Thus, if there is no *eiruv*, so that carrying articles about is prohibited, latecomers must not bring their prayer books and so forth to the synagogue after this time.

c. 1) Where there are several synagogues, those who pray at one are not affected when Shabbath is received at another (even if those who have received Shabbath are in the majority).

2) Moreover, the reception of Shabbath in a particular synagogue by the majority of those who usually attend does not affect even its own congregants who have not yet arrived, so long as most of the other synagogues in town have still not received Shabbath.

3) a) A synagogue in which evening services are held at two different times on Friday is regarded as two synagogues.

b) In summertime, for instance, Shabbath might be received at the first service at *pelag ha-minchah* (as in paragraph 4 above) and, at the second, shortly before sunset.

c) Those who pray at the second service are not affected when Shabbath is received at the first service.

tosefeth Shabbath still part of previous day

8. Although, as stated in paragraph 1 above, it is a mitzva to receive a holy day early and thereupon to desist from all forbidden activity, the time added is deemed, for the purpose of other laws, to be part of the previous day, as can be seen in the following instances:

a. 1) A baby born on Friday,

a) after both the public and the individual have received Shabbath, but

b) before the sun has set,

is circumcised on the following Friday.

2) If the baby is born after sunset, one should ask a rabbi versed in the Halacha when to perform the

circumcision.

b. 1) It is a mitzva to eat a *ka-zayith* of matza on the night of Passover.

2) The matza should not be eaten until after the stars come out, even if the congregation received the Festival before sunset and also recited the evening prayer.

c. 1) One may intone the Friday evening *kiddush* before dark.

2) Notwithstanding this, one should be careful to eat at least a *ka-zayith* of bread after the stars come out.

d. 1) On the evening of Sh^{e}mini Atzereth, one should not make *kiddush* before nightfall.

2) Otherwise, one will be faced with the dilemma of,
   a) on the one hand, having to eat one's Sh^{e}mini Atzereth meal in the *sukka*, because Sukkoth has not yet terminated, and,
   b) on the other hand, being unable to recite the blessing appropriate to Sukkoth, since one has already made *kiddush* for Sh^{e}mini Atzereth.

e. 1) One should not say the evening prayer for the night of Shavuoth before nightfall.

2) This is in order to allow the period of forty-nine days during which the *omer* is counted to be fully completed before one "starts" the next day.

f. 1) A person who forgets to count the *omer* on Thursday night, and remembers before sunset on Friday evening, can still count the number appropriate for Friday, even if
   a) he has already received Shabbath, and even if
   b) the congregation has already received Shabbath and recited the evening prayer.

2) a) He counts without pronouncing the blessing, but,
   b) on the remaining days, he should count with the blessing.

g. 1) a) A woman must wait at least five days, starting with the day she first finds signs of menstruation, before she can examine herself to make sure the flow has completely ceased.

b) If the signs first became apparent on Friday or on the day prior to Yom Tov, before sunset, then that day is counted as the first of the five, even if she had already kindled lights and received Shabbath or Yom Tov.

c) This means that, if the first day is Friday, she can make the examination on the Tuesday of the following week.

2) Similarly, if

a) the fifth day is Friday or the day preceding Yom Tov and

b) she does not manage to make the examination before kindling Shabbath or Yom Tov lights,

she may do so later, as long as she completes it before sunset.

praying minchah after congregation has received Shabbath

9. *a.* 1) If, when a congregation receives Shabbath, a minority of its members

a) has not yet recited the *minchah* prayer, and yet

b) joins the congregation in responding to *Bar^echu*,

those who respond can no longer say the *minchah* prayer* (except as mentioned below).

2) They will have to make up for the missed prayer by saying the Friday night *Amidah* twice.

b. 1) The situation is different if the congregants comprising this minority

a) are not in the synagogue when the congregation receives Shabbath, or

b) are in the synagogue, but do not join in the response to *Bar^echu*, or

c) do join in the response, but have in mind not thereby to receive Shabbath.

2) In these circumstances,

a) they are indeed bound by the action of the majority in receiving Shabbath, as explained in para-

* The individual, by responding, personally receives Shabbath and may, therefore, neither perform prohibited activities, nor recite the *minchah* prayer.

graph 7 above, to the extent that they have to refrain from prohibited activity, but, this notwithstanding,

b) they can still recite the *minchah* prayer.*

3) They should not, however, do so (even if they pray individually) inside the synagogue where Shabbath has been received, but should go out into the entrance hall, or into another room, and pray there.

c. The case of a woman who does not manage to say the *minchah* prayer before she has to kindle the Shabbath lights is dealt with in Chapter 43, paragraph 18.

10. *a.* 1) Someone who comes to the synagogue so late that the congregation will receive Shabbath while he is in the course of saying the *minchah* prayer should preferably not start to pray inside the synagogue.

praying minchah while congregation receives Shabbath

2) What he ought to do is go out into the entrance hall, or into another room, and recite the *minchah* prayer there.

b. Nevertheless, if he has nowhere else to pray, he should begin to say the *minchah* prayer in the synagogue, despite the fact that the congregation will receive Shabbath before he finishes.

c. He should not delay beginning the *minchah* prayer in order to respond to *Bar^e^chu* with the congregation.

PERFORMING FORBIDDEN ACTIVITIES DURING TOSEFETH SHABBATH AND BEIN HA-SH^e^MASHOTH

11. As will be seen below, in order to know which activities are still permitted during *tosefeth* Shabbath (that is to say after the reception of Shabbath, but before sunset), a distinction must be made between

distinguishing between individual and congregation

---

* An individual who has not personally received Shabbath, but is merely bound by the congregation's receiving Shabbath, is indeed forbidden to perform prohibited activities, but may still recite the *minchah* prayer.

a. an individual who receives Shabbath and

b. a congregation which receives Shabbath, and thereby binds even that minority of its members which is not present (as explained in paragraph 7 above).

after woman kindles lights

12. *a.* 1) The custom is for a woman to receive Shabbath when she kindles the lights.

2) The laws applicable in her case are explained in Chapter 43, paragraphs 18 to 20.

b. 1) In case of need, however, she can stipulate, before lighting, that she is not yet receiving Shabbath.

2) In that event, she will still be permitted to perform otherwise forbidden activities until just before sunset, as explained in Chapter 43, paragraph 22.

c. See also paragraph 15*b* below.

after man kindles lights

13. *a.* A man who kindles Shabbath lights does not thereby receive Shabbath, as detailed in Chapter 43, paragraph 26.

b. Still, as explained there, if he has already said the *minchah* prayer and wishes, after kindling lights, to do something which is forbidden on Shabbath, it is well for him to stipulate, prior to kindling, that he is not thereby receiving Shabbath.

c. 1) If he neither

a) made such a stipulation, nor

b) received Shabbath expressly,

he may, in case of need, still perform activities forbidden on Shabbath (so long as the community has not yet received Shabbath by saying *Bo'i v^e^-shalom*, *Mizmor shir l^e^-yom ha-Shabbath* or *Bar^e^chu* prior to the evening service).

2) Thus, for example, if he kindles the lights for Shabbath which falls during Chanuka before he kindles the Chanuka lights, he may still kindle the latter. (See also paragraph 23 below.)

14. *a.* As stated in paragraph 3 above, an individual can receive Shabbath early by reciting, before sunset, *after individual says Shabbath prayers*
1) the Shabbath evening prayer, or
2) *Bo'i v^e-shalom* or *Mizmor shir l^e-yom ha-Shabbath*.

b. Should he do so, he will be prohibited from performing forbidden activities, as if it were actually Shabbath.

c. He cannot stipulate that he will pray without thereby receiving Shabbath.

d. See, however, paragraphs 19 and 22 below.

e. 1) In a place where there is no *eiruv*, a person who has received Shabbath in this way may not take his prayer book or his *Chumash* to the synagogue, even if the sun has not yet set (and it goes without saying that he must not bring them back home from the synagogue after the service).
2) With regard to asking somebody else to take them, see paragraph 21 below.

f. See also paragraph 15*b* below.

15. *a.* 1) Paragraph 7 above particularizes how a congregation can receive Shabbath early by reciting, before sunset (but after *p^elag ha-minchah*, as mentioned in paragraph 4 above), *after congregation receives Shabbath*
a) the Shabbath evening prayer, or
b) *Bo'i v^e-shalom* or *Mizmor shir l^e-yom ha-Shabbath*.
2) In the conditions explained there, the minority of the congregation which is not in the synagogue is bound when Shabbath is received by the majority.
3) See also paragraph 22 below.

b. Nonetheless, authoritative sources are lenient in permitting, for the purpose of a mitzva which one would otherwise miss, the performance of a forbidden act after the congregation has received Shabbath (but before sunset),
1) even if they have already recited the evening prayer,
2) even if the mitzva is only a Rabbinical one, and
3) even if one has oneself received Shabbath.

c. 1) A case in point is where
  a) Rosh Hashana falls on Thursday and Friday,
  b) due to the force of circumstances a congregation has not been able to hear the *shofar* blown,
  c) the congregation has already received Shabbath and recited the evening prayer, but
  d) the sun has not yet set, and now
  e) the opportunity arises for them to have the *shofar* blown.

  2) The *shofar* may be blown, but
  a) the usual blessings should not be said and
  b) not more than thirty blasts (as opposed to the customary one hundred) should be blown.

d. A person who has a son to circumcise on Friday is still obliged to have him circumcised that day,
  1) even if he, the *mohel* and the congregation have all already received Shabbath,
  2) as long as the sun has not yet set.

bein ha-sh^e^mashoth: meaning and nature

16. *a.* It is uncertain at which moment, during the period between sunset and the time when the stars come out, the previous day ends and the following night (and consequently the next day) begins.

b. This period is called *bein ha-sh^e^mashoth.**

c. During *bein ha-sh^e^mashoth*, activities which are forbidden on Shabbath are prohibited as if it were definitely Shabbath, except to the extent specified below, even if one has not received Shabbath.

doubt as to whether it is bein ha-sh^e^mashoth

17. If there is a doubt as to whether it is *bein ha-sh^e^mashoth*, that is to say if one is not sure whether the sun has already set, one should apply the same restrictions as if it were definitely *bein ha-sh^e^mashoth*.

---

* Since there are varying views as to the actual delimitation of *bein ha-sh^e^mashoth*, that view is usually followed which makes for greater stringency in the particular case in question.

Rabbinical prohibitions during bein ha-shemashoth: general rule

18. The Rabbis permitted one to violate Rabbinical prohibitions during *bein ha-sh^{e}mashoth*, in the special circumstances defined and described in the paragraphs below,

a. provided the congregation to which one belongs has not received Shabbath,

b. even if one has oneself received Shabbath.

when Rabbinical prohibitions permitted during bein ha-shemashoth

19. *a.* The circumstances referred to in the previous paragraph are that

1) the Rabbinical prohibition involved is not one which is likely to lead to the transgression of a Torah prohibition and

2) the act in question is being done

a) for the purpose of a mitzva which one will otherwise miss, or

b) in honor of guests, or

c) for the purposes of Shabbath, or

d) because one will be caused considerable loss if it is not performed now, or

e) to answer a pressing need.

b. 1) The Rabbinical prohibition may be violated even if one has oneself privately received Shabbath (as stated in the preceding paragraph), but,

2) if the public has already received Shabbath, all of the laws of Shabbath apply in full also to the individual (as set out in paragraph 7 above), and one may not violate any prohibitions, even in the above circumstances.

instances of Rabbinical prohibitions permitted during bein ha-shemashoth

20. *a.* The following are examples of the rule expressed in the preceding two paragraphs.

1) a) If one forgot to separate *t^{e}rumoth* and *ma'asroth* from food, and has no other suitable food to eat, one may separate them even though it is already *bein ha-sh^{e}mashoth*.

b) The same applies if one forgot to separate *challa*

from baked products in Eretz Yisrael,* and has no other suitable food, for instance no other loaves for *lechem mishneh*.

c) Separation of the *terumoth* and *ma'asroth* or *challa* is permitted, even though the individual has received Shabbath, since the public has not.

d) If it is certain that separation has not taken place previously, the appropriate blessings should also be recited.

2) a) Someone whose eating utensils have not been halachically immersed in a *mikveh*, and has no others which he can use for the Shabbath meal, may immerse them during *bein ha-shemashoth*.**

b) He should pronounce the appropriate blessing at the time of the immersion.

3) One may wrap a pot of food during *bein ha-shemashoth**** in the same way as one may do before Shabbath starts, as detailed in Chapter 1, paragraph 65c.

4) a) In the event that one did not manage to make an *eiruv chatzeiroth* earlier, one may say the blessing and make the *eiruv* during *bein ha-shemashoth*. (See Chapter 17, paragraph 13.)

b) One may similarly make an *eiruv tavshilin*. (See Chapter 2, paragraph 10.)

5) One may bathe in honor of Shabbath during *bein*

---

* *a*. This is so only in Eretz Yisrael, where, at the time when the Temple stood, there was a Torah obligation to separate *challa*.

b. Elsewhere, since the obligation, even at that time, was only Rabbinical, one is allowed to eat on Shabbath and separate the *challa* after Shabbath from what is left, as explained in Chapter 31, paragraph 41.

c. Consequently, one may not separate *challa* outside Eretz Yisrael during *bein ha-shemashoth* any more than one may on Shabbath itself.

d. The one exception occurs when Shabbath is the day before Pesach, because one will not be able to leave the *chametz* for *challa* to be separated after Shabbath.

** See *c* above.

*** See note to paragraph 16 above.

*ha-sh^{e}mashoth,** if one did not manage to do so previously (but see Chapter 43, paragraph 19).

b. As mentioned in paragraph 18 above, all of the above activities are permitted during *bein ha-sh^{e}mashoth* only if the public has not yet received Shabbath.

c. As soon as one suspects that one may be approaching the end of *bein ha-sh^{e}mashoth*, that is to say about a quarter of an hour after sunset,** it is forbidden to perform any act which is prohibited on Shabbath, even if

1) it is needed for the purposes of a mitzva, or for Shabbath, and
2) the prohibition is only Rabbinical.

asking Jew who has not received Shabbath to do prohibited act

21. *a.* 1) Somebody who has received Shabbath individually may ask another Jew who has not yet received Shabbath to do something for him which involves even a Torah prohibition, as in Chapter 43, paragraph 20, provided that

a) the time of *bein ha-sh^{e}mashoth* has not yet arrived and
b) the public has not yet received Shabbath.

2) It makes no difference whether the person making the request

a) has received Shabbath by kindling lights, in prayer or by some other form of verbal acceptance, or
b) has simply made up his mind that he is accepting Shabbath.

b. 1) If there is more than one synagogue in town, it may be that

a) one congregation receives Shabbath early and recites the evening prayer before sunset (from *p^{e}lag ha-minchah* onwards, as stated in paragraph 4 above), whereas
b) another does not receive Shabbath until later.

---

* See note to paragraph 16 above.

** See note to paragraph 16 above.

2) During the intervening period, those who pray with the former may ask those who pray with the latter to do for them even something which involves a Torah prohibition.

asking non-Jew to do prohibited act during tosefeth Shabbath

22. *a.* During *tosefeth* Shabbath, one may request a non-Jew to do any act which a Jew is forbidden to do on Shabbath, if indeed it is required
1) for an important purpose,
2) for Shabbath or
3) for a mitzva.

b. This is permitted even if
1) Shabbath has been received, not only by oneself, but by the whole public,
2) it is *bein ha-sh^e^mashoth* (but there is still a little while to go before the stars come out), and
3) the performance of the act by a Jew would involve the trangression of a Torah prohibition.

c. Therefore, one may, during this period of time, ask a non-Jew to put on
1) a light for Shabbath or
2) a memorial light.

d. 1) If a woman remembers, during *bein ha-sh^e^mashoth*, that she has forgotten to kindle Shabbath lights, she should tell a non-Jew to kindle her usual Shabbath lights for her, as is explained in Chapter 43, paragraph 14, but
2) she should not recite a blessing on the lights kindled by the non-Jew.

e. See further Chapter 30, paragraph 24, and Chapter 43, paragraphs 14 and 19.

f. Before the sun sets, one may ask a non-Jew to perform forbidden acts as above, even if they are not required for an important purpose, for Shabbath or for a mitzva.

Chanuka lights

23. *a.* 1) When Shabbath occurs during Chanuka, one should kindle the Chanuka lights before the Shabbath lights.

2) Nevertheless, if one
   a) has kindled the Shabbath lights, but
   b) has not thereby received Shabbath (as to which see Chapter 43, paragraph 26),

   one may still kindle the Chanuka lights.

b. 1) A woman, however, who has kindled the Shabbath lights should not subseqently kindle the Chanuka lights.

2) This is because, according to custom, women do receive Shabbath upon kindling the Shabbath lights. (See Chapter 43, paragraph 18.)

3) a) She should tell someone else to kindle the Chanuka lights on her behalf.
   b) That other person should also say for her the specific blessing on kindling.
   c) On the other hand, she can herself say the blessing *she-assa nissim* and, on the first day of Chanuka, the *she-hecheyanu* blessing.

Chapter 47

Kiddush on Shabbath and Yom Tov: The Obligation, the Cup, the Wine and the Order

THE OBLIGATION

source

1. *a.* 1) There is a positive commandment in the Torah to sanctify the Shabbath day in words.

2) This is derived from the verse in Exodus 20:8, "Remember the Shabbath day to sanctify it," that is to say, remember it in praise and sanctification.

3) One has to remember it

a) at its commencement, with *kiddush*, and

b) at its termination, with *Havdalah*.

b. 1) That is the source for making *kiddush* on Friday evening.

2) However, we also "remember the Shabbath **day**," by making *kiddush* on Shabbath morning.

Yom Tov

2. *a.* As in the case of Shabbath, one also makes *kiddush* at the commencement of Yom Tov and *Havdalah* when Yom Tov terminates.

b. Similarly, one makes *kiddush* on Yom Tov morning.

types of kiddush

3. *a.* 1) Only the *kiddush* made on Friday evening is the subject of an obligation imposed by the Torah.

2) Making *kiddush*

a) on Shabbath morning or

b) on Yom Tov, whether in the evening or in the morning,

is only a Rabbinical obligation.

b. In spite of this, the same rules are applicable to *kiddush* on Yom Tov evening as to *kiddush* on Friday evening. (See paragraph 9 below.)

c. 1) There are some who make an additional *kiddush* with a cup of wine before the third Shabbath meal.

2) However, there is no halachic obligation to make *kiddush* before the third Shabbath meal, unless one had no wine or other acceptable beverage* with which to make *kiddush* before the morning meal. (See Chapter 50, paragraph 14.)

3) In any event, it is a fine practice to drink wine at the third meal.

d. So far as the obligation to make *Havdalah* at the end of Shabbath and Yom Tov is concerned, see Chapter 58, paragraphs 5 and 6.

4. *a.* 1) In the opinion of some authorities, the Torah does not require either wine or bread for making *kiddush*. *requirements of the Torah*

2) They hold that one discharges one's Torah obligation to make *kiddush* when one mentions matters relating to Shabbath and Yom Tov in the evening prayer.

3) What is more, the obligation is fulfilled by the expression of any praise or exaltation in honor of Shabbath or Yom Tov, as we find in the Talmud (*Shabbath* 119a):

a) Rabbi Chanina used to say, "Come, let us go out to meet Shabbath, the Queen!"

b) Rabbi Yannai used to extol Shabbath, "Come, O bride, come O bride!"

4) In all of the above instances,

a) saying the appropriate words discharges one's obligation only if one intends it to do so, and, even then,

b) one discharges the Torah obligation alone, and not the Rabbinical obligation, as to which see the following paragraphs.

b. Other authorities hold that, once the Members of the Great Assembly formulated the *kiddush*, one could no

* See Chapter 53, paragraph 9.

longer fulfill even the Torah obligation in the course of prayer, and one now has to recite *kiddush* in the form which they prescribed.

rabbinical requirement for wine:

5. The Rabbis laid it down that one should make *kiddush* over wine, as will be explained below.

women

6. Not only men, but women too, have to make *kiddush*

a. at the beginning of both
   1) Shabbath and
   2) Yom Tov

   and also

b. during the daytime of Shabbath and Yom Tov.

children

7. *a.* Children (boys under thirteen and girls under twelve) who know what Shabbath is are under an obligation to make *kiddush.**

b. One must accustom them to hearing *kiddush*.

c. See further Chapter 51, paragraphs 10 to 15, regarding children making *kiddush* for others and listening to others making *kiddush*.

omission to make kiddush

8. *a.* If one did not make *kiddush* in the evening, before the meal, one should not defer the mitzva until the next meal, but should make *kiddush* as soon as one remembers.

b. This is so,
   1) whether one's omission was unintentional or on purpose, and
   2) whether one remembers in the evening or during the day.

c. One should, after *kiddush*,
   1) eat a *ka-zayith* of bread or cake or
   2) drink as much as a *r^e^vi'ith* of wine,

---

* Usually, this obligation will be fulfilled by their hearing an adult make *kiddush*.

so as to satisfy the requirement of making *kiddush* in the place where one has one's meal. (See Chapter 54, paragraphs 1 and 21 to 23.)

d. 1) In the event that one does not remember during the evening, but only during the day, one should, nevertheless, recite the form of *kiddush* which is said in the evening, with the omission of the verses which precede the blessings.

2) This one *kiddush* will discharge both

a) the obligation to make the evening *kiddush* and

b) the obligation to make *kiddush* in the daytime.

3) Indeed, when reciting this *kiddush*, one should have in mind to discharge both obligations.

e. For the case where one does not eat bread at the evening meal, see Chapter 54, paragraph 32.

f. There is no difference between the laws of Shabbath and the laws of Yom Tov with regard to the contents of this paragraph.

THE CUP AND THE WINE

9. *a.* 1) a) The cup of wine which is required in the performance of a mitzva must contain at least a quarter of a *log* (a *r*e*vi'ith*). *quantity required*

b) This measure was equal to the volume of an egg and a half, including the shell.

2) Recent halachic authorities vary in their estimates of today's equivalent.

a) There are those, including the members of the Sephardi communities, who follow the ancient Jerusalem custom of using a cup containing 86 cubic centimeters of wine.

b) Others are stricter, in requiring a cup which holds 137 cubic centimeters, and this is a common practice.

c) Those who adopt the opinion of the Chazon Ish are stricter still and take a cup which holds 150 cubic centimeters.

b. 1) At the Friday night *kiddush* and at *Havdalah* after Shabbath, one ought to satisfy the most demanding of these requirements, since making *kiddush* and *Havdalah* at these times is essentially a Torah obligation.

2) a) One should do the same at the Yom Tov evening *kiddush* and at *Havdalah* after Yom Tov.

b) Although the obligations in this case are Rabbinical, they have been put on the same footing as the corresponding Shabbath obligations.

3) At the daytime *kiddush*, which is purely Rabbinical, one can rely on the general practice of using a cup which contains only the least of the above quantities.

c. 1) One may put ice cubes into the *kiddush* cup, in order to cool the wine (but see Chapter 53, paragraph 6).

2) The volume of the cubes cannot, however, be taken into account to make up the required *r^e^vi'ith*, as if they were part of the wine in the cup, so long as they have not yet melted.

insufficient quantity

10. *a.* If one's *kiddush* cup does not contain a *r^e^vi'ith*,

1) one does not fulfill one's obligation to make *kiddush* and

2) one is guilty of pronouncing the blessing of the *kiddush* in vain.

b. See, however, the end of paragraph 16 below.

nature of cup

11. *a.* One should beautify the mitzva by being particular to use a handsome cup.

b. One should not use a disposable cup unless one has no other.

c. In the event that one does not have even this, one should make *kiddush* on the wine in the bottle.

cup to be whole

12. *a.* 1) One should be particular to use a cup which is whole.

2) That is to say,

a) it should not be broken or chipped, however little,

b) nor should it be cracked, whether at the rim or at the side, and

c) its base also should be unbroken.

b. One may make *kiddush* with a cup which is not altogether whole if one cannot obtain one which is, but

c. the following cannot be used for making *kiddush*, and indeed the *kiddush* made with them is invalid:

1) a cup which has a hole in it, and does not contain a *revi'ith* below the hole, and

2) a glass cup which is cracked, and so would not hold hot liquid.

13. *a.* The *kiddush* cup should be washed, or wiped over with a cloth, both inside and out, to make sure it is clean and free from, for example, crumbs. *washing cup*

b. Even if the cup does not contain crumbs and so forth, it is good to wash it, unless it is clean and spotless.

c. Indeed, in accordance with the Zohar (*Parashath Pinchas*), it is customary to wash the cup even if it is clean and spotless.

14. The best way of beginning the mitzva is to pour the wine into the cup from the bottle *filling cup*

a. just before making *kiddush*,

b. specifically for that purpose.

15. *a.* 1) One should not make *kiddush* with a cup of wine from which somebody has already drunk. *tasted wine*

2) One should be strict about this,

a) however small a sip may have been taken from it, and

b) even if whoever drank from the wine did so through a straw.

3) Similarly, if someone drank straight from the bottle, one should not pour any of the remaining wine into a cup in order to make *kiddush*.

b. 1) Still, after the event, if one has made *kiddush* and then discovers that the wine was previously tasted, one has discharged one's duty to make *kiddush*.

2) Moreover, in time of difficulty, if one only has wine which has previously been tasted (and one cannot cure the defect in the manner described below), one may use it to make *kiddush*.

c. 1) The defect inherent in a cup of wine which has been tasted may be put right by adding a little wine or other drink from the bottle (out of which nobody has drunk) to the cup.

2) It is even sufficient to add a little water out of a cup of water from which no one has drunk, or even from the tap, so long as the water does not weaken the strength of the wine too much.

d. 1) a) Wine left in the *kiddush* cup after one has drunk from it (as explained in Chapter 48, paragraph 9), should not be returned directly to the bottle.

b) Were one to do this, the tasted wine in the cup would spoil all of the wine in the bottle for making *kiddush*.

2) What one should do is

a) first add a little wine from the bottle to the cup and

b) only then pour all of the wine in the cup back into the bottle.

e. If one wants to make *kiddush* with a cup of wine which someone else has already used for *kiddush* and partially drunk, one would do well

1) first to add a little wine from the bottle to the wine remaining in the cup,

2) next to pour all of the wine in the cup back into the bottle and

3) then to refill the cup for the mitzva of *kiddush*. (See paragraph 14 above.)

cup to be full

16. *a.* The mitzva is to make *kiddush* with a full cup, even if it contains several *r^evi'ioth*.

b. However, in the event that one only has a large cup, and not enough wine to fill it, one may make *kiddush* with it, even if it is not full, provided it does indeed contain at least a *reviʿith* of wine. (See paragraph 9 above.)

c. 1) If some of the wine spills from the cup during *kiddush*, one fulfills one's obligation to make *kiddush* even if there is not a whole *revi'ith* left in the cup.

2) Nonetheless, one would do well to make up the deficiency.

3) See also Chapter 48, paragraphs 15 and 16.

type of wine

17. *a.* One should perform the mitzva in the finest manner, by choosing for *kiddush* a good wine, whose *kashruth* is impeccable.

b. All other things being equal, it is a mitzva to use red wine.

c. See also Chapter 53, paragraphs 1 and 2.

wine left uncovered

18. One should be particular, to the extent one can, not to make *kiddush* with wine which has been left standing uncovered (even if not for any great length of time).

boiled or pasteurized wine

19. *a.* Some have the custom of

1) boiling the wine with which they are going to make *kiddush* or

2) buying pasteurized *kiddush* wine.

b. This is because wine which has not been treated in this way would be made unfit for drinking if it came to be touched by a non-Jew, or by a Jew who violates Shabbath in public, whereas

c. wine which has been boiled and, according to some authorities, wine which has been pasteurized, can no longer be made unfit for drinking by being touched.

d. There are, however, authorities who hold that pasteurization does not have the same effect as boiling for the purposes under discussion, and does not prevent wine from being spoiled by touch.

THE ORDER OF KIDDUSH

preferred time for kiddush

20. *a.* As mentioned in paragraph 1 above, our Sages learn from the verse, "Remember the Shabbath day to sanctify it" (Exodus 20:8), that one should remember Shabbath at its commencement.

b. From here we have the mitzva of making *kiddush* close to the inception of Shabbath.

c. Consequently, as soon as one comes home from the synagogue on Friday evening, one should make *kiddush* and eat the Shabbath meal.

delaying kiddush

21. *a.* This notwithstanding, someone who does not have the appetite to eat his Shabbath meal can wait to make *kiddush* and eat until such time as he does have appetite, provided indeed that

1) the delay will not be a source of interference with domestic harmony and
2) he does not have guests who are hungry.

b. See also Chapter 42, paragraph 29.

kiddush after early evening prayer

22. *a.* The contents of paragraph 20*c* above apply also (except as stated below) to a person whose custom is to receive Shabbath at *p^e^lag ha-minchah*, as stated in Chapter 46, paragraph 4, and who recites the evening prayer while it is still day.

b. He should make *kiddush* straight after praying and eat his Shabbath meal right away, in spite of the fact that it is not yet dark (and even if the sun has not yet set).

c. 1) If, however, there is less than half an hour to go before the time when the stars come out at night, he should wait, and then repeat the *Sh^e^ma* before making *kiddush*.

2) a) Nevertheless, no objection should be raised if somebody is not strict about waiting and makes *kiddush* during this half hour, but
b) an individual who does this should remember to read the three paragraphs of the *Sh^e^ma* again after nightfall.

d. 1) During the days when the *omer* is counted, one should not be lenient in either
a) counting before the time when the stars come out or
b) making *kiddush* in the half hour preceding nightfall.
2) One should wait until nightfall and then
a) read the *Sh^{e}ma*,
b) count the *omer* and
c) make *kiddush*.

e. See also Chapter 52, paragraph 5.

23. *a.* 1) A person who receives Shabbath early (from *p^{e}lag ha-minchah* onwards, as mentioned above), may *making kiddush early and praying later*
a) make *kiddush* and eat* while it is still daytime and
b) say the evening prayer later, after nightfall.
2) He must not, however, make *kiddush* in the half hour prior to the time when the stars come out.

b. 1) One may also make *kiddush* early on the eve of Yom Tov, except on the eve of *early kiddush on Yom Tov*
a) the second day of Rosh Hashana,
b) *yom tov sheini shel galuyoth* or
c) Yom Tov following on immediately after Shabbath.**
2) On these evenings, one should not make *kiddush* until
a) after the time when the stars come out and
b) after one has said the evening prayer.

24. *a.* 1) One should arrange the table before Shabbath commences, so that one will find it set and ready when one comes home from the synagogue. *setting the table*
2) This is part of the mitzva of honoring Shabbath.

---

* See, nevertheless, Chapter 54, paragraph 33.

** One should also not make *kiddush* early on seder night or on the eve of Shavuoth.

b. The custom is to have the Shabbath loaves already on the table before *kiddush*, even if one is going to make *kiddush* over wine (and not over the loaves).

covering the bread

25. *a.* The bread should be covered with a clean cloth,

1) even if one is making *kiddush* on the loaves, and not on wine, and
2) even if one only has cut bread, and is making *kiddush* on that.

b. 1) Some have the custom of spreading a cloth under the loaves too, in addition to the tablecloth.

2) There is also a custom to leave the loaves covered until after *kiddush* and the blessing on the bread.

c. 1) When one makes *kiddush* with wine, one should also cover, until the end of *kiddush*, any cut bread lying on the table.

2) The same applies to cake.

d. 1) Whilst one of several individuals round a table is making *kiddush*, those who have made, or will be making, *kiddush* separately need not cover the bread in front of them.

2) However, all those for whom he is making *kiddush* must cover the bread in front of them, even if they are sitting at different tables.

washing hands

26. *a.* The prevalent custom is to make *kiddush* on the wine before washing one's hands for the meal.

b. 1) Nonetheless, if one forgot and washed one's hands for the meal before *kiddush*, one should

a) proceed to make *kiddush* over the wine and drink it, and,
b) immediately thereafter, pronounce the blessing over the bread.

2) a) The *kiddush* itself is not considered to be an interruption between washing and saying the blessing over the bread, since it is a prerequisite to starting the meal, but

b) one should take care not to allow anything else to intervene between *kiddush* and the blessing on the bread.

c. Some have the custom that

1) the members of the household and guests for whom *kiddush* is being made wash their hands for the meal before *kiddush*, whereas

2) the person actually making *kiddush* washes his hands after *kiddush*.

d. Still others have the custom that the person actually making *kiddush* also washes his hands before *kiddush*.

e. See also Chapter 50, paragraph 12.

27. *a.* A person who is inspired with a proper awe of the Almighty should not make *kiddush* with just a skullcap on his head, but should put on a hat. *dressing for kiddush*

b. Similarly, it is customary to wear an outer garment (such as a jacket) during *kiddush*.

28. *a.* 1) It is the custom of some to stand all the time while they recite the *kiddush*. *standing*

2) The members of their families and guests for whom they are making *kiddush* should likewise stand.

b. 1) a) It is the custom of others to begin by standing, and to sit down just before saying the blessing for the wine.

b) Those for whom they are making *kiddush* should do likewise.

2) This custom is the preferred one for those who have no other.

c. It is the custom of still others to sit during the whole of *kiddush*.

d. 1) When the person making *kiddush* does so standing, those for whom he is making *kiddush* should be particular to stand around his table.

2) They should not be just scattered around the dining room, since

a) the *kiddush* is being recited in fulfillment of the

obligations of all of them and,

b) for this purpose, it is important that they should collectively be in position as a unit.

3) See also paragraph 33 below (and, for a case which is difficult to reconcile with the rule, paragraph 34 below).

e. Even those whose practice is to stand during *kiddush* sit when drinking the wine.

holding the cup

29. *a.* When making *kiddush*, one

1) takes the cup in both hands, as a sign of one's attachment to the mitzva, and then
2) puts it into one's right hand and
3) raises it a *tefach* above the table.

b. One should not use one's left hand to help one hold the cup in one's right* (although, if one is left-handed, one should hold the cup in one's left hand instead of one's right).

c. It is proper to hold the cup by standing it on one's right palm, surrounded by the upright fingers of one's right hand.

the initial words

30. One starts to say the Friday night *kiddush* aloud with the words, "יוֹם הַשִּׁשִּׁי: וַיְכֻלּוּ הַשָּׁמַיִם — *Yom ha-shishi: Va-yechulu ha-shamayim*"** since the initial letters of these four words, when put together, make up the name of God.

looking at the lights and the cup

31. *a.* 1) When beginning to say *Va-yechulu*, one should look at the Shabbath lights.

2) It is proper to read *Va-yechulu*, rather than to say it by heart.

---

* Someone who would have difficulty holding the cup otherwise may place his left hand under his right, to support it, so long as his left hand is not touching the cup.

** There is a custom to preface these words with the preceding phrase of the verse (in Genesis 1:31), "וַיְהִי עֶרֶב וַיְהִי בֹקֶר — *Va-yehi erev va-yehi voker*" (which some say in an undertone).

b. When saying the blessing on the wine and the subsequent blessing of the ***kiddush***, one should look at the cup with which one is making ***kiddush***, so that one's attention should not be diverted from it.

c. Those for whom ***kiddush*** is being made should also glance at the lights and the cup.

32. *a.* The person making ***kiddush*** should have the intention to discharge not only his own obligation (if he indeed desires to do so), but also the obligations of those listening to him. *desired intention*

b. Those listening
1) should intend to have their obligations discharged by the person making ***kiddush*** and
2) should listen to the ***kiddush*** carefully from beginning to end.

(See also paragraphs 36 and 39 below.)

c. It is right for the person making ***kiddush*** to warn the others to have the requisite intention.

d. Ideally, those who are listening to the ***kiddush*** should look at the words of the ***kiddush*** while they are being recited (so that their attention should not wander).

33. *a.* 1) Notwithstanding the contents of the preceding paragraph, after the event, those who are listening have discharged their obligations to make ***kiddush*** even if *lack of desired intention*
a) the person making ***kiddush*** did not intend to discharge his own obligation,
b) he did not expressly have in mind to discharge their obligations and
c) they did not expressly have in mind to discharge their obligations by listening,

provided that they were collectively in position as a unit, as set out in paragraph 28 above.

2) The latter would be the case if they were, for instance,
a) standing around the person making ***kiddush*** or

b) sitting in their places at the table.

b. 1) Their obligations are not discharged if

a) the person making *kiddush* expressly has in mind that he is not making *kiddush* for them or

b) they expressly have in mind not to discharge their obligations by listening.

2) Examples are where either he or they think

a) that they are going to make *kiddush* themselves or

b) that someone else is going to make *kiddush* for them.

3) Their obligations remain unfulfilled, even if it subsequently transpires that it is not possible for them to make *kiddush* again, either because there is not enough wine left, or for any other reason.

making kiddush for person who is not nearby

34. *a.* A person may make *kiddush* also for someone who is listening in another room, or even in another house, and who is going to eat his Shabbath meal there, so long as both of them intend thereby to discharge the obligation of the listener.

b. If one can, one should ensure that, between the person making *kiddush* and those listening, there does not intervene a place which is unclean, in the sense that one would be forbidden to pray there.

"Baruch Hu u-varuch sh^e^mo"

35. *a.* Generally, when hearing somebody reciting a blessing, it is customary to respond, "*Baruch Hu u-varuch sh^e^mo*" ("Blessed be He and blessed be His name") upon his mentioning the name of the Almighty.

b. Persons for whom *kiddush* is being made should not interrupt the blessings of *kiddush* by responding in this fashion.

c. Still, even if they do, the *kiddush* to which they are listening fulfills their obligations, provided they have not missed hearing a single word.

36. *a.* 1) Immediately after the person making *kiddush* finishes each blessing,* those listening must answer "Amen," without interruption. *answering "Amen"*

2) In this manner, they actively demonstrate

a) that they reinforce and affirm his words and

b) that they desire the blessing on the wine and the blessing of the *kiddush* pronounced by him to fulfill their own obligations in respect of each.

b. Nonetheless, even if they have not answered, their obligations are discharged, in accordance with the rule that a person who listens (with the requisite intentions) is treated as if he responded.

c. See also paragraph 46 below and Chapter 48, paragraphs 7 and 13.

37. The person making *kiddush* should not commence the blessing of the *kiddush* until all of those responding to the blessing on the wine finish saying the word "Amen," even if some of them prolong its intonation. *waiting for "Amen"*

38. *a.* 1) During *kiddush*, *place should be clean*

a) the place where one is should be clean and

b) one's body should be clean, that is to say, one should not be in need of relieving oneself.

2) A place is not clean if there are in it such items as

a) excrement,

b) a baby's potty or

c) diapers (nappies) that exude a bad smell.

b. These requirements apply not only to the person reciting the *kiddush*, but also to those for whom he is making it, since they are in the same situation as if they themselves are saying *kiddush*.

c. What one should do if one made *kiddush* in a place

---

* Special care must be taken not to answer "Amen" before the end of the last word of the blessing, because, over and above the general prohibition on proclaiming "Amen" prematurely, there is an obligation to hear the blessings to the very end.

which one ought to have suspected might not be clean, for instance in a place where there are babies, depends on the circumstances.

1) If one subsequently found
   a) that there was excrement on the floor or
   b) that the babies' diapers were not clean, and stank,
   one should make *kiddush* again.
2) If one found
   a) that the babies' diapers were not clean, but did not stink, or even
   b) that there was urine on the floor (but no smell of urine),
   one should not make *kiddush* again.

saying kiddush with person who recites it aloud

39. *a.* 1) Some have the custom that those for whom *kiddush* is being made repeat it, word for word, together with the person reciting it.
2) They do this for fear that they might fail
   a) to direct their attention to all of the words of the person making *kiddush*, as required, or
   b) to hear all the words of the *kiddush*.
3) In any event, they should only repeat the words in an undertone, so as not to confuse the person who is making *kiddush* aloud.
4) Moreover, they should not say "Amen" at the end of his blessings. (See Chapter 48, paragraph 7.)
5) a) They should all drink from the *kiddush* wine immediately afterwards.
   b) Indeed, if they do not all do so, it is doubtful whether the *kiddush* made discharges them all from their obligations, even if one of them does drink the required quantity.
   c) This is because they could be regarded as having in effect made *kiddush* themselves, without wine.

b. 1) Others have the custom, when saying in an undertone the blessing of the *kiddush* together with the person who is reciting it aloud, to omit its opening and closing words and not to repeat the blessing on the wine.

2) They should
   a) finish as far as they are accustomed to do, before he begins the conclusion of the blessing of the *kiddush*,
   b) listen to his words and
   c) answer "Amen."

3) If they wish to drink from the wine, they should not say another blessing on it, provided that both they and the person who made *kiddush* intended the blessing he made on the wine to be for them too. (See Chapter 48, paragraph 13.)

interruptions and failure to hear part

40. *a.* 1) As mentioned in paragraph 32 above, when one person makes *kiddush* for others, the mitzva is for those listening to hear all of the words from beginning to end.

2) Nevertheless, their obligations to make *kiddush* are fulfilled even if they fail to hear
   a) the verses preceding the blessing of the *kiddush** or
   b) the blessing on the wine.

3) However, should they miss any integral part of the blessing of the *kiddush* (as distinct from his blessing on the wine), their obligations remain unfulfilled, and they must make *kiddush* again with another

---

* *a.* Someone who did not hear the verses preceding the blessing of the *kiddush* should take a cup of wine in his hand, even in the middle of his meal, and recite them.

b. He should drink the wine, without repeating the appropriate blessing over it, if he drank from the *kiddush* wine and
  1) had in mind to drink more wine during the meal or
  2) is accustomed to drinking wine during the meal.

c. He should repeat the blessing on the wine,
  1) if he drank from the *kiddush* wine, but
    a) neither had in mind to drink more wine during the meal,
    b) nor is accustomed to drinking wine during the meal, or
  2) if he did not drink from the *kiddush* wine.

cup of wine.*

b. 1) Neither the person reciting *kiddush*, nor those listening, should speak until the wine is drunk. (See Chapter 48, paragraph 3.)

2) Nevertheless, their obligations are discharged (subject to what is stated in *a*3) above and in *c* below),

a) even if they did speak and

b) even if what they said had nothing to do with *kiddush* or the drinking of the wine.

c. In the following cases, a person who has heard *kiddush* should not drink from the wine unless he repeats the blessing over the wine himself:

1) where he did not hear the blessing over the wine;

2) where he (or the person making *kiddush*) had in mind that the blessing on the wine was not being made for him;

3) where he spoke (about matters not connected with *kiddush* or the drinking of the wine) after hearing the blessing over the wine;

4) where his mind was occupied with extraneous matters in the period between the blessing on the wine and drinking;

5) where he left the house or apartment in the meantime.

d. 1) It may happen that, for one reason or another, somebody is unable to hear the whole of *kiddush* from the person reciting it, but has no cup of wine or bread with which to make *kiddush* himself.

2) He should direct his attention to the cup of the person who is reciting *kiddush*, and quietly repeat the whole order of the *kiddush* to himself. (See paragraph 39 above.)

---

* Someone who does this should not repeat the blessing on the wine, except in one of the circumstances mentioned in *c*.

saying Shabbath kiddush on weekday Yom Tov

41. *a.* 1) a) If one makes the Shabbath *kiddush* on the eve of Yom Tov (falling on a weekday), one has failed to fulfill one's obligation, and must make *kiddush* again.

b) The same applies (with the exception mentioned immediately below) even if one did recite the *kiddush* prescribed for Yom Tov, but concluded the blessing as one would for Shabbath.

2) Nonetheless, in the latter case, if, and only if,

a) one realizes one's mistake before the elapse, from the end of the blessing, of the time it would take to say, "*Shalom aleicha rabi*," **and**

b) one has not begun to say even the first word of another blessing (for example *she-hecheyanu*),

one should just add the appropriate conclusion for Yom Tov, and that is sufficient.

3) Where one

a) does have to make *kiddush* again and,

b) at the time of the original *kiddush*, said the *she-hecheyanu* blessing (or the blessing on being in the *sukka* in the event that it is Sukkoth),

one repeats only the blessing of the *kiddush* itself, and not the *she-hecheyanu* blessing (or the blessing on the *sukka*).

4) When one has already started drinking the wine,

a) one should take another cupful in one's hand and repeat both the blessing on the wine and the blessing of the *kiddush*, unless one intended to drink more wine during the meal, or is used to doing so, in which case

b) one should repeat the blessing of the *kiddush*, but not the blessing on the wine.

5) When one has not yet drunk any of the wine, one should repeat the blessing of the *kiddush* **without** the blessing over the wine, if

a) one did not interrupt, after the original blessing over the wine, by speaking about matters not connected with *kiddush* or the drinking of the wine,

b) one did not in the interval leave the place where one heard the blessing **and**

c) one's mind was not in the meantime diverted to extraneous matters.

6) Should any of these three eventualities have occurred, one will have to say the blessing on the wine as well as the blessing of the *kiddush*.

errors on Yom Tov falling on Shabbath

b. 1) If, on the eve of Yom Tov which falls on Shabbath, one makes either

a) the Shabbath *kiddush*, without mentioning Yom Tov, or

b) the Yom Tov *kiddush*, without mentioning Shabbath,

one has not fulfilled one's obligation, and must make *kiddush* again, using the form appropriate when Yom Tov falls on Shabbath.

2) The contents of *a*3) to 6) above apply here too.

3) In the event that one has indeed recited the *kiddush* for Yom Tov which occurs on Shabbath, but mentioned only Shabbath in the conclusion of the blessing, one has, after the event, fulfilled one's obligation.

4) When one has mentioned only Yom Tov in the conclusion of the blessing, then, if

a) one has realized one's mistake within the time it would take to say, "*Shalom aleicha rabi*," **and**

b) one has not begun to say even the first word of another blessing,

one should just add the appropriate conclusion for Yom Tov which occurs on Shabbath, and that is sufficient.

5) a) Where either of these two conditions is absent, it does not help to add the correct ending, and it is doubtful whether or not one has fulfilled one's obligation by saying the wrong one.

b) The solution would be to hear *kiddush* said by somebody else, who has in mind to fulfill one's obligation thereby.

c) When there is no such person, one should not make *kiddush* again oneself, due to the doubt.*

6) If one made the proper *kiddush* for Yom Tov occurring on Shabbath, but forgot to say the verses preceding the blessings, one should take a cup of wine in one's hand, even in the middle of one's meal, and recite them (as in the note to paragraph 40*a*2) above).

substituting one Yom Tov for another

42. *a.* In the following cases, one has not fulfilled one's obligation, and must make *kiddush* again:

1) if, on Pesach, Shavuoth or Sukkoth, one
   a) mistakenly said the *kiddush* for Rosh Hashana or
   b) said the right *kiddush*, but concluded the blessing with the ending appropriate for Rosh Hashana;

2) if, on Rosh Hashana, one
   a) mistakenly said the *kiddush* for Pesach, Shavuoth or Sukkoth, or
   b) said the right *kiddush*, but concluded the blessing with the ending appropriate for Pesach, Shavuoth and Sukkoth;

3) if, on Pesach, Shavuoth or Sukkoth, one said the correct *kiddush*, and concluded the blessing in the proper way, but
   a) mistakenly omitted the name of the Festival, merely referring to Yom Tov in general terms, or
   b) mistakenly mentioned the wrong Festival, for instance Shavuoth when making *kiddush* on Pesach.

b. The contents of paragraph 41 above, adapted to suit the circumstances, apply also in these cases.

c. 1) There is a difference of opinion amongst the authorities as to whether one has to make *kiddush* again in a case where, on Shemini Atzereth (or Simchath Torah outside Eretz Yisrael), one

---

* One may, nevertheless, eat.

a) erroneously referred to Sukkoth in the *kiddush* and
b) has already completed the blessing.

2) a) Since the matter is in doubt, one should not make *kiddush* again.
b) This is in accordance with the rule we have that blessings are not said if it is uncertain whether they are required.
c) It is as well, in such an eventuality, to hear *kiddush* from somebody else, who says it with the intention of fulfilling one's obligation thereby.

she-hecheyanu on Pesach, Shavuoth and Sukkoth

43. *a.* The *she-hecheyanu* blessing is recited during *kiddush* on the eve of Yom Tov (including *yom tov sheini shel galuyoth*), except on the seventh day of Pesach (and the eighth day, where it is observed).

b. 1) If one forgot to say the *she-hecheyanu* blessing at the time of *kiddush*, one should say it whenever during the Festival one remembers,
a) even if some considerable time has elapsed,
b) even if it is already *chol ha-mo'ed* and
c) even if it is the last day of Pesach.

2) In such a case, one can say the *she-hecheyanu* blessing wherever one happens to be and one does not require a cup of wine for the purpose.

3) a) If one forgot the *she-hecheyanu* blessing on the eve of Sukkoth and did not remember until Shemini Atzereth, one cannot make up the omission, since Shemini Atzereth is a separate Festival.
b) One should just recite the *she-hecheyanu* blessing for Shemini Atzereth itself.

c. 1) If one mistakenly says the *she-hecheyanu* blessing on the eve of the seventh (or eighth) day of Pesach, one is guilty of reciting a blessing in vain.

2) Nevertheless,
a) the interruption does not break the continuity between the blessing on the wine and the drinking;

therefore,

b) one should drink from the wine without making an additional blessing.

3) a) Generally, if, when one has said the first three words of a blessing, בָּרוּךְ אַתָּה יהוה, one realizes that one has no reason for saying it, one should just add the two words, לַמְּדֵנִי חֻקֶּיךָ.

b) In this way, one converts it into the verse in Psalms 119:12, "בָּרוּךְ אַתָּה יהוה לַמְּדֵנִי חֻקֶּיךָ — Blessed art Thou, O Lord; teach me Thy statutes."

c) In the case under discussion, however, one should not interrupt by adding these two words, but should rather stop short, immediately drink the required quantity of wine and then say, "בָּרוּךְ שֵׁם כְּבוֹד מַלְכוּתוֹ לְעוֹלָם וָעֶד — Blessed is the name of His glorious kingdom for ever and ever."

d) This is the phrase usually said if one does not realize until one has completed a blessing that it was recited in vain.

she-hecheyanu on Rosh Hashana

44. *a.* On the eve of the second day of Rosh Hashana too, one says the *she-hecheyanu* blessing when making *kiddush*, but,

b. if one can, one should make a point of

1) a) having a fruit which one has not yet eaten that season on the table during *kiddush* or

b) wearing an important, new article of clothing and

2) having in mind that this *she-hecheyanu* blessing should also be in fulfillment of one's obligation to say that blessing over the new season's fruit or the new article of clothing.

c. Nonetheless, one says the *she-hecheyanu* blessing during *kiddush* even if one has neither new season's fruit nor new clothes.

d. 1) If one has new season's fruit, the earliest one should eat it is straight after drinking the *kiddush* wine.

2) Yet it is preferable to eat it only after one has eaten a *ka-zayith* from the Yom Tov loaf.

3) It goes without saying that someone who washed his hands before *kiddush*, following the custom mentioned in paragraph 26 above, should not eat the fruit before eating from the loaf.

e. 1) a) Those present can also fulfill their obligation to make the *she-hecheyanu* blessing by hearing it from the person making *kiddush*.

b) This is so even if they did not have in mind to eat the same fruit as the person making *kiddush*, as long as the fruit they did have in mind was before them when *kiddush* was being made.

c) The person reciting *kiddush* should inform those present that he is making the *she-hecheyanu* blessing for them on the new fruit as well (if that is indeed the case).

2) Still, it is usual for each individual, after the *kiddush* wine is drunk (or after eating from the Yom Tov loaf), to take a new fruit and himself recite over it the *she-hecheyanu* blessing, as well as the regular blessing for the fruit.

f. 1) Somebody who

a) **said** the *she-hecheyanu* blessing on new fruit when reciting *kiddush*, but

b) forgot to eat it that evening,

should not repeat the *she-hecheyanu* blessing when he eats the fruit the next day.

2) Somebody who

a) **listened** to *kiddush* and the *she-hecheyanu* blessing being recited, but

b) did not eat any of the new fruit that evening,

should repeat the *she-hecheyanu* blessing when he eats the fruit the next day (since he presumably intended to recite the blessing himself, in accordance with the custom mentioned in sub-paragraph *e*2) above).

g. 1) The rules in this paragraph apply also, where relevant, and with suitable changes, to a woman who says the *she-hecheyanu* blessing when kindling lights on the second day of Rosh Hashana, according to the custom mentioned in Chapter 44, paragraph 4.

2) She should not, of course, eat the fruit until after *kiddush*. (See Chapter 43, paragraph 45.)

yom tov sheini shel galuyoth falling on Shabbath

45. *a.* 1) A problem regarding *kiddush* arises when a person living outside Eretz Yisrael is the guest of a resident of Eretz Yisrael on the eve of *yom tov sheini shel galuyoth* which falls on Shabbath.

2) The guest is obliged to make the *kiddush* appropriate to a Yom Tov occurring on Shabbath.

3) He cannot discharge this obligation by listening when his host recites the ordinary Shabbath *kiddush*. (See paragraph 41 above.)

b. In the converse case, where the guest is from Eretz Yisrael and the host lives outside it, the situation is as follows:

1) If he can, the guest should make *kiddush* for himself and not rely on his host's *kiddush*.

2) a) Otherwise, it is sufficient for him to listen to his host, provided he has in mind to fulfill his obligation by hearing that part of the *kiddush* which is relevant to him.

b) If it is Shavuoth,* the host will recite the *she-hecheyanu* blessing in the course of making *kiddush*, but the guest should not answer "Amen" to that blessing.

reciting kiddush together

46. *a.* 1) Where

a) two families are eating together and

b) the head of each family makes *kiddush* for his

* According to the way in which the calendar is constructed, *yom tov sheini shel galuyoth* can coincide with Shabbath only on the eighth day of Pesach, when the *she-hecheyanu* blessing is not recited in any case, and on the second day of Shavuoth.

family and guests,

they should not both recite the *kiddush* at the same time.

2) This is because the listener will presumably be unable all the time to distinguish the voice and words of the one who is saying *kiddush* specifically for him, and, as a result, his obligation to make *kiddush* will remain unfulfilled.

b. 1) However, where

a) each of two individuals wishes to make *kiddush* for himself and

b) neither of them is fulfilling the obligation of anybody else,

it is permissible for both of them to recite the *kiddush* at the same time.

2) Neither should answer "Amen" to the other's blessing if he himself has not yet drunk from the wine, as explained in Chapter 48, paragraph 7.

Chapter 48

Kiddush on Shabbath and Yom Tov: Drinking the Wine

drinking right away

1. *a.* Immediately after the person reciting *kiddush* has finished doing so, he should drink the wine, in a sitting position, provided that most of those answering "Amen" have finished responding.

b. 1) He should not pause for longer than it would take to say, "*Shalom aleicha rabi.*"

2) Nor should he speak, wink, or gesture with his fingers, before drinking the wine.

c. Nevertheless, if he does interrupt in any of these ways, he does not have to repeat the blessings, so long as, in the meantime,

1) his mind was not diverted to extraneous matters (as to which see paragraph 5 below) and

2) he did not speak about matters unconnected with *kiddush* or the drinking of the wine (as to which see paragraph 3 below).

not interrupting

2. Until the person making *kiddush* has drunk *ki-m*ᵉ*lo logmav** of the *kiddush* wine or, at least, until he has tasted a little of it, neither he nor those for whom he is making *kiddush* should

a. talk, even

1) for the purpose of *kiddush* or

2) for the purpose of another mitzva or

3) about matters required for the meal,

or

b. leave the room.

* See paragraph 9 below.

speaking before drinking

3. *a.* In a case where the person who recited *kiddush* has wrongfully spoken before drinking any of the wine, then,
1) if
   a) he spoke only about matters relating to *kiddush* or to the meal,
   b) his mind was not diverted from the *kiddush* (as in paragraph 5 below) and
   c) he did not leave the house or apartment,

   both he and those listening have discharged their obligations to make *kiddush*, and he should proceed to drink the required quantity of wine without saying another blessing, but,
2) if he spoke even one word about matters unconnected with *kiddush* or the meal,
   a) he must, before drinking, repeat the blessing on the wine, but
   b) he should not repeat the *kiddush*, since both he and his audience have discharged their obligations in that respect, provided indeed that his mind was not diverted from *kiddush* and he did not leave the house or apartment.

b. 1) In the event that the person who recited *kiddush*
   a) tasted the wine, but did not drink the required quantity (as specified in paragraph 9 below), and then
   b) spoke about matters unconnected with *kiddush* or the meal,

   he should drink again, this time *ki-m^e^lo logmav.*
2) However, he should not say the blessing on the wine again, unless,
   a) when he said the blessing the first time, he intended to drink only the small quantity which he in fact drank before speaking, and no more, or
   b) he left the house or apartment in the meantime.
3) In either of these last two eventualities, he must recite the blessing on the wine again.

speaking when someone else drinks

4. *a.* If

1) the person who recited *kiddush* did not taste the wine, but proceeded to speak about matters not related to *kiddush* or the meal, and
2) the wine was tasted (whether before or after the interruption) by one of those for whom he was making *kiddush*,

all of the company have fulfilled their obligations, provided that, in the meantime, the individual who drank the wine neither diverted his attention to extraneous matters nor left the house or apartment.

b. 1) The individual in question should drink *ki-m^e^lo log-mav* of the wine.

2) a) If he did not intend the blessing on the wine pronounced by the person who recited *kiddush* to be on his behalf also, or

b) if he too spoke after the blessing about matters not related to *kiddush* or the meal,

he should himself pronounce a blessing on the wine before drinking. (See paragraph 13 below.)

c. It is better, in these circumstances, for the others present not to drink the wine in reliance on the blessing said by the person who recited *kiddush*, but to avail themselves of one of two possibilities:

1) either somebody
   a) who now wishes to drink and
   b) whose obligation to say the blessing on the wine was not discharged when it was said by the person reciting *kiddush*

   should say the blessing on the wine for himself and for them or
2) they too should speak about matters not related to *kiddush* or the meal, so that they will then have to say another blessing on the wine before they drink.

5. *a.* 1) a) If the attention of a person who makes *kiddush* has been diverted to extraneous matters (for example when he went to pacify a crying baby)

attention diverted before drinking

before he has drunk *ki-m^elo logmav* of the wine, he has to make *kiddush* again.

b) The same is true where he has left the house or apartment, even if, at the time of the blessing, he had in mind to do so.

2) a) However, if it is Yom Tov, and he has pronounced the *she-hecheyanu* blessing, he should not say it again when making *kiddush* the second time.

b) Similarly, if it is Sukkoth, he should not repeat a second time the blessing on being in the *sukka*.

b. 1) Where, in these same circumstances, someone for whom the *kiddush* was being said drinks *ki-m^elo logmav* of the wine, all of the company have fulfilled their obligations and need not hear *kiddush* a second time.

2) If the individual who drinks did not intend the blessing on the wine made by the person who recited *kiddush* to be on his behalf too, he should himself pronounce a blessing on the wine before drinking.

3) Compare paragraph 4 above.

leaving the room before drinking

c. 1) When the person who made *kiddush*

a) has merely gone from one room to another in the same house or apartment, and

b) has not meanwhile diverted his attention to extraneous matters,

he should drink the wine and not make *kiddush* again.

2) a) Nor should he say a second blessing on the wine, as long as he did not, in the meantime, speak about matters unconnected with *kiddush* or the meal.

b) This is so, even if, when he first made the blessing, he had no intention of leaving his place.

interruption by those listening

6. *a.* Despite the fact that those for whom *kiddush* was made have wrongfully

1) spoken, even about matters unconnected with *kiddush* or the meal,

2) left the room, or even the house or the apartment, or
3) diverted their attention from *kiddush*,
even before the wine was tasted, their obligation to make *kiddush* is discharged, so long as they sit down to eat in the place where the *kiddush* was made.

b. 1) However, should they themselves wish to drink any of the wine, they must first repeat the blessing on it, except where
a) they spoke only about matters connected with *kiddush* or the meal and
b) did not divert their attention from *kiddush*, or leave the house or apartment.

2) Illustrations of conversation connected with *kiddush* or the meal are requests
a) to pass the cup of wine or
b) to put on the table the salt which will be required when the Shabbath loaves are cut.

"Amen" to another blessing before drinking

7. *a.* 1) A person who has recited *kiddush* should not interrupt by talking before the drinking of the wine, even in order to answer "Amen" to somebody else's blessing on wine or *kiddush*.

2) Still, if he did answer "Amen" to somebody else's blessing on wine or *kiddush*, he does not make another blessing on the wine before drinking it.

3) Where, however, he answered "Amen" to a different blessing (unrelated to *kiddush*), he should say the blessing on the wine again before drinking.

4) In any event, he should not make *kiddush* again. (See paragraph 3 above.)

b. 1) As stated in Chapter 47, paragraph 36, those listening should answer "Amen" when the person saying *kiddush* for them recites
a) the blessing over the wine and
b) the blessing of the *kiddush*.

2) a) They should not interrupt before the person making *kiddush* for them drinks the wine, even in order to answer "Amen" to somebody else's blessing

on wine or *kiddush*.

b) Likewise, they should not interrupt before they themselves drink, if they are relying on the blessing over the wine made by the person who recited *kiddush*.

c) See also Chapter 44, paragraph 4.

3) Still, if they did answer "Amen" to somebody else's blessing on wine or *kiddush*, they do not say another blessing on the wine before drinking it, nor do they make *kiddush* again.

4) Where, however, they answered "Amen" to a different blessing (unrelated to *kiddush*), and wish to drink the wine, they should repeat the blessing on the wine first (but should not make *kiddush* again).

women answering "Amen" on Sukkoth

8. *a.* 1) a) A woman who recites *kiddush* in the *sukka* on Sukkoth eve, and wishes to say the blessing on being in the *sukka*, should preferably do so after she has drunk from the wine.

b) This is because that blessing could be deemed an unwarranted interruption between making the blessing on the wine and drinking, since women are not bound to observe the mitzva of sitting in the *sukka*.

2) a) There are in fact those who hold that she can say the blessing on being in the *sukka* in the same order as men do.

b) In their view, since she desires to sit in the *sukka* and keep the Almighty's commandment, the blessing is not considered an unwarranted interruption.

b. 1) As to a woman's responding "Amen" to the blessing on being in the *sukka* when she hears someone else making *kiddush*, the position is as follows:

a) if she wishes the blessing to be also on her behalf, she should indeed answer "Amen";

b) if she does not wish to rely on the blessing of the person reciting *kiddush*, but wants to say the blessing herself, it is better for her not to answer "Amen";

c) if she is sitting outside the *sukka*, or in a part of the *sukka* which is not halachically fit to be used as such, she should not answer "Amen."

2) Nevertheless, there are those who hold that a woman may answer "Amen" to this blessing in any event, because it is being said as part of the accepted order of *kiddush*.

9. *a.* 1) The person making *kiddush* should drink *ki-m^elo logmav* from the *kiddush* cup. *quantity*

2) This is the amount of wine which would fill one half of his mouth when his cheeks are puffed out.

3) It is estimated in relation to the individual concerned and so will vary, depending on how big or small his mouth is.

4) It is sufficient for him to drink *ki-m^elo logmav*, even if the cup holds much more.

b. 1) a) So long as he has not drunk *ki-m^elo logmav*, he has not finished fulfilling the mitzva and

b) he should drink more, until he has consumed the required quantity.

2) If he had intended to drink only the smaller quantity which he originally drank, and no more, he has to repeat the blessing on the wine before he continues to drink.

3) He does not have to recite *kiddush* again, provided that, in the interval, he has not

a) diverted his attention from *kiddush* or

b) left the house or apartment.

c. 1) On seder night, one should do one's best to drink the whole cup, however large it is.

2) Nonetheless,

a) if one has been unable to do so, or

b) in a place where wine is expensive,

one's obligation to make *kiddush* is discharged by drinking *ki-m^elo logmav*.

time limit

10. *a.* 1) If one can, one ought to drink *ki-m^elo logmav* without stopping or
2) one should at least drink it within the time that it is possible to drink a *r^evi'ith*.
3) Still, even if one takes two minutes or, at the very most, four minutes, to drink it, one has discharged one's obligation.

b. 1) If it takes one longer than four minutes, one has not properly fulfilled one's obligation to make *kiddush* and should drink again, this time *ki-m^elo logmav* within the prescribed time.
2) See paragraph 9 above for the rules applicable in this case.
3) At any rate, one does not have to recite *kiddush* again, provided one has not
a) diverted one's attention from *kiddush* or
b) left the house or apartment.

listeners drinking

11. *a.* The recommended practice is that all those for whom *kiddush* was made taste some of the wine in the *kiddush* cup, to show how dear the mitzva is to them.
b. Even a small sip is enough.
c. It is preferable for them all to sip from the *kiddush* cup itself, after the person who recited *kiddush* has drunk from it, rather than to pour the wine into their own cups.*

---

* *a.* If one's wife is in a state of *nidda*, one should not hand her the cup, but should put it down on the table, from where she should take it herself and drink.
b. In any event, in the presence of other people, this should be done unobtrusively.
c. Should one wish, in such a case, to drink from the wine which one's wife has left over, one should not do so from the same cup, unless somebody else drinks from it in between.
d. Alternatively, one can transfer the wine she has left over into a different cup, and drink from that.

d. However, there is also authority to support the practice of those who pour the wine into the cups of the company.*

e. This should be done in the following way:

1) If the cup of the person making *kiddush* holds enough wine to leave a *r^e^vi'ith* behind after he has poured some into the cups of the company,
   a) he should pour the wine into their cups before he drinks, but
   b) they should not drink before he does.

2) If his cup is not so big, he should
   a) first drink *ki-m^e^lo logmav* from it and
   b) only then pour wine from his cup into theirs.

12. If *kiddush* is being made for a large company, and there is not enough wine in the *kiddush* cup for all of them to taste, more should be added to what is left in the cup after the person reciting *kiddush* has drunk *ki-m^e^lo logmav*. *adding wine for listeners*

13. *a.* 1) When listening to *kiddush*, the participants should have in mind thereby to discharge their obligations to make the blessing on the wine too, so that they will not have to say it themselves over the wine they drink. *listeners saying blessing on wine*

2) However, those whose custom is to say the blessing themselves also have authorities to support them.

b. 1) When a large number of people are present, anyone who is doubtful whether there will be wine left for him to drink by the time the cup reaches him should wait to make the blessing himself, in the event that the cup indeed reaches him with wine in it.

2) Still, if he does intend that the blessing on the wine of the person making *kiddush* should discharge his own potential obligation to say it in the event that

---

* *a.* If one's wife is in a state of *nidda*, one should not pour the wine into a cup specially for her.
b. One should just pour out an extra cup among the others one pours out for the company, and she should take one for herself and drink it.

wine reaches him, it is indeed discharged, and he drinks without an additional blessing.

who has to drink?

14. *a.* If he can, the person making *kiddush* should drink the whole of the required amount of wine, *ki-melo logmav*, himself.

b. If he cannot, he should sip a little himself and then let one of those for whom he made *kiddush* drink *ki-melo logmav*.

c. The *kiddush* is effective even if the individual who drank *ki-melo logmav* is under thirteen years of age, so long as he has some idea of what reciting a blessing means.

d. 1) In any event, it is preferable for the whole *ki-melo logmav* to be drunk by one person.

2) However, even if it took two or more individuals to drink this quantity between them, that is sufficient, so long as it was consumed within the allotted time (as detailed in paragraph 10 above).

e. When one is unable to drink wine at all, it is better not to make *kiddush* with the intention that somebody else should drink it, but either

1) to make *kiddush* over bread (as described in Chapter 53, paragraphs 15 to 17), or

2) a) to let another person in the company, who is capable of drinking *ki-melo logmav* of wine, make *kiddush*, and

b) to have in mind that that person is doing so also in discharge of one's own obligation.

f. See further Chapter 53, paragraph 5.

g. 1) Notwithstanding the above, the obligations of all the company to make *kiddush* can be discharged, even though the person who recited *kiddush* tasted no wine at all.

2) That is so, provided one or more of those for whom the *kiddush* was said drinks *ki-melo logmav* (as in *d* above).

3) Such a situation could occur where, for example, after reciting *kiddush* over wine, one realizes that one

cannot drink it, because it is not sweet, or because it is too strong.

h. If those who drink did not intend the blessing on the wine pronounced by the person who recited *kiddush* to be on their behalf too, they should of course repeat that blessing prior to drinking. (See also paragraph 13 above.)

i. 1) For *kiddush* to be effective, those drinking the prescribed *ki-m^elo logmav* must have participated in it.

2) A person cannot be said to be a participant if he intended neither his obligation to say the blessing on the wine, nor his obligation to make *kiddush*, to be discharged by the person who recited *kiddush*.

j. See also paragraphs 3 and 4 above.

k. If

1) one is unable to drink *ki-m^elo logmav* of the wine within the prescribed time, as specified in paragraph 10 above, and

2) there is nobody else who can drink it in one's place,

one's obligation to make *kiddush* remains undischarged.

where some wine spilled

15. *a.* If a person recited *kiddush* and, before he or any of the other participants tasted it, the cup of wine was spilled,

1) they have all discharged their obligations to make *kiddush* (except as specified otherwise in paragraph 16 below), but

2) the person who recited *kiddush*, or one of the participants, has to drink wine, and may even have to recite another blessing on the wine, as explained in this and the following paragraphs.

b. 1) In a case where not all of the wine in the cup was spilled, he should

a) first drink from what is left and then

b) pour out another cup, from the bottle in front of him, or, if there is none, from wine brought in from his kitchen cupboard or refrigerator, and drink *ki-m^elo logmav* within the prescribed time.

2) If he has not in the meantime diverted his mind from drinking, he should not make another blessing over the new wine, provided that, at the time when the original blessing on the wine was said,
   a) he had the intention of drinking more wine, in addition to the *kiddush* wine, or
   b) he had no particular thoughts as to how much wine he would drink.
3) Where, at the time of the original blessing on the wine, he had in mind to drink no more than the wine in the *kiddush* cup, he must repeat the blessing over the second cup of wine, even if it came from the bottle standing on the table in front of him.

where all of wine spilled, but there is more

16. In a case where all the wine in the cup is spilled, the position is as follows:

a. If
   1) the bottle of wine is in front of him on the table and
   2) he has not diverted his attention from drinking,
   he does **not say** the blessing on the wine again (unless he had in mind, at the time when he originally recited the blessing, not to drink more than was in the cup before him).

b. If he had to bring more wine from the kitchen cupboard or the refrigerator, he **should say** the blessing on the wine again (unless he had in mind, at the time when he originally recited the blessing, to drink more wine during the meal).

c. For the rules where his attention was diverted in the meantime, or where he spoke about matters unconnected with the *kiddush*, see paragraphs 3 and 5 above.

d. 1) If indeed he did not have more wine in the house and went to bring some from a neighbor, he has to recite again both
   a) *kiddush* and
   b) the blessing on the wine.
   2) a) However, if it is Yom Tov, and he has pronounced the *she-hecheyanu* blessing, he should not say it

again when making *kiddush* the second time.

b) Similarly, if it is Sukkoth, he should not repeat a second time the blessing on being in the *sukka*.

3) a) Where the person who made *kiddush* did not himself leave the house to go to the neighbor, but the wine was brought to him from there by somebody else, he should say the blessing on the wine again, but not the blessing of the *kiddush*.

b) If the person who brought the wine from the neighbour was one of those for whom the *kiddush* was said, and wishes to drink, he too should say (or listen to) the blessing on the wine again, but not the blessing of the *kiddush*. (See paragraph 6 above.)

where all of wine spilled, and there is no more

17. *a.* When
1) all the wine in the cup is spilled and
2) there is no other wine in front of him, but
3) there is some other acceptable beverage (as defined in Chapter 53, paragraph 9) in front of him and
4) it is in sufficient quantity, namely *ki-m^e^lo logmav*,

he should say the blessing appropriate to that beverage and drink it, without reciting *kiddush* again.

b. Similarly, when
1) all the wine is spilled and
2) there is no other wine in front of him, but
3) he washed hands for the meal prior to *kiddush* (in accordance with the custom mentioned in Chapter 47, paragraph 26), and
4) there is bread in front of him (even if it is only a slice the size of a *ka-zayith*),

he should not go to his neighbor and ask for wine, but should say the blessing appropriate to bread and eat at least a *ka-zayith* of it, without reciting *kiddush* again.

wine during meal covered by blessing

18. *a.* The blessing on the wine made by the person reciting *kiddush* covers not only the wine in the *kiddush* cup, but wine drunk during the ensuing meal, either by himself or by any person listening to him, provided the individual in question

1) in fact drank wine at the time of *kiddush* and
2) a) intended that it should cover the wine he would consume during the meal or
   b) is used to drinking wine at the Shabbath meal.

b. 1) An individual who did not drink any of the wine in the *kiddush* cup has to make a separate blessing on the wine he consumes during the meal.

2) It is of no avail that, when the blessing on the wine was said at the time of *kiddush*, he had the intention of drinking wine during the meal.

intention not to drink wine during meal

19. *a.* Someone who drinks the *kiddush* wine, and had in mind not to drink any wine other than what is in the cup, cannot drink additional wine without pronouncing another blessing.

b. 1) Even if a little additional wine is poured into the cup which still contains a larger quantity of *kiddush* wine, it is doubtful whether the blessing which was recited on the *kiddush* wine extends to cover the new wine.

2) What one should do in such an event* is
   a) to pour some other wine into a second cup,
   b) to pronounce a blessing on it, intending it also to cover the wine added to the *kiddush* cup,
   c) to drink some of the wine in the second cup and then

---

* This somewhat involved procedure is adopted in order to avoid the following dilemma:
a. One cannot drink the mixture without a new blessing, because the first blessing did not cover the additional wine.
b. On the other hand, one cannot pronounce a blessing over the added wine, since it could be said to have lost its identity by merger in the original *kiddush* wine.

d) to drink the wine in the *kiddush* cup.

20. The blessing made when drinking wine covers also all other beverages consumed, subject to the conditions set out in Chapter 54, paragraph 26.

other drinks covered by blessing on wine

21. *a.* The person who has drunk the *kiddush* wine need not say the blessing usually recited after drinking wine.

b. He is discharged from that obligation by saying *birkath ha-mazon* after the ensuing meal.

c. This is so even if, during the actual meal, he drank no additional wine which, together with the *kiddush* wine he previously drank, could perhaps have been said to form part of the meal covered by the *birkath ha-mazon*.

d. Since not all of the authorities agree that *birkath ha-mazon* automatically covers wine drunk before the meal, the proper course is specifically to have in mind, at the time of *birkath ha-mazon*, that it should also cover the *kiddush* wine.

not saying blessing after wine

Chapter 49

Kiddush in the Synagogue

the practice

1. *a.* The practice was instituted of making *kiddush* in the synagogue on the eve of Shabbath and the eve of Yom Tov, for visitors who used to eat there.

b. Nowadays, in many places it remains the practice to make *kiddush* in the synagogue, in spite of the fact that no visitors eat there.

c. At any rate, the custom in Eretz Yisrael is not to make *kiddush* in the synagogue, neither on Shabbath eve nor on Yom Tov eve.

seder night

2. Even in places where it is the practice to make *kiddush* in the synagogue, one does not do so on the seder nights of Pesach.

Sukkoth

3. *a.* 1) There are places where *kiddush* is not said in the synagogue on Sukkoth eve, nor on the eve of Shabbath falling on one of the intermediate days of Sukkoth.

2) In addition, others do not say *kiddush* in the synagogue on the eve of Sh^emini Atzereth (since one sits in the *sukka* on that day outside Eretz Yisrael).

b. 1) The correct practice, however (where *kiddush* is made in the synagogue), is to say it there even on Sukkoth eve.

2) The wine is given to a child to drink (as detailed in paragraph 8 below).

3) If there is no child, an adult may also drink the wine (as in paragraph 10 below), and there is nothing wrong with his doing so, even though he is drinking outside the *sukka*.

only over wine

4. *a.* The *kiddush* in the synagogue is recited only over wine.

b. If wine fit for making *kiddush* is unobtainable, one does not say *kiddush* in the synagogue at all.

5. *a.* 1) It is the custom to sell the right to donate wine for *kiddush* and *Havdalah* in the synagogue for appreciable amounts. *selling the mitzva*

2) This is a well-established custom and should not be abrogated.

3) The whole congregation prays for the purchasers of this mitzva every Shabbath, after the reading of the Torah, and asks the Almighty to reward them and send them blessing and success in all they do.

b. There is also a custom for individual members of the congregation to donate a silver cup, in order to beautify the mitzva of making *kiddush* and *Havdalah* in the synagogue.

6. It is the practice for both the person making *kiddush* and the congregation to stand during *kiddush* in the synagogue (even if they normally sit when making *kiddush* at home, in accordance with the custom mentioned in Chapter 47, paragraph 28). *standing*

7. *a.* As stated in Chapter 54, paragraph 1, the rule is that *kiddush* must be made in the place where one eats one's Shabbath meal. *not drinking the wine*

b. Since the person who makes *kiddush* in the synagogue does not eat there, he cannot thereby discharge even his own obligation to make *kiddush* (except as mentioned in paragraph 10 below).

c. Consequently, after making *kiddush* in the synagogue, he is not allowed to drink the wine (except as mentioned in paragraph 10 below).

8. *a.* 1) One gives the wine to a child under the age of thirteen to drink. *giving a child the wine*

2) The child must have reached an age where he has some idea of what reciting a blessing means, that is to say, about five or six.

b. He should have in mind that the blessing on the wine made by the person reciting *kiddush* is being said for him, and he should not himself repeat the blessing before he drinks.

how much the child drinks

9. *a.* 1) If possible, one child should drink *ki-m^e^lo logmav* of the wine.

2) According to the principle mentioned in Chapter 48, paragraph 9, this amount is measured according to the size of the child's mouth.

b. Where one child cannot drink so much, the amount should be shared between several children.

c. 1) The view has been expressed that the child should drink a *r^e^vi'ith*.

2) This is the quantity of wine which is in itself deemed to be a meal where there is nothing else acceptable that one can eat after *kiddush*. (See Chapter 54, paragraph 23.)

3) In practice, however, this view is not followed.

if there is no child

10. *a.* If there is no child of suitable age present, the person making *kiddush* in the synagogue should have the intention of thereby discharging his own obligation to make *kiddush*.

b. Alternatively, he

1) should tell another member of the congregation who is there to have a similar intention and

2) should have in mind to discharge that person's obligation when he recites the *kiddush*.

c. 1) The person who made *kiddush* (or the other member of the congregation whose obligation is being discharged by the *kiddush*), should

a) drink a *r^e^vi'ith* of the wine and

b) subsequently recite the usual blessing after wine.

2) The *r^e^vi'ith* of wine takes the place of the meal which the *kiddush* should precede. (See Chapter 54, paragraph 23.)

making kiddush again at home

11. *a.* Whoever recites *kiddush* in the synagogue may make *kiddush* again at home, for the members of his household.

b. This applies even to a person whose own obligation to make *kiddush* was discharged by the *kiddush* in the synagogue, as set out in the previous paragraph.

c. In the latter circumstance, however, it is better if he does not repeat *kiddush* at home, unless he does so for someone who does not know how to, or cannot, make *kiddush* for himself. (See Chapter 51, paragraph 5.)

she-hecheyanu

12. *a.* The custom on reciting *kiddush* in the synagogue on Yom Tov eve is also to pronounce the *she-hecheyanu* blessing.

b. When the person who recited *kiddush* in the synagogue later makes *kiddush* again at home, for his wife and the members of his household, he should repeat the *she-hecheyanu* blessing.

c. However, if

1) his wife said the *she-hecheyanu* blessing when kindling the Yom Tov lights (according to the custom referred to in Chapter 44, paragraph 4), and
2) there is no other member of his household present who has not yet fulfilled his obligation to say this blessing,

he should not repeat it when making *kiddush* again at home (except on Sukkoth, as mentioned below).

d. 1) On Sukkoth, the *she-hecheyanu* blessing relates not only to the Festival itself, but also to the mitzva of *sukka*.

2) As a result, he should
   a) repeat the *she-hecheyanu* blessing when he says *kiddush* again in the *sukka*, even if there is nobody else whose obligation requires to be discharged, and
   b) have in mind that he is saying it with reference to the mitzva of *sukka*.

when omer is counted

13. *a.* During the days of the counting of the *omer* (from Pesach to Shavuoth), *kiddush*, when made in the synagogue, is said before counting.

b. 1) An exception occurs when the eighth day of Pesach (outside Eretz Yisrael) falls immediately after Shabbath.

2) On that occasion, the Yom Tov eve *kiddush* is said after counting, since, by postponing the *kiddush*, one prolongs the sanctity of the Shabbath.

Chapter 50

The Morning Kiddush

1. *a.* The table should be prepared on Shabbath morning, so that one will find it ready and laid when one comes back from the synagogue. *preparing the table*

b. This is part and parcel of the mitzva of honoring the Shabbath.

c. See, however, Chapter 3, paragraph 79.

2. *a.* It is a mitzva to make *kiddush* before the first meal on Shabbath morning. *the obligation on Shabbath*

b. This obligation applies equally to men and to women.

c. 1) Our Sages related the morning *kiddush* to the verse in Exodus 20:8, "Remember the Shabbath **day** to sanctify it."

2) That is to say, in addition to making *kiddush* at the beginning of Shabbath, one should remember Shabbath also during the daytime.

d. 1) This is done by

a) simply saying the blessing on the wine, and drinking it, and then

b) washing one's hands and eating the meal.

(See, however, Chapter 47, paragraph 26.)

2) Alternatively, one can

a) say the blessing on the wine, and drink it, and then

b) make the appropriate blessing for cake, cookies (biscuits) or other acceptable food (as specified in Chapter 54, paragraph 22), and eat that.

3. On Yom Tov morning too, as on Shabbath, one makes *kiddush*. *the obligation on Yom Tov*

in honor of the meal

4. *a.* This *kiddush*, whether on Shabbath or on Yom Tov, is said exclusively in honor of the ensuing meal.

b. The day, in its turn, is sanctified by the importance attributed to the Shabbath or Yom Tov meal through its initiation with wine (or bread, where there is no wine or other acceptable drink). (See Chapter 53, paragraphs 9 to 12.)

how kiddush sanctifies the day

5. *a.* The day is sanctified through the medium of the blessing on the wine, in spite of the fact that the blessing itself

1) does not intrinsically contain any element which can serve to sanctify the day, but
2) is simply an indispensible prerequisite to drinking wine, as on any other day of the week.

b. The logic of this is as follows:

1) it was laid down that wine must be drunk in honor of the meal, in order to sanctify the day (as stated in paragraph 4*b* above);
2) consequently, one is obliged to recite the blessing on the wine;
3) thus, the blessing on the wine itself is an integral part of the process of sanctifying the day.

making kiddush for others

6. *a.* A person may recite *kiddush* for others on Shabbath morning, even if he

1) has already made *kiddush* on his own behalf or
2) does not at present desire to fulfill his own obligation to make *kiddush*.

b. He recites the blessing on the wine (or other acceptable beverage) and either he drinks it or they drink it.

c. See also Chapter 51, paragraph 5.

wine

7. As in the evening, the best way of performing the mitzva of making *kiddush* in the morning is over wine (but see further Chapter 53, paragraph 9).

sitting

8. *a.* It is preferable for both the person reciting *kiddush* and his family and guests to sit during the morning *kiddush*.

b. Even those whose practice it is to stand during *kiddush* sit when drinking the wine.

c. See further Chapter 47, paragraph 28.

9. *a.* There are those who say that, at the morning *kiddush*, each of those whose obligation is being discharged should be particular to drink from the wine in the *kiddush* cup. *drinking*

b. Nevertheless, most people are not strict about this.

10. *a.* The morning *kiddush* in essence comprises merely the blessing on the wine. *prefatory verses on Shabbath*

b. Despite this, it is customary to preface the blessing with verses 16 and 17 in Exodus, Chapter 31, beginning "*Ve-shamᵉru*," and verses 8 to 11 in Exodus, Chapter 20, beginning "*Zachor*."

c. Some also preface with verses 13 and 14 in Isaiah, Chapter 58, beginning "*Im tashiv mi-Shabbath raglecha*."

d. However, the practice which exists of commencing from the middle of the last verse of "*Zachor*," with the words "*al kein beirach*," is not to be recommended.

11. *a.* On Pesach, Shavuoth, Sukkoth, Shᵉmini Atzereth and Simchath Torah, it is customary to commence the morning *kiddush* with verse 44 in Leviticus, Chapter 23, beginning "*Va-yᵉdaber Moshe*." *prefatory verses on Yom Tov*

b. On Rosh Hashana, the custom is to say Psalm 81, verses 4 and 5, beginning "*Tik'u va-chodesh*."

c. Some have the custom to say "*Va-yᵉdaber Moshe*" on Rosh Hashana too.

d. Others are accustomed to say both "*Tik'u va-chodesh*" and "*Va-yᵉdaber Moshe*" on Rosh Hashana.

e. Each person should follow his own custom.

f. When Yom Tov occurs on Shabbath, the verses appropriate to Shabbath should be said before those appropriate to Yom Tov.

washing before kiddush

12. *a.* 1) Those whose practice it is to wash their hands before *kiddush*, as mentioned in Chapter 47, paragraph 26, may also say the above verses.

2) This is not considered to be an interruption between washing hands and the blessing over the bread.

b. 1) Those for whom the *kiddush* is made may also drink from the wine and

2) their drinking is not considered an interruption either.

c. 1) However, immediately after the drinking of the wine, the blessing on the bread should be recited.

2) They should not talk about anything, nor should they divert their minds from the meal, in the meantime.

other laws

13. All the other laws of the morning *kiddush* are the same as those of the evening *kiddush*, as explained in the preceding chapters and in those that follow.

making up omission

14. *a.* If one did not make *kiddush* prior to the first meal on Shabbath morning (the second Shabbath meal), one ought to honor the third Shabbath meal by preceding it with *kiddush*.

b. It makes no difference, for this purpose, whether one's omission to make *kiddush* was

1) unintended,

2) on purpose or

3) due to there being no beverage available with which one could have made *kiddush* (as explained in Chapter 53, paragraphs 9 to 12).

c. See also Chapter 53, paragraph 13.

Chapter 51

Making Kiddush for Others

1. *a.* A person may make *kiddush* for others even if he does not eat with them. *without eating*

b. He may do so even if

1) he has already fulfilled his own obligation to make *kiddush* or

2) he has not yet fulfilled his own obligation, but does not wish to fulfil it at present (perhaps because he does not intend to eat immediately).

2. *a.* 1) The person making *kiddush* should have the intention of thereby discharging the obligations of those listening and *requisite intentions*

2) those listening need to have the intention of having their obligations discharged thereby,

as particularized in Chapter 47, paragraphs 32 and 33.

b. Those for whom *kiddush* is being made *responding*

1) should respond with "Amen" to the blessings of the person reciting the *kiddush*, as explained in Chapter 47, paragraph 36, but

2) should not interrupt his blessings with "*Baruch Hu u-varuch sh^e^mo.*" (See Chapter 47, paragraph 35.)

3. *a.* 1) Where the person reciting *kiddush* has already discharged his own obligation, one of those for whom he is making *kiddush* should drink the wine. *who drinks?*

2) However, the person reciting *kiddush* could also drink it himself.

b. Where he has not yet discharged his own obligation, but does not at present wish to do so, as when he intends to go home to make *kiddush* and dine there,

1) he must not taste the wine,

2) nor may he eat anything else.

where to make it

4. *a.* If one makes *kiddush* for others, one should do so in the place where they are going to eat, as stated in Chapter 54, paragraph 14 (but see Chapter 47, paragraph 34).

b. One should not make *kiddush* for them in one's own house, if they are going to go home to eat afterwards.

when better not to

5. It is preferable not to make *kiddush* for others, if one has already discharged one's own obligation in that respect, or does not at present wish to discharge one's own obligation, unless

a. one is doing so for somebody who does not know how, or is unable, to make *kiddush* for himself or

b. there is some other reason for doing so.

when blessing on the wine or bread may be said for others

6. *a.* A person making *kiddush* for others, whether on Shabbath or Yom Tov, should recite the blessing on the wine, even if, at the present moment, he personally has no obligation to pronounce that blessing. (See paragraph 19 below for an exception.)

b. The same applies with regard to the blessing on bread, in a case where he is making *kiddush* for them over bread.*

c. This situation (where he has no personal obligation to pronounce the blessing) would arise, for example,

1) if he did not at present desire to fulfill his own obligation to make *kiddush* or

2) if he were reciting *kiddush* for them in the middle of his own meal, having already pronounced the blessing on wine or bread, as the case may be.

d. 1) The obligations of the listeners are discharged, provided one of them has drunk *ki-melo logmav* of the wine (or has eaten a *ka-zayith* of the bread), and

2) they must not talk or leave the room until the one

---

* *a.* See Chapter 53, paragraphs 15 and 16.

b. Those who wish to have their obligations discharged by listening to someone making *kiddush* over bread should wash their hands before *kiddush*.

who is drinking has done so, or has at least tasted a little of it, as mentioned in Chapter 48, paragraph 2.

3) For the situation where they have wrongfully spoken or left the room, see Chapter 48, paragraph 6.

when blessing on the wine or bread may be said for others

7. *a.* As stated in paragraph 1 above, one may make *kiddush* for others (subject to the reservation mentioned in paragraph 5 above), and so discharge them from their obligations in this regard, even if

1) one has already discharged one's own obligation or
2) one does not at the moment want to discharge one's own obligation.

b. 1) If one makes *kiddush* over wine, one at the same time discharges them from their obligation to say the blessing on wine before drinking.

2) If one makes *kiddush* over bread, one at the same time discharges them from their obligation to say the blessing on bread before eating.

c. 1) It is otherwise if one has already made *kiddush* over wine and now wishes to say the blessing on bread over the *lechem mishneh*.

2) One cannot discharge the obligation of others to say the blessing on bread in this case unless one eats with them, failing which, they have to pronounce the blessing themselves.*

d. See also Chapter 55, paragraph 20.

in the morning

8. *a.* 1) In the morning too, one can make *kiddush* for others, even though one does not eat with them.

2) Despite the fact that the morning *kiddush* consists essentially of nothing more than the blessing on the wine,** one can pronounce the blessing for the others, and one then gives the wine to them to drink.

b. 1) The situation is different, however, where one

* See footnote to Chapter 55, paragraph 20.

** Contrast paragraph 7c above and see the footnote to Chapter 55, paragraph 20.

a) has no wine or other acceptable beverage on which to make the morning *kiddush*, and so
b) makes *kiddush* on the *lechem mishneh*, as described in Chapter 53, paragraph 12.

2) In such event, if one does not intend the blessing on the bread to discharge one's own obligation, it cannot discharge the obligations of others, and they have to say the blessing themselves.*

by women

9. *a.* As mentioned in Chapter 47, paragraph 6, a woman has the same obligation to make *kiddush* as a man.

b. Consequently, she can recite *kiddush* in discharge of the obligations of her husband and the members of her household, even if she

1) has already fulfilled her own obligation to make *kiddush* or
2) has no desire to fulfil her own obligation with this *kiddush*.

c. For reasons of modesty, it is proper for a woman to avoid saying *kiddush* for men who are not members of her family, unless there is no alternative.

obligation of child to make kiddush

10. *a.* The Rabbis imposed upon children (boys under thirteen and girls under twelve) an obligation to make *kiddush*, as part of the process of educating them.

b. A child may not only make *kiddush* for himself, but may, in certain circumstances, do so in discharge of the obligations of others, as detailed in paragraphs 13 and 15 below.

c. An adult may make *kiddush* for a child who is old enough to be educated,

1) even for a child who is not a member of his household, and
2) even when he has already discharged his own obli-

---

* This is because it is not recognizable whether one is saying the blessing on the bread in fulfillment of the mitzva of making *kiddush*, or merely as a preliminary to eating bread at the beginning of the meal.

gation to make *kiddush*, or does not wish to eat at the moment, if the child cannot recite *kiddush* by himself.

11. Since a child's obligation is only Rabbinical (being imposed for educational purposes), he cannot discharge the obligation of an adult by saying *kiddush* for him, except in the instance mentioned in paragraph 13 below. *by child for adult: general inability*

12. *a.* An adult's Torah obligation to make *kiddush* at the commencement of Shabbath may be discharged when he recites the Friday evening prayer. (See Chapter 47, paragraph 4.) *making kiddush after praying*

b. His obligation to make *kiddush* over wine after he has prayed would then be only rabbinical. (See Chapter 47, paragraph 5.)

13. *a.* A child, whose obligation to make *kiddush* is always only **Rabbinical** (even before he recites the evening prayer), cannot say *kiddush* in discharge of the **Torah** obligation of an adult (that is to say where the adult has not yet prayed).* *by child for adult: when possible*

b. 1) However, a child may say *kiddush* for an adult if
   - a) the child has not yet recited the evening prayer,
   - b) the adult has already recited the evening prayer,
   - c) the adult does not know how to make *kiddush* himself, or is physically incapable of doing so, and
   - d) there is nobody there but the child who can make *kiddush* for him.

2) The reason for this is that the obligations of both are now Rabbinical,
   - a) the child's because it is never more than Rabbinical and
   - b) the adult's because he discharged his Torah obligation when he prayed. (See paragraph 12 above.)

---

* See paragraph 14 below.

c. 1) A child who has recited the evening prayer cannot say *kiddush* for an adult, even if the adult has also prayed.

2) The reason for this is that their obligations, while both Rabbinical, are not on the same level, since

a) the child, having discharged his primary Rabbinical obligation by praying, is now subject to a **secondary** Rabbinical obligation to make *kiddush* over wine, whereas

b) the adult, having discharged his Torah obligation by praying, is now subject to a **primary** Rabbinical obligation to make *kiddush* over wine.

duration of childhood

14. The incapacity of a child, mentioned above, to discharge the Torah obligation of an adult continues even after the age of thirteen (or twelve in the case of a girl), until the development of the required physical indications of adolescence.

by child for child

15. *a.* A child who has already recited the Shabbath evening prayer cannot say *kiddush* for another child who has not yet prayed, but

b. a child who has not yet prayed can say *kiddush* for another child who has not yet prayed either.

c. They may likewise make *kiddush* for each other if both of them have prayed, and

d. it goes without saying that a child who has not yet prayed may make *kiddush* for a child who has already prayed.

for women

16. *a.* 1) Some authorities hold that, even though a woman is ordinarily free from the obligation to say the evening prayer, she would do well to recite it on Friday night.

2) Her obligation to make *kiddush*, like that of her husband (who will also have said the evening prayer), will thus be only rabbinical, so that he will have no problem in making *kiddush* for her.

b. In the view of others, even if she did not recite the

evening prayer, her husband can say *kiddush* for her.

17. *a.* A person discharges his obligation to make *kiddush* even if he hears it from someone whose pronunciation of Hebrew is different from the pronunciation to which he is accustomed. *differences in pronunciation*

b. For instance, someone with an Ashkenazi accent can make *kiddush* for a person who is used to praying in a Sephardi accent.

18. *a.* It is doubtful whether one can make *kiddush* for others on Friday afternoon *before receiving Shabbath*

1) before one has received Shabbath and
2) before the public has received Shabbath,
3) if one does not oneself want to receive Shabbath with that same *kiddush*.

b. This question can arise in the case, for example, of a person who

1) makes *kiddush* for patients in a hospital and
2) wishes to travel home before Shabbath commences.

c. In practice, one can make *kiddush* in these circumstances, provided that it is after *p^elag ha-mincha*, if

1) there is no other practicable alternative and
2) one does not make a regular habit of it.

19. *a.* Someone who is making *kiddush* for others should **not** repeat the blessing on the wine **if** *in middle of one's meal*

1) he is in the middle of his meal, having already said the blessing on wine,* and
2) those listening will not be drinking any of the wine.

b. He should

1) take a cup of wine,
2) say *Va-y^echulu* and the blessing of the *kiddush* (without the blessing on the wine) and

---

* He does have to repeat the blessing if he had in mind not to drink any more wine.

3) drink the requisite quantity.

in hospital wards

20. *a.* A person who makes *kiddush* several times, in different places, all of which are in the same building,

1) should say the blessing on the wine only the first time,
2) should drink the appropriate quantity* each time (unless one of those for whom he is making *kiddush* does so) and
3) should say the blessing usually recited after wine only after the last time he drinks.

b. This situation can happen when someone makes *kiddush* for hospital patients in several different wards in succession.

c. 1) After saying the blessing on the wine in the first ward, he should not repeat it in a subsequent ward, unless

a) he says it for one of those for whom he is making *kiddush* and
b) that person tastes the wine.

2) When making *kiddush* in a subsequent ward where none of those present will drink from the wine, he should

a) take the cup of wine,
b) say *Va-yᵉchulu* and the blessing of the *kiddush* (without the blessing on the wine) and
c) drink the requisite quantity.

e. Those listening do not discharge their obligations to make *kiddush* unless they eat immediately afterwards. (See Chapter 54, paragraph 15.)

---

* The appropriate quantity, if he has already discharged his own obligation to make *kiddush*, is *ki-mᵉlo logmav*, but,

a. if he is now also discharging his own obligation, he should drink an additional *rᵉvi'ith* (to serve as the meal which he must eat immediately following *kiddush*), and,

b. in any event, in order to be able to recite the blessing after wine, he should drink a *rᵉvi'ith* in at least one place.

21. A resident of Eretz Yisrael, who only observes one day of Yom Tov, cannot make *kiddush* on the eve of *yom tov sheini shel galuyoth* for a Jew who lives outside Eretz Yisrael, even though the latter does not know how to make *kiddush* by himself.

on yom tov sheini shel galuyoth

Chapter 52

Prohibition against Eating before Kiddush

on Shabbath

1. *a.* It is forbidden to taste anything before *kiddush*, whether on Friday evening or on Shabbath morning.*

b. One may not even drink water.

c. The prohibition is applicable equally to men and to women.

on Yom Tov

2. *a.* It is likewise forbidden to taste anything before *kiddush* on Yom Tov, whether on the eve of the Festival or in the morning.

b. Here too, one may not even drink water.

mouth rinsing

3. *a.* One may rinse one's mouth out with water before *kiddush*, because one does not intend, in so doing, to derive any benefit from the taste.

medicine

b. A person who is under doctor's orders to take medicine before his meal

1) may take it prior to *kiddush* and
2) may also drink a little water to help him swallow it, but
3) should not use any other drink for this purpose.

commencement of prohibition in evening

4. *a.* The prohibition against tasting anything on the eve of Shabbath commences

1) with sunset or
2) when one receives Shabbath,

whichever is the earlier.

b. For the position with regard to women who kindle lights, see paragraph 8 below.

---

* See, however, paragraphs 3, 9 and 11 below.

5. *a.* 1) A person who recites the Friday night evening prayer while it is still day* (but after *p^elag ha-minchah***), may make *kiddush* and eat immediately thereafter.*** *eating after early kiddush*

2) He should, however, be particular not to make *kiddush* and eat within the half hour before the stars come out.

3) If this latter period has already commenced, he ought to

a) wait for nightfall, then

b) recite the *Sh^ema* again and, only then,

c) make *kiddush* and eat.

b. Nonetheless, no objection should be raised if someone is more lenient, and does make *kiddush* and eat in the half hour preceding the stars' coming out, before the time for reading the *Sh^ema* has arrived.***

c. In any event, it is proper to extend the meal until after nightfall and eat at least a *ka-zayith* of bread then.

d. See also Chapter 47, paragraph 22 (where the situation during the days of the *omer* is also discussed).

e. In the opinion of the Vilna Gaon, it is better not to say the evening prayer until the stars come out, even at the cost of praying by oneself, without a *minyan*.

6. It often happens that in institutions, such as hospitals, the evening meal is served before the commencement of Shabbath. *hospitals, etc.*

a. Where the meal is served after *p^elag ha-minchah*, one should receive Shabbath, make *kiddush* and eat.

b. Where the meal is served before *p^elag ha-minchah*, and

---

* Somebody who does this should recite the *minchah* prayer before *p^elag ha-minchah*.

** *P^elag ha-minchah* is one and a quarter hours before sunset, where one hour is defined as one twelfth of the time between sunrise and sunset on the day in question.

*** After nightfall, he should remember to read all three paragraphs of the *Sh^ema*.

it is not possible to keep it till afterwards, one should
1) eat it and,
2) in the evening, ask for some wine or bread and make *kiddush*, and then
3) eat at least a *ka-zayith* of bread or cake.*

eating before going to mikveh

7. *a.* 1) A married woman, the time for whose immersion in the *mikveh* occurs on Friday night, should not make *kiddush* and eat before her immersion.
2) This is because she is not allowed to eat between
a) cleaning herself in preparation for immersion (which she must do before Shabbath begins) and
b) the actual immersion (which takes place at night).

b. 1) A problem arises where
a) nightfall, and consequently the time for immersion, in the summer is at a late hour and
b) the woman will be embarrassed when her family and guests eat early and she does not eat with them.
2) In these circumstances, there is room for relaxing the prohibition and permitting her to participate in the Shabbath meal, provided that, prior to her immersion (after nightfall), she
a) again cleans her teeth carefully with a toothpick and
b) checks her hands to make sure there is nothing stuck to them.
3) She should **not** perform the immersion before nightfall, with the object of coming home early and making *kiddush* and eating with the others.
4) In the opinion of some authorities, the prohibition on eating prior to immersion should not be relaxed, due to the apprehension that the woman may not clean her teeth properly after the Shabbath meal.

---

* See also Chapter 53, paragraph 7.

8. *a.* According to the accepted custom, upon kindling the Shabbath lights a woman receives Shabbath. *eating after kindling lights*

b. Consequently, she should not subsequently eat or drink before *kiddush*.

c. See further Chapter 43, paragraphs 45 to 47, from which it will be seen that

1) sometimes it may be permissible to drink and,

2) in case of difficulty, she may even be allowed to eat.

9. *a.* 1) Notwithstanding the contents of paragraph 1 above, on Shabbath morning before praying one may, without making *kiddush* first, drink a cup of tea or coffee containing neither sugar nor milk. *morning drink: general rule*

2) One may even drink with sugar, if one does not stir it into the tea or coffee, but just keeps it in one's mouth while drinking.

b. Many are, nevertheless, accustomed to putting milk (or sugar, or both) into the tea or coffee, because they find that this helps them to compose their minds more readily for prayer.

10. *a.* Somebody who did not make *kiddush* in the evening should make *kiddush* in the daytime, as explained in Chapter 47, paragraph 8. *kiddush in morning after omission in evening*

b. He must not taste anything before making *kiddush*,

1) not even water, whether cold or hot,

2) even if he has not yet said the morning prayer.*

11. The prohibition on tasting anything before *kiddush* on Shabbath or Yom Tov morning begins straight after the morning prayer is said (even before *mussaf*).** *commencement of prohibition in morning*

12. *a.* 1) An ill person who, on Shabbath morning before his *illness*

---

* See paragraph 11 below.

** It must not be forgotten that there is also a prohibition on tasting anything before saying the morning prayer, but this is subject to exceptions (as in paragraph 9 above).

prayers, has to eat baked products made from wheat, barley, rye, oats or spelt should first recite *kiddush*.

2) He would also do well to precede this with at least the *birchoth ha-Torah* and the initial paragraph of the *Sh^e^ma*.

b. 1) If it is sufficient for him to eat something else, such as fruit, he should eat as much as he needs, without making *kiddush* first.

2) Nonetheless, he ought, before doing so, to say the *birchoth ha-Torah* and the first paragraph of the *Sh^e^ma*, as above.

morning drink: women

13. *a.* The contents of paragraph 9 above, in connection with drinking before reciting the morning prayer, apply also to a woman who is accustomed always to say the morning prayer before eating.

b. 1) It is otherwise, however, if she

a) is in the habit of eating after she has made just a brief supplication, and

b) does not recite the morning prayer at all, or does so only after eating.

2) In that case, as soon as she has made the supplication, she

a) is subject to the obligation to make *kiddush* and

b) may not even drink water before *kiddush*.

(See also paragraph 15 below.)

c. 1) In spite of the above, in time of need, a woman may eat before praying, without making *kiddush* first.

2) This would be so where, for example, the woman is weak and has no wine or anything else with which to make *kiddush*.

weakness

14. *a.* Someone who has a weak constitution, and cannot wait until the end of the service in the synagogue, should preferably

1) recite the morning prayer at home, by himself,

2) make *kiddush*,

3) eat (within the limits described below), and then
4) go to the synagogue to hear *kaddish*, *Barechu*, *kedushah* and the reading of the Torah.

b. 1) The amount he may eat after making *kiddush* is
a) up to *ka-beitzah** of bread, cake or cookies and
b) as much fruit as he wants.
(See paragraph 17 below.)
2) He should not, however, eat a proper meal before reciting the *mussaf* prayer, unless he is so weak that eating only a little is insufficient for him.

c. The above applies also on Rosh Hashana to a person who, owing to weakness, needs to eat before he has first heard the blowing of the *shofar* and before he has recited *mussaf*.

feeling faint before mussaf

15. *a.* 1) Somebody who
a) feels faint after the Shabbath morning prayer and
b) has no wine or other suitable beverage (as specified in Chapter 53, paragraph 9) with which to make *kiddush*,

may, to a limited extent, eat before the *mussaf* prayer.
2) He may eat
a) as much fruit as he wants and
b) up to *ka-beitzah* of cake or cookies.

b. However, a person who has wine or some other suitable beverage with which to make *kiddush* should not taste anything prior to making *kiddush*.

making kiddush a second time after mussaf

16. If one made *kiddush* before *mussaf* (subsequent to the morning prayer), one would do well to make *kiddush* again, prior to the meal one has after *mussaf*.

* See Glossary.

kiddush before mussaf without a proper meal

17. *a.* A person who makes *kiddush* with wine before the *mussaf* prayers and does not immediately eat a proper meal,* should
1) drink at least *ki-m^e^lo logmav* of the wine and then
2) eat a *ka-zayith* of bread, cake or cookies (as in paragraph 14 above), in order to satisfy the requirement that *kiddush* must be made in the place where one eats one's meal.

b. Nevertheless, since there is a doubt whether a blessing has to be recited after drinking so small a quantity, it is better
1) to drink a whole *r^e^vi'ith* of wine and,
2) when subsequently reciting the concluding blessing, to include in it reference to both the wine and the cake or cookies.

c. 1) If one does not eat cake or cookies, but only fruit, one should drink an additional *r^e^vi'ith* of wine, over and above the *ki-m^e^lo logmav* one drinks for *kiddush*, to take the place of the meal one must have after *kiddush*.**
2) When there is no alternative, one can discharge this latter obligation even if one drinks only the contents of the *kiddush* cup, namely, no more than one *r^e^vi'ith* of wine.
3) See further Chapter 54, paragraph 23.

children

18. One may give a child something to eat before *kiddush*,
a. whether in the evening or in the morning,
b. even though the child is old enough to know what *kiddush* is, and is, consequently, obliged to make (or hear) *kiddush*,
c. provided that the child is under thirteen, if a boy, or under twelve, if a girl.

---

* See paragraph 14 above.
** See Chapter 54, paragraph 24.

19. *a.* If somebody *forgetting to make kiddush: remembering after blessing on food (not bread)*

1) forgets to make *kiddush* and
2) recites the blessing preliminary to eating,* but,
3) before tasting the food, remembers that he has not yet made *kiddush*,

he should taste a little of the food, so that the blessing will not have been said in vain, and should then make *kiddush* over a cup of wine.

b. 1) In the event that, on a Friday night, one *remembering after blessing on washing hands*

a) washes one's hands for the meal, and says the blessing on washing hands, and then
b) remembers that one has not yet made *kiddush*,

one should there and then recite *kiddush* over the wine.

2) The *kiddush* is not considered an unwarranted interruption between washing one's hands and saying the blessing over the bread, since it is an indispensable preliminary to proceeding with the meal.
3) One should drink from the *kiddush* wine (and so may the other participants in the *kiddush*), but should not interrupt with anything else between *kiddush* and the blessing over the bread.

20. *a.* Where one has said the blessing for bread over a whole loaf, or even over a slice of bread comprising at least a *ka-zayith*, and then, before starting to eat, remembers that one has not yet made *kiddush*, one should *remembering after blessing on bread*

1) take, or have brought before one,** an additional loaf, or at least an additional slice,
2) recite the blessing of the *kiddush* (without *Va-y^e^chulu*),
3) eat at least a *ka-zayith* of the bread over which one originally said the blessing, and then
4) take a cup of wine, and say over it *Va-y^e^chulu* and

---

* Except in the case of bread, as to which see paragraph 20, below.

** One must try to do this without speaking, even though it would be for the purpose of the *kiddush*.

the blessing for wine.

b. Should one have no more than the one loaf or slice (comprising at least a *ka-zayith*) over which one said the blessing for bread, one should
1) recite the blessing of the *kiddush* (without *Va-y^echulu*) over that loaf or slice,
2) eat from it and then
3) say *Va-y^echulu*.

remembering after starting to eat

21. *a.* 1) If one has already started eating when one remembers that one has not made *kiddush*, one should
a) interrupt one's meal,
b) make *kiddush* over wine and then
c) continue one's meal, without reciting the blessing over the bread again.

2) In the event that one has no wine, one should
a) take two loaves, or, failing that, one whole loaf and one slice of bread, or even two slices,* and
b) recite *Va-y^echulu* and the blessing of the *kiddush*, but not repeat the blessing for bread.

remembering after meal

b. 1) If one remembers only after one has finished eating on Friday night that one has not made *kiddush*, one should take a cup of wine and make *kiddush* then.

2) Should one not have an appetite, one does not have to eat bread again in order to fulfill the obligation of making *kiddush* in the place where one eats, since that requirement is satisfied by the meal one has already eaten.

in the morning

22. *a.* Where one has mistakenly recited the blessing for wine on Shabbath morning, without intending thereby to make *kiddush*, one should taste a little of it, so that the blessing will not have been in vain, and then proceed as follows:

---

* See further Chapter 53, paragraph 17.

1) In a case where one had in mind not to drink any more wine, one should take another cup of wine and recite over it the blessing for wine, by way of *kiddush*.

2) a) In a case where one did have in mind to drink more wine, or if one is accustomed to drinking wine during the course of the meal, one need not, and indeed must not, recite the blessing on further cups of wine one drinks.

b) In the absence of a blessing, the act of drinking an additional cup would not be any indication that it was Shabbath.

c) Consequently, in those circumstances, one should make *kiddush* over the *lechem mishneh*.* (See Chapter 53, paragraph 12.)

b. 1) If one has forgetfully washed one's hands (and said the appropriate blessing) for the Shabbath morning meal before making *kiddush*, one should make *kiddush* over wine prior to the blessing over the bread, as in paragraph 19 above.

2) In the event that one has already pronounced the blessing on the bread, and only then remembers that one has omitted to make *kiddush*, one should

a) eat a little of the bread, so that the blessing will not have been in vain, and subsequently

b) make *kiddush* over wine and continue with one's meal.

waiting for wine or bread

23. *a*. 1) Somebody who

a) has no wine or bread** for *kiddush* on the eve of Shabbath or Yom Tov, but

b) expects to receive them after a while,

would do well to wait before beginning his meal.

2) He should not, however, wait longer than midnight,*** since

a) the distress caused is inconsistent with the

---

* The use of *lechem mishneh* manifestly shows that it is Shabbath.

** See Chapter 53, paragraph 7.

*** That is to say, halfway between sunset and sunrise.

mitzva of enjoying Shabbath or Yom Tov and
b) he is not performing the mitzva of eating the Shabbath or Yom Tov meal.

b. 1) In the following situations, he should not wait, but should eat right away:
a) if he is weak, and finds it difficult to wait until wine or bread is brought;
b) if there are pressing reasons for not waiting, as where waiting a long time for wine or bread could disturb matrimonial harmony;
c) if he does not expect to receive wine or bread at all, or even if he doubts whether he will receive them.

2) See also paragraph 25 below.

3) When wine or bread eventually arrives (after he has eaten), he should make *kiddush* over it* and
a) eat at least a *ka-zayith* of bread** or
b) eat a *ka-zayith* of cake or cookies or, if neither of these is possible,
c) drink a *r^e^vi'ith* of wine (preferably exclusive of the *ki-m^e^lo logmav* he has to drink for *kiddush*).

c. 1) Somebody who, on Shabbath or Yom Tov morning, has neither wine or any other suitable drink (as to which see Chapter 53, paragraph 9) nor bread*** with which to make *kiddush* may eat without waiting.

2) This is so, even if he knows that, after a while, he will have wine or bread to make *kiddush*.

3) When wine or bread eventually arrives, he should make *kiddush* over it and
a) eat at least a *ka-zayith* of bread, or of cake or cookies, or
b) drink a *r^e^vi'ith* of wine.

---

* If it is already daytime, he should say the form of *kiddush* for the evening, but without *Va-y^e^chulu*.

** See Chapter 54, paragraph 21.

*** See Chapter 53, paragraph 12.

24. *a.* One needs to have a minimum of a *r^evi'ith* of wine, or of a *ka-zayith* of bread,*

lack of wine or bread: hearing kiddush from another

1) with which to make *kiddush* and
2) to serve as the meal which one must eat immediately after *kiddush*.

b. If one has neither, one should at least try to hear *kiddush* from someone who does have wine or bread, and one can then eat whatever one has.

c. Someone who is ill, and is forbidden to drink wine and eat bread, should try to do likewise.

d. 1) Should one later on during Shabbath obtain sufficient wine or bread, or,
2) if one is ill, and is subsequently permitted to drink wine or eat bread,

one must (except in the case mentioned immediately below) make *kiddush*** and eat at least a *ka-zayith* of bread (or cake) or drink at least a *r^evi'ith* of wine (as amplified in paragraph 23 above).

e. One need not make *kiddush* again if, after originally hearing *kiddush* (as in *b* and *c* above), one ate at least a *ka-zayith* of some cooked product made from wheat, barley, rye, oats or spelt (such as cereal).

25. *a.* Somebody who knows in advance

evening prayer as kiddush

1) that he will have no opportunity of making *kiddush* and
2) that there is no one else who can make *kiddush* for him

should have the intention to perform the mitzva of making *kiddush* by the very act of saying the Friday (or Yom Tov) night *Sh^emoneh Esrei* prayer.

b. He should then eat his meal, despite the fact that he has not made *kiddush* with wine or bread.

c. In the event that he does after all manage to obtain wine

---

* See Chapter 53, paragraph 7.

** If it is Shabbath morning or afternoon by the time one can make *kiddush*, one should say the form of *kiddush* for the evening, but without *Va-y^echulu*.

or bread during the course of the Shabbath, he should make *kiddush* and act as set out in the comparable situation in paragraph 23*b* above.

kiddush in morning also in lieu of evening kiddush

26. *a.* A person who makes *kiddush* on Shabbath morning, not having made *kiddush* the previous evening (as could be the case in the circumstances discussed in the preceding paragraphs), discharges simultaneously

1) his obligation to make *kiddush* in the evening and
2) his obligation to make *kiddush* in the morning.

b. Indeed, he should have the intention thereby to discharge both obligations.

Chapter 53

Kiddush With or Without Wine

CHOICE OF WINE

1. *a.* As mentioned in Chapter 47, paragraph 5, it is a Rabbinical mitzva to make *kiddush* over wine. *quality*

b. One should make an effort to fulfill the mitzva in the best possible manner, by making *kiddush* over a superior-quality wine, even if it costs up to a third more to buy.

c. Nevertheless, it is preferable to buy a wine which is to one's taste, and to which one is accustomed, even if other wines of a better quality are available, so that one can perform the mitzva wholeheartedly.

2. *a.* If one can, one should use, for *kiddush*, wine which was pressed from the grape at least forty days before. *types*

b. 1) Still, someone who finds it difficult to drink wine in the required quantity may make *kiddush* with grape juice.

2) One may even use juice which has been freshly squeezed out of the grapes (before the commencement of Shabbath, of course).

c. A person may also say *kiddush* over wine which was made from raisins, even if they were boiled in the process.

d. 1) a) One ought not to make *kiddush* over reconstituted wine, that is to say, over wine which was concentrated by evaporation and subsequently reconstituted by the addition of water.

b) There is also a doubt whether one can at all say the blessing for wine before drinking it.

2) Nonetheless, according to an opposing view, reconstituted wine is considered to be perfectly proper wine, both as regards the blessing and in regard to making *kiddush*.

e. See also Chapter 47, paragraph 17.

preferability

3. So long as Kosher wine is obtainable in town, one should buy it, even if it is expensive, rather than make *kiddush* over bread or over a beverage other than wine.*

KIDDUSH WITHOUT WINE ON FRIDAY NIGHT

bread where there is no wine

4. Whoever does not have wine for *kiddush* on Friday night should make *kiddush* over bread. (See paragraph 15 below.)

inability to drink wine

5. *a.* 1) Someone who cannot drink wine, not even a small quantity, should
- a) ask a friend to make *kiddush* for him and to drink the required quantity of wine (*ki-m^e^lo logmav*) or
- b) make *kiddush* over bread. (See paragraph 15 below.)

2) This situation could arise where, for example, the person in question
- a) does not like the taste of wine or
- b) is forbidden to drink wine for medical reasons.

3) Although he could recite *kiddush* himself, and let his friend drink the wine, it is better not to do so.

b. 1) If he can drink a little wine, but not as much as *ki-m^e^lo logmav*, he may
- a) recite *kiddush* over the wine,
- b) taste it and then
- c) give it to one of those who participated in the *kiddush* to drink *ki-m^e^lo logmav*.

2) a) While it is preferable for one person to drink the whole *ki-m^e^lo logmav*, the duty to make *kiddush* has been fulfilled even if two or more participants drank that quantity between them. (See Chapter 48, paragraph 14.)

---

* With regard to the morning *kiddush*, see paragraphs 9 and 10 below.

b) They must, however, have drunk it within the prescribed time limit, as specified in Chapter 48, paragraph 10.

6. *a.* One should not make *kiddush* over wine with the intention of adding an inordinate amount of water before drinking it. *diluting between kiddush and drinking*

b. This is because excessively diluted wine* ceases to be wine, and consequently cannot be used to discharge the obligation to drink the *kiddush* wine.

c. Moreover, one will have recited the blessing over wine in vain.

7. *a.* If one has no wine, or finds it difficult to drink wine, then one should make *kiddush* in the evening over bread (as to which see paragraph 15 below) rather than over some other beverage. *order of preference in absence of wine*

b. If one has no bread either, one should say *kiddush* over cake or cookies made from wheat, barley, rye, oats or spelt (and see paragraph 18 below).

c. Only if one has no such cake or cookies either, should one recite *kiddush* over some other drink which is customarily consumed as a beverage of consequence in the locality (as in paragraph 9 below) rather than neglect to make *kiddush* altogether.

8. *a.* On seder night, if one has no wine, not even grape juice or raisin wine, one should make *kiddush* over some other beverage of consequence customarily consumed in the locality, even if its importance is confined to the duration of Pesach. *seder night*

b. One should not make *kiddush* over matzoth unless one has no such beverage either.

---

* It must still taste like wine, and must not have a greater water content than that to which people are accustomed when drinking wine.

KIDDUSH WITHOUT WINE IN THE MORNING

other drinks

9. *a.* In the morning, too, the mitzva of making *kiddush* is best performed with wine.

b. Nevertheless, since the morning *kiddush* is only a Rabbinical institution, in the following situations one can instead use any other drink* which is customarily consumed in the locality as a beverage of consequence:
1) if wine is unobtainable in the town;
2) if wine is expensive;
3) if one cannot bear to drink wine.

c. Examples of such drinks are
1) beer and
2) natural fruit juice, but

d. one should not make *kiddush* over
1) water,
2) "fruit juice" or "squash" which is really a concoction of water, essence and sweetener,
3) soda water or even
4) milk.

strong liquors

10. On Shabbath morning, a person who likes drinking brandy, whisky or similar strong liquors can make *kiddush* over them, even if wine is available, so long as
a. the liquor in question is customarily drunk in that place as a beverage of consequence and
b. he complies with the requirements set out in paragraph 19 below.

milk, coffee and tea

11. When one has no drink of consequence which is customarily consumed in the locality, one may go so far as to make *kiddush* on Shabbath morning over
a. a cup of milk,
b. a cup of coffee (whether ground or instant) or even
c. a cup of sweetened tea.

---

* In the morning, unlike the evening, it is preferable to make *kiddush* over an alternative drink rather than over bread.

12. *a.* In time of difficulty, when one has no drink other than water, one should make *kiddush*, before eating one's meal, *bread or cake*
1) over two loaves of bread, or even
2) over two slices of bread, each of which is at least a *ka-zayith* in size.

b. When one has no more than one slice of bread, one can make *kiddush* even over that, provided it is at least a *ka-zayith* in size.

c. 1) If one has no bread at all, one should make *kiddush* over a cake, and say the usual blessing for cake, before eating one's meal.
2) See further paragraph 18 below.

d. In all the above cases, one should specifically have the intention of making *kiddush* over the bread or cake, as well as using it for the Shabbath meal.

13. *a.* In any event, if one is subsequently brought wine during the meal, one should fill a cup and make *kiddush* over it. *arrival of wine after start of meal*

b. If one had no wine at the morning meal, one should try to obtain it for *kiddush* before the third Shabbath meal.

14. Where *eating when making kiddush is impossible*

a. one has neither wine (or any other suitable drink) nor bread (or cake) over which to make *kiddush*, either in the evening or in the morning, and

b. there is no one from whom one can hear *kiddush*,

one is permitted, and is indeed obliged, to eat one's meal without *kiddush*, but see Chapter 52, paragraphs 23 to 25 for details of the rules applicable.

KIDDUSH OVER BREAD

15. A person making *kiddush* over bread on Friday night, as in the circumstances mentioned in paragraph 4 above, should proceed in the following way: *procedure*

a. He should take two loaves as *lechem mishneh* and cover them with a cloth.

b. He and those participating in the *kiddush* should wash their hands in the same manner as they normally should before eating bread.

c. He should place his hands on the cloth covering the loaves and say *Va-y^echulu*.

d. 1) After finishing *Va-y^echulu*, he should uncover the *lechem mishneh*, place his hands on them and say the blessing on bread.

2) While saying the name of God in the blessing, he should raise the loaves, but not yet cut them.

e. 1) He should then cover the loaves again, place his hand on them and recite the blessing of the *kiddush*.

2) It is as well for him to raise the *lechem mishneh* also during the time he says the blessing of the *kiddush*.

f. 1) When he has ended reciting *kiddush*, he should cut the bread and eat at least a *ka-zayith* of it.

2) He should be particular to eat this quantity within a period of two or, at the very most, four minutes.

3) See further the comparable case in Chapter 48, paragraph 10.

saying blessing over bread for others

16. *a.* When making *kiddush* with bread, one should have the intention, while saying the blessing on the bread, of discharging also the obligations which the other participants will have to recite that blessing before eating.

b. They should have a corresponding intention to have their obligations discharged, so that they will not have to repeat the blessing themselves prior to eating.

c. Nevertheless, those who say the blessing on bread themselves also have authorities to support them.

in absence of two whole loaves

17. *a.* Someone who does not have two loaves for *lechem mishneh* should take one whole loaf, together with a piece of bread at least a *ka-zayith* in size.

b. If he does not have a whole loaf at all, he can also make *kiddush* over two pieces of bread, or even over one piece which is a *ka-zayith* in size.

18. *a.* 1) If one has to make *kiddush* over cake or cookies, as mentioned in paragraph 7 above, it is as well to eat them as a meal. *over cake*

2) That is to say, one should eat as much cake, or as many cookies, as people would eat at a proper daytime or evening meal where they formed the main item of the menu.*

b. 1) When one indeed proposes to eat such a quantity of cake or cookies, one should

a) wash one's hands, as before eating bread, reciting the appropriate blessing,

b) take two whole cakes or cookies (a *ka-zayith* in size) as *lechem mishneh* and

c) make *kiddush* over them, as over bread, including the blessing normally said before eating bread.

2) However, even if one has no more than one whole cake or only pieces of cake (of sufficient quantity), one should make *kiddush* over them in this way.

c. Where one makes *kiddush* over cake or cookies, but will not be eating the quantity mentioned in *a* above, one should recite the blessing appropriate to cake or cookies (and not the blessing appropriate to bread) prior to the blessing of the *kiddush*.

KIDDUSH OVER BRANDY

19. *a.* A person who makes *kiddush* on Shabbath morning over brandy or some other strong drink should, nonetheless, be particular *brandy*

1) to take a cup containing a *r^evi'ith* (as in Chapter 47, paragraph 9), and

2) to drink from it at least *ki-m^elo logmav*.

---

* *a.* On the first night of Sukkoth (and on the second night outside Eretz Yisrael) the mitzva is to eat a *ka-zayith* specifically of bread in the *sukka*; cake or cookies will not do.

b. Consequently, if one has no wine for *kiddush*, one should make *kiddush* specifically over bread, and not over cake or cookies, even if one intends to eat as much of them as is mentioned in *a* above.

b. Still, if he finds that too difficult, it is sufficient if he and the other participants between them drink *ki-m^e^lo logmav*, provided they together consume it within the prescribed time, as detailed in Chapter 48, paragraphs 10 and 14.

KIDDUSH WHEN THERE IS WINE, BUT NOT ENOUGH

insufficient wine

20. *a.* 1) One requires a minimum of one *r^e^vi'ith* of wine for *kiddush* in the evening and one *r^e^vi'ith* for *kiddush* in the morning (as detailed in Chapter 47, paragraph 9).

2) Yet, one need drink only *ki-m^e^lo logmav* in the evening, and can leave the rest of the *r^e^vi'ith* for the morning *kiddush*.*

3) Thus, the total quantity of wine required for *kiddush* is one *r^e^vi'ith* plus *ki-m^e^lo logmav*.

4) Somebody who does not have that much should, if possible, dilute what wine he has with water, so that there will be enough for *kiddush* both in the evening and in the morning.**

b. In the event that the wine is not strong enough to be diluted, he should use it for the evening *kiddush*, and make *kiddush* over beer, or some other beverage of consequence, in the morning, as set out in paragraph 9 above.

c. Even if he will have no beer or other suitable beverage for the morning *kiddush*, he should not refrain from using wine for *kiddush* on Friday night, and should make *kiddush* with bread in the morning.

---

* See, however, Chapter 47, paragraph 15.

** See note to paragraph 6 above.

Chapter 54

The Rule That Kiddush Must Be Followed by a Meal — the Shabbath and Yom Tov Meals in General

THE RULE THAT KIDDUSH MUST BE IN PROXIMITY TO A MEAL

1. *a.* The prophet Isaiah (in Chapter 58, verse 13) states, "Call Shabbath a joy." *source*

b. This has been expounded as follows: In the place where you call Shabbath, namely where you pronounce the *kiddush*, shall there be joy, namely the enjoyment of the meal.

c. A corollary of this is that one must eat immediately in the place where one has made *kiddush*, as will be explained below.

2. The necessity for the meal to be in close proximity to *kiddush*, both in regard to place and time, applies equally *when applicable*

a. on Friday night and on the eve of Yom Tov and

b. on Shabbath and on Yom Tov morning.

KIDDUSH MUST BE IN THE PLACE WHERE ONE EATS

3. *a.* A person who makes *kiddush* on wine, but does not eat in the same place afterwards (in accordance with the requirements set out in paragraphs 21 to 24 below), has not discharged his obligation to make *kiddush*. *failure to observe rule*

b. This is so even if he does eat elsewhere and, indeed,

1) he is regarded as having eaten without *kiddush*, as will be explained below, and
2) the blessing of the *kiddush* which he recited was said in vain.

effect of intention to eat elsewhere

4. If, during *kiddush*, one had the intention to eat elsewhere, even outside the house altogether, but subsequently changed one's mind and ate in the place where one made *kiddush*, one has discharged one's obligation to make *kiddush*.

to whom applicable

5. *a.* Regarding this requirement, there is no difference between the person making *kiddush* and those for whom he is making *kiddush*.

b. 1) Each of the latter too, whether or not he himself drank from the *kiddush* cup, must eat his meal in the place where he heard *kiddush* and intended to fulfil his obligation.

2) He cannot rely on what the person who recited the *kiddush* ate, but must himself consume a sufficient quantity of food (as specified in paragraphs 21 to 24 below) in the place where he heard *kiddush*.

3) Should he not do so, he will not have discharged his obligation, and must make *kiddush* again.

effect of non-observance by person making kiddush for others

6. If the person reciting *kiddush* did not eat a meal in the same place, in accordance with the requirements set out in paragraphs 21 to 24 below, but the other participants did, then they have fulfilled their obligations, but he has not.

changing place: general rule

7. *a.* It is best not to change one's place at all for the meal, after *kiddush*, even from one side of the room to another (subject to what is mentioned in paragraph 8 below).

b. See also paragraph 13 below, concerning leaving the room to wash hands.

eating in another part of the same room

8. *a.* 1) Notwithstanding the contents of paragraph 7 above, there is nothing wrong with eating in another part of the same room, if, at the time when *kiddush* is being recited, one has the intention of doing so.

2) This would be the case in the dining room of an institution where

a) everyone gathers round to hear the person making *kiddush*, but

b) each of them intends to eat at his allotted table, in his own individual place.

b. 1) If, at the time of *kiddush*, one did not have the intention of eating in another part of the room, one should eat a little (enough to satisfy the requirements set out in paragraphs 21 to 24 below) in the place where one made or heard *kiddush*.

2) In the event, however, that one did not eat even a little where one made *kiddush*, but ate all one's meal in a different part of the same room, one does not make *kiddush* again.

9. *a.* 1) One should not eat in a different room from that in which one made *kiddush*, unless *eating in a different room*

a) one can see the other room from the place where one made *kiddush*,

b) the other room is in the same apartment **and**

c) at the time of *kiddush* one had in mind to eat in the other room.

2) One may, therefore, make *kiddush* in a room, with the intention of eating on the adjoining balcony, even if the door to the balcony is closed during *kiddush*, provided the balcony is visible through the window.

b. 1) If one did make *kiddush* with the intention of eating in another room (in the same apartment), despite the fact that one could not see the place where one wishes to eat, one is not obliged to make *kiddush* again in the second room.

2) Nevertheless, one would do well to eat enough to satisfy the requirements set out in paragraphs 21 to 24 below, before moving to the other room.

c. 1) If one

a) made *kiddush* with the intention of eating in the same room, but

b) has changed one's mind and wishes to eat in a different room in the same apartment, one should not move there until one eats, in the place where one made *kiddush*, enough to satisfy the requirements set out in paragraphs 21 to 24 below.

2) In the event that one did move before eating that much, then,
   a) if the room where one wishes to eat could be seen from the place where one made *kiddush*, one does not make *kiddush* again, whereas,
   b) if it could not be seen, one strictly speaking should make *kiddush* again, although
   c) it is preferable* to return to one's original place and eat as much as is required there, so that one should not have to make *kiddush* again. (See paragraph 13 below.)

eating outside the house

10. *a.* One should not make *kiddush* inside the house and eat outside it, for instance in the yard or garden,** or in a *sukka**** which is in the yard or garden, even if,
1) at the time of *kiddush*, one intended to do so and
2) one could see the place where one wants to eat, for instance the *sukka*, from the house.

b. 1) Where one has made *kiddush* in the house
   a) with the intention of eating outside it or
   b) with the intention of eating where one made *kiddush*, but has changed one's mind and decided to eat outside the house,

one should not leave the house until one has eaten the small amount required to satisfy the requirements set out in paragraphs 21 to 24 below.

---

* This is because, by staying where one is and making *kiddush* again, one creates a situation where the blessing of the *kiddush* one recited previously could be regarded as having been made in vain.

** With respect to eating in a garden, see Chapter 26, paragraph 5.

*** See further paragraph 12 below.

If the garden is for the private use of the family occupying the house, and is enclosed by the same fence or wall, it may be that it should be treated as another room of the same house and, in that case, the rules set out in paragraph 9 above would apply.

2) When one has already left the house, and is not returning, one must make *kiddush* again (except in the case mentioned immediately below), even if one left through force of circumstances, and not as a matter of choice.

3) Due to a difference of opinion among the authorities, and to prevent the risk of reciting a blessing in vain, one should not make *kiddush* again if
   a) the place where one is going to eat was visible from the place where one made *kiddush* and
   b) there is no road or path dividing between the two places.

4) One would be well advised to avoid this situation of uncertainty by
   a) hearing *kiddush* again at the house of a neighbor who has not yet made *kiddush*,
   b) eating a little at the neighbor's (sufficient to fulfil the requirements set out in paragraphs 21 to 24 below), and only then
   c) going to the place where one intends to eat and having one's Shabbath meal there.

11. *a.* It follows from the above that one cannot discharge one's obligation to make *kiddush* by hearing the cantor recite it in the synagogue on Friday night, if one does not eat there enough to satisfy the requirements in paragraphs 21 to 24 below.* *in the synagogue*

b. Not even the person reciting the *kiddush* fulfils his obligation.

c. Consequently, neither he nor those listening are allowed to taste the wine.

d. See Chapter 49, paragraphs 7 to 10, for the way in which they should proceed.

12. *a.* The above rules relating to making *kiddush* in the place where one eats are relevant also in the case of *the sukka*

---

* See also Chapter 51, paragraph 2.

1) a person who makes *kiddush* in the *sukka* and, before he has succeeded in eating even the small amount specified in paragraphs 21 to 24 below, moves into the house to eat, because of rain, and
2) a person who makes *kiddush* in the house, because it is raining, and then wishes to eat in the *sukka*, because the rain has stopped.

b. The rules applicable differ in accordance with the position of the *sukka*.

c. Moving to or from the *sukka* is considered to be like moving from room to room, and the rules set out in paragraph 9 above are applicable, if the *sukka* is
1) on the balcony of the house or apartment or
2) in the yard or garden, but with its entrance directly off the house or apartment, so that one can go straight in, without passing through the yard or garden.

d. Moving to or from the *sukka* is considered to be like moving from house to house, and the rules set out in paragraph 10 above are applicable, if the *sukka* is
1) in the yard or garden,* and one has to go through the yard or garden to reach it, or
2) on the roof, and one has to go through a shared staircase to reach it.

e. 1) It may happen that there is not enough place in the *sukka* for the whole family to eat their Yom Tov meal there together.
2) In such event, those for whom there is no room should not move into the house to eat straight after hearing *kiddush*, but should first eat in the *sukka* enough to satisfy the requirements set out in paragraphs 21 to 24 below.

in hospital

f. Similar considerations apply when *kiddush* is made for patients in a hospital.
1) Where the person reciting *kiddush* is in the corridor and the patients are in their rooms,

---

* See note **** to paragraph 10 above.

a) their obligations to make *kiddush* are discharged, but
b) they should take care that they hear every word of the blessings of the *kiddush* and
c) they should eat in their rooms, as required in accordance with the rules in paragraphs 21 to 24 below, since that is where they fulfilled their duty to make *kiddush*.

2) If the patients come out into the corridor to hear *kiddush*, it is better for them to eat a little in the corridor, since that is where they have fulfilled their duty to make *kiddush*. (See further paragraph 9 above.)

leaving and returning

13. *a.* Like rules also apply to someone who wishes to leave the house after *kiddush*, but intends to come back and eat there.

b. He should not, therefore, leave the house without first eating, in the place where he made *kiddush*, sufficient to fulfil the requirements set out in paragraphs 21 to 24 below.

c. Nonetheless, if he did leave the house after *kiddush* without doing so, and returned to eat, his obligation to make *kiddush* has been discharged, and he should not make *kiddush* again.

d. This is all the more so the case where he left in order to do something for the purpose of the meal, for example if he
1) made *kiddush* in the *sukka* and then
2) washed his hands for the meal into a receptacle which was standing outside the *sukka*.*

e. 1) There is nothing wrong with going from the dining room into the kitchen after *kiddush*, in order to wash one's hands for the meal, and then returning to one's place to eat.

---

* As explained in Chapter 26, paragraph 5, one must not wash one's hands onto a garden or any other sown land.

2) This is not deemed an unwarrantable interruption between *kiddush* and the meal, since it is for the purpose of the meal.

making kiddush only for another

14. *a.* From Chapter 51, paragraph 1, it can be seen that one may make *kiddush* for somebody else, even if one does not wish thereby to discharge one's own obligation to make *kiddush*.

b. When one does so, the person for whom *kiddush* is being made must be in the place where he is going to eat.

c. One should not invite him into one's own house to hear *kiddush* in discharge of his obligation, unless, immediately afterwards, one gives him a little to eat (as in paragraphs 21 to 24 below), so that he makes *kiddush* where he eats.

KIDDUSH MUST BE IMMEDIATELY BEFORE ONE EATS

scope of rule

15. *a.* Just as the mitzva is to make *kiddush* in the place where one eats, so is it to eat immediately after *kiddush*.

b. That is to say, one should not make even a short break between *kiddush* and the meal.

c. Where one has wrongfully done so, then, if, at the time of *kiddush*, one did not have the intention to eat immediately afterwards, one must recite *kiddush* again.

d. This is so even in a case where one had to make the break through force of circumstances and not choice.

delay contrary to intention

16. If one

a. intended, at the time of *kiddush*, to eat straight away afterwards, but,

b. contrary to one's wishes, is able to eat only after a delay, one's obligation to make *kiddush* is discharged, provided one does not leave one's place between *kiddush* and the meal in circumstances which would require one to make *kiddush* again. (See paragraphs 8 to 10 and 13 above.)

lack of appetite

17. When one does not wish to eat right away, for instance, if one is not hungry, one should wait and make *kiddush* when one does want to eat (but see Chapter 47, paragraph 21).

eating immediately contrary to initial intention

18. *a.* If a person
1) intended, at the time of *kiddush*, to eat only after an interval, as where he did not know of the rule that the meal should follow immediately, but
2) changed his mind and ate right away,

he has fulfilled his duty to make *kiddush*.

b. Moreover, even if he
1) intended, at the time of *kiddush*, not to eat at all afterwards, as where he did not know of the rule that *kiddush* must be made in the place where one is going to eat, but
2) changed his mind and ate right away in the place where he made *kiddush*,

he has fulfilled his duty to make *kiddush*.

permissible interruptions

19. *a.* Despite what has been stated in the preceding paragraphs, one may interrupt between *kiddush* and eating in order to do things which have a connection with the meal.

b. Thus,
1) it is permissible to bring food from the kitchen to the dining room after *kiddush*, before washing one's hands for the meal;
2) a person is allowed to go to the bathroom after *kiddush* to relieve himself, before washing his hands for the meal;
3) one may quench one's thirst with water or some other drink after *kiddush*, before washing hands for the meal, as long as one washes immediately after drinking;*
4) when several people who are eating together in one room each have their own cup and recite *kiddush* in-

---

* *a.* So far as pronouncing a blessing before drinking is concerned, see paragraph 26 below.
b. One should not pronounce a separate blessing when one has finished drinking, since quenching one's thirst makes it easier for one to eat, so that the drink becomes part of the meal which follows, and can be covered by the Grace one says afterwards.

dividually, one after the other, they may wait, before washing hands, until they have all finished making *kiddush*.

when one person makes kiddush for others

20. *a.* Regarding the subject matter of the previous paragraphs, there is no difference between the actual person reciting *kiddush* and those for whom he is making *kiddush*.

b. 1) Both he and they must eat meals sufficient to meet the requirements set out in paragraphs 21 to 24 below immediately after *kiddush*.

2) They cannot rely on what he ate immediately afterwards, but each of them must himself consume a sufficient quantity of food straight after *kiddush*.

3) Whoever does not do so, will not have discharged his obligation, and must make *kiddush* again.

4) If the person reciting *kiddush* did not eat a meal right away, but the other participants did, then they have fulfilled their obligations, but he has not.

AMOUNT TO BE EATEN AFTER KIDDUSH

bread

21. *a.* 1) How much should one eat to satisfy the requirement that *kiddush* must be in the place where one is going to have one's meal?

2) It is best to eat at least a *ka-zayith* of bread (but see paragraph 30 below, regarding the quantity to be eaten for a Shabbath meal).

b. 1) This is applicable also to someone who has made *kiddush* over bread (as detailed in Chapter 53, paragraphs 4 and 15) and has already eaten a *ka-zayith* of bread in discharge of his obligation to make *kiddush*.

2) He ought to eat at least another *ka-zayith* of bread, by way of the meal which must follow *kiddush*.

full meal

22. *a.* 1) It is good to wash hands and eat the whole Shabbath meal straight after *kiddush*, whether it be Friday night or Shabbath morning.

2) The same applies to the eve of Yom Tov and Yom Tov morning.

b. 1) Nevertheless, a person who is accustomed to eating cake or cookies straight after *kiddush* on Shabbath or Yom Tov morning* also discharges thereby his obligation to make *kiddush* in the place where he eats, but *cake and cookies*

a) he should eat at least a *ka-zayith* of cake or cookies** and

b) see Chapter 55, paragraph 4.

2) He can also discharge his obligation by eating a *ka-zayith* of *kugel**** or cooked cereal which are made from wheat, barley, rye, oats or spelt.

3) a) After an interval (prior to which he would have recited the blessings appropriate after whatever he ate or drank), he should eat his Shabbath or Yom Tov meal.

b) In the event that he starts his meal without a break, then, if all he has eaten following *kiddush* is cake or cookies, he should not recite *al ha-michya* (nor the usual blessing after wine) before washing for the meal.

c) If he has also eaten other things, such as fruit, or

---

* This is relevant also in the case of someone who makes *kiddush* after the morning prayer, but before *mussaf*, as in Chapter 52, paragraphs 15 to 17.

** *a.* Where he eats other food, such as *kugel* or fish, as well as cake or cookies, he should be careful not to eat as much cake or cookies as, together with the other items, would normally satisfy a person's appetite.

b. If he did eat so much, he would be required, in the view of some authorities, to wash his hands first, as before a meal eaten with bread, to pronounce the blessing for washing hands, to say, prior to eating, the blessing normally said before bread and to recite *birkath ha-mazon*.

*** *a.* As explained in Chapter 1, paragraph 58, one should not place pickled gherkin on hot *kugel* which still retains a temperature of 45 degrees centigrade.

b. When eating *kugel* with gherkin, one should not pronounce a blessing over the gherkin, if it is subsidiary to the *kugel*, since it is then covered by the blessing pronounced over the *kugel*.

if he ate *kugel* or cooked cereal, he should, before washing, recite the blessing usually pronounced after eating them.*

c. In the evening too, although it is a mitzva to eat a meal with bread, one can fulfill one's obligation to make *kiddush* where one eats by eating at least a *ka-zayith* of cake or cookies, or even of *kugel* or cooked cereal, as above.

wine

23. *a.* 1) In circumstances of difficulty, one can discharge one's obligation to make *kiddush* in the place where one eats, even in the evening, by drinking one *r^e^vi'ith* of wine, including the wine one drank for *kiddush*, but

2) there are authorities who require one to drink a *r^e^vi'ith* of wine in addition to the *ki-m^e^lo logmav* one drinks in discharge of one's obligation to make *kiddush*, and

3) one ought to act in accordance with this latter, stricter view

a) at the evening *kiddush* and

b) at the morning *kiddush*, if one has sufficient wine.

4) Nevertheless, someone who intends to fulfill his obligation by listening to another person making *kiddush* need drink no more than one *r^e^vi'ith* in order to discharge his duty to make *kiddush* in the place where he eats.

b. 1) a) When there is a circumcision on Shabbath or Yom Tov morning, the person making the blessing over the wine may drink a *r^e^vi'ith*, and this is regarded

---

* *a.* A person who eats cake, cookies, *kugel* or cereal following *kiddush* (as above) and does not wash for the meal straight afterwards, should drink at least a *r^e^vi'ith* of the wine on which he makes *kiddush* (and not just *ki-m^e^lo logmav*).

b. This is because there is a doubt whether somebody who drinks a lesser quantity has to say the usual blessing after wine.

c. If, however, he does drink less, he should, due to the doubt, add, in the *al ha-michya* blessing he will in any case have to recite, the words appropriate when one has drunk wine.

as being by way of both *kiddush* and the meal which must follow.

b) Where he can, it is better for him to drink *ki-melo logmav* for *kiddush* and an additional *revi'ith* as the meal, as mentioned above.

c) Notwithstanding the above, the custom followed is to have the cup of wine drunk by a child under thirteen who has some idea what reciting a blessing means (as in Chapter 49, paragraph 8).

2) a) If, however, the person saying the blessing is going to eat cake or cookies afterwards, he should not give the wine to a child, but should drink it himself for *kiddush*, and eat the cake or cookies for the meal.

b) He should eat at least a *ka-zayith* of the cake or cookies, as in paragraph 22 above.

c) He should also drink at least a *revi'ith* of the wine, to avoid the doubt which would arise regarding the blessing normally pronounced after wine, as explained in the last note to paragraph 22 above.

24. *a.* One does not fulfill one's duty to make *kiddush* in the place where one has one's meal by eating food other than that mentioned above, however much of it one eats (except in the circumstances specified in *d* below). *other food or drink*

b. Similarly, one does not discharge one's duty if one makes *kiddush* on Shabbath or Yom Tov morning over beer or some other drink one likes, within the limits delineated in Chapter 53, paragraph 9 (however much of it one drinks), but

1) neither eats a sufficient quantity of bread or cake,

2) nor drinks at least a *revi'ith* of wine.

c. Therefore,

1) if one is preparing *kiddush* for after the service in the synagogue on Shabbath or Yom Tov morning, one

a) should not provide just fruit or similar snacks, but

b) should see to it that there will be enough cake

or cookies (or *kugel* made from the ingredients specified in paragraph 22*b*2) above) for everyone, and

2) a person who is invited to *kiddush* after the service, and sees that there is not at least a *ka-zayith* of cake or cookies (or of *kugel* made as in paragraph 22 above, or a *r^evi'ith* of wine) left for him,
   a) should not taste any food or drink at all and,
   b) when he comes home, should make *kiddush* with wine and eat in the normal way.

d. Nevertheless, someone who feels a little faint, and does not have sufficient bread, cake or wine, can rely on a minority opinion that fruit too can serve as the meal one has to eat after *kiddush*, but,
   1) if possible, he should be particular that the fruit is stewed and
   2) he can rely on this opinion only at the morning *kiddush*, and not on Shabbath or Yom Tov eve.

time for consumption

25. *a.* One should take care to consume the *ka-zayith* one has to eat after *kiddush* (as detailed in paragraphs 21 and 22 above) within a period of two, or at most four, minutes.

b. 1) When one's "meal" consists of wine (as in paragraph 23 above), one should drink the *r^evi'ith* straight down, without a pause, although,
   2) if one drinks it within two, or at most four, minutes, that is also good enough.

blessing over other drinks after wine

26. *a.* Where one has pronounced the usual blessing before drinking wine, one does not have to pronounce an additional blessing before other drinks one consumes,* provided
   1) the other drinks were on the table at the time one pronounced the blessing on the wine or,

---

* There is a difference of opinion among the authorities (reflected below in this paragraph) regarding the quantity of wine one has to drink for this to be effective.

2) at the time one pronounced the blessing on the wine, one had in mind to consume the other drinks as well.

b. As a result, somebody who
1) makes *kiddush* on wine,
2) drinks at least *ki-melo logmav** of it,
3) does not eat bread afterwards,** but only cake, *kugel* or cereal (as detailed in paragraph 22 above), and
4) wishes to partake of different drinks too,

does not recite a further blessing prior to consuming the other drinks.***

c. 1) However, participants in the *kiddush* who did not themselves taste any of the wine have to say separate blessings both before and after consuming other drinks.
2) Since they did not drink wine at all, the person who recited *kiddush* discharged them from their obligation to say the blessing on the wine only in so far as it forms part of *kiddush*.

d. 1) It is uncertain whether or not participants (including the person reciting *kiddush*)**** who drink from the wine, but less than *ki-melo logmav*, have to say a blessing over other drinks they consume afterwards.
2) They would thus do well, before having the other drink,
a) to ask someone who did not taste the wine, and is about to say a blessing over a different drink, to have in mind to discharge also their obligations to say the blessing, or
b) to take some food the blessing over which is the same as for the drink, and to have both the food

---

* As indicated in the last note to paragraph 22 above, the person making *kiddush* should drink at least a *revi'ith*, since there is a doubt whether the usual blessing after wine has to be recited after drinking less.

** If he does eat bread, the blessing on the bread itself covers the other drinks consumed during the meal.

*** If he desires to drink them with a lump of sugar in his mouth, it is proper for him to say a blessing over the sugar (and eat some of it) first.

**** See Chapter 48, paragraph 14.

and the drink in mind while saying the blessing.

e. Just as

1) the blessing said before wine covers also other drinks, as above,

so

2) the blessing said after drinking a *revi'ith* of wine obviates the need to recite a separate blessing after other drinks one also consumed.

THE SABBATH AND YOM TOV MEALS: GENERAL RULES

number

27. *a.* There is an obligation to eat three meals during Shabbath,

1) one on Friday evening,
2) one on Shabbath morning and
3) one on Shabbath afternoon.

b. One should see to it that even a poor man, who lives on charity, has enough for three meals.

c. Each of these three meals should be commenced with two loaves. (See Chapter 55, in general, and Chapter 56, paragraphs 5 and 6, with particular reference to the third meal.)

d. 1) On Yom Tov, the obligation is to eat two meals (also commencing with two loaves).

2) It is not the custom to eat a proper third meal on Yom Tov (but see Chapter 56, paragraph 1).

who is obliged?

28. *a.* Both men and women are obliged to eat three meals on Shabbath.

b. With regard to Yom Tov, however, there is a difference of opinion.

1) According to one view, women, like men, have to eat two meals.
2) According to another, they have no such obligation at all.

bread

29. *a.* The Friday evening and Shabbath morning meals should both be eaten with bread.

b. The same applies to the Yom Tov eve and Yom Tov morning meals.
c. As to the third Shabbath meal, the best way to perform the mitzva is to eat this also with bread (but see Chapter 56, paragraph 5).

30. *a.* If one can, one should eat at least a little more than a *ka-beitzah* of bread at each of the Shabbath or Yom Tov meals. *quantity*
b. At any rate, one should not eat less than a *ka-zayith*.
c. One should be particular to eat this amount of a *ka-zayith* within two, or at most four, minutes.

31. *a.* Someone who has no bread can eat cake or cookies. *cake or cookies*
b. 1) He should consume as much of them* as a person needs in order to eat to satisfaction.**
2) In the event that he eats such a quantity, he should
a) wash his hands, as before eating bread,
b) recite the blessing appropriate when washing hands,
c) recite the blessing normally said prior to eating bread and,
d) after the meal, recite *birkath ha-mazon*.
c. 1) If he does not have so much cake or cookies, he should rely on those authorities who hold that it is sufficient to eat a *ka-zayith* of them (and see further, paragraph 32 below).
2) In that event, he should not, of course, wash his hands or say the blessings appropriate when eating bread, as above.
d. 1) Without either bread or cake or cookies, one cannot fulfill one's duty to eat the Shabbath or Yom Tov meals, however much one may eat of different kinds of delicacies or of a variety of dishes (but see Chapter

* For a fuller definition of the quantity, see Chapter 53, paragraph 18.
** He should be careful to consume at least a *ka-zayith* of the cake or cookies within two, or at most four, minutes.

56, paragraph 5, for the third Shabbath meal).
2) Concerning the separate obligation to make *kiddush* in the place where one eats, see paragraph 24 above.

omission of evening meal

32. *a.* A person who, at the Shabbath eve meal, ate
1) neither bread,
2) nor such a quantity of cake or cookies as is needed in order to eat to satisfaction,

should eat three meals during the daytime on that Shabbath.

b. 1) The first two of those meals should be eaten with bread. (Compare Chapter 47, paragraph 8.)
2) As to the necessity for eating the third meal with bread, see Chapter 56, paragraph 5.

c. If it was not Shabbath, but Yom Tov, he has to eat only two meals during the daytime, both of them with bread.

eating early

33. *a.* Somebody who receives Shabbath or Yom Tov early, and makes *kiddush* before nightfall, as described in Chapter 47, paragraphs 22 and 23, and Chapter 52, paragraph 5, should try and eat at least a *ka-zayith* of bread after nightfall.

b. However, if this presents a difficulty, he may make *kiddush* and eat while it is still daytime, even if he will finish the meal before nightfall.

c. As mentioned in Chapter 46, paragraph 4, one cannot receive Shabbath before *p^e^lag ha-minchah*.

light

34. *a.* One ought preferably to make *kiddush* and eat the whole of one's evening meal by the glow of the lights which were kindled with a blessing in honor of Shabbath or Yom Tov, even if there are other lights on in the house by which one could eat. (See Chapter 43, paragraph 15.)

b. Still, if one moves to a place which is better illuminated, it does not matter, provided one keeps to the rules concerning making *kiddush* in the place where one eats, as detailed in paragraphs 9 and 10 above.

c. Furthermore, subject to the same proviso, in the event that
1) one is seriously bothered by, for instance, mosquitoes or
2) the place where the lights were kindled is too hot, and one desires to go to somewhere cooler, for example a balcony,

one may move even to a place which is not lit at all.

35. *a.* The Shabbath and Yom Tov meals are intended to be for pleasure. *exemption*

b. As a result, somebody who is worried the food may harm him has no obligation to eat.

36. *a.* It is a mitzva for each person to enjoy Shabbath and Yom Tov according to the means which the Almighty has bestowed upon him. *liberality*

b. He should be liberal with meat, wine and other delicacies to the extent that he is able and should also eat fish at each one of the three Shabbath meals.

c. See also Chapter 42, paragraph 16.

37. *a.* One should eat Shabbath meals with appetite. (See Chapter 42, paragraph 25.) *appetite*

b. Consequently, on Shabbath morning too, it is proper to take the preferable course of washing one's hands for the meal straight after *kiddush*, rather than to fill one's stomach with a variety of "snacks" first. (See paragraph 22 above.)

38. Someone who is accustomed, when laying the table for guests, purposely to omit some small item of food and to leave a place free of a dish which should be there, in memory of the destruction of the Temple, should not do so on Shabbath or Yom Tov. *commemorating the destruction of the Temple*

39. *a.* Although the custom is to cover the knives during *birkath ha-mazon*, or to remove them from the table, *removing knives* *b.* on Shabbath and Yom Tov, the practice is to leave them on the table and not cover them.

c. Yet, there are some who do not depart from their usual custom, and cover or remove the knives even on Shabbath or Yom Tov.

Chapter 55

Laws Relating to Lechem Mishneh and the Cutting of the Loaves

LECHEM MISHNEH

1. It is a mitzva to start each Shabbath and Yom Tov meal with two whole loaves, namely *lechem mishneh*. *the mitzva*

2. *a.* However many times a day one eats, one should start each meal with *lechem mishneh*, although, *when required*
b. in case of difficulty, one whole loaf will suffice,
1) at the third Shabbath meal,
2) at additional meals one has on Shabbath and
3) at meals one has on Yom Tov over and above the two obligatory meals.

3. *a.* The mitzva of *lechem mishneh* is applicable to both men and women. *women*
b. One can observe it by *how to perform the mitzva*
1) listening to someone reciting the blessing on bread over the *lechem mishneh* and then
2) eating a piece of one of the loaves.
c. See also paragraphs 19 and 22 below.

4. *a.* Somebody who, after *kiddush* on Shabbath morning, eats not bread, but cake or cookies, following the practice mentioned in Chapter 54, paragraph 22, should try and say the blessing over two whole cakes or cookies (each at least a *ka-zayith* in size). *when eating cake or cookies*
b. Nonetheless, according to a different view, there is no obligation to be particular about *lechem mishneh*, unless one is eating
1) a meal with bread or
2) as much cake, or as many cookies, as a person needs

in order to eat to satisfaction, in which case one should

a) wash one's hands, as before eating bread,
b) recite the blessing appropriate when washing hands,
c) recite, over two whole cakes or cookies, the blessing normally said prior to eating bread and,
d) at the end of the meal, recite *birkath ha-mazon.*

size

5. *a.* One should make a point of taking, for *lechem mishneh,* loaves which are each at least a *ka-zayith* in size.

seder night

b. It is also as well, if possible, that there should be sufficient to distribute to each of those around the table.

c. 1) Consequently, on seder night, it is advisable to give each of those around the table three matzoth of their own.

2) In this way, everyone will have *lechem mishneh* and will be able to perform the mitzva of eating matza in the proper way.

joined loaves

6. *a.* Two loaves which became stuck together whilst being baked may be used as *lechem mishneh,* even if they are still attached to each other.

b. However, there is a view which disputes this and holds that one must first separate them.

c. 1) In the event that one separates them from each other, and they remain whole, they are indeed considered whole loaves, even if one can tell they were joined together.

2) Where part of one loaf remains stuck to the other, it is well to remove the piece, so that the loaf to which it is stuck should indeed look whole.

burned loaves

7. *a.* One may use as *lechem mishneh* a loaf which was burned while baking, provided it is whole, but,

b. if one can avoid it, one should not use a loaf which was burned to such an extent that the burned part is inedible.

8. *a.* Where possible, one ought to be particular that the loaves should be perfectly whole. *loaves should be whole*

b. Thus, if there is a label stuck to the loaf itself, one should not remove it until after one has cut the bread, so that the loaf remains whole at the time of the blessing.*

c. Similarly, if one takes matzoth for *lechem mishneh*, one should see to it that they are whole, and not cracked.

d. Nevertheless, it does not matter if a little of the bread has been removed by way of separating *challa*. (See the following paragraph.)

9. *a.* 1) Subject to what is stated below, if *challa* has not been separated, before Shabbath or Yom Tov, from bread which was kneaded in Eretz Yisrael, one cannot separate it on Shabbath or Yom Tov. (See Chapter 11, paragraph 16.) *when challa not separated*

2) Nor is one permitted to extricate oneself from the difficulty by leaving over some of the bread, with the intention of separating *challa* from it after the end of Shabbath or Yom Tov.

3) Since one, therefore, cannot eat the bread, the result is that

a) it is *muktzeh* and

b) one cannot use it as one of the loaves for *lechem mishneh* (even if one wishes to eat only from the other loaf). (See also paragraph 14 below.)

b. 1) Outside Eretz Yisrael, the position is different.

2) The obligation to separate *challa* from dough kneaded there, even at the time when the Temple stood and the whole of the Jewish people lived in Eretz Yisrael, was only a Rabbinical one.

3) Consequently, the Rabbis took a more lenient attitude and (as stated in Chapter 31, paragraph 41) ruled that one should

---

* Labels should be removed together with a little of the bread to which they are attached, so as not to tear through the lettering on them, as explained in Chapter 11, paragraph 9.

a) leave a piece of bread uneaten and
b) separate *challa* from that after the termination of Shabbath or Yom Tov.

4) The result is that, since one is allowed to eat the bread from which *challa* was not separated, one may also use it for *lechem mishneh*.

c. 1) Notwithstanding the above, if, before Shabbath or Yom Tov, one made the stipulation referred to in Chapter 11, paragraphs 18 and 21, one may separate *challa* on Shabbath or Yom Tov, even in Eretz Yisrael.

2) When separating *challa* on Shabbath or Yom Tov, one proceeds as follows:
a) One determines the place in the loaf where the *challa* is to be, at that end of it which one is not going to eat.
b) One pronounces the blessing said before the separation of *challa*.*
c) One verbally designates what one wishes to separate as *challa*.
d) One pronounces the usual blessing over bread and eats some.
e) One then takes off the *challa*, together with some of the bread which is not *challa* (since the portion actually designated as *challa* is itself *muktzeh*).

3) a) Better still, one should not wait to take off the *challa* until one has pronounced the blessing over the bread, but should separate it earlier.
b) Although, when one comes to pronounce the blessing over the bread, the piece removed for *challa* will be missing, this does not prevent one from using the loaf for *lechem mishneh*. (See paragraph 8 above.)
c) It is as well to take off only a few crumbs as

---

* The blessing is only pronounced if
a. 1) the quantity of bread is enough to make separating *challa* obligatory, as to which see Chapter 42, paragraph 9, or
2) the original dough contained a sufficient quantity, and
b. *challa* has definitely not yet been separated.

challa, so that the loaf should remain as near whole as possible.

10. *a.* 1) Bread from which a piece has been cut or broken may be put into the oven and rebaked (if it is not yet Shabbath). *broken loaves*

2) The rebaked loaf is regarded by the Halacha as being whole.

b. 1) If this possibility is not open to one, and one has no other whole loaf, one can join the severed piece to the loaf with, for example, a toothpick.

2) The reconstituted loaf can then be used for *lechem mishneh*, so long as one cannot readily tell that it has been cut or broken.

3) The loaf may be joined together in this way even on Shabbath or Yom Tov (provided one does not do so with a piece of wood which is *muktzeh mei-chamath gufo*).

c. 1) A matza, part of which has broken off, may also be put into the oven (before Shabbath) to rebake (or even held over an open flame).

2) If one cannot readily tell that the edges are broken, one may then use it for *lechem mishneh*.

11. Sliced bread which is held together by virtue of being inside a plastic wrapper is not regarded as a whole loaf. *sliced bread*

12. One may use a frozen loaf, which has just been taken out of the freezer, for *lechem mishneh*.* *frozen loaf*

13. If one is lacking a second loaf for *lechem mishneh*, one may *borrowed loaf*

---

* *a.* It is better not to put a frozen loaf onto the special electric plate used on Shabbath, in order to defrost, but
b. one may put an empty pot, or an upside-down plate, onto the electric Shabbath plate, and place the loaf on that, or on the lid of a pot containing food, even if it is on the flame.
c. In any event, one should not cover the loaf, for instance with a towel, while it is on the lid, if one indeed covers it on all sides.

a. borrow a loaf from a neighbor,
b. say the blessing over bread, cutting one's own loaf, and then
c. return the borrowed loaf to its owner.

loaf one cannot eat

14. *a.* A person who has only one whole loaf that he is able to eat may take, to make up *lechem mishneh*, a second loaf which, for any one of the following reasons, he will not eat at the present time.

1) a) The second loaf is not fit for the mitzva which he is performing.
   b) For example, even though, for the mitzva of eating matza on seder night, one requires matza *sh^emura*, if he only has one such matza, he may take, as the second matza, one which is not *sh^emura*.

2) a) He has taken upon himself to be stringent in a respect not demanded by the Halacha.
   b) For example, even though he is particular, throughout Pesach (and not just on seder night), to eat only matza which is *sh^emura*, he may take a second matza which is not *sh^emura*.

3) a) The halachic practice is not to eat the second loaf in the currently existing circumstances.
   b) For example, even if he is going to eat meat during the meal, he may take, for his second loaf, one which may not be eaten with meat.

4) a) The Halacha forbids the loaf to be eaten at the present time.
   b) For example, when the day before Pesach occurs on Shabbath, even though it is forbidden to eat matza, he may add a matza to the single loaf of bread which he has, as *lechem mishneh*.*

b. Similarly, there are grounds for permitting someone who does not eat bread baked by a non-Jew, and has only one

---

* The matza which he has placed with the loaf of bread should not be eaten on Pesach.

loaf from a Jewish baker and the other from a non-Jewish baker, to use also the bread from the non-Jew for *lechem mishneh*.

c. 1) On the other hand, bread which the Halacha absolutely forbids one to eat cannot be used to make up *lechem mishneh*.

2) a) An example of this is bread from which *t^e^rumoth* and *ma'asroth* have not been separated, except when the omission can be rectified. (See Chapter 11, paragraphs 18 to 28.)

b) A further example is bread kneaded in Eretz Yisrael, from which *challa* has not been taken, except when the omission can be rectified. (See paragraph 9 above.)

3) Such bread is *muktzeh* and may not even be moved.

15. *a.* Two whole rusks (zwieback) may also be used as *lechem mishneh*. *rusks*

b. According to another view, however, rusks should not be used for this purpose.

16. *a.* Someone who eats cake or cookies instead of bread, and consumes as much of them as a person needs in order to eat to satisfaction, may start his meal with two whole cakes or cookies (each at least a *ka-zayith* in size) as *lechem mishneh*, but *using cake or cookies*

b. 1) a person who has washed his hands in order to eat his meal with bread should not take a cake or cookie as one of his *lechem mishneh*, if he can help it, even if he intends to eat from it during the course of the meal, although

2) a different opinion argues as follows:

a) if he decided to eat his meal with cake or cookies instead of bread, as in *a* above, he would use them to fulfil his obligation to take *lechem mishneh*;

b) since they are themselves fit for *lechem mishneh*, it is perfectly in order to use them, with a loaf of bread, to make up *lechem mishneh* when he eats his meal with bread, even if he has no intention to eat them during the meal.

c. Certainly, somebody who has only one whole loaf of bread would do well, according to all opinions, to place a whole cake or cookie with it, as *lechem mishneh.*

in absence of whole loaves

17. *a.* When one does not have two whole loaves, one should take one whole loaf together with one which has been started.

b. If one does not even have one whole loaf, one should take two which have been started.

c. At the very least, one should take two slices of bread.

CUTTING THE SHABBATH LOAF

when to cut

18. *a.* 1) While, on an ordinary weekday, one should cut into the loaf a little, before pronouncing the blessing on the bread,

2) on Shabbath and Yom Tov, one should not actually cut into it at all, until after the blessing, so that the loaf will be completely whole when the blessing is being said.

b. 1) There are, however, those who are particular to make a practice, on Shabbath and Yom Tov, of marking the bread with the knife, before the blessing, so that they will know where to cut it.*

2) This is intended to minimize the delay between reciting the blessing and tasting the bread.

3) At any rate, if one forgets, and cuts into the loaf a little, as on a weekday, one can still use it for the mitzva of *lechem mishneh.*

---

* The position of the mark should be such that one will cut off enough of the loaf to last all those round the table for the whole meal. (See paragraph 24 below.)

19. *a.* 1) It is proper that, when the person who cuts the Shabbath loaf says the blessing over the bread, he should intend it to be on behalf of all those present, and *how to say the blessing for others*

2) they

a) should have a corresponding intention to discharge their obligations by listening to his blessing and

b) should answer "Amen."

b. 1) The correct procedure is for all those participating to be seated in their places when the blessing on the bread is being recited.

2) Nevertheless, even if it happened that they were not all sitting in their places, they have discharged their duty to say the blessing, as long as

a) the person who recited the blessing had the intention of thereby discharging their obligations and

b) they themselves intended to discharge their obligations by hearing his blessing.

c. 1) a) The person reciting the blessing should, immediately prior thereto, request the permission of the other participants, with the words "*Bir^e^shuth rabbothai.*"

b) Even if he is their senior, this does not exempt him from asking their permission.

2) After the blessing, he should cut the loaf, but not before most of those who answer "Amen" have finished doing so.

3) Neither he nor they should interrupt by speaking, even

a) for a purpose connected with the *lechem mishneh* or

b) for the purpose of another mitzva or

c) about matters required for the meal,

until they have eaten some of the bread (preferably the amount of a *ka-zayith*).

4) The rules in Chapter 48, paragraphs 2 and 7, apply

here too, with appropriate changes.

d. 1) If it should happen that, when the blessing on the bread is being said, some of the participants
a) have not yet said the blessing on washing hands, or have not yet dried their hands, or
b) have not yet even managed to wash their hands,
they have nonetheless discharged their duty to say the blessing on the bread.

2) However,
a) both they and the person reciting the blessing must have had the requisite intentions (as above),
b) they should be particular to respond with "Amen," and
c) it is better not to let such a situation arise at all.

3) In any event, they should not interrupt between hearing the blessing on the bread and tasting the bread (except for washing their hands, with the usual blessing).

e. 1) Notwithstanding the above, those who are accustomed to saying their own blessing, on the piece of bread given them by the person who cut it, also have authority to support them, but

2) a) the person saying the blessing over the bread must have the intention to discharge the obligations of the participants with regard to the mitzva of *lechem mishneh* and
b) the participants must have the intention thereby to discharge their obligations in this respect.

when one can say the blessing for others

20. *a.* 1) Someone who makes *kiddush* for others, as explained in Chapter 51, paragraphs 1 and 6, says the blessing on the wine for them, even if
a) he himself does not wish thereby to discharge his own obligation to make *kiddush* and
b) only they, and not he, will be drinking the wine.

2) This is so both on Shabbath and Yom Tov eve and during the day.

b. 1) It is different,* however, with regard to the blessing on bread to be recited over the *lechem mishneh* after *kiddush.*

2) He cannot say the blessing for them if he does not eat bread himself, and they must recite the blessing for themselves.

3) See further Chapter 51, paragraph 7.

c. 1) On Passover eve, it is a mitzva to eat a *ka-zayith* of matza.

2) Consequently, even if he is not eating with the other people present, he can say on their behalf both blessings over the matza, that is to say,

a) the blessing usually recited over any bread, as well as

b) the special blessing over the mitzva of eating matza,

although

3) it is preferable for him not to do so (when he is not himself eating), if they know how to say the blessings themselves.

d. 1) Similarly, on the eve of Sukkoth, he can say the blessing on the bread for the others present, since it is a mitzva to eat a *ka-zayith* of bread in the *sukka.*

2) There is, however, this difference: namely, that, if he is not eating with them, he can say the blessing only for the men, and not for the women, as the latter are free from the mitzva of eating in the *sukka.*

---

* It is difficult to state a general rule which precisely covers this and all similar situations, but it seems that the following distinctions should be made:

a. blessings over a mitzva (for example the blessing of *kiddush* and the blessing in *c*2)b) of this paragraph) may be said for others even when one is not saying them for oneself, whereas

b. if a blessing is said before eating, or enjoying a similar benefit, then,

1) if the principal reason for eating is to perform a mitzva (as in *c*2)a) and in *d* above), one may say it for others even when one is not saying it for oneself, but,

2) if the principal reason for eating is because one wants to eat (even where a mitzva is involved, as in *b* above), one may say it for others only if one is at the same time saying it for oneself.

holding the loaves

21. *a.* The person reciting the blessing over the *lechem mishneh* should hold both loaves.

b. It is as well for them to be covered until after the blessing.

c. One should raise them when mentioning the name of God.

separate blessings over the same loaves

22. *a.* Participants may, contrary to the recommendation in paragraph 19 above, wish to have neither their duty to take *lechem mishneh*, nor their obligation to say the blessing over them, discharged by the person who cuts the loaves.

b. If they only have two loaves between them, they should each, in turn, hold the loaves and pronounce the blessing themselves.

c. Each should be very careful not to interrupt between his own blessing and tasting the bread, by answering "Amen" after the blessings of the others. (Compare Chapter 48, paragraph 7.)

d. When they have all individually pronounced their blessings, the bread should be cut and distributed amongst all of them.

which loaf to cut

23. *a.* One should put the two loaves of *lechem mishneh* one on top of the other.

b. On Friday evening, one should
   1) take care to place the lower loaf nearer to one than the upper and,
   2) at the end of the blessing, hold and cut the lower loaf.

c. On Shabbath during the day, and on Yom Tov (both in the evening and during the day), one should cut the upper loaf (which should be nearer to one, so that it comes readily to hand).

cutting, distributing and eating

24. *a.* If one marked the loaf, as mentioned in paragraph 18 above, one should cut it where marked.

b. 1) It is a mitzva to cut off sufficient bread to last all those round the table for the whole meal.

2) This is a demonstration of one's enthusiasm in fulfilling the mitzva of eating the Shabbath or Yom Tov meal.

c. One should distribute* at least a *ka-zayith*** of the bread one has cut off to each of the participants.

d. Nevertheless, the participants have discharged their duty to eat *lechem mishneh*, even if they

1) received only a small piece of the *lechem mishneh* to eat and

2) added other bread to it to make up the quantity of a *ka-zayith*.

e. The others round the table should not eat the bread until the person cutting it has started doing so (except as mentioned below).

f. Indeed, it is better for the person cutting the bread to start eating his piece before distributing the rest.

g. 1) If, however, each of those present has his own *lechem mishneh* in front of him, they can start eating, even when the person pronouncing the blessing has not yet done so.

2) This might be the case on Pesach eve, if one followed the recommendation mentioned in paragraph 5 above.

25. Some have the custom of starting each of the meals by cutting both loaves of the *lechem mishneh*. *cutting both loaves*

MISCELLANEOUS

26. *a.* 1) On a weekday, if one eats bread at a meal, not from a desire to eat bread, but only to avoid separate blessings before other food one is going to eat, it is *eating bread to avoid repeating blessings*

---

* *a.* One should neither hand each person his piece of bread, nor throw it down in front of him.
b. What one should do is put it down in front of him, so that he can take it and eat it himself.

** Each person should be particular to eat a *ka-zayith* of bread within two, or at most four, minutes, as explained in Chapter 54, paragraph 30.

doubtful whether the blessing on the bread in fact obviates the need for the other blessings.

2) This is because it could be said that the other food is not ancillary to the bread, but rather the reverse.

b. 1) On Shabbath, the blessing on the bread does cover the rest of the meal too (except for the dessert eaten as the last course), even in these circumstances.

2) This is because the mitzva to eat a *ka-zayith* of bread at the Shabbath meal makes the bread the most important item on the menu.

leaving food for after the meal

27. *a.* 1) It is forbidden to bring about a situation where a blessing will have to be said unnecessarily.

2) Thus, one

a) should not recite *birkath ha-mazon*, so long as one still intends to eat, but

b) should finish the whole meal, and only then say *birkath ha-mazon*.

b. 1) On Shabbath and Yom Tov, one can take into account that it is more difficult to recite the one hundred blessings one ought to pronounce every day, since there are fewer blessings in the *Amidah* prayer.

2) One may, therefore, leave fruit or a piece of cake, for example, from one's Shabbath or Yom Tov meal, to be eaten subsequent to *birkath ha-mazon*, so that one will then have to say blessings before and after eating it.

loaf of eiruv tavshilin

28. *a.* As mentioned in Chapter 2, paragraph 10, one may cook on Yom Tov for Shabbath occurring on the subsequent day only if one made an *eiruv tavshilin* before Yom Tov.

b. It is proper to use the loaf (or matza) of the *eiruv* as one of the *lechem mishneh* at all of the Shabbath meals, cutting it only at the last of them.

c. Those who are accustomed to starting each meal by cutting two loaves, as mentioned in paragraph 25 above, should preferably cut the loaf of the *eiruv* on Friday night.

Chapter 56

The Third Shabbath Meal

days applicable

1. *a.* 1) One should make a particular point of observing the mitzva of eating a third meal on Shabbath.

2) One should try to do so even if one has already eaten one's fill and is not yet hungry again (but see paragraph 5 below).

b. 1) On Yom Tov, it is not customary to eat a third meal.

2) Nevertheless, one would do well

a) to eat fruit on Yom Tov, in place of a third meal, or

b) to serve an extra dish at the morning meal.

c. 1) There are some who follow the custom of the Vilna Gaon in eating a third meal in the afternoon of the last day of Pesach, but not on any other Yom Tov.

2) He used to wash hands and eat matza, out of his attachment to the mitzva of eating matza on Pesach, the time for which was about to expire.

to whom applicable

2. Women too have an obligation to eat the third Shabbath meal.

praying first

3. *a.* The custom is to say the afternoon prayer before the third Shabbath meal.

b. 1) In any event, a person who finds it difficult to eat the meal subsequent to the afternoon prayer can eat first, from half an hour after midday* onwards.

2) The practice is to permit this even if it is late in the day, so long as one takes care not to miss the time for the afternoon prayer altogether.

c. If the third Shabbath meal is one at which *sheva beracho*th are to be said (and which is, therefore, likely to be more protracted than usual), one should not sit

* A "day," for these purposes, means the hours between sunrise and sunset.

down to eat until one has recited the afternoon prayer.

d. Nor should one do so in the event that one
   1) is going to say the afternoon prayer privately, that is to say without a congregation, and
   2) is already in the last quarter of the day.*

before sunset

4. *a.* If one can, one should eat at least a *ka-zayith* of the bread of the third meal before sunset.

b. Where one cannot manage this, one may, nonetheless, start to eat, but one should wash one's hands and pronounce the blessing on the bread prior to sunset.

c. See further Chapter 59, paragraphs 11 and 12.

d. Whoever is anxious to act in the proper manner ought not to wash his hands and start to eat after sunset.**

what to eat

5. *a.* 1) The best course is
      a) to wash one's hands for the third meal,
      b) to start with *lechem mishneh*, as stated in Chapter 55, paragraph 2, and
      c) to eat more than a *ka-beitzah* of bread, as mentioned in Chapter 54, paragraph 30.
   2) At any rate, one should eat not less than a *ka-zayith* of bread.***

b. 1) If one is not hungry, and finds it difficult to eat bread at all, one should eat baked or cooked food made from wheat, barley, rye, oats or spelt.
   2) If that also is not possible, one should eat meat or fish.
   3) Failing that, one should at least
      a) eat fruit (according to some authorities, cooked fruit) or
      b) drink a *rᵉvi'ith* of wine.

c. Should one find it hard to eat or drink anything at all,

---

* A "day," for the purposes, means the hours between sunrise and sunset.

** In places where Shabbath ends a long time after sunset, there is room for being more lenient and starting to eat a few minutes after sunset.

*** It should be noted that, if one is going to eat less than a *ka-beitzah* of bread, one should not say a blessing when washing one's hands.

one need not force oneself to do so, since the purpose of the Shabbath meal is to give pleasure and not pain.

6. *a.* As mentioned in the preceding paragraph, one ought to be particular about starting with *lechem mishneh*, that is to say, two whole loaves, at the third meal too. *the loaves*

b. In any event, one should make every effort to have at least one whole loaf.

c. Still, even if one has no more than one slice of bread, one should observe the mitzva of having a third Shabbath meal by eating that.

7. *a.* It is not the custom to cover the *lechem mishneh* with a cloth at the third Shabbath meal. *covering the loaves*

b. There are, however, those who hold that, at the third meal also, the loaves should be covered, with one cloth over them and another beneath them.

8. Although one does not make *kiddush* before the third Shabbath meal, *wine*

a. there are some whose custom is to make *kiddush* (over wine) then too (as explained in Chapter 47, paragraph 3), and

b. it is certainly a good practice to say a blessing over wine during the meal.

9. *a.* 1) When holding a meal in honor of a bride and groom, during the seven days of feasting which begin with the wedding, *sheva beracoth* are said. *sheva berachoth*

2) However, if it is an ordinary day of the week, *sheva berachoth* are said only if there is present, in their honor, a person who did not attend any of the previous meals.

b. 1) On Shabbath and Yom Tov, at the first two meals, that is to say, in the evening and in the morning, the custom is to say *sheva berachoth* even when there is no such new person present.

2) At the third Shabbath meal, it is also customary

to say *sheva b^e^rachoth* even when there is no new guest, provided the groom gives an exposition on some Torah subject.

3) See also Chapter 59, paragraphs 17 and 18.

eating early before Yom Tov

10. *a.* When Shabbath is the day before Yom Tov, it is a mitzva to eat the third Shabbath meal early, before the last quarter of the day* begins, so that one will have an appetite to eat the Yom Tov meal in the evening.

b. If it is later than that, one should still eat the third meal, but should only have a little bread, that is to say, somewhat more than a *ka-beitzah*.

finishing before Yom Tov

11. When Shabbath is the day before Yom Tov, then, even if one began the third meal before the last quarter of the day, one should not prolong it later than sunset, since one then becomes subject to the duty of making *kiddush* for Yom Tov.

day before Pesach

12. *a.* When the day prior to Pesach is Shabbath, there is a problem with respect to eating the third Shabbath meal.

1) One cannot eat bread which is *chametz*, because it is forbidden to eat *chametz* after the first third of the day.**

2) On the other hand, one is not allowed to eat matza either, on the day before Pesach.

b. 1) What one can do is eat, for example, matza balls.

2) Since the matza balls are cooked,

a) one cannot use them to fulfil the mitzva of eating matza on Pesach, and is, therefore, allowed to eat them on the day before Pesach, and,

b) no matter how much of them one eats, one first recites the blessing usually said before cooked food made from wheat, barley, rye, oats or spelt, and,

---

* A "day," for these purposes, means the hours between sunrise and sunset.

** See previous note.

afterwards, one recites the *al-hamichya* blessing.*

3) a) However, one should not start a meal comprising cooked matza if one is already in the last quarter of the day;**

b) nor should one do so even when it is earlier, if one can see that one would not finish eating until after the last quarter of the day has begun.

c. In the event that

1) one has not prepared a dish made from cooked matza, or

2) one does not want to eat such a dish, or

3) it is too late to eat it (as in *b*3) above),

one should observe the mitzva of the third Shabbath meal by eating meat or fish, or at least fruit (as in paragraph 5 above).

d. 1) There are those who are accustomed, in addition to eating a meal in the afternoon, as detailed above, to divide into two the meal eaten in the morning with bread.

2) That is to say, they

a) start by eating some bread,

b) recite *birkath ha-mazon*,

c) allow a little time to elapse,

d) wash their hands again and then

e) eat a third meal (also with bread).

e. Others express the view that, when Shabbath is the day before Pesach,

1) there is no duty to eat a third meal and

2) one should occupy oneself with studying Torah, instead of with feasting.

meat and wine during the Nine Days

13. See Chapter 59, paragraph 19, for what one ought to do with regard to eating meat and drinking wine at the third meal, when Shabbath occurs in the Nine Days beginning

---

* Contrast the situation in Chapter 54, paragraph 31, where cake or cookies, which are baked, are eaten.

** A "day," for these purposes, means the hours between sunrise and sunset.

with the first of Av, and one prolongs the meal beyond the time for the expiration of Shabbath.

before Fast of Av

14. *a.* 1) When the Ninth of Av falls

a) on Sunday, or

b) on Shabbath, so that the Fast is put off to Sunday, one must finish eating on Shabbath (preceding the Fast) before sunset.

2) Nevertheless, at the concluding meal before the Fast, one may eat meat and drink wine, and may indeed serve a feast fit for a king.

3) Moreover, it is forbidden to omit from one's third meal anything one is accustomed to have on other Shabbathoth during the year.

b. 1) Whoever is in the habit of eating with company at the third meal on other Shabbathoth of the year should do so on this Shabbath too.

2) In any event, it is permitted

a) to eat with one's family in the usual way and

b) to say *birkath ha-zimun* (even though one does not say *birkath ha-zimun* after eating the concluding meal before the Fast on a weekday).

c. 1) When the day before the Fast of the Ninth of Av occurs on a weekday, and one wishes to eat something after the concluding meal, it is as well to stipulate, before *birkath ha-mazon*, that one is not yet taking upon oneself to start the Fast.

2) On Shabbath, however, there is no need to make any such stipulation, and one may eat even after *birkath ha-mazon*, until sunset.

Chapter 57

Mentioning Special Days During Birkath Ha-Mazon

1. *a.* On special days, one is required to mention the occasion in the third blessing of *birkath ha-mazon.* *the rule*

b. That is to say,

1) on Shabbath, one should add the *Retzei* prayer,

2) on Yom Tov, *chol ha-mo'ed* and *rosh chodesh*, one should add the *Ya'aleh Ve-yavo** prayer and,

3) when one of these latter days falls on Shabbath, one should add both, saying first *Retzei* and then *Ya'aleh Ve-yavo.*

c. 1) If, in this last case, one has mistakenly said *Ya'aleh Ve-yavo* before *Retzei*, one has, nonetheless, discharged one's obligation.

2) Where, however, one remembers, in the middle of *Ya'aleh Ve-yavo*, before one has mentioned *rosh chodesh* or the name of the particular Festival, that one has omitted *Retzei*, one has to

a) stop,

b) say *Retzei*, and afterwards

c) go back to the beginning of *Ya'aleh Ve-yavo.*

d. 1) Somebody who has to eat on Yom Kippur should add, in *birkath ha-mazon*,

a) *Ya'aleh Ve-yavo*, with the insertion of the words, "*be-Yom Ha-kippurim ha-zeh*," and,

b) if it is Shabbath too, *Retzei* (before *Ya'aleh Ve-yavo*).

---

* *a.* It is customary to respond "Amen" after each of the words, "*le-tovah*," "*li-vrachah*" and "*le-chayim*," towards the end of *Ya'aleh Ve-yavo*, when one hears someone else saying them.
b. One should not do so if one is oneself reciting *birkath ha-mazon* and is in the middle of one of the blessings.
c. One may do so if one is in between blessings, or after the fourth blessing (which ends "*al yechassreinu*").

2) See also Chapter 39, paragraph 31.

in the "three-in-one" blessing

2. The occasion is also mentioned on Shabbath, Yom Tov, *rosh chodesh* and *chol ha-mo'ed*, when saying the "three-in-one" blessing* recited after cake, cookies, certain fruits and wine.

remembering before name of God

3. If one

a. mistakenly omits the appropriate addition in the third blessing of *birkath ha-mazon* on Shabbath, Yom Tov, *chol ha-mo'ed* or *rosh chodesh*, and

b. remembers before mentioning the name of God at the end of the third blessing,

one should recite the additional passage (or passages) right away and then repeat the last part of the third blessing, from "*U-venei Yerushalayim.*"

remembering after name of God

4. If one remembers only after mentioning the name of God, one should

a. prevent the name of God one has pronounced from being in vain, by adding the words, "לַמְּדֵנִי חֻקֶּיךָ — *lamdeini chukecha*" so completing verse 12 of Chapter 119 of Psalms, "בָּרוּךְ אַתָּה יהוה לַמְּדֵנִי חֻקֶּיךָ — Blessed art Thou, O Lord, teach me Thy statutes,"

b. recite the appropriate additional passage (or passages) and

c. then repeat the last part of the third blessing, from "*U-venei Yerushalayim.*"

remembering between third and fourth blessings

5. *a.* If one has already completed the third blessing (ending, "*bonei berachamav Yerushalayim amen*") when one remembers that one has not said *Retzei* or *Ya'aleh Ve-yavo* (or when one begins to entertain a doubt in that respect), one should

1) add a special, separate blessing (as detailed in paragraphs 14 and 15 below), and then

---

* See Glossary.

2) continue with the usual fourth blessing:
(בָּרוּךְ אַתָּה יהוה אֱלֹהֵינוּ מֶלֶךְ הָעוֹלָם, הָאֵל אָבִינוּ...)

b. In the event that one erroneously recited *Retzei* or *Ya'aleh Ve-yavo* after the end of the third blessing, instead of saying the special blessing, one has achieved nothing, and the rules set out in paragraph 7 below apply.

6. If one has already started reciting the fourth blessing, but has only said as far as the words "מֶלֶךְ הָעוֹלָם" when one remembers that one has not said *Retzei* or *Ya'aleh Ve-yavo* (or when one begins to entertain a doubt in that respect), one should

remembering at start of fourth blessing

a. finish with the words of the appropriate special blessing, as detailed below, and then

b. return to the beginning of the fourth blessing.

7. *a.* However, in a case where one has continued with the fourth blessing, and has already said the words "הָאֵל אָבִינוּ", two distinctions must be made (with the practical results detailed below, in this and the following paragraph):

remembering in middle of fourth blessing or afterwards

1) between
   a) Shabbath and Yom Tov, on the one hand,
   and
   b) *rosh chodesh* and *chol ha-mo'ed*, on the other hand,

and

2) between
   a) the first two Shabbath and Yom Tov meals
   and
   b) other Shabbath and Yom Tov meals.

b. On Shabbath and Yom Tov,

on Shabbath or Yom Tov

1) at the evening meal and the first meal in the morning, one has to go back to the beginning of *birkath ha-mazon*;

2) at the third, or any subsequent, meal,
   a) one neither goes back to the beginning of *birkath*

ha-mazon, nor recites *Retzei* or *Ya'aleh Ve-yavo* later on in *birkath ha-mazon*, although

b) there is a view that, at the third Shabbath meal, one should say *Retzei* in the concluding part of *birkath ha-mazon* (when one says "*Ha-Rachaman*").

on Rosh Hashana

c. On Rosh Hashana,

1) at the evening meal, one has to go back to the beginning of *birkath ha-mazon*,

2) at the first meal in the morning,

a) one also has to go back to the beginning of *birkath ha-mazon*, although

b) some authorities hold that one should not do so, and

3) at any additional meals, one neither goes back to the beginning of *birkath ha-mazon*, nor recites *Ya'aleh Ve-yavo* later on in *birkath ha-mazon*.

on rosh chodesh or chol ha-mo'ed

d. On *rosh chodesh* or *chol ha-mo'ed*, one neither goes back to the beginning of *birkath ha-mazon*, nor recites *Ya'aleh veyavo* later on in *birkath ha-mazon*.

forgetting when rosh chodesh or chol ha-mo'ed occur on Shabbath

8. *a.* When *rosh chodesh* or *chol ha-mo'ed* occur on Shabbath, the position is as follows:

1) if one has forgotten *Retzei*, whether or not one remembered to say *Ya'aleh Ve-yavo*,

a) the rules applicable are those set out in paragraph 7*b* above and,

b) when one has to repeat the *birkath ha-mazon* of the first two meals, one says both *Retzei* and *Ya'aleh Ve-yavo*;

2) if one has forgotten *Ya'aleh Ve-yavo*, but said *Retzei*, the rules applicable are those set out in paragraph 7*d* above.

forgetting when Yom Tov occurs on Shabbath

b. If Yom Tov occurs on Shabbath, and one has forgotten either *Retzei* or *Ya'aleh Ve-yavo* (or both), then

1) the rules applicable are those set out in paragraph 7*b* and *c* above and,

2) when one has to repeat the *birkath ha-mazon* of the

first two meals, one says both *Retzei* and *Ya'aleh Ve-yavo*.

effect of eating cake for first morning meal

9. *a.* A person who
1) eats cake or cookies for his first morning meal, as described in Chapter 54, paragraph 22,
2) recites the "three-in-one" blessing* afterwards, and then
3) eats a proper Shabbath or Yom Tov meal, but
4) forgets to say *Retzei* or *Ya'aleh Ve-yavo* in *birkath ha-mazon*,

does not say *birkath ha-mazon* again.**

b. There are, however, those who hold the opinion that, in these circumstances too, one should repeat *birkath ha-mazon*.

where some of the company forget

10. *a.* Three or more people who
1) ate together,
2) said *birkath ha-zimun*, and then
3) forgot to say *Retzei* or *Ya'aleh Ve-yavo* in *birkath ha-mazon*,

have fulfilled their duty so far as concerns *birkath ha-zimun*.

b. Yet, each of them individually has to say *birkath ha-mazon* again from the beginning (where this is required by the rules set out in paragraphs 7 to 9 above).

c. The same applies to ten or more, who add the name of God in *birkath ha-zimun*, as they should do.

forgetting in the "three-in-one" blessing

11. Somebody who forgets to mention the occasion of the day in the "three-in-one" blessing should not go back and say it again.

---

* See Glossary.

** This is because it may be that the cake or cookies should be regarded as his second Shabbath meal, in which case the subsequent meal is the third, and the rule set out in paragraph 7*b*2) above would apply.

third meal continuing after night

12. *a.* If one's third Shabbath or Yom Tov meal continues until after nightfall, one should still say *Retzei* or *Ya'aleh Ve-yavo*, as appropriate, in *birkath ha-mazon* (except in the situations mentioned in *d* and perhaps in *e* below),

1) provided one ate at least a *ka-zayith* of bread prior to sunset,
2) even if the meal is prolonged for a considerable time into the night.

(See Chapter 59, paragraphs 11 and 12.)

b. Should one forget to say *Retzei* or *Ya'aleh Ve-yavo* after nightfall (in the above circumstances),

1) one should not go back and repeat *birkath ha-mazon* from the beginning and,
2) in the situation described in paragraph 5 above,
    a) one adds the special blessing specified in paragraph 14 below, but without the name of the Almighty; that is to say,
    b) one begins, ...בָּרוּךְ אֲשֶׁר, and, where the termination of the blessing is in the form, ...בָּרוּךְ אַתָּה יהוה מְקַדֵּשׁ, one ends instead, ...בָּרוּךְ מְקַדֵּשׁ.

c. See also Chapter 59, paragraph 4.

d. One does not mention *Retzei* or *Ya'aleh Ve-yavo* in *birkath ha-mazon* if

1) one has already said the evening prayer in the middle of the meal or
2) one has already recited *Havdalah* over a cup of wine (or other suitable drink) in the middle of the meal.*

e. If, in the middle of the meal, one said, *"Baruch Ha-Mavdil bein kodesh l^e^-chol,"*** to enable one to do something which is forbidden on Shabbath, it is doubtful whether one has to say *Retzei* or *Ya'aleh Ve-yavo* in *birkath ha-mazon*.

---

* If three people ate the third Shabbath or Yom Tov meal together, and one of them said the evening prayer or made *Havdalah* over a cup in the middle of the meal, they still remain obliged to recite *birkath ha-zimun*.

** See Chapter 58, paragraph 7.

Shabbath followed by rosh chodesh

13. *a.* When
1) *rosh chodesh* occurs immediately following Shabbath and
2) one is reciting *birkath ha-mazon* after nightfall, following a meal which one commenced on Shabbath,

the position is as follows.

b. 1) If one actually finished eating before sunset, one should say only *Retzei* (and not *Ya'aleh Ve-yavo*).
2) Should one forget to do so, one
   a) neither says *birkath ha-mazon* again,
   b) nor adds the special blessing set out in paragraph 14 below.

c. 1) If, however, one's meal continued until after dark,
   a) some authorities hold that one should add only *Ya'aleh Ve-yavo* in *birkath ha-mazon*, since the conclusion of the meal was on the night of *rosh chodesh*, whereas,
   b) in the view of others, one should say both *Retzei* and *Ya'aleh Ve-yavo*.
2) It is better not to continue eating after dark, so as to avoid the uncertainty of whether or not one is obliged to say *Retzei*.

forms of special blessing

14. *a.* There are set out below the forms of the special blessings which one is required to say in the circumstances described in paragraphs 5 and 6 above.

b. They all open with the words בָּרוּךְ אַתָּה יהוה אֱלֹהֵינוּ מֶלֶךְ הָעוֹלָם ("Blessed art Thou, O Lord our God, King of the universe"), and continue,
1) if one has forgotten *Retzei* on Shabbath,
   ...אֲשֶׁר נָתַן שַׁבָּתוֹת לִמְנוּחָה לְעַמּוֹ יִשְׂרָאֵל בְּאַהֲבָה לְאוֹת וְלִבְרִית, בָּרוּךְ אַתָּה יהוה מְקַדֵּשׁ הַשַּׁבָּת
   ("...Who gave Shabbathoth for rest to His people Israel with love, as a sign and as a covenant, blessed art Thou, Sanctifier of the Shabbath");
2) if one has forgotten *Ya'aleh Ve-yavo* on Yom Tov (other than Rosh Hashana),
   ...אֲשֶׁר נָתַן יָמִים טוֹבִים לְעַמּוֹ יִשְׂרָאֵל לְשָׂשׂוֹן וּלְשִׂמְחָה אֶת יוֹם

חַג...הַזֶּה, בָּרוּךְ אַתָּה יהוה מְקַדֵּשׁ יִשְׂרָאֵל וְהַזְּמַנִּים
("...Who gave Yamim Tovim to His people Israel for rejoicing and happiness, this day of the Festival of..., blessed art Thou, Sanctifier of Israel and the festive occasions");

3) if one has forgotten *Ya'aleh Ve-yavo* on Rosh Hashana,
...אֲשֶׁר נָתַן יָמִים טוֹבִים לְעַמּוֹ יִשְׂרָאֵל אֶת יוֹם הַזִּכָּרוֹן הַזֶּה
("...Who gave Yamim Tovim to His people Israel, this Day of Remembrance"),
without a specific conclusion on the lines of the previous blessings, although, in the opinion of many authorities, one should conclude,
בָּרוּךְ אַתָּה יהוה מְקַדֵּשׁ יִשְׂרָאֵל וְיוֹם הַזִּכָּרוֹן
("blessed art Thou, Sanctifier of Israel and the Day of Remembrance");

4) if one has forgotten *Ya'aleh Ve-yavo* on *chol ha-mo'ed*,
...אֲשֶׁר נָתַן מוֹעֲדִים לְעַמּוֹ יִשְׂרָאֵל לְשָׂשׂוֹן וּלְשִׂמְחָה אֶת יוֹם חַג...הַזֶּה
("...Who gave appointed times to His people Israel for rejoicing and happiness, this day of the Festival of.......");

5) if one has forgotten *Ya'aleh Ve-yavo* on *rosh chodesh*,
...אֲשֶׁר נָתַן רָאשֵׁי חֳדָשִׁים לְעַמּוֹ יִשְׂרָאֵל לְזִכָּרוֹן
("...Who gave *rashei chodashim* to his people Israel as a remembrance");

6) if one has forgotten both *Retzei* and *Ya'aleh Ve-yavo* on a Yom Tov (other than Rosh Hashana) which occurs on Shabbath,
...אֲשֶׁר נָתַן שַׁבָּתוֹת לִמְנוּחָה לְעַמּוֹ יִשְׂרָאֵל בְּאַהֲבָה לְאוֹת וְלִבְרִית וְיָמִים טוֹבִים לְשָׂשׂוֹן וּלְשִׂמְחָה אֶת יוֹם חַג...הַזֶּה, בָּרוּךְ אַתָּה יהוה מְקַדֵּשׁ הַשַּׁבָּת וְיִשְׂרָאֵל וְהַזְּמַנִּים
("...Who gave Shabbathoth for rest to His people Israel with love, as a sign and as a covenant, and Yamim Tovim for rejoicing and happiness, this day of the Festival of...., blessed art Thou, Sanctifier of the Shabbath, Israel and the festive occasions");

7) if one has forgotten both *Retzei* and *Ya'aleh Ve-yavo* on a Rosh Hashana which occurs on Shabbath,

...אֲשֶׁר נָתַן שַׁבָּתוֹת לִמְנוּחָה לְעַמּוֹ יִשְׂרָאֵל בְּאַהֲבָה לְאוֹת וְלִבְרִית וְיָמִים טוֹבִים לְיִשְׂרָאֵל אֶת יוֹם הַזִּכָּרוֹן הַזֶּה, בָּרוּךְ אַתָּה יהוה מְקַדֵּשׁ הַשַּׁבָּת וְיִשְׂרָאֵל וְיוֹם הַזִּכָּרוֹן

("...Who gave Shabbathoth for rest to His people Israel with love, as a sign and as a covenant, and Yamim Tovim to Israel, this Day of Remembrance, blessed art Thou, Sanctifier of the Shabbath, Israel and the Day of Remembrance");

8) if one has forgotten both *Retzei* and *Ya'aleh Ve-yavo* on Shabbath during *chol ha-mo'ed*,

...אֲשֶׁר נָתַן שַׁבָּתוֹת לִמְנוּחָה לְעַמּוֹ יִשְׂרָאֵל בְּאַהֲבָה לְאוֹת וְלִבְרִית וּמוֹעֲדִים לְשָׂשׂוֹן וּלְשִׂמְחָה אֶת יוֹם חַג...הַזֶּה, בָּרוּךְ אַתָּה יהוה מְקַדֵּשׁ הַשַּׁבָּת וְיִשְׂרָאֵל וְהַזְּמַנִּים

("...Who gave Shabbathoth for rest to His people Israel with love, as a sign and as a covenant, and appointed times for rejoicing and happiness, this day of the Festival of......., blessed art Thou, Sanctifier of the Shabbath, Israel and the festive occasions");

9) if one has forgotten both *Retzei* and *Ya'aleh Ve-yavo* on a *rosh chodesh* which occurs on Shabbath,

...אֲשֶׁר נָתַן שַׁבָּתוֹת לִמְנוּחָה וְרָאשֵׁי חֳדָשִׁים לְזִכָּרוֹן, בָּרוּךְ אַתָּה יהוה מְקַדֵּשׁ הַשַּׁבָּת וְיִשְׂרָאֵל וְרָאשֵׁי חֳדָשִׁים

("...Who gave Shabbathoth for rest and *rashei chodashim* as a remembrance, blessed art Thou, Sanctifier of the Shabbath, Israel and the *rashei chodashim*").

special blessing when only one of two occasions forgotten

15. When

a. Rosh Hashana, another Yom Tov, *chol ha-mo'ed* or *rosh chodesh* occur on Shabbath and, in the third blessing of *birkath ha-mazon*, one

b. 1) says *Ya'aleh Ve-yavo*, but forgets *Retzei*, or

2) says *Retzei*, but forgets *Ya'aleh Ve-yavo*,

one should say the special blessing appropriate to the occasion one forgot, without referring to the occasion one did mention.

ignorance of special blessing

16. *a.* Someone who
1) forgot to say *Retzei* or *Ya'aleh Ve-yavo* and
2) a) does not know the form of the appropriate special blessing, as set out above, but
b) does know a few words from its beginning and its conclusion which express the essence of the blessing,

should say as much as he knows.

b. Failing that, the rules set out in paragraph 7*b* to *d* above apply.

Chanuka and Purim

17. *a.* On Chanuka and Purim, one adds *al ha-nissim* in the second blessing of *birkath ha-mazon*

b. In the event that one forgets *al ha-nissim*, then,
1) when one remembers before one has mentioned the name of God at the end of the second blessing, one goes back and says it; however,
2) when one remembers only subsequently, one does not go back, but adds it in the concluding part of *birkath ha-mazon*, with a slight change of form, "הָרַחֲמָן הוּא יַעֲשֶׂה לָנוּ נִסִּים וְנִפְלָאוֹת כְּשֵׁם שֶׁעָשִׂיתָ...בִּימֵי."

c. One does not make any special addition in the "three-in-one" blessing for either Chanuka or Purim.

mentioning an occasion erroneously

18. *a.* If one erroneously mentions an occasion in *birkath ha-mazon* on an inappropriate day, then,
1) where one realizes one's mistake before saying the name of God at the end of the blessing in which one made the insertion, one should stop right away and go back to the beginning of that blessing, but,
2) where one realizes only afterwards, one is no longer allowed to go back, but should continue with the rest of *birkath ha-mazon* as usual.

b. For example,
1) if one finds oneself saying *Retzei* on a weekday, one should immediately break off and start the third blessing again, whereas,

2) if one has already finished *Retzei*, and pronounced the name of God at the conclusion of the blessing, one should carry on with *birkath ha-mazon* and not go back.

Chapter 58

When Shabbath and Yom Tov End, and the Principles of the Mitzva of Havdalah

THE TIME WHEN SHABBATH AND YOM TOV END

prolonging Shabbath and Yom Tov

1. *a.* Just as there is a mitzva to add to a holy day, when it commences, whether it be Shabbath or Yom Tov, at the expense of the ordinary weekday, so is there a mitzva to add to it when it concludes. (See Chapter 46, paragraph 1.)

b. This addition is over and above the time of *bein ha-sh^e^mashoth*, during which one must in any case observe Shabbath or Yom Tov, due to the doubt as to whether it is day or not. (See Chapter 46, paragraph 16.)

recognizing the time

2. *a.* The time for the end of Shabbath and Yom Tov, including the addition mentioned in the preceding paragraph, is when three small stars are visible in the sky, not scattered, but close together.

b. It is proper to be particular and wait for a further period, until all trace of red has disappeared from the sky in the west.

c. There are, however, those who are more strict, in accordance with the opinion of Rabbeinu Tam, and do not consider it night until 72 minutes after sunset.

d. According to another view, the time for the conclusion of Shabbath, as determined at the latitude of Eretz Yisrael, varies between forty-five and fifty minutes after sunset.

calendars

3. *a.* Annual calendars are printed, containing the times for the termination of Shabbath and Yom Tov.

b. One must be sure that the publishers can be relied upon for the precision of the times.

c. If they are reliable, one may make use of calendars,

provided, of course, one has an accurate watch.

d. Generally, the times are calculated only for the place where the calendars are intended to appear, and one cannot assume that they hold good for a different geographical location.

e. In countries which adopt daylight-saving time, one must check whether the editors took this into account.

delaying evening prayer

4. *a.* It is proper and correct to delay commencing the evening prayer at the conclusion of Shabbath or Yom Tov.

b. Some have the custom to sing psalms before the evening prayer at the conclusion of Shabbath (but not at the end of Yom Tov, or when Yom Tov or the Fast of Av occur immediately after Shabbath).

THE MITZVA OF HAVDALAH

essence and source

5. *a.* There is a positive commandment to sanctify the Shabbath day in words at its termination (with *Havdalah*), just as there is at its commencement (with *kiddush*).

b. That is to say, we mention the holiness of the day, its preeminence and its distinction from the days which follow.

c. Whether the mitzva to make *Havdalah* is a Torah obligation or a Rabbinical one is a matter of dispute among the authorities.

Yom Tov and Yom Kippur

6. *a.* Just as one makes *Havdalah* at the termination of Shabbath, so does one make *Havdalah* at the termination of Yom Tov and of Yom Kippur.

b. One makes *Havdalah* even when

1) Yom Tov is immediately followed by *chol ha-mo'ed* or

2) Shabbath is immediately followed by Yom Tov.

(See Chapter 62, paragraph 9.)

c. In the view of all authorities, the obligation to make *Havdalah* on the termination of Yom Tov is only Rabbinical.

in prayer and mere words

7. *a.* 1) a) The bare requirement to make *Havdalah* is satisfied by saying the passage commencing *"Atah chonantanu"* in the *Sh^e^moneh Esrei* prayer on the expiration of Shabbath.

b) This is so even according to those authorities who hold that making *Havdalah* on the termination of Shabbath is a Torah obligation.

2) When it is Yom Tov at the termination of Shabbath, one inserts instead the passage beginning *"Vatodi'einu."*

b. Indeed, the same effect results from any expression of praise of the Almighty as being He Who differentiates holiness, for instance

1) *Baruch ha-mavdil bein kodesh le-chol* — בָּרוּךְ אַתָּה הַמַּבְדִּיל בֵּין קֹדֶשׁ לְחוֹל. ("Blessed is He Who divides between the holy and the profane), or

2) *Baruch ha-mavdil bein kodesh le-kodesh* — בָּרוּךְ אַתָּה הַמַּבְדִּיל בֵּין קֹדֶשׁ לְקֹדֶשׁ. ("Blessed is He Who divides between one holiness and another"), when it is Yom Tov on the expiration of Shabbath.

importance of cup

8. *a.* Notwithstanding the above, our Sages laid down a rule that one should make *Havdalah* over a cup (of wine or other suitable drink), even though one has made *Havdalah* during the evening prayer (as stated in the preceding paragraph).

b. One should be as diligent in one's efforts to make *Havdalah* over a cup as one is in observing all the other mitzvoth by which one is bound.

c. Only when there is no possibility of making *Havdalah* with a cup can one discharge one's liability with the *Havdalah* included in the evening prayer.

necessity in prayer

9. *a.* Likewise, even if one made *Havdalah* over a cup before saying the evening prayer, one has to make *Havdalah* during the evening prayer.

b. Similarly, if one said *"Baruch ha-mavdil bein kodesh le-chol"* or *"Baruch ha-mavdil bein kodesh le-kodesh"*

before the evening prayer, so that one would be able to perform a forbidden activity (as explained in Chapter 59, paragraph 1), one still has to make *Havdalah*
1) in the evening prayer and also
2) over a cup.

omission from prayer where there is drink

10. *a.* 1) Someone who
a) forgets to say "*Atah chonantanu*" and
b) remembers only after he has mentioned the name of God in the conclusion of the blessing beginning "*Atah chonein*"

should not go back and repeat the whole *Shemoneh Esrei*, since he will be saying *Havdalah* over a cup anyway.

2) The same applies to someone who, when Yom Tov occurs immediately after Shabbath,
a) forgets to say "*Va-todi'einu*" and
b) remembers only after he has mentioned the name of God in the conclusion of the blessing beginning "*Atah vechartanu.*"

b. It is possible for somebody who has forgotten to recite "*Atah chonantanu*" or "*va-todi'einu*" to say them at the end of the *Shemoneh Esrei*, after the verse commencing "*Yiheyu le-ratzon.*"

c. 1) See Chapter 59, paragraph 7, for the case where one forgets to make *Havdalah* in the evening prayer and by mistake performs a forbidden activity before making *Havdalah* over a cup.

2) See Chapter 59, paragraph 22, for the case where one forgets to make *Havdalah* in the evening prayer and by mistake tastes something before making *Havdalah* over a cup (contrary to the prohibition set out in Chapter 59, paragraph 10).

omission from prayer where there is no drink

11. *a.* The following is the situation where
1) one forgets to say "*Atah chonantanu,*"
2) one has no wine or other suitable drink over which to make *Havdalah* and
3) one knows that one will not have any the next day

either.

b. 1) If one remembers just after mentioning the name of God in the termination of the blessing commencing "*Atah chonein,*" one should

a) end with the words "*lamdeini chukecha,*"* and then

b) insert "*Atah chonantanu*" and conclude the blessing.

2) If one has already finished the blessing, but remembers before starting the blessing which begins "*Hashiveinu,*" one should

a) then and there say, "*Atah chonantanu,*" ending with the words "*u-m^edubakim b^e-yir'atecha,*" and

b) continue, "*Hashiveinu.*"

3) If one remembers only afterwards, but before saying the name of God at the end of the blessing which concludes "*shome'a t^efila,*" one should say "*Atah chonantanu*" in that blessing, after the words "*al t^eshiveinu.*"

4) If one remembers just after mentioning the name of God in the conclusion of the blessing which ends "*shome'a t^efila,*" one should

a) end with the words "*lamdeini chukecha,*"** and then

b) repeat the blessing, this time inserting "*Atah chonantanu*" after the words "*al t^eshiveinu.*"

5) If one has already finished "*shome'a t^efila,*" but remembers before starting the blessing which begins "*Retzei,*" one should

a) then and there say, "*Atah chonantanu,*" ending with the words "*u-m^edubakim b^e-yir'atecha,*" and

b) continue with "*Retzei.*"

6) If one remembers only after one has begun "*Retzei,*" one should go back and begin again from "*Atah chonein.*"

---

* See Chapter 57, paragraph 4*a*.

** See previous note.

7) If one remembers only after saying the verse commencing "*Yiheyu le-ratzon,*" at the end of *Shemoneh Esrei*, one should go back and start again from the beginning of *Shemoneh Esrei.*

c. When Yom Tov falls immediately after Shabbath,

1) one can make *Havdalah* over the loaves at the same time as one uses them to make *kiddush*, as explained in Chapter 62, paragraph 14, and, if that possibility exists, then

2) the rule contained in paragraph 10 above (and not those contained in this paragraph) applies.

in evening after missing afternoon prayer

12. *a.* Somebody who forgets to say the afternoon prayer should say *Shemoneh Esrei* again after the *Shemoneh Esrei* of the ensuing evening prayer, in place of the one he missed.

b. 1) The *Shemoneh Esrei* to be repeated is always that appropriate to the time when it is being said.

2) For instance, when Shabbath or Yom Tov is followed by an ordinary weekday, and he omitted the Shabbath or Yom Tov afternoon prayer, he repeats, after the evening prayer, the weekday *Shemoneh Esrei* he has just said.

c. "*Atah chonantanu*" or "*Va-todi'einu*" should be said in the first *Shemoneh Esrei*, since that is the one which belongs to the evening prayer.

d. If he said them in the second, and not in the first, he should recite a further *Shemoneh Esrei* to make up for the afternoon prayer he missed.*

e. If, however, he said *Havdalah* in both the first and the second *Shemoneh Esrei*, or in neither of them, he does not recite a further prayer.

---

* *a.* By making *Havdalah* in the second *Shemoneh Esrei* and not in the first, he has shown his intention that the second one should be that of the evening prayer, but

b. the first one cannot be in place of the afternoon prayer he missed, as a prayer in compensation for one missed must be recited after, and not before, the ensuing prayer.

in morning after missing evening prayer

13. *a.* Somebody who forgets to say the evening prayer should say *Shemoneh Esrei* again after the *Shemoneh Esrei* of the ensuing morning prayer, in place of the one he missed.

b. If the evening prayer he missed was that which he should have recited on the expiration of Shabbath or Yom Tov, the position is as follows:

1) If he **has** already made *Havdalah* over a cup of wine or other suitable drink, he should not say "*Atah chonantanu*" in either the first or the second *Shemoneh Esrei* in the morning.
2) In the event that he has **not** yet made *Havdalah* with a cup,*
   a) he should say "*Atah chonantanu*" in the second *Shemoneh Esrei*, which is the one he says in compensation for the evening prayer he missed, and
   b) he will still, of course, have to make *Havdalah* over a cup.
3) There are, however, some authorities who hold that, in this latter event, he should say "*Atah chonantanu*" in the first *Shemoneh Esrei*, as that is the first he is reciting since the termination of Shabbath or Yom Tov.

dispute regarding liability of women

14. There is a difference of opinion among the authorities as to the liability of a woman to make *Havdalah* after Shabbath or Yom Tov.

a. According to those who hold that the mitzva to make *Havdalah* on the termination of Shabbath is a Torah obligation, as mentioned in paragraph 5 above, a woman is also subject to the Torah obligation.

b. On the other hand, amongst those who hold that the

---

* This would be the case if, for example,
a. the Fast of Av occurred immediately after Shabbath or
b. he did not have any wine or other suitable drink with which to make *Havdalah*.

mitzva to make *Havdalah* on the termination of Shabbath is a Rabbinical obligation, there are two views.

1) Some hold that a woman has to make *Havdalah*, because
   a) making *Havdalah*, like making *kiddush*, is part of a general precept to mention Shabbath and its sanctity, and
   b) our Sages constructed the obligation to make *Havdalah* on the lines of the obligation to make *kiddush*.
2) Others hold that the obligation to make *Havdalah*
   a) is not part of any such general precept, but
   b) is an independent mitzva which the Sages instituted to divide between the holy and the profane, and so
   c) falls within the overall category of mitzvoth which apply only at particular times, and from which, by and large, a woman is free.

preferable course for women

15. *a.* Having regard to the above conflict of opinions, it is better for a woman
   1) not to say herself the usual *Havdalah* blessing which is pronounced over a cup, but
   2) to hear *Havdalah* recited by a man.

b. Nevertheless, if she recites the evening prayer, she has to say,
   1) "*Atah chonantanu*" in the blessing commencing "*Atah chonein*" or,
   2) when it is Yom Tov immediately after Shabbath, "*Va-todi'einu*" in the blessing commencing "*Atah vechartanu*."

c. Moreover, should she wish to perform an activity which is prohibited on Shabbath, before hearing *Havdalah* or before praying, she should say,
   1) "*Baruch ha-mavdil bein kodesh le-chol*" or,
   2) when it is Yom Tov immediately after Shabbath, "*Baruch ha-mavdil bein kodesh le-kodesh*."

woman making Havdalah for herself

16. *a.* A woman who has nobody to make *Havdalah* for her should make *Havdalah* herself and drink the wine. (See Chapter 60, paragraph 38.)

b. She should not, however, pronounce the blessing on the light. (See further Chapter 61, paragraph 24.)

man making Havdalah for woman

17. *a.* It is a matter of dispute among the authorities whether a man who has already made *Havdalah* over a cup, or has discharged his own liability by hearing *Havdalah* in the synagogue, or from somebody else, is allowed to make *Havdalah* for a woman.

b. Consequently, if there is no man available who has not yet made (or heard) *Havdalah*, it is better for the woman to make *Havdalah* for herself. (See also Chapter 61, paragraph 24.)

c. 1) It is as well, in order to avoid this problem, for husbands to have in mind, when hearing *Havdalah* in the synagogue, not thereby to discharge their own obligations.

2) They can then return home and recite *Havdalah* for themselves and all the members of their households.

woman making Havdalah for others

18. *a.* A woman who makes *Havdalah* can at the same time discharge the obligation of another woman who is listening, but

b. she cannot discharge the obligation of a man.

children

19. *a.* 1) A child who knows what Shabbath is is bound by the mitzva of *Havdalah*.

2) One must accustom him to hearing *Havdalah*.

3) He may also make *Havdalah* for himself.

4) He may even make *Havdalah* for another child, as detailed below.

b. 1) An adult may make *Havdalah* for a child, even if the child is not a member of his household, but,

2) in the event that the adult has already discharged his own obligation to make *Havdalah*, he should

make *Havdalah* for the child only if the child
a) is old enough to have some idea what reciting a blessing means, that is to say he is about five or six years old, and
b) does not know how to make *Havdalah* himself.

c. A child who is making *Havdalah* over a cup for himself cannot at the same time discharge the obligation of an adult, unless
1) the child has not yet said "*Atah chonantanu*" in the evening prayer, or "*Baruch ha-mavdil bein kodesh le-chol*," **and**
2) the adult has said one or other of them.
(See, by way of comparison, Chapter 51, paragraph 13.)

d. 1) A child cannot make *Havdalah* over a cup for another child, if
a) he himself has said "*Atah chonantanu*" or "*Baruch ha-mavdil bein kodesh le-chol*," but
b) the other child has said neither.
2) He may do so if
a) he himself has so far said neither **or**
b) he himself, as well as the other child, has said one or both.
3) Compare Chapter 51, paragraph 15.

e. In the view of those authorities who hold that a woman is liable to make *Havdalah*, as mentioned in paragraph 14 above, small girls also have such an obligation, and one must accustom them to hearing *Havdalah*.

f. 1) Regarding saying the blessing over the spices for a child when one cannot smell them oneself, see Chapter 61, paragraph 5.
2) Regarding a blind man's saying the blessing over the light for a child, see Chapter 61, paragraph 21.

20. *a.* 1) A person who did not make *Havdalah* over a cup after Shabbath, whether accidentally or on purpose,

failure to make Havdalah with drink

should do so as soon as he remembers.*

2) It does not matter whether it is night or during the day, except that, if it is daytime, he should not make *Havdalah* until after he has recited the morning prayer.

3) He can make *Havdalah* until the sun sets on Tuesday, but

4) he does not say the blessings on the spices or on the light, except on the evening when Shabbath expires.

b. 1) If he did not make *Havdalah* after Yom Tov or Yom Kippur (which fell on a weekday), he can do so until the sun sets on the following day, but not later.**

2) The blessing on the light which one says after Yom Kippur should be recited only on the evening when Yom Kippur expires.

c. As soon as a person remembers that he has not made *Havdalah*, he is forbidden to eat, provided he is now in a position to make *Havdalah*. (For further particulars, see Chapter 59, paragraph 10.)

before burial

21. Concerning the obligation of a mourner to make *Havdalah*, where the burial will take place only after Shabbath or Yom Tov, see Chapter 64, paragraph 25.

Sukkoth

22. *a.* On *chol ha-mo'ed* of Sukkoth, one should make *Havdalah* with a cup in the *sukka*, but without saying the special blessing one pronounces over being in the *sukka*.

---

* *a.* There are places where Shabbath and Yom Tov end very late, so that the children of the family are no longer up when *Havdalah* is recited.
b. The practice to be followed in such circumstances is for one of the children to recite *Havdalah* over a cup, for himself and the others, the next morning.
c. He should not, however, pronounce the blessings on the spices and the light.

** *a.* Somebody who failed to make *Havdalah* with a cup after Rosh Hashana should do so the following day, despite the fact that it is the Fast of Gedaliah.
b. He should give the wine to a child who has some idea what reciting a blessing means, that is to say, at the age of about five or six.

b. 1) However, after making *Havdalah* and drinking the wine, one should eat more than a *ka-beitzah* of bread or of some other baked or cooked food made from wheat, barley, rye, oats or spelt, and say the blessing on the *sukka*.

2) If one eats food (as above) other than bread, one ought to have in mind that the special blessing should cover not only eating the food, but also one's stay in the *sukka* afterwards.

c. Those who are accustomed to discharging their obligation to make *Havdalah* over a cup by listening to the cantor making *Havdalah* in the synagogue may do this on *chol ha-mo'ed* of Sukkoth too, in accordance with their usual practice.

Chanuka

23. *a.* At the termination of Shabbath during Chanuka, in the synagogue the Chanuka lights are kindled first and then *Havdalah* is recited over a cup (where the custom is to make *Havdalah* in the synagogue).

b. What one does at home depends on the local custom.

1) There are some who make *Havdalah* first and then kindle the Chanuka lights, since the fact that the mitzva of *Havdalah* is more frequent gives it precedence.

2) Others kindle the Chanuka lights first, in order to proclaim the miracle at the earliest opportunity, and only then recite *Havdalah* over the cup.

Jew from Eretz Yisrael abroad

24. *a.* 1) A resident of Eretz Yisrael who happens to be abroad should be careful to make *Havdalah*

a) in the evening, on the expiration of the first day of Yom Tov, or,

b) at latest, during the following day, *yom tov sheini shel galuyoth*, before sunset.

2) He should not wait until the next evening, since it will then be too late, as explained in paragraph 20 above.

3) In any event, when making *Havdalah*, he should be

particular to do so in private, as it is still Yom Tov for the local residents.

b. 1) a) When the first day of Yom Tov occurs on Shabbath, he should also make *Havdalah* on the evening of its expiration, that is to say on the expiration of Shabbath, but

b) he should not extinguish the *Havdalah* light, since, generally speaking, it is forbidden for him, on *yom tov sheini shel galuyoth*, to perform, even in private, an act which is forbidden to the local residents.

2) a) If, however, he did not make *Havdalah* on the expiration of Shabbath, but hears a local resident making *Havdalah* at the end of *yom tov sheini shel galuyoth*, his obligation is discharged.

b) For cases in which a resident of Eretz Yisrael and someone who lives elsewhere cannot discharge each other's obligations, see Chapter 62, paragraph 22.

Chapter 59

Performing Prohibited Activities, Eating and Drinking before Havdalah

PROHIBITED ACTIVITIES BEFORE HAVDALAH

1. *a.* 1) The Rabbis prohibited one from performing forbidden activities, even after the expiration of Shabbath or Yom Tov, until one has made *Havdalah*, either in prayer or with a cup or, at least, by saying, "*Baruch ha-mavdil bein kodesh le-chol.*" *general rule*

2) When Yom Tov occurs after Shabbath, one says, "*Baruch ha-mavdil bein kodesh le-kodesh*" to permit activities which are prohibited on Shabbath, but allowed on Yom Tov.

b. The acts one may not perform before *Havdalah* include

1) not only those prohibited by the Torah, but
2) those subject to Rabbinical prohibitions,
3) just moving *muktzeh* objects and even
4) everyday activities specified in Chapter 29, paragraphs 13 to 43, which are forbidden, not under the head of any specific act prohibited on Shabbath, but by reference to Isaiah 58:13 and 14.

c. There is Talmudical authority for the assertion that whoever performs a forbidden activity before *Havdalah* on the expiration of Shabbath or Yom Tov will not profit thereby.

2. *a.* 1) By virtue of the above, a person who has not made *Havdalah*, either in prayer, or with a cup, or by saying, "*Baruch ha-mavdil...*," *lights*

a) may not kindle a light,
b) may not transfer articles from one *reshuth* to another, where there is no *eiruv*, and
c) may not smoke.

2) Similarly, one should say, "*Baruch ha-mavdil...*", before turning on the light in the synagogue for the evening prayer.
3) One should do likewise before lighting the *Havdalah* candle, in the event that one
   a) forgot "*Atah chonantanu*" in the evening prayer or
   b) is going to make *Havdalah* with a cup before one has said the evening prayer.

Yom Tov after Shabbath

b. When it is Yom Tov immediately after Shabbath, one is not allowed
1) to cook for the Yom Tov meal,
2) to kindle the Yom Tov lights,
3) to wash the dishes and set the table for Yom Tov evening, or
4) to prepare the candles in the candlesticks so that one will be able to light them at the time of the meal,

before saying, "*Baruch ha-mavdil bein kodesh le-kodesh.*"

c. For the manner in which a mourner should conduct himself when Shabbath and Yom Tov end, see Chapter 65, paragraph 33.

women

3. Women too who do not say the evening prayer after Shabbath or Yom Tov should not perform any forbidden activity before saying, "*Baruch ha-mavdil bein kodesh le-chol*" (or "*Baruch ha-mavdil bein kodesh le-kodesh,*" if it is Yom Tov straight after Shabbath).

asking others to do forbidden acts

4. *a.* Things which one may not speak about on Shabbath or Yom Tov, as specified in Chapter 29, paragraphs 51 to 65, may be spoken about straight after Shabbath or Yom Tov, even if one has not yet made *Havdalah* in any form whatsoever.

b. Consequently,
1) one may ask a non-Jew, or even a Jew who has

already made *Havdalah*,* to perform for one an activity which is forbidden on Shabbath or Yom Tov, for example to turn on the light, or to cook, and

2) one may enjoy the benefit of that activity and eat any food produced by it.

c. One may request the performance of the activity, and benefit from it, even if one has not yet finished eating one's third meal and will be saying *Retzei* in *birkath ha-mazon* afterwards (as to which see Chapter 57, paragraph 12).

effect of Havdalah by congregation

5. *a.* As stated in Chapter 46, paragraph 7, regarding the commencement of Shabbath, an individual must not perform prohibited activities once the public has received Shabbath, even though he himself has not yet done so.

b. 1) It is otherwise when the time comes for the termination of Shabbath.

2) Even if the congregation has not yet said the evening prayer, an individual is at liberty to make *Havdalah* himself (in prayer, over a cup or by saying "*Baruch ha-mavdil...*") and forthwith perform hitherto forbidden activities.

3) Conversely, even if the congregation has already said the evening prayer or made *Havdalah*, an individual who has not yet made *Havdalah* in any form (as above) is not allowed to perform an activity that is forbidden on Shabbath.

c. Similarly, where a husband has not yet recited the evening prayer, or even if he has not yet finished his third Shabbath meal, his wife may make *Havdalah* for herself (as above) and proceed to perform hitherto forbidden activities.

behaving more strictly than required

6. *a.* A person who feels a sensitivity to the sanctity of Shabbath should be strict in his behavior and not perform

---

* It does not matter whether he has made *Havdalah* with a cup, in prayer or by saying, "*Baruch ha-mavdil....*"

forbidden activities on the expiration of Shabbath until he has

1) not only made *Havdalah* in prayer, but has also
2) recited the verses beginning, "*Vi-y^e^hi no'am,*" and the prayer commencing, "*V^e-atah kadosh,*" after the evening *Amidah.*

b. Nevertheless, there is nothing wrong with turning on the light in the synagogue, in honor of the congregation, as soon as

1) the time for the expiration of Shabbath has arrived and
2) one has made *Havdalah*, either in prayer or by saying "*Baruch ha-mavdil....*"

c. It is also perfectly permissible to perform activities which are subject only to a Rabbinical prohibition, for instance, moving objects which are *muktzeh*, as soon as one has made *Havdalah* in prayer or by saying, "*Baruch ha-mavdil....*"

mistakenly doing forbidden act before Havdalah

7. *a.* Someone who mistakenly performs a forbidden activity before making *Havdalah* after Shabbath or Yom Tov is not penalized by having to repeat the *Amidah* (as is the case in certain circumstances specified in paragraph 22 below).

b. This is so, even if he **neither**

1) remembered to insert "*Atah chonantanu*" in the evening prayer,

nor

2) said "*Baruch ha-mavdil...*"

nor

3) made *Havdalah* with a cup.

acts of people who do not make Havdalah

8. One is allowed to benefit when somebody who does not keep the mitzvoth, and so does not make *Havdalah*, performs, after the expiration of Shabbath or Yom Tov, an activity which is forbidden on Shabbath or Yom Tov.

a. As a result, one may deliver work to be done after Shabbath or Yom Tov, even to a person one knows did not make *Havdalah.*

b. 1) One may also travel on a bus with a Jewish driver after Shabbath or Yom Tov, even if one knows the driver did not make *Havdalah*.

2) Some people are particular, on entering the bus, to wish the driver "*Shavua tov*" ("A good week") with the object that he should reply likewise and so perhaps fulfil at least his basic obligation to make *Havdalah*.

9. One should not, if one can possibly help it, travel on a bus (owned by a Jew, or with a Jewish driver) which leaves its departure point before Shabbath or Yom Tov ends, and arrives to pick up passengers immediately on its expiration. *buses leaving before Shabbath ends*

EATING AND DRINKING BEFORE HAVDALAH

10. *a.* 1) It is forbidden to eat or drink anything, other than water, from sunset until after one has made *Havdalah* over a cup. *general rule*

2) The prohibition continues even after one makes *Havdalah* in prayer.

b. Someone who did not make *Havdalah* over a cup on the evening Shabbath or Yom Tov expired

1) should do so as soon as he remembers, as explained in Chapter 58, paragraph 20, and,

2) in the meantime, is forbidden to eat or drink.

c. See Chapter 56, paragraph 4, with respect to not managing to eat the third meal before sunset.

d. One may give a child (under thirteen if a boy and under twelve if a girl) something to eat before *Havdalah*, even though the child is old enough to know what Shabbath is and, so, is liable to make (or hear) *Havdalah*.

11. *a.* If one started eating a meal with bread before sunset, one may continue eating, even after the time for the expiration of Shabbath has passed. *continuation of meal permitted*

b. This is because, when one started eating, it was perfectly proper to do so, since it was not yet sunset.

c. Indeed, it is sufficient if one only manages to say the blessing on the bread before sunset.

d. One should not be strict to stop eating in these circumstances.

e. See further Chapter 60, paragraph 25.

interrupting a meal

12. *a.* Even if one interrupted the meal to say "*Baruch ha-mavdil bein kodesh le-chol,*" so that one could perform an activity which is forbidden on Shabbath, one may continue eating afterwards.

b. On the other hand, if one recited the evening prayer in the middle of the meal, there is room for saying that one has become bound to make *Havdalah*, and one should, therefore, not continue eating until one makes *Havdalah* with a cup.

c. With regard to inserting *Retzei* or *Ya'aleh Ve-yavo* in *birkath ha-mazon*, see Chapter 57, paragraph 12.

at the end of Pesach

13. *a.* 1) A person who began eating towards evening on the last day of Pesach, and continued until night, should not eat *chametz*, despite the fact that the time for the expiration of the Festival has passed.

2) The reason for this is that, when he comes to *birkath ha-mazon*, it would be incongruous to have refer to "this Festival of matzoth" in *Ya'aleh Ve-yavo*, if he is already eating *chametz*.

b. 1) If, however, he recited the evening prayer, or made *Havdalah* with a cup, in the middle of his meal, he may eat *chametz* when he continues eating.

2) The reason for this is that, in these circumstances, he will not be saying *Ya'aleh veyavo* in *birkath ha-mazon*, as stated in Chapter 57, paragraph 12.

interrupting snacks

14. *a.* 1) If one does not start a proper meal, but sits down to drink, one has to stop at sunset.

2) This is so even if a number of people sit down to drink together, as might be the case at a prolonged Yom Tov celebration.

b. The same applies if one is eating fruit, confectionery or even cake or cookies, but did not wash one's hands for a meal.*

15. *a.* Someone who washes his hands and recites the blessing to eat a proper meal before sunset can continue drinking and eating, not only bread, but any other food, during the course of the meal, even beyond sunset or nightfall. *extent of continued meal*

b. What is more, even if, after he has finished eating, but before he has recited *birkath ha-mazon*, he sits down to drink, he need not stop at sunset (or nightfall), in spite of the fact that the drinking is not part of the main meal.

16. *a.* 1) If, when one has finished one's meal, *drinking the wine of birkath ha-mazon*

a) the sun has already set, but

b) the stars have not yet come out,**

one may drink the cup of wine over which one recited *birkath ha-mazon*.

2) One should drink a *revi'ith* of the wine, and follow it with the appropriate "three-in-one" blessing.

3) The "three-in-one" blessing should include reference to the day which is ending, that is to say, Shabbath or Yom Tov or both, as the case may be.

4) Others participating may also drink from the wine.

b. 1) If

a) the stars have already come out*** **and**

b) one is always careful to recite *birkath ha-mazon* over a cup of wine,

then one should drink a *revi'ith*, and follow it with the appropriate blessing, as above.

2) That blessing should include reference to the day, as in *a* above, but there are those who hold otherwise,

---

* In connection with washing one's hands when eating cake or cookies, see Chapter 54, paragraph 31.

** For the purpose in question, the practice adopted in Eretz Yisrael is to take this as being about twenty-five minutes after sunset. (For other purposes, see Chapter 58, paragraph 2.)

*** See previous note.

on the grounds that the day ended when the stars came out.

3) Here too, others of the company may also drink from the wine, but only if they are always particular to say *birkath ha-mazon* over a cup.

c. 1) If
   a) the stars have already come out and
   b) one is **not** always careful to recite *birkath ha-mazon* over a cup of wine,

   one may now recite *birkath ha-mazon* over a cup, but should not drink any of the wine* before *Havdalah*.

2) One should
   a) say the evening prayer,
   b) fill another cup of wine (if one has one) for *Havdalah*,
   c) recite *Havdalah* and drink from the *Havdalah* cup, as required (and as set out in Chapter 60, paragraph 35), and then
   d) drink at least *ki-melo logmav* of the wine from the cup over which one said *birkath ha-mazon*, making up a total of at least a *revi'ith* of wine drunk, and
   e) say the "three-in-one" blessing after the wine.

3) Alternatively, another of the company who heard *Havdalah* may drink from the wine over which *birkath ha-mazon* was said, but he should drink a whole *revi'ith*, so that he will be able to conclude with the "three-in-one" blessing.

4) a) Where the person who recited *Havdalah* is the one who drinks the wine from the cup over which *birkath ha-mazon* was said, he should not say the blessing prior to drinking wine a second time.
   b) Where another of the company drinks it, he can have in mind to discharge his obligation to say the blessing over the wine by hearing it from the

---

* It goes without saying that one does not recite the blessing on the wine after *birkath ha-mazon*.

person reciting *Havdalah*, so long as the latter intends to say it also on his behalf.

5) Notwithstanding the above, the custom is to make *Havdalah* and say *birkath ha-mazon* over the same cup of wine, and drink a *r^e^vi'ith* of that, even if one has another cup of wine available.

6) In any event, one should not allow a lengthy interval to elapse between *birkath ha-mazon* and *Havdalah*, but should recite the evening prayer, whether at home or in the synagogue, and immediately make *Havdalah*.

sheva b^e^rachoth ending after sunset

17. *a.* When the third Shabbath meal

1) is held in honor of a bride and groom, during the seven days of feasting which begin with the wedding, and

2) ends at, or even after, sunset, but before the stars come out,*

one should recite *birkath ha-mazon*** over one cup of wine and *sheva b^e^rachoth* over another, and drink both as usual. (See paragraph 16 above.)

b. 1) Even if the meal finishes only after the stars come out, the custom is to say *birkath ha-mazon* and *sheva b^e^rachoth*, and for the bride, the groom and other participants to drink*** the wine from the cups, as usual.****

2) Others have the custom, when the meal finishes after the stars come out,

a) to recite *birkath ha-mazon* and *sheva b^e^rachoth* with two cups, but

---

* See note ** to paragraph 16 above.

** It is customary not to recite "*D^e^vy haseir*" before *birkath ha-zimun* on Shabbath or Yom Tov, but to say "*Nodeh l^e^-shimcha*" instead.

*** This is so, even if they do not usually say *birkath ha-mazon* with a cup of wine.

**** Whoever drinks a *r^e^vi'ith* should follow it with the "three-in-one" blessing, including reference to the day, as in 16*a*3) above, although there are those who hold otherwise, on the grounds that the day ended when the stars came out.

b) not to say the blessing before wine, either over the cup with which one recited *birkath ha-mazon* or over that with which one recited *sheva b^e^rachoth*,
c) to leave both cups of wine until after the evening prayer,
d) then to make *Havdalah* over the cup with which one recited *birkath ha-mazon* and,
e) finally, to drink the cup with which one recited *sheva b^e^rachoth*, in the usual manner, that is to say, the wine from both cups is mixed and given to the bride, the groom and the others present to drink.

last day of sheva b^e^rachoth

18. *a.* If the third Shabbath meal being given in honor of the bride and groom is on the last of the seven days of feasting (that is to say, the wedding was on Sunday, before sunset), one should
1) conclude the meal,
2) recite *birkath ha-mazon* over a cup of wine and
3) say the *sheva b^e^rachoth*,
all before sunset.

b. In the event that the meal
1) lasts until after sunset, or even
2) ends before sunset, but *sheva b^e^rachoth* were not recited before sunset,
one should no longer recite *sheva b^e^rachoth*.

Nine Days

19. *a.* The custom is not to eat meat or drink wine during the Nine Days beginning with *Rosh Chodesh* Av, except on Shabbath.

b. 1) If, during this period, one's third Shabbath meal continues until after nightfall, and the congregation has already recited the evening prayer after Shabbath, one should no longer eat meat or drink wine.
2) The reason for this is that one has a duty to participate in the public grief over the destruction of the Temple.

c. 1) There are, however, authorities who differ and hold

that one may continue to eat meat and drink wine, as

a) one has not oneself either said the evening prayer or pronounced *Havdalah* over a cup and

b) one will still be saying *Retzei* in *birkath ha-mazon*, as stated in Chapter 57, paragraph 12.

2) According to this view, someone who is always careful to recite *birkath ha-mazon* with a cup of wine may drink that cup too, as in paragraph 16 above.

d. Concerning the third Shabbath meal when the Fast of Av takes place immediately after Shabbath, see Chapter 56, paragraph 14.

e. Concerning the making of *Havdalah* by a person who is ill and has to eat, when the Fast of Av takes place immediately after Shabbath, see Chapter 62, paragraph 46.

starting to eat between sunset and night

20. *a.* Where one began to eat or drink and then realized that one did so later than was permissible, that is to say after sunset, or less than half an hour before the stars come out if one is in a place where sunset is earlier than that, one must stop right away.

b. If one has repeated a blessing over some food, but, before tasting it, realizes that it is already too late to start eating, one should taste a little, so that the blessing will not have been in vain, and eat no more.

saying blessing on food before Havdalah

21. *a.* If one by mistake pronounces a blessing over food after the expiration of Shabbath or Yom Tov and, before starting to eat, remembers that one has not yet made *Havdalah* over a cup, one should

1) taste a little, so that the blessing will not have been in vain, and then

2) make *Havdalah* over a cup, before continuing to eat.

b. If, however, one washes one's hands for a meal, pronouncing the appropriate blessing upon washing hands, and remembers before pronouncing the blessing over the bread, one should

1) make *Havdalah* with a cup, drinking from the wine, and only afterwards
2) pronounce the blessing over the bread and eat.

starting to eat between night and Havdalah

22. Where a person has made a mistake after the expiration of Shabbath or Yom Tov and eaten, or even just tasted something, before making *Havdalah* with a cup, the position is as follows:

a. 1) In the event that he also forgot to say, "*Atah chonantanu*" (or "*Va-todi'einu*" if it is Yom Tov on the expiration of Shabbath), in the evening prayer, he
   a) has to repeat the *Amidah* (this time with "*Atah chonantanu*" or "*Va-todi'einu*") as a penalty for his improper conduct, and
   b) should then make *Havdalah* over a cup.

2) Where he has contravened the penal provision, and not said the *Amidah* again, but just made *Havdalah* over a cup and then eaten, he should not go back and repeat the *Amidah*, since the authorities differ as to whether he must do so.

b. In the event that he said, "*Atah chonantanu*" (or "*Va-todi'einu*" if appropriate), there is no penalty, and he does not say the *Amidah* again.

when there is no wine

23. If one has no wine or other suitable drink (as particularized in Chapter 60, paragraphs 3 to 8) with which to make *Havdalah*, the position is as follows:

a. When one knows that one will have drink with which to make *Havdalah* by noon on the next day, one should be strict in one's behavior and not eat until one has made *Havdalah* over a cup.

b. 1) However, if
   a) one is weak and finds it difficult to wait a long time without eating, or
   b) one estimates that one will be able to obtain wine (or other drink) only on the afternoon of the next day, or

c) one estimates that one will not have anything at all with which to make *Havdalah*,

then one may eat immediately after saying the evening prayer, with the inclusion of "*Atah chonantanu*" or "*Va-todi'einu*," as appropriate.

2) When one does obtain wine (or other drink), one should immediately make *Havdalah* (as in Chapter 58, paragraph 20).

Chapter 60

Havdalah with Wine and the Order of Havdalah

THE OBLIGATION TO USE WINE,
AND WHEN OTHER DRINKS MAY BE USED

importance of wine

1. *a.* It is a Rabbinical mitzva to make *Havdalah* over a cup of wine.

b. Although, as will be seen below, certain other drinks may be used, the mitzva is best performed with wine,* provided one has it in the house.

c. When one has neither wine nor any other suitable drink (as explained below), one cannot make *Havdalah* over bread,** even if, as a result, one will not be able to make *Havdalah* at all (other than in prayer or by saying "*Baruch ha-mavdil...*").

expense

2. So long as wine is available in town, even if it is expensive, one should use wine, and not any other drink, for *Havdalah* (except as mentioned in paragraphs 3 and 8 below).

other drinks: general rule

3. *a.* One may make *Havdalah* with a drink other than wine which is customarily consumed in the locality as a beverage of consequence (as detailed below),

1) if one has no wine with which to make *Havdalah*, or
2) if one likes the other drink better, or
3) if
   a) one is unable to drink *ki-m^e^lo logmav* of wine and
   b) there is nobody for whom one is making *Havdalah* (even a child, so long as he is old enough to have some idea of what reciting a blessing means) who can drink it in his place.

---

* Wine, for this purpose, includes natural grape juice.

** But see Chapter 62, paragraph 14.

b. 1) The other drink must be one which, in the locality, is not drunk merely to quench thirst, but serves a social function, in gracing the dinner table and being offered to guests.

2) Examples are to be found below.

4. *a.* It follows that, subject to the conditions set out in paragraph 3 above, one can make *Havdalah* with beer. *beer, brandy: quantity*

b. Subject to the same conditions, one can use brandy, or some other strong drink, but one should be particular to fill a cup which holds a *r^evi'ith* and to drink at least *ki-m^elo logmav.*

5. One can also make *Havdalah* over orange or grapefruit juice, or over cider, provided they conform to the requirements described in paragraph 3 above, and the other conditions set out there are fulfilled. *fruit juice, cider*

6. *a.* In time of difficulty, one can rely on the lenient view that one may make *Havdalah* over sweetened tea, or over coffee, whether with or without milk (if they are drinks of consequence, as defined in paragraph 3 above), but *tea, coffee*

b. there are opposing authorities, in whose view one cannot make *Havdalah* over sweetened tea or over coffee.

7. One should not make *Havdalah* over water, soda water or soft drinks other than those mentioned above, even if one has nothing else. *water, soft drinks*

8. *a.* Many people have the habit of making *Havdalah* over beer, even when there is wine available, either because they find the wine difficult to drink or because they like beer. *preference for beer*

b. This is in conformity with the rules set out above, provided, of course, that beer is a drink of social significance in the locality, as defined in paragraph 3 above.

wine from which someone drank

9. If

a. one only has wine from which somebody has already drunk and

b. there is no possibility of putting right the defect by adding wine from the bottle or, at least, by adding water, as described in Chapter 47, paragraph 15,

it is better to make *Havdalah* over beer (which does not suffer from a like defect), provided that beer is a drink of social significance in the locality (as defined in paragraph 3 above).

HAVDALAH IN THE SYNAGOGUE

the practice

10. *a.* 1) There is a practice to make *Havdalah* over a cup in the synagogue, in order to discharge the obligation to make *Havdalah* of whoever has no wine.

2) Regarding the form of *Havdalah*, see paragraph 23 below.

b. 1) The practice is to sell the right to supply wine for *Havdalah* for sizeable amounts of money, and there is much competition to acquire this mitzva.

2) Indeed, the congregation, in its prayers, requests a special blessing for those who donate the wine for *Havdalah*.

c. It is forbidden, while it is still Shabbath or Yom Tov, to bring wine to the synagogue to be used for *Havdalah* afterwards (but see Chapter 28, paragraph 73).

mutual intentions required

11. *a.* The person reciting the blessings during *Havdalah* must have the intention to discharge the obligations of all who wish to have their obligations discharged thereby, and

b. those listening must have a corresponding intention, if they want the blessings they hear to be in discharge of their own obligations.

intention not to discharge obligation

12. *a.* 1) Despite the above, someone who has wine, or some other suitable drink (as defined in paragraph 3 above) in his house

a) should not rely on the *Havdalah* being made in the synagogue, but
b) should make *Havdalah* at home, in order to discharge the obligations in that regard of the members of his family.

b. Anyone listening who does not intend his own obligations to be discharged responds, "*Baruch Hu u-varuch sh*ᵉ*mo*," whenever the person reciting *Havdalah* mentions the name of God, but he should not respond in a loud voice,
1) so as not to confuse those who do wish to have their obligations to make *Havdalah* discharged and
2) so that those whose obligations are being discharged should not be misled into thinking that they too may answer, "*Baruch Hu u-varuch sh*ᵉ*mo*."

when nobody needs it

13. If
a. there is nobody in the synagogue who wishes to fulfill his obligation to make *Havdalah* by listening to the person who recites it there and
b. the latter wishes to make *Havdalah* at home for his family,
then one should not make *Havdalah* in the synagogue.

Havdalah again at home

14. *a.* 1) The person reciting *Havdalah* in the synagogue may intend it to be also in discharge of his own obligations.
2) He may, nevertheless, make *Havdalah* again, in order to discharge the obligations of others, whether members of his family or not, who do not know how to make *Havdalah* themselves.*
3) He should not, however, make *Havdalah* only for a woman. (See Chapter 58, paragraph 17.)

b. Someone making *Havdalah* for others should pronounce the usual blessing before wine (or whatever other suitable beverage he has) even if he is not

---

* It is preferable for someone who has already made *Havdalah* not to make *Havdalah* for others who know how to do so themselves, but to let them indeed make *Havdalah* themselves, unless there is reason to act otherwise.

going to drink any himself, as long as one of those for whom he is making *Havdalah*

1) relies on that blessing in order to drink the wine (or other beverage) and
2) drinks *ki-m^elo logmav.**

c. With respect to saying the blessings on the spices and on the light in discharge of the obligations of others, when one has already discharged one's own obligations, see Chapter 61, paragraphs 6 and 22 respectively.

drinking the wine

15. *a.* 1) The custom is to give the wine from *Havdalah* made in the synagogue to a child under the age of thirteen to drink.

2) The child must have reached the age where he has some idea of what reciting a blessing means, that is to say, about five or six.

b. However, the person who recites *Havdalah*, or any other adult, can also drink from it, if he indeed intended the *Havdalah* and the accompanying blessing on the wine to be in discharge of his own obligations.

c. Conversely, somebody who did not have in mind that the *Havdalah*, or at least the blessing on the wine, recited in the synagogue should be in discharge of his own obligations should not drink from the wine.

when one is still praying

16. *a.* If one is praying in the synagogue, and is still saying the *Amidah* when one hears that *Havdalah* is being recited over a cup, one should continue praying, with the specific intention of not having one's obligations with regard to *Havdalah* discharged.

b. 1) Nevertheless, if one did interrupt one's prayer to listen to the blessings being recited by the person making *Havdalah*, one has indeed fulfilled one's obligations.

---

* From paragraph 35 below, it will be seen that it is best to drink a whole *r^evi'ith.*

2) In any event, one must not respond "Amen" to the blessings one hears while one is still in the middle of the *Amidah*.

THE HAVDALAH CUP AND THE ORDER OF HAVDALAH

17. *a.* One should not change out of one's Shabbath clothes in the evening after Shabbath ends before one has made *Havdalah* over a cup. *clothes and tablecloth*

b. Similarly, the cloth should remain on the table at least until after *Havdalah*.

c. See further Chapter 63, paragraph 2.

18. *a.* The laws applicable to the cup used for *Havdalah* are the same as those applicable to the cup used for *kiddush*. *the cup*

b. Thus,

1) the cup must contain at least a quarter of a *log* (a *r^evi'ith*),
2) the cup should be whole, and not broken or chipped,
3) the cup should to be washed, or wiped with a cloth, both inside and out, and
4) one should be particular to use a handsome cup.

c. For the detailed rules, see Chapter 47, paragraphs 9 to 16.

19. *a.* The mitzva is to make *Havdalah* with a full cup of wine, as explained in Chapter 47, paragraph 16. *filling the cup*

b. It is also customary to fill the cup to such an extent that a little of the wine spills over onto the floor, or into the *Havdalah* plate, as an indication of the plenty for which one hopes at the start of the new week.

20. *a.* 1) The person reciting *Havdalah* must have the intention to discharge the obligations to make *Havdalah* of all those listening, and *intentions required*

2) those listening must intend to have their obligations to make *Havdalah* discharged by him.

b. See the detailed rules in Chapter 47, paragraph 32.

c. Both the person reciting *Havdalah* and those listening with the object of having their obligations discharged ought to keep their eyes on the cup and on the *Havdalah* light, so as not to divert their attention to other matters.

responding to blessings

21. *a.* Those who wish to discharge their obligation to make *Havdalah* by listening to it

1) should not respond, "*Baruch Hu u-varuch shemo*," but
2) are obliged to answer "Amen," after each blessing pronounced by the person reciting *Havdalah*.

b. For details of the rules applicable, see Chapter 47, paragraphs 35 and 36, which contain the parallel laws relating to *kiddush*.

c. See also paragraphs 37 to 39 there, for additional laws which are as relevant to *Havdalah* as to *kiddush*.

sitting and standing

22. *a.* 1) It is the custom of some to stand while they recite *Havdalah*.

2) In that case, those for whom they are making *Havdalah* should also stand.

b. If one is making *Havdalah* for others, it is indeed best for all to sit, in the absence of a custom to the contrary.

c. 1) When, however, the person reciting *Havdalah* does so standing, those for whom he is saying it should be particular to stand around him.

2) They should not be just scattered around the room, since
   a) the *Havdalah* is being recited in fulfillment of the obligations of all of them and,
   b) for this purpose, it is important that they should collectively be in position as a unit.

d. In any event, when drinking the wine one should sit.

e. 1) When Yom Tov occurs immediately following Shabbath, the *Havdalah* after Shabbath is incorporated in the *kiddush* of Yom Tov.

2) The rule applicable is the same as that for *kiddush* on Friday night, and it is best to sit. (See Chapter 47, paragraph 28).
3) See also Chapter 62, paragraph 17.

23. *a.* 1) When *Havdalah* is said at home on the expiration of a Shabbath which is followed by an ordinary weekday, the custom is to begin with the verses commencing, "*Hinei Keil yeshuathi...*" *preliminary verses*

2) These verses are recited as an expression of our reliance on the blessings of the Almighty and by way of prayer for success.
3) It is not the custom to say them on the expiration of Yom Tov.

b. On the following occasions, the preliminary verses are omitted, and *Havdalah* (even after a Shabbath which is followed by an ordinary weekday) starts with the usual blessing on wine:

1) when the person leading prayers recites *Havdalah* in the synagogue;
2) when somebody who failed to make *Havdalah* in the evening after Shabbath does so on one of the succeeding three days, as mentioned in Chapter 58, paragraph 20;
3) when a mourner recites *Havdalah* during his first seven days of mourning.

24. *a.* Initially, one takes the *Havdalah* cup in both hands, out of attachment to the mitzva. *procedure*

b. One then puts it into one's right hand (unless one is left-handed, in which case one places it in one's left hand).

c. It is proper to hold the cup by standing it on the palm, surrounded by the upright fingers of the hand.

d. One

1) raises the cup a *tefach* above the table,
2) holds the spices in one's other hand,
3) says the verses commencing, "*Hinei Keil yeshuathi*," and

4) recites the blessing on the wine.

e. Afterwards, one

1) transfers the cup to one's left hand and the spices to one's right,

2) pronounces the blessing over the spices, smells them and puts them down on the table.

f. Next, one pronounces the blessing over the light* and looks at the fingers of one's right hand, as detailed in Chapter 61, paragraph 35.

g. Finally, one takes the cup back in one's right hand and finishes reciting *Havdalah*.

in mid-meal

25. *a.* 1) It is in order (subject to what is stated later in this paragraph) for someone whose third meal lasts until after dark (as in Chapter 59, paragraph 11,) to make *Havdalah* with wine in the middle of the meal, although

2) one should not do so unless one has to, since, as mentioned below, one will thereby lose the opportunity of inserting in *birkath ha-mazon* the passages relating to the day which has expired.

b. 1) There is a dispute amongst the authorities as to whether a person who has already pronounced the blessing on wine during the meal has to say the blessing on wine again if he recites *Havdalah* before the meal ends.

2) So as to avoid this quandary, somebody in this situation should not make *Havdalah* in the middle of the meal, if he can help it (unless he previously decided not to drink any more wine, in which case the original blessing is no longer effective).

---

* *a.* A woman in a state of *niddah* may hold the *Havdalah* candle in her hand and

b. her husband may benefit from its light, but

c. he should not

1) hand her the candle,

2) light the candle while she is holding it,

3) take the candle from her hand or

4) pour wine onto the candle in her hand to put it out.

c. 1) Similarly, one should not make *Havdalah* in the middle of the meal over a drink other than wine (as detailed in paragraphs 3 to 8 above), even if one has not drunk any of it during the course of the meal.

2) Since one does not recite a separate blessing over such drinks during a meal (eaten with bread), it is doubtful whether one ought to say such a blessing when making *Havdalah* with them in the middle of the meal.

d. 1) If one is compelled to do so by the pressure of circumstances, one may make *Havdalah* over wine in the middle of the meal, even if one has drunk wine, and recited a blessing over it, during the meal, but

2) one should not pronounce the blessing over wine again when making *Havdalah* (unless one previously decided not to drink any more wine).

e. Likewise, if one makes *Havdalah* over a different drink in the middle of the meal, one should say the blessing of the *Havdalah*, but should not say a separate blessing over the drink (even if one did not have any during the meal).

f. In the same way, if one did not begin a proper meal, but sat down to drink wine before dark (as might be the case at a Yom Tov celebration), one must make *Havdalah* as soon as Shabbath or Yom Tov terminate, but should not say the blessing on wine again.

g. 1) Somebody who makes *Havdalah* in the middle of the meal, and wants to continue eating afterwards, need not say the blessing on the bread again.

2) Whether or not he continues eating after *Havdalah*, he should not include in *birkath ha-mazon* the passages relating exclusively to the day which has expired (*Retzei* or *Ya'aleh Ve-yavo*).

saying blessings on spices and light for others

26. *a.* Those who are listening to *Havdalah* being said for them should have the intention to discharge their obligations also with respect to the blessings on the wine, the spices and the light, rather than individually pronounce these blessings themselves.

b. They

1) should be particular to smell the spices and enjoy the benefit of the light immediately and
2) should not divert their attention from the *Havdalah* when the person reciting it continues with the blessings.

Havdalah continued before others enjoy spices and light

c. 1) It may happen that the person reciting *Havdalah* continues with his blessings before they have smelt the spices or enjoyed the light (for example, because the spices and the light have not yet reached them).

2) In such event, they should smell the spices and enjoy the light (without pronouncing any additional blessing) only after he has concluded the blessing of the *Havdalah*.

3) a) If, for some reason, they did not have the intention of discharging their own obligations by listening to the blessings on the spices and the light, or

b) if, in the meantime, the intention of benefitting from the spices or the light left their minds,

they should repeat the respective blessings after the end of *Havdalah*, prior to smelling the spices and enjoying the light.

d. See further Chapter 61, paragraphs 8 and 23.

others saying blessings on spices and light themselves

27. *a.* Despite the contents of the previous paragraph, there are some whose practice is

1) to have in mind not to discharge their obligations in respect of the blessings on the spices and the light when they hear them pronounced by the person making *Havdalah*, but
2) to say these blessings for themselves.

b. 1) Nevertheless, they may intend to drink from the *Havdalah* wine afterwards, in reliance upon the blessing on the wine pronounced by the person reciting *Havdalah*.

2) If they do, they should be careful not to respond, "*Baruch Hu u-varuch sh^e^mo*"* or "Amen" to the blessings on the spices and the light, when the person making *Havdalah* (or anybody else) recites them.
3) This is because responding to blessings which are not in fulfillment of their own obligations is an unwarranted interruption between their hearing the blessing on the wine and their drinking it.
4) For the same reason, the person reciting *Havdalah* should not answer, "*Baruch Hu u-varuch sh^e^mo*" or "Amen" to blessings pronounced by others present.

c. If those listening to *Havdalah* wish to say the blessings on the spices and the light themselves, they may do so only so long as the person reciting *Havdalah* has not yet continued and started the blessing of the *Havdalah* itself ("*Ha-mavdil*").

Havdalah continued before others enjoy spices and light

d. In the event that
1) they have said these blessings, but have not yet managed to enjoy the benefit of the spices or of the light, as the case may be, and
2) the person reciting *Havdalah* continues with "*Ha-mavdil*,"

they should direct their attention to the blessing which he is saying, and not smell the spices, or enjoy the light, until he has ended.

Havdalah continued before others end blessings on spices and light

e. Should they still be in the process of saying the blessing on the spices or on the light when the person reciting *Havdalah* continues with "*Ha-mavdil*,"
1) they have not fulfilled their duty to make *Havdalah* and
2) they should, therefore, take one of the courses set out below.

f. Where possible, one of them should
1) take the *Havdalah* cup in his hand, after the per-

---

* From Chapter 47, paragraph 35, it can be seen that one should also not respond "*Baruch Hu u-varuch sh^e^mo*" to a blessing which somebody else is reciting for one.

son reciting *Havdalah* has finished "*Ha-mavdil*," but before he drinks the wine,

2) say "*Ha-mavdil*" for all those who did not hear it from beginning to end and

3) return the cup to the person who first recited *Havdalah*, for him to drink.

g. 1) Where this possibility is not open to them, then, if there is more wine on the table, one of them should pour out another cup and recite *Havdalah* again for all those who did not hear the whole of "*Ha-mavdil*," but

2) he should not say the blessings on the spices and the light,

3) nor should he repeat the blessing on the wine before drinking it, provided that the following three conditions are all fulfilled:

a) he did indeed intend the blessing on the wine of the person who originally recited *Havdalah* to be on his behalf too;

b) he did not divert his attention to extraneous matters in the meantime;

c) when he listened to the blessing on the wine, he had in mind to drink also other wine, in addition to that in the original *Havdalah* cup.

h. 1) However, if

a) there is no more wine on the table in front of him, or

b) one of the three conditions in *g*3) above is unfulfilled,

there are two ways in which they can proceed.

2) Either

a) one of them can say "*Ha-mavdil*" for them all, with his eyes and his attention on the cup held in the hand of the person who first started reciting *Havdalah*,

or

b) he can bring another cup of wine, recite the blessing on wine and "*Ha-mavdil*" over it and drink the prescribed amount (but without repeating the blessings on spices and on the light).

reversing order of blessings on spices and light

28. *a.* If one has made a mistake and said the blessing on the light before one has said the blessing on the spices, one should

1) proceed to enjoy the light (as in Chapter 61, paragraph 35), and then
2) say the blessing on the spices and smell them.

b. Even if one merely has the mistaken intention, when mentioning God's name in the blessing, to end with the words of the blessing on the light, but, before saying them, remembers that one has not yet recited the blessing on the spices, one should

1) finish, as one intended to do, with the words of the blessing on the light,
2) enjoy the light, and, only afterwards,
3) say the blessing on the spices and smell them.

correcting errors in blessings on spices and light

29. *a.* If one had the intention, when mentioning God's name at the beginning of the blessing, to say the blessing on the spices, but mistakenly ended with the words of the blessing on the light ("*borei m*e*'orei ha-eish*"), then,

1) in the event that one did not correct oneself, one
   a) has fulfilled one's duty to say the blessing on the light, and
   b) should now say the blessing on the spices (ending, "*borei minei b*e*samim*"), but
2) in the event that one corrected oneself immediately, and in effect said, "*borei m*e*'orei ha-eish minei b*e*samim*," one
   a) has fulfilled one's duty to say the blessing on the spices, and
   b) should now say the blessing on the light.

b. 1) However, it is otherwise if one
   a) had the erroneous intention, when mentioning God's name in the first blessing after that on the wine, to end with the words of the blessing on the

light, and
b) did indeed say the blessing on the light.
2) In that case, even if one immediately added, "*borei minei b^e^samim*," one
a) has fulfilled one's duty to say the blessing on the light, and
b) should now say the blessing on the spices.

missing part of Havdalah

30. *a.* 1) Somebody who comes into the room after the person reciting *Havdalah* has already pronounced the blessing on the wine can still discharge his own obligation by listening to the blessing "*ha-mavdil*" being recited, provided
a) he hears it from beginning to end, without missing any integral part, and
b) he (as well as the person who is reciting *Havdalah*) has the intention of fulfilling his obligation in this way.
2) This is so, even if he also missed the blessings on the spices and on the light, but, in that case, he should say them (and enjoy the spices and the light) after he has heard "*ha-mavdil*."
3) If he wants to drink some of the wine, he should recite the blessing on the wine (which he missed) before he does.
4) On the other hand, if he missed any integral part of "*ha-mavdil*," he has not discharged his obligation, and he should adopt one of the courses set out in paragraph 27*f*, *g* or *h* above.

b. 1) The above contents of this paragraph apply equally to someone who talks while the order of *Havdalah* is being recited, and so misses part of it.
2) Moreover, a person who talks about matters unconnected with the order of *Havdalah*, between
a) the blessing on the spices, the light or the wine, and
b) smelling the spices, enjoying the light or drinking the wine, respectively,

has to repeat the appropriate blessing before deriving the relevant benefit from them.

31. *a.* One may recite *Havdalah* for somebody else, even when one has already discharged one's own duty in that respect, but, in that eventuality, only if the other person does not know how, or is unable, to make *Havdalah* for himself. *saying Havdalah for others*

b. One may do this even for a child (subject to the same conditions), as long the child is old enough to be educated, that is to say, he is about five or six years old.

c. See further paragraph 14 above.

32. A person who, when making *Havdalah* over a cup, forgets to say the blessing on the spices or on the light, and remembers after he has finished "*ha-mavdil*," but before he has tasted the wine, should *Forgetting blessings on spices and light*

a. say immediately the blessing he omitted,

b. enjoy the spices or the light and, only then,

c. drink the wine.

33. *a.* Someone who intends to eat a meal immediately after he has made *Havdalah* over wine should not put the bread on the table until he has finished *Havdalah*. *eating after Havdalah*

b. If

1) he wants to drink wine during the course of the meal or

2) he is accustomed to drinking wine during the course of the meal,

he should specifically have in mind not to include that wine in the blessing on wine which he says when reciting *Havdalah*.

c. Following *Havdalah*, he should recite the "three-in-one" blessing over the *Havdalah* wine, prior to washing his hands for the meal.

d. In the event that he did put the bread on the table before he made *Havdalah*, he should

1) place a cloth over the bread, and keep it covered

during *Havdalah,**

2) say the "three-in-one" blessing after *Havdalah* and then

3) wash his hands for the meal.

e. If, notwithstanding what is stated in *c* above, he washed hands for the meal after *Havdalah*, without first saying the "three-in-one" blessing, he should no longer say the "three-in-one" blessing.

f. 1) If, contrary to what is stated in *b* above, he did not specifically intend to exclude wine he would have during the meal from the blessing on wine which he made as part of *Havdalah* and, all the more so,

2) if he intended that blessing to cover also wine he would have during the meal,

he should not say a blessing on wine again before he drinks in the course of the meal, (since there is a difference of opinion among the authorities on the point).

DRINKING THE WINE

drinking immediately

34. *a.* Immediately one has finished reciting *Havdalah*, one should drink the contents of the cup while sitting, provided that most of those answering "Amen" have finished responding.

b. One must not interrupt by speaking between *Havdalah* and drinking, not even with the customary greeting, "*Shavua tov*" ("A good week").

c. Nor ought one to pause, even without speaking, for longer than it takes to say "*Shalom aleicha rabi.*"

d. See Chapter 48, paragraphs 1 to 7, for the comparable rules in relation to *kiddush*.

e. One should not even extinguish the *Havdalah* candle before drinking at least a little of the wine.

---

* If he does not intend to eat right after *Havdalah*, he need not cover bread which is on the table.

35. *a.* 1) If one can, one ought to drink a whole *r^evi'ith* from the *Havdalah* cup without stopping. *quantity required*

2) In this connection, there is no difference between wine and any other drink one is permitted to use for *Havdalah.*

3) Subsequent to drinking, one should pronounce the blessing appropriate after the particular drink one used.

b. Despite the above, provided one drank *ki-m^elo logmav*,* one has discharged one's duty, but

1) one should not pronounce a blessing after drinking, since there is a doubt as to whether a blessing is required after drinking less than a *r^evi'ith* and

2) one should at least try to drink the amount of *ki-m^elo logmav* without stopping.

c. See Chapter 48, paragraph 10, regarding the time within which one should finish drinking.

d. If the wine is too strong for one to drink the appropriate quantity within the prescribed time, one should not dilute it with so much water that it can no longer be described as wine, since one cannot make *Havdalah* with mere flavored water.

36. *a.* If one *drinking insufficient*

1) did not drink as much as *ki-m^elo logmav* or

2) took more than four minutes to drink *ki-m^elo logmav*,

one has not properly fulfilled one's obligation, and should drink again, this time *ki-m^elo logmav* within the prescribed limit.

b. 1) In a case where, at the time of reciting the original blessing on wine, one

a) intended to drink more wine, in addition to that one drank for *Havdalah*, or

b) did not think at all about whether or not to drink more,

* See Chapter 48, paragraph 9, as to how this is measured.

one does not need to pronounce the blessing on wine before drinking the second time.

2) If, however, one intended to drink only the small amount of wine one originally drank for *Havdalah*, and no more, one has to repeat the blessing on wine before drinking the second time.

c. In any event, there is no need to repeat "*ha-mavdil*" a second time.

who drinks

37. *a.* If he can, the person reciting *Havdalah* should

1) drink the whole *r^e^vi'ith* of wine himself, and say the appropriate blessing afterwards, or, at least,

2) drink *ki-m^e^lo logmav*, as in paragraph 35 above.

b. 1) Still, the obligations of the company to make *Havdalah* are discharged, even though the person reciting *Havdalah* tasted no wine at all, provided one of the participants drank a *r^e^vi'ith*, or at least *ki-m^e^lo logmav*.

2) The individual who drank the wine may even be a child under the age of thirteen, so long as he has some idea what reciting a blessing means.

3) It is even sufficient if two or more participants drank *ki-m^e^lo logmav* between them.

c. 1) Nevertheless, if he can help it, a person should not recite *Havdalah* with the intention that somebody else participating should drink all of the wine in his place.

2) Where he is unable, for some reason, to drink a sufficient quantity, he should either

a) recite *Havdalah* with the intention of tasting a little wine himself and then letting another participant drink a whole *r^e^vi'ith*, or at least *ki-m^e^lo logmav*, or

b) let another participant, who will himself drink the required quantity, recite *Havdalah*.

d. See Chapter 48, paragraph 14, for further details of the corresponding rules relating to *kiddush*, which are applicable also here (with appropriate changes).

38. *a.* The custom among women is not to drink from the *Havdalah* wine. *women*

b. When, however, they make *Havdalah* for themselves, as stated in Chapter 58, paragraph 17, they also have to drink the wine.

39. *a.* Until the person reciting *Havdalah* has drunk the amount of *ki-m*^{e}*lo logmav*, neither he nor the other participants (whether or not they wish to taste the wine) *speaking or leaving the room*

1) should speak, not even to say "*Shavua tov*," or
2) leave the room.

b. See Chapter 48, paragraphs 1 to 7, for further details of the corresponding rules relating to *kiddush*, which are applicable also here (with appropriate changes).

40. *a.* 1) a) After drinking the required quantity (as specified in paragraph 35 above) from the cup over which one said the blessing, one should pour a little of the remainder into the plate and put out the *Havdalah* candle in it. *extinguishing candle*

b) In this way, it is made clear to all that the candle was lit purely for the purpose of a mitzva, namely, so that one can say a blessing over it.

2) If one uses, not a special *Havdalah* candle, but a light which is burning in the house, one need not extinguish it after *Havdalah*.

b. There is a custom to dab one's eyelids with the wine spilled in the *Havdalah* plate, as a demonstration of one's attachment to the mitzva.

41. *a.* If a person recited *Havdalah* and, before he or any of the other participants tasted it, the cup of wine was spilled, the rules applicable are the same as those set out in connection with *kiddush*, in Chapter 48, paragraphs 15 to 17. *cup of wine spilled*

b. As mentioned in paragraph 1 above, even if one has no more wine, one cannot make *Havdalah* over bread.

c. 1) There are cases (for example where the circumstances are analogous to those described in Chapter 48, paragraphs 5*a* and 16*d*1) and 2)) in which one has to make *Havdalah* again.

2) In such a situation, one does not also repeat the blessings on the spices and the light a second time (except in the eventualities described in paragraph 26*c*3) above).

Chapter 61

The Spices and the Light at Havdalah

THE BLESSING ON THE SPICES

the practice

1. *a.* Our sages ordained that one should
1) take spices in one's hand at *Havdalah* after Shabbath,
2) say a blessing over them and then
3) smell them.

b. The blessing to be said is:

בָּרוּךְ אַתָּה יהוה אֱלֹהֵינוּ מֶלֶךְ הָעוֹלָם בּוֹרֵא מִינֵי בְשָׂמִים

("Blessed art Thou, O Lord our God, King of the universe, Who creates varieties of spices").

c. For the order of *Havdalah*, see Chapter 60, paragraph 24.

when applicable

2. *a.* This applies at *Havdalah* on the evening Shabbath expires, but not
1) on the expiration of a Yom Tov (occurring on an ordinary weekday), whether the next day be an ordinary day of the week or *chol ha-moed*, nor
2) on the expiration of a Shabbath which is immediately followed by Yom Tov.

b. 1) One does not pronounce the blessing on spices on the expiration of Yom Kippur either, but,
2) at the end of a Yom Kippur which occurred on Shabbath, there are those whose custom is to say the blessing on the spices, either
   a) among the other blessings in the order of *Havdalah* or
   b) after they have drunk the *Havdalah* wine.

c. Somebody who did not make *Havdalah* on the evening Shabbath expired, and so recites *Havdalah* subsequently, during the first three days of the week, should not pronounce the blessing on the spices, as explained in Chapter 58, paragraph 20.

effect of omission

3. *a.* The omission of the blessing on the spices does not affect the validity of *Havdalah.*

b. Therefore, if one has no spices, one should make *Havdalah* without them.

c. Nonetheless, in the event that one obtains spices later on, during the course of Saturday night, one should say the blessing over them.

in absence of wine

4. *a.* Even someone who has no wine (or other acceptable drink) with which to make *Havdalah* is required to pronounce the blessing on the spices.

b. If, however, he estimates that, during the course of the night, he will be able to obtain wine (or some other acceptable drink) with which to make *Havdalah*, it is better to wait and pronounce the blessing on the spices over the same cup.

inability to smell

5. *a.* 1) If one is unable to smell, for instance because one has a cold, one should not pronounce the blessing on the spices (except as mentioned below).

2) This is so, even if one's intention is to say the blessing for the members of one's family, so that they can smell the spices.

3) In such a case, one should

a) let another member of the family say the blessing on the spices, for himself as well as for oneself,

b) answer "Amen" to the blessing and then also

c) try to smell the spices.

b. 1) Even if one cannot smell, one may pronounce the blessing on the spices for small children who do not know how to say the blessing themselves, whether or not they are one's own children, and they should smell the spices immediately afterwards, but,

2) in these circumstances, one should not pronounce the blessing in the order usual when making *Havdalah*, but only after one has drunk from the *Havdalah* wine.

6. A person making *Havdalah* for others should say the blessing on the spices, even if he has already fulfilled his own obligation (as in Chapter 60, paragraph 14), but he must also smell the spices himself straight after the blessing. *saying it a second time for others*

7. *a.* It is a mitzva for everyone to smell the spices himself and, when the person reciting *Havdalah* smells them, that does not discharge the obligations of the other participants. *everyone should smell the spices*

b. If there is a large number of participants, one should try to prepare several lots of spices, so that one will be able to hand them out and not pause for an inordinate length of time between the blessings one recites at *Havdalah*.

8. *a.* 1) Those listening to *Havdalah* being said for them should listen also to the blessing over the spices with the intention of thereby discharging their obligations in that respect. *listening to the blessing*

2) See further Chapter 60, paragraphs 26 and 27.

b. Nevertheless, if they estimate that they will not manage to smell the spices before the person reciting *Havdalah* continues with the other blessings, they have two courses open to them.

1) They may

a) have in mind not to discharge their obligations in respect of the blessing on the spices when they hear it pronounced by the person making *Havdalah* (in which case they should not respond to it with "Amen" either),

b) say the blessing on the spices themselves after the person making *Havdalah* has finished reciting all the blessings and then

c) smell the spices.

2) They may even

a) have in mind to discharge their obligations in respect of the blessing on the spices when they hear it pronounced by the person making *Havdalah* and

b) respond to it with "Amen," but
c) smell the spices only after the end of "*ha-mavdil.*"

spices to use

9. *a.* One should try to obtain for *Havdalah* a spice of the kind over which one says the blessing ending with the words, "*borei minei b^e^samim,*" such as cloves.

b. In any event, one says this blessing at *Havdalah* even over those spices on which one at other times says the blessings ending

1) "*borei atzei b^e^samim*" ("Who creates sweet-smelling woods") or
2) "*borei issvei b^e^samim*" ("Who creates sweet-smelling herbs").

c. The reason is that

1) not all are well-versed in the different blessings over smell, and some people might come to say the wrong blessing, whereas
2) someone who has said the blessing "*borei minei b^e^samim*" has discharged his obligation with regard to spices of all kinds.

using plants

10. If one says the blessing on spices over plants, it is proper to hold them the same way up as they grow, that is root down and leaves up.

spice box

11. *a.* It is the practice to keep a special box for the *Havdalah* spices used after Shabbath, and in this way to enhance the performance of the mitzva.

b. One should, if possible, open the box for the blessing, and not just smell the spices through the lid, even if it has perforations.

perfume

12. One should not use liquid perfume in place of spices, since there is a doubt whether one says the blessing at all when smelling it.

disposal of spices

13. *a.* Spices over which the blessing has been said at *Havdalah* should not just be emptied into the garbage like ordinary refuse.

b. Since they have been used for performing a mitzva, they should be disposed of in a more dignified manner.*

14. *a.* 1) If, after saying the blessing on the spices, one discovers that they do not exude a smell, one has to repeat a second time the blessing on the wine. *spices which have no smell*

2) This is because it has transpired that the blessing on the spices was out of place (in the absence of proper spices) and was, therefore, an unjustified interruption between the original blessing on the wine and drinking it.

3) In the event that one is brought other spices, one should also repeat again the blessing on the spices and smell them.

b. Regarding whether a mourner pronounces the blessing on the spices on the expiration of Shabbath, see Chapter 65, paragraph 35.

THE BLESSING ON THE LIGHT

15. *a.* Our sages ordained that one should make a blessing on the light at *Havdalah*, in remembrance of the creation of fire, which took place after the end of the first Shabbath, when the Almighty gave the first man the insight to produce fire from stones. *the custom*

b. The blessing to be said is:

בָּרוּךְ אַתָּה יהוה אֱלֹהֵינוּ מֶלֶךְ הָעוֹלָם בּוֹרֵא מְאוֹרֵי הָאֵשׁ

("Blessed art Thou, O Lord our God, King of the universe, Who creates the lights of the fire").

16. *a.* This applies *when applicable*

1) on the expiration of every Shabbath, even if the day after Shabbath is Yom Tov, as explained in Chapter 62, paragraph 18, and

2) on the expiration of Yom Kippur, whether it occurred

---

* They can, for instance, be put in the garbage wrapped in a plastic bag.

on a weekday or on Shabbath, as explained in Chapter 62, paragraph 29.

b. It does not apply on the expiration of Yom Tov (which did not occur on Shabbath), whether the ensuing day is *chol ha-mo'ed* or whether the Festival is over.

c. Somebody who did not recite *Havdalah* on the evening when Shabbath expired, and so recites it subsequently, during one of the first three days of the week, should not say the blessing on the light, as explained in Chapter 58, paragraph 20.

effect of omission

17. *a.* The omission of the blessing on the light on the expiration of Shabbath does not affect the validity of *Havdalah*.

b. Therefore, in the event that one has no light, one should make *Havdalah* without it.

c. Nonetheless, if one obtains a light later on, during the course of Saturday night, one should say the blessing over it.

in absence of wine

18. *a.* Even someone who has no wine (or other acceptable drink) with which to make *Havdalah* should pronounce the blessing on the light.*

b. If, however, he estimates that, during the course of the night, he will be able to obtain something with which to make *Havdalah*, it is better to postpone saying the blessing on the light, and pronounce it later over the *Havdalah* cup.

on Purim

19. *a.* When Purim falls immediately after Shabbath, one uses the light, before making *Havdalah*, in order to read the scroll containing the Book of Esther.

b. Nevertheless, the custom is to pronounce the blessing on the light later, over the *Havdalah* cup, and not to say it earlier, before the reading of the scroll.

---

* The same applies when the Fast of the Ninth of Av occurs immediately after Shabbath. (See Chapter 62, paragraph 43.)

20. *a.* It is a mitzva for everyone to enjoy the benefit of the light himself and, when the person reciting *Havdalah* enjoys it, that does not discharge the obligations of the other participants. *everyone should enjoy the light*

b. See further paragraph 23 below.

21. *a.* 1) Someone who is so unfortunate as to be blind does not say the blessing on the light (except as mentioned below). *the blind*

2) He should not do so even for others who will enjoy the benefit of the light immediately following the blessing.

b. 1) Nonetheless, he may pronounce the blessing on the light for small children, whether or not his own, if

a) they do not know how to say the blessing themselves and

b) they enjoy the benefit of the light right after the blessing,

but,

2) he should pronounce the blessing only after he has drunk from the *Havdalah* wine.

22. *a.* It may happen that a person makes *Havdalah* for others, even though he himself has already fulfilled his own obligations in that respect, as in the situation described in Chapter 60, paragraph 14. *saying it a second time for others*

b. The authorities differ as to whether, in such circumstances, the person making *Havdalah* can also say the blessing on the light for the other participants.

c. As a result, it is better for the person making *Havdalah* to avoid the dilemma, by letting one of those whose obligations are in the process of being discharged pronounce the blessing on the light.

d. If, however, none of them knows how to say a blessing, then the person who is reciting *Havdalah* should say that blessing for them too, but they must benefit from the light.

e. In the event that he says the blessing on the light for them, he can say it in its usual place in *Havdalah*.

listening to the blessing

23. *a.* 1) Those listening to *Havdalah* being said for them should listen also to the blessing over the light with the intention of thereby discharging their obligations in that respect.

2) See further Chapter 60, paragraphs 26 and 27.

b. However, their obligations are not discharged unless they are close to the light, so that they can enjoy its benefit after the blessing.

c. If they are not near enough to the light, they have two courses open to them.

1) They may

a) have in mind not to discharge their obligations with respect to the blessing on the light when they hear it pronounced by the person making *Havdalah* (in which case they should not respond to it with "Amen" either),

b) say the blessing on the light themselves after the person making *Havdalah* has finished reciting all the blessings and then

c) enjoy the benefit of the light.

2) They may even

a) have in mind to discharge their obligations in respect of the blessing on the light when they hear it pronounced by the person making *Havdalah* and

b) respond to it with "Amen," but

c) enjoy the benefit of the light only after the end of "*ha-mavdil.*"

d. 1) Sometimes, many of those who wish to discharge their obligations by listening to the blessing on the light are not close enough to it.

2) In that case, it is a good idea to prepare several lights and hand them out, so that one will not have to pause for an inordinate length of time between the blessings one recites at *Havdalah*.

3) See also paragraph 33 below.

24. *a.* A woman who recites *Havdalah* for herself, as in Chapter 58, paragraph 16, should not pronounce the blessing on the light in its usual place in the order of the *Havdalah* ceremony. *women*

b. This is because it might be considered an unwarranted interruption in the order of *Havdalah*, since in fact the woman has no obligation to pronounce the blessing on the light.

c. Still, she can pronounce the blessing after she has drunk from the *Havdalah* cup.

25. *a.* The custom is to keep a special *Havdalah* candle, made out of wax, for the blessing to be recited after Shabbath. *Havdalah candles*

b. 1) One should enhance one's performance of the mitzva by using a burning torch, comprising two or more flames held together, which throws out a great deal of light, and

2) the *Havdalah* candles in general use are indeed made of a number of wax-covered tapers plaited together to form a torch.

c. One should take care that the individual flames are touching each other.

d. A number of wicks (as opposed to wax-covered tapers) plaited together is not considered a torch (but merely one thick wick).

26. *a.* When one has no specially made *Havdalah* candle, one should hold two candles, or even two matches, together, so that their flames unite. *lack of Havdalah candle*

b. However, even if one has only one light, one can recite the blessing on the light over it.

27. *a.* 1) The blessing on the light may be recited only over a light which has been lit for the purpose of illumination. *lights not intended for illumination*

2) It may not be said* (as amplified further in this paragraph) over a light which has been lit
   a) for a mitzva (other than the mitzva of saying the blessing on the light),
   b) as a mark of honor or reverence, or
   c) to provide heat, for instance for the purpose of cooking.

b. 1) Consequently, one does not recite the blessing over those lights which are lit in the synagogue to burn as a sign of reverence during the service.
   2) The custom is to ignite a special candle for *Havdalah* in the synagogue.
   3) If one has no such candle, one should extinguish those which are burning in front of the person who is leading the prayers, and kindle them again specially for *Havdalah*.

c. One should not say the blessing over
   1) a memorial light kindled to commemorate a departed soul or
   2) the Chanuka lights.

d. 1) Nor should one recite it over a light put on, over and above the usual lighting, to add dignity or a festive atmosphere on the occasion of a visit by an important personage.
   2) It is otherwise if the light is put on to provide illumination for the guest.

e. The blessing on the light should not be pronounced on the flame of a gas or kerosene cooker or heater, which is not burning for the purpose of illumination.

f. It should not be pronounced even on a flame which was lit both

---

* *a.* If one has said the blessing over a light which was not lit for illumination, one has not discharged one's duty and must say the blessing again over another light.

b. What is more, one also has to say again the blessing on the wine, because it now transpires that it was out of place to pronounce the original blessing on the lights, which was thus an unwarranted interruption between the original blessing on the wine and drinking.

1) for a mitzva, or as a mark of honor or reverence, or to provide heat, as above,

and

2) for illumination.

g. If one wishes to say the blessing at *Havdalah* over a light which

1) was lit for a mitzva, or as a mark of honor or reverence, or to provide heat, but

2) is now being used for illumination,

it is better to extinguish it and then rekindle it for *Havdalah*.

lights kindled on Shabbath

28. *a.* One does not recite the blessing

1) over a light which was kindled in breach of the laws of Shabbath,* nor

2) over a light which was kindled on Shabbath by a non-Jew (except as mentioned below), even if he kindled it for his own use.**

b. One may recite the blessing over a light

1) which was permissibly kindled on Shabbath, for example, for the purposes of a dangerously ill person, or

2) which was kindled on Shabbath by a non-Jew for the purposes of a person who is ill, even though not dangerously so.

lights kindled before Shabbath

29. The blessing may be pronounced over a light which has been burning since before Shabbath.

lights kindled by non-Jew

30. *a.* 1) One may say the blessing over a light kindled by a non-Jew after Shabbath, but,

2) if one can help it, one should not say it over a second

---

* *a.* If one did recite the blessing over such a light, one has not discharged one's duty, and must say the blessing again over another light.

b. See also the note to paragraph 27 above.

** See preceding note.

b. 1) Therefore, one may say the blessing over a match which a non-Jew struck in order to provide light, but
2) one ought not to say it over a candle which the non-Jew ignited with a match.

covered flames

31. *a.* One should not pronounce the blessing over a flame which is covered, and so not visible, even when one can see the light which it radiates.
b. If possible, one should be strict, and not say the blessing even over a flame which is visible, but only through glass, as in the case of a kerosene lamp.

electric lights

32. *a.* One may not say the blessing over a fluorescent light, since there is nothing burning.
b. One may not say the blessing over an ordinary electric light bulb either, if its glass is opaque.
c. 1) As to a transparent electric light bulb, the authorities hold differing opinions as to whether it may be used to make the blessing.
2) According to those who permit it, one can say the blessing over it even if it was lit on Shabbath by means of a preset time switch.

closeness to light

33. *a.* 1) One does not discharge one's duty with respect to the blessing on the light unless one is in a position to benefit from it.
2) One should be close enough to be able to distinguish between two different coins.
b. 1) If one is not standing near the *Havdalah* candle, so that one's main benefit is from the electric light in the room, it is best to make a point of turning off the electric light, so that one can enjoy the light of the *Havdalah* candle.
c. 2) Alternatively, one can adopt either of the two courses suggested in paragraph 23*c* above.

34. *a.* One should not pronounce the blessing, even over a light the benefit of which one enjoys, if one cannot see the flame. *flame not in one's sight*

b. See also paragraph 32 above.

35. *a.* The custom, on saying the blessing over the light, is to make use of it by looking at the palm and finger nails of one's right hand. *looking at fingers*

b. Some bend the fingers over into the hand, so that they see the finger nails and the palm at the same time.

c. One should not stretch out the fingers and look at their palm side, but should specifically look at their backs, where the finger nails are.

d. Some have the custom of

1) bending the fingers over into the hand and then

2) straightening them and looking at their backs.

e. 1) The blessing on the light should be recited after looking at the fingers, although

2) there are those who are particular to adopt the reverse procedure and recite the blessing first.

f. Failure to comply with any of these customs does not invalidate the blessing and, so long as one enjoys the benefit of the light, one may recite the blessing over it.

36. One should not ignite a light whose kindling is not a mitzva from a candle one has lit for *Havdalah*, unless one has already made *Havdalah* over the candle. *use of Havdalah light*

37. Some have the custom of smelling the *Havdalah* candle after they have extinguished it. *smelling Havdalah candle*

Chapter 62

Havdalah on Special Days

HAVDALAH AFTER YOM TOV

adding time

1. Just as it is a mitzva to add time to Shabbath at its conclusion, at the expense of the ordinary weekday, so is it a mitzva to add time on the conclusion of a Festival.

activities forbidden before Havdalah

2. *a.* Just as one makes *Havdalah* on the termination of Shabbath, so does one make *Havdalah* on the termination of Yom Tov, whether the ensuing day is an ordinary weekday or *chol ha-mo'ed.* (See Chapter 58, paragraph 6, and also paragraph 9*b* below.)

b. 1) It is forbidden to perform activities which are prohibited on Yom Tov until one has made *Havdalah*, either in prayer, or with a cup, or by saying, "*Baruch ha-mavdil bein kodesh le-chol.*" (For the similar position after Shabbath, see Chapter 59, paragraph 1.)

2) Thus, on the one hand, one may, even before *Havdalah*, perform activities which are not prohibited on Yom Tov itself, such as

a) cooking,

b) smoking or

c) lighting a fire with a flame taken from a fire which is already burning.

whereas,

3) on the other hand, one may not, unless one has at least said, "*Baruch ha-mavdil bein kodesh le-chol,*"

a) light a "new" fire or

b) extinguish a fire.

c. It is forbidden to eat after Yom Tov until one has made *Havdalah* over a cup.

in prayer

3. *a.* One makes *Havdalah* in the evening prayer by inserting the passage commencing, "*Atah chonantanu.*"

b. The rules applicable if one forgets to say "*Atah chonantanu*" on the expiration of Yom Tov are the same as those applicable if one forgets to say it on the expiration of Shabbath. (See Chapter 58, paragraphs 10 and 11.)

4. One makes *Havdalah* over a cup, as after Shabbath, but it is not customary to preface *Havdalah* with the verses commencing, "*Hinei Keil y^eshuathi.*" (See Chapter 60, paragraph 23.) *over a cup: form*

5. On the expiry of a Yom Tov which fell on an ordinary weekday, one does not recite the blessings on the spices and on the light. *no spices or light*

6. If one did not make *Havdalah* over a cup after Yom Tov in the evening, one can do so until the sun sets on the following day, but not later. *on the next day*

7. *a.* One makes *Havdalah* with a full cup of wine, as after Shabbath (and as mentioned in Chapter 60, paragraph 19), but *full cup*

b. it is not customary, after Yom Tov, to fill the cup to such an extent that it spills over.

8. Regarding *Havdalah* in the *sukka* on *chol ha-mo'ed* of Sukkoth, both after Shabbath and after the first day (or days) of Yom Tov, see Chapter 58, paragraph 22. *in the sukka*

HAVDALAH AFTER SHABBATH WHEN THE ENSUING DAY IS YOM TOV

9. *a. Havdalah* is made on the termination of Shabbath, even when the ensuing day is Yom Tov, since the holiness of Yom Tov is of a lesser degree than that of Shabbath. *the rule*

b. On the other hand, *Havdalah* is not made on the termination of Yom Tov when the ensuing day is Shabbath, since one is proceeding from a lesser to a higher degree of holiness.

c. The form of *Havdalah* said when Shabbath is followed

immediately by Yom Tov differs from that recited after other Shabbathoth during the year, and can be found in the prayer book.

in prayer

10. *a.* One makes *Havdalah* in the evening prayer by inserting the passage commencing "*Va-todi'einu*" in the blessing which begins "*Atah v^e^chartanu.*"

b. The rules applicable if one forgets to say "*Va-todi'einu*" are similar to those applicable if one forgets to say "*Atah chonantanu*" on the expiration of Shabbath. (See Chapter 58, paragraphs 10 and 11.)

activities forbidden before Havdalah

11. *a.* One must not eat or perform forbidden activities before making *Havdalah*, as after any other Shabbath. (See Chapter 59.)

b. 1) In the event that one needs to perform a forbidden activity before one has made *Havdalah* with a cup or in the evening prayer, one must first make *Havdalah* by saying, "*Baruch ha-mavdil bein kodesh l^e^-kodesh.*"

2) This would be applicable, for instance, in the case of a woman who wants
  a) to kindle her Yom Tov lights,
  b) to cook for the Yom Tov evening meal, or even
  c) to set the table for Yom Tov evening.

c. One is not, however, permitted to eat until one has made *kiddush* and *Havdalah* over a cup in the proper manner.

combining kiddush and Havdalah

12. *a.* One makes *Havdalah* over a cup by adding the appropriate blessings for *Havdalah* in the Yom Tov evening *kiddush.*

b. The following blessings are made, in the order in which they appear:
1) the blessing on the wine;
2) the blessing of *kiddush*;
3) the blessing on the light;
4) the blessing of *Havdalah*;
5) the *she-hecheyanu* blessing.

c. When the Yom Tov which occurs immediately after Shabbath is the eighth day of Pesach (ouside Eretz Yisrael), the *she-hecheyanu* blessing is omitted.

13. When it is Yom Tov on the expiry of Shabbath, the custom is not to say the blessing on the spices. *no spices*

14. *a.* As mentioned in paragraph 12 above, when Yom Tov occurs on the expiry of Shabbath, one makes *kiddush* and *Havdalah* together. *bread*

b. Someone who is allowed to make *kiddush* over bread, as in the circumstances mentioned in Chapter 53, paragraph 4, may, thus, make *Havdalah* over the bread incidental to making *kiddush* over it.

c. Nevertheless, if he has any possibility of obtaining wine for *kiddush* and *Havdalah*, he should do so, even if he has a predilection for bread.

15. *a.* There is a practice, when making *Havdalah* after Shabbath, to fill the cup to such an extent that it spills over onto the floor or into the *Havdalah* plate, as mentioned in Chapter 60, paragraph 19. *filling the cup*

b. It is not the custom to do this when one makes *kiddush* and *Havdalah* together on a Yom Tov eve which immediately follows Shabbath.

16. *a.* 1) As stated in Chapter 58, paragraph 15, it is better if a woman does not herself recite *Havdalah* over a cup after Shabbath. *women*

2) Consequently, when it is Yom Tov after the end of Shabbath, and *Havdalah* is combined with *kiddush*, she should, if possible, not recite *kiddush* herself.

b. 1) Chapter 60, paragraph 38, refers to the custom of women not to drink from the *Havdalah* wine.

2) Nonetheless, it is the custom for women to drink from the combined *kiddush* and *Havdalah* wine when Yom Tov falls immediately after Shabbath.

17. *a.* An apparent conflict arises if a person *standing or sitting*

1) has the custom to stand during *Havdalah* after Shab-

bath (as mentioned in Chapter 60, paragraph 22) and also

2) has the custom in general to sit during *kiddush* (as mentioned in Chapter 47, paragraph 28).

b. When *kiddush* and *Havdalah* are combined, as above, he should sit during both *kiddush* and *Havdalah*.

the light

18. *a.* When saying the blessing on the light at *Havdalah*, on the expiration of a Shabbath which is followed by Yom Tov, one should hold two candles next to each other, so that the two flames join together into one combined flame.

b. There are, however, those whose custom in this case is to pronounce the blessing

1) on two individual candles, without holding them together, or even

2) on a single candle which is standing on the table.

c. One should certainly not extinguish the *Havdalah* candle, even though one is accustomed to doing so after *Havdalah* on the termination of an ordinary Shabbath (as in Chapter 60, paragraph 40).

forgetting Havdalah on Yom Tov

19. *a.* 1) Somebody who makes *kiddush* on a Yom Tov eve which occurs immediately after Shabbath, but forgets to make *Havdalah*, should, as soon as he remembers,

a) interrupt his meal,

b) make *Havdalah* over a cup, saying the blessing on the light and the blessing of *Havdalah* (in the form mentioned in paragraph 9 above), and then

c) continue with his meal.

2) So far as the blessing on the wine is concerned,

a) if **either** he is used to drinking wine during the meal **or**, at the time of *kiddush*, he had in mind to do so, he should not say the blessing again, but,

b) if **neither** of these preconditions exists, he has to say the blessing on the wine again (prior to the blessing on the light).

b. If he did not make *Havdalah* during the meal, he should take a cup and make *Havdalah* afterwards, reciting the blessing on the wine, the blessing on the light and the blessing of *Havdalah* (in the form appropriate when it is Yom Tov after Shabbath).

c. 1) If he did not make *Havdalah* on a cup at all during Saturday night, he should do so in the course of the following day, but

2) he cannot say the blessing over the light, except on Saturday night.

d. 1) If Yom Tov falls on Sunday and Monday, he can make *Havdalah* (in the above form) up to the end of the second day of Yom Tov.

2) This could happen, for example, in the case of the first two days of Pesach, outside Eretz Yisrael, where *yom tov sheini shel galuyoth* is observed.

e. If he did not make *Havdalah* by the end of Yom Tov (whether one or two days), he should just make *Havdalah* in the normal way on the expiry of Yom Tov. (See paragraph 4 above.)

forgetting Havdalah on seder night

20. *a.* 1) If, after making *kiddush* and drinking the wine on a Pesach seder night which occurs immediately following Shabbath, one remembers that one has omitted *Havdalah*, one should

a) continue reciting the *haggada* until after the blessing which concludes "*ga'al Yisrael*" and

b) make *Havdalah* over the second of the four cups one is obliged to drink.

2) That is to say, before drinking the second cup, one pronounces

a) the blessing on the wine,

b) the blessing on the light and

c) the blessing of *Havdalah* in the form appropriate to Yom Tov.

b. 1) If one has already drunk the second cup when one remembers that one has forgotten *Havdalah*, one should make *Havdalah* then.

2) In the event that one is in the middle of one's meal, one must interrupt it and make *Havdalah* right away.

3) With respect to the blessing on the wine, the position is as set out in paragraph 19*a* above.

c. When one remembers after the meal, subsequent to eating the *afikoman*, or during *birkath ha-mazon*, one makes *Havdalah* immediately after *birkath ha-mazon*, over the third of the four cups.

d. Should one remember only after drinking the third cup, one should make *Havdalah* over the fourth cup.

e. If one does not remember until after drinking the fourth cup, one has to take an additional cup and say over it the blessings on the wine, on the light and of *Havdalah*.

saying wrong form of Havdalah

21. *a.* 1) a) As mentioned in paragraph 9 above, there is a special form for *Havdalah* made on the termination of a Shabbath which is followed by Yom Tov.

b) A person who makes a mistake, and recites the blessing of *Havdalah* in the form appropriate when Shabbath is followed by an ordinary weekday, has not fulfilled his duty and must say it again in the correct form.

2) However, provided he has not in the meantime

a) diverted his attention from the blessing on the wine nor

b) spoken about matters unconnected with *kiddush* or *Havdalah*,

he should not repeat the blessing on the wine again (but see *c* below).

3) Where he has caused an interruption in either of these ways,

a) he has to pronounce again the blessing on the wine, as well as repeating the blessing of *Havdalah* in the form appropriate to Yom Tov, but,

b) he should not again recite the blessing of *kid-*

dush, as explained in Chapter 48, paragraph 3 (except in the circumstances set out in *d* below) nor the blessing on the light or the *she-hecheyanu* blessing.

b. 1) It can happen that one starts saying the correct form of the blessing of *Havdalah* for Yom Tov, but, instead of concluding, "*Baruch atah Ha-shem Ha-Mavdil bein kodesh le-kodesh*," mistakenly concludes as on a weekday, "*Baruch atah Ha-shem Ha-Mavdil bein kodesh le-chol*."

2) In that case, if one

a) remembers, within such time after finishing the blessing as it takes to say, "*Shalom aleicha rabi*," and

b) has not yet said even one word of the next blessing (*she-hecheyanu*),

one should quickly add, "*Ha-Mavdil bein kodesh le-kodesh*," and this is enough to discharge one's obligation.

3) a) If one remembers later, or if one has already started the next blessing, one must repeat the whole of "*ha-mavdil*," in the proper form.

b) As to the blessing on the wine, the rule is as in *a* above (subject to what follows immediately below).

c. 1) Should one not remember, until after one has drunk from the wine, that one made a mistake when saying "*Ha-Mavdil*," one

a) should take another cup of wine and repeat the blessing of *Havdalah* properly, but

b) should not make *kiddush* again (except in the circumstances mentioned in *d* below).

2) Whether or not one says a blessing on wine over this second cup depends on the considerations set out in paragraph 19 above.

d. 1) If, before one has drunk *ki-melo logmav* of the wine, one has

a) diverted one's attention from the combined *kid-*

dush and *Havdalah* or

b) left the house or apartment,

one must make *kiddush* and *Havdalah* again, as explained in Chapter 48, paragraph 5, but

2) one should not say the blessing on the light and the *she-hecheyanu* blessing again.

e. 1) If one erroneously says the blessing on the spices at *Havdalah* after a Shabbath which is followed immediately by Yom Tov, one should still go ahead and drink the wine without further ado.

2) Although the blessing on the spices, and smelling the spices, is an unauthorized interruption between the blessing on the wine and drinking it, one is not required to (and indeed may not) say the blessing on the wine a second time.

yom tov sheini shel galuyoth

22. *a.* 1) A resident of Eretz Yisrael who makes *Havdalah* at the end of a Shabbath which is followed immediately by *yom tov sheini shel galuyoth* cannot thereby discharge also the obligation to make *Havdalah* of a person who lives outside Eretz Yisrael.*

2) Likewise, the person who lives outside Eretz Yisrael, and combines *Havdalah* with *kiddush*, cannot discharge the obligation of the resident of Eretz Yisrael to make *Havdalah*.

b. They have to make *Havdalah* separately, because one of them is obliged to recite *Havdalah* in the form appropriate on Yom Tov and the other in the form appropriate on a weekday.

c. The resident of Eretz Yisrael should not extinguish the candle after making *Havdalah* outside Eretz Yisrael, since he is not allowed, even in private, to perform, on *yom tov sheini shel galuyoth*, activities which are forbidden on Yom Tov. (See Chapter 31, paragraph 37.)

---

* The situation can arise if, by way of example, the person who lives outside Eretz Yisrael forgets to make *Havdalah* at the same time as he makes *kiddush*.

HAVDALAH AFTER YOM KIPPUR

23. *a.* It is a mitzva to add to Yom Kippur, both when it begins and when it ends, at the expense of the ordinary weekday. *adding time*

b. See further Chapter 58, paragraphs 1 to 4.

24. During the additional time, it is forbidden to perform *prohibitions during additional time*

a. not only those activities which are prohibited on Shabbath, but also

b. those which are specifically prohibited on Yom Kippur, namely, eating and drinking, washing, oiling the skin, wearing leather shoes and engaging in marital relations.

25. *a.* As soon as the additional time at the end of Yom Kippur is over, the prohibitions on washing, oiling the skin, wearing leather shoes and engaging in marital relations cease, but *prohibitions before Havdalah*

b. one should not eat or drink (except for water, as detailed below) until one has made *Havdalah* with a cup.

c. 1) With regard to the performance of activities which are prohibited on Shabbath, before making *Havdalah* over a cup, the rules are the same as on the expiry of Shabbath. (See Chapter 59, paragraphs 1 and 2.)

2) a) One may perform them if one has made *Havdalah* in prayer;

b) failing that, one should say, "*Baruch Ha-Mavdil bein kodesh le-chol,*" before performing them.

d. 1) Someone who is thirsty may drink water (once the stars have come out) before he has made *Havdalah* with a cup, as on the expiration of Shabbath. (See Chapter 59, paragraph 10.)

2) Nevertheless, before doing so, he should make *Havdalah*

a) by saying "*Atah chonantanu*" in the evening prayer, or

b) by saying, "*Baruch Ha-Mavdil bein kodesh le-chol.*"

the next day

26. *a.* One makes *Havdalah* over a cup at the end of Yom Kippur, as at the end of Shabbath.*

b. 1) If one did not make *Havdalah* at the end of Yom Kippur (which fell on a weekday), one can do so until the sun sets on the following day, but not later than that.

2) The blessing on the light can, however, only be said on the evening on which Yom Kippur expired.

c. Should one fail to make *Havdalah* after a Yom Kippur which fell on a Shabbath, one can make *Havdalah* until the sun sets on Tuesday.

d. See further Chapter 58, paragraph 20.

form of Havdalah

27. *a.* After a Yom Kippur which occurred on a weekday, it is not customary to begin *Havdalah* with the preliminary verses, commencing, "*Hinei Keil yeshuathi...*" (as mentioned in Chapter 60, paragraph 23), but,

b. if Yom Kippur occurred on Shabbath, it is customary to say them.

spices

28. *a.* The blessing on the spices is not recited at *Havdalah* on the termination of Yom Kippur, although,

b. after a Yom Kippur which fell on Shabbath, some do have the custom to say it.

c. At any rate, it ought not to be said in the course of the order of *Havdalah*, but subsequently, after drinking the wine.

d. Nonetheless, there are those whose custom is to say the blessing on the spices in its usual place in the order of *Havdalah*.

reason for blessing on light

29. *a.* One recites the blessing on the light upon the expiry of Yom Kippur, even if it fell on a weekday, and not on Shabbath, despite the fact that the reason for reciting

---

* See Chapter 60, paragraph 33, concerning the "three-in-one" blessing after the *Havdalah* wine, prior to washing hands for a meal.

the blessing after Shabbath (outlined in Chapter 61, paragraph 15) is not applicable.

b. 1) When said at the termination of Yom Kippur, this blessing is analogous to the blessing of *Havdalah* itself.

2) We are pronouncing a blessing to the Almighty, solely because He made a distinction for us between Yom Kippur and other days, in that

3) during the whole of Yom Kippur we were forbidden to use a flame for preparing even food (unlike on every other Yom Tov, when we are permitted to use a flame for this purpose), whereas now we are permitted to do so.

nature of mitzva to say blessing on light

30. *a.* Thus, the blessing on the light said after Yom Kippur differs in its nature from that said after Shabbath, since it is more akin to *Havdalah* itself, in that it signifies the demarcation between the holy and the secular.

b. As a result, there are those who hold that one must exert oneself to obtain a light after Yom Kippur to the same extent as one does to obtain wine (or some other suitable drink) for *Havdalah*.

use of new light forbidden

31. *a.* For the same reason, one can, on the expiration of Yom Kippur, pronounce the blessing only over a light which symbolizes this differentiation between the holy and the secular.

b. In other words, one should pronounce the blessing

1) over a light

a) which has been burning throughout Yom Kippur, or

b) which was permissibly lit on Yom Kippur in the circumstances explained in paragraph 32*b* below,

or

2) over a light which was kindled from such a light after Yom Kippur.

c. One should not use for this purpose

1) a light*
   a) which was newly created (as opposed to being kindled from another light) after the expiry of Yom Kippur, or
   b) which was wrongfully kindled on Yom Kippur,

   or

2) a light which was kindled from such a light.

lights one may use

32. *a.* From the preceding paragraph, it emerges that there are two limitations with regard to the light one may use for *Havdalah* after Yom Kippur:
   1) like the *Havdalah* light used after Shabbath (as to which, see Chapter 61, paragraph 28), it must not have been wrongfully lit on the holy day;
   2) in addition, it must not be a new light, created after the expiry of Yom Kippur.

b. At all events, one may recite the blessing on a light
   1) which was permissibly kindled on Yom Kippur, for example for the purposes of a dangerously ill person, or
   2) which was kindled on Yom Kippur by a non-Jew for the purposes of a person who is ill, although not dangerously so.

light must be for illumination

33. *a.* As on the expiry of Shabbath, so on the expiry of Yom Kippur, one recites the blessing only over a light intended for illumination.

b. As amplified in Chapter 61, paragraph 27, one may not use a light which has been lit for a mitzva, or as a mark of honor or reverence, or to provide heat (but see paragraph 34 below).

c. Consequently, one should not say the blessing

---

* *a.* If one pronounces the blessing over a light of this kind, one has not fulfilled one's duty and must repeat the blessing over another light (but see paragraph 35 below).

b. Furthermore, one has to say the blessing on the wine again before drinking it, as in the comparable situations mentioned in Chapter 61, paragraph 14, and in the note to paragraph 27 there.

1) over lights lit in the synagogue as a sign of reverence, even if they have been burning since before Yom Kippur, nor
2) over a light kindled in memory of a departed soul.

34. *a.* The right thing to do is to leave a light burning at the commencement of Yom Kippur, to be used specifically for the purpose of saying the blessing during *Havdalah* at the end of the day. *leaving a light burning*

b. If one has not left such a light burning, one should
1) light a candle from a light one has left burning in honor of Yom Kippur since the previous day, and
2) say the blessing over both of them together.

c. Alternatively, one can
1) light a candle from a gas flame one has had burning since before Yom Kippur for the purpose of heating food during the day* (for instance for children or for somebody who is ill), and
2) say the blessing over that.

35. When Yom Kippur falls on Shabbath, it is indeed permitted to say the blessing over a light which was kindled after the expiry of Yom Kippur, but the custom is to act strictly and not use such a light. *light to use when Yom Kippur was on Shabbath*

36. *a.* If one can, one ought to say the blessing on the expiry of Yom Kippur (as on the expiry of Shabbath) over a burning torch comprised of two or more flames held together which throws out a good deal of light. (See Chapter 61, paragraph 25.) *burning torch*

b. However, it is also in order to say it over a single light.

37. *a.* There is a strict halachic opinion which holds that, if she can possibly avoid it, a woman *women*

---

* One may also light the candle from a gas flame ignited by a pilot light that has been burning since before Yom Kippur.

b. should not herself recite *Havdalah* over a cup after Yom Kippur, but

c. should be particular to discharge her duty in that respect by listening to a man making *Havdalah*.

HAVDALAH WHEN THE FAST OF THE NINTH OF AV OCCURS AFTER SHABBATH

wine during the Nine Days

38. *a.* In spite of the restriction on drinking wine during the nine days from the first of Av to the Fast of the Ninth of Av, one makes *Havdalah* with wine as usual at the end of Shabbath (except when the Fast begins immediately after Shabbath, as to which see the following paragraphs); however,

b. one should not drink it oneself, if one has the possibility of giving it to a young child who,

1) on the one hand, is old enough to have some notion of what reciting a blessing means, but,
2) on the other hand, is not yet old enough to have any idea what it is to mourn the destruction of Jerusalem.

restrictions applicable towards end of Shabbath

39. *a.* When the Ninth of Av falls

1) on a Sunday, or
2) on Shabbath, so that the Fast is put off to Sunday,

one must stop eating before sunset on Shabbath (preceding the Fast), as detailed in Chapter 56, paragraph 14.

b. At the same time, the obligations to abstain from washing and applying oil to the body take effect.

c. One does not, however, show any external sign of mourning until after Shabbath.

d. Thus, one should not change out of one's Shabbath clothes until nightfall,

e. nor should one remove one's leather shoes in the synagogue until after the intonation of *Bar^echu*.*

f. See further, Chapter 28, paragraph 77.

---

* The person who is leading prayers should say, "*Baruch Ha-Mavdil bein kodesh l^e-chol*," and then take off his shoes, before *Bar^echu*.

40. *a.* If one takes off one's leather shoes or changes one's clothes at home before going to the synagogue, one should first say, "*Baruch Ha-Mavdil bein kodesh le-chol.*" *changing at home*

b. Indeed it is a good thing to begin the evening prayer somewhat later than usual, so as to give everyone enough time to change at home before coming to the synagogue.

41. *a.* The leather-free shoes one is going to wear on the Fast should not be brought to the synagogue on Shabbath; *bringing slippers and Book of Lamentations to synagogue*

b. nor should one bring the Book of Lamentations to the synagogue before Shabbath ends, unless one reads from it a little there, while it is still Shabbath.

c. See Chapter 28, paragraph 77.

42. *a.* When the Fast of the Ninth of Av occurs upon the expiration of Shabbath, one should say "*Atah chonantanu*" by way of *Havdalah* in the evening prayer, as usual. *Havdalah in prayer*

b. If one forgets "*Atah chonantanu,*" one does not have to repeat the *Amidah*, since one will be making *Havdalah* with a cup anyway after the Fast (as stated in paragraph 44 below).

c. Nevertheless, one must not

1) perform an activity which is prohibited on Shabbath, nor

2) remove one's shoes or change one's clothes,

so long as one has not said, "*Baruch Ha-Mavdil bein kodesh le-chol.*" (See Chapter 59, paragraph 1.)

43. *a.* On the actual evening of the Fast (occurring on the expiry of Shabbath), *on eve of the Fast*

1) one does not recite *Havdalah* over a cup, nor does one say the blessing on the spices, but

2) one does say the blessing on the light.

b. The custom is to say the blessing before the reading of the Book of Lamentations.

c. Should one forget, one can pronounce the blessing afterwards, during the course of the night.

d. If one can, one should say the blessing over a burning

torch comprised of two or more flames held together, as explained in Chapter 61, paragraph 25.

at end of Fast

44. *a.* After the end of the Fast, one does not make *Havdalah* in one's prayer, even if one forgot to do so the previous evening, when Shabbath expired.

b. 1) Before beginning to eat, however, one makes *Havdalah* with a cup.*

2) The person reciting *Havdalah* may drink the wine himself, and does not need to give it to a child to drink.

c. One does not say the blessing on the spices.

d. Likewise, one does not say the blessing on the light, even if one forgot to say it the previous evening, when Shabbath expired.

e. The custom is not to commence *Havdalah* with the preliminary verses beginning, "*Hinei Keil yeshuathi....*" (See Chapter 60, paragraph 23.)

children eating

45. *a.* A child (under thirteen if a boy and under twelve if a girl) who eats on the Fast of the Ninth of Av

1) when it falls on Shabbath, and is therefore postponed to Sunday, or

2) when it falls on Sunday,

is allowed to eat even though he has not made *Havdalah* after the expiry of Shabbath.

b. He should listen to *Havdalah* when it is made after the end of the Fast.

ill people eating

46. *a.* An ill person who has to eat on the Fast of the Ninth of Av should say *Havdalah* over a cup beforehand.

b. 1) If he has to eat right away in the evening, he should

---

* See Chapter 60, paragraph 33, regarding the "three-in-one" blessing to be said after the wine, before washing one's hands for the meal.

make *Havdalah* in the evening.*

2) If he does not have to eat till the morning, he should make *Havdalah* in the morning.**

c. When reciting *Havdalah*, he can thereby discharge also the obligations of the members of his household to make *Havdalah*.

d. 1) He would do well

a) not to make *Havdalah* with wine, but with some other beverage over which one can make *Havdalah*, as detailed in Chapter 60, paragraphs 3 to 8, or

b) to give the *Havdalah* wine to a young child (as in paragraph 38 above) to drink.

2) In the eventuality that he does not have available an alternative beverage, or a suitable child, the ill person should use wine, and himself drink only the required quantity, and no more.

47. *a.* 1) In the following conditions, the parents of a baby being circumcised, the *mohel* and the *sandak* may eat after midday on the day of the Fast: *circumcisions*

a) the Fast has been postponed to that day from the previous day, because the Ninth of Av fell on Shabbath,*** and

b) the circumcision is taking place, as it should normally do, on the eighth day, counting from the day of the birth.

2) They should, however, make *Havdalah* over a cup before eating.

---

* *a.* He should not say the blessing over the spices, but

b. he should say the blessing over the light.

c. He should not say the verses commencing "*Hinei Keil y^eshuathi*..." before the blessing of *Havdalah*.

** *a.* He should say neither the blessing over the spices, nor that over the light.

b. He should just say the blessing appropriate to the particular beverage he is using and the blessing of *Ha-Mavdil*.

*** When the Fast is not postponed, but is actually on the Ninth of Av, they must fast to the end of the day as usual.

3) When making *Havdalah*, they can also thereby discharge the obligations of anybody else who cares to listen (as in the case in paragraph 46 above).

b. 1) Similar rules apply when a firstborn son is redeemed, if
   a) the Fast has been postponed from the previous day, because the Ninth of Av fell on Shabbath,* and
   b) the period which the Halacha requires to pass before the redemption can take place expires on that very day.

2) In those circumstances, the father of the baby and the *kohen* from whom the baby is being redeemed may eat after midday, but should make *Havdalah* first.

women who must eat

48. *a.* 1) If a woman is ill, and has to eat on the Fast of the Ninth of Av, her husband would do well to
   a) make *Havdalah* over a cup for himself, his wife and his family, and
   b) let a young child (as in paragraph 38 above) drink the wine.

2) Better still, he should not use wine, but some other drink over which one is permitted to make *Havdalah*. (See Chapter 60, paragraphs 3 to 8.)

3) In the event that there is no young child, and no suitable drink other than wine, the woman should drink from the wine, but only the required quantity and no more.

b. 1) If there is no man available who can make *Havdalah* for her, the woman should make *Havdalah* herself, as stated in Chapter 58, paragraph 16, and

2) the same rules as in *a* above apply with regard to the beverage used and drinking it.

---

* When the Fast is not postponed, but is actually on the Ninth of Av, they must fast to the end of the day as usual.

restrictions after the Fast

49. *a.* 1) The practice is, except in specified circumstances, to avoid situations in which one will have to recite the *she-hecheyanu* blessing during the three weeks leading up to the Fast of the Ninth of Av.

2) It is, however, allowed to say the *she-hecheyanu* blessing over new season's fruit on the evening the Fast ends, at least when that is the eve of the eleventh of Av, in other words when the Fast was postponed from Shabbath to Sunday.

b. Immediately after a postponed Fast, one may also cut one's hair, wash clothes and bathe in hot water, but

c. one should not drink wine (other than the *Havdalah* wine, as in paragraph 44 above) or eat meat until the next morning, except at a meal eaten in honor of a mitzva.

Chapter 63

M^e^laveh Malkah

nature of mitzva

1. *a.* One should lay the table for a meal after the end of Shabbath, even if one does not feel like eating very much.

b. The purpose is to honor Shabbath at its termination, as one does at its commencement.

c. Although many people are not particular about eating this *m^e^laveh malkah* meal, a God-fearing person should exert himself in order to do so.

d. 1) One should have in mind to eat it as a *m^e^laveh malkah* meal.

2) Indeed, it is proper to declare that one is eating "for the mitzva of the *m^e^laveh malkah* meal."

clothes and tablecloth

2. *a.* One should not take off one's Shabbath clothes until after the *m^e^laveh malkah* meal.

b. Moreover, the table should be covered with a cloth at this meal. (See Chapter 42, paragraph 55.)

women

3. *a.* It is fitting also for women to eat the *m^e^laveh malkah* meal.

b. Some even say one should insist that they keep this mitzva.

after Yom Tov

4. It is not the practice to eat a *m^e^laveh malkah* meal on the expiry of Yom Tov (which did not fall on Shabbath).

time

5. *a.* It is well to eat the *m^e^laveh malkah* meal early, soon after the end of Shabbath, although,

b. if one does not feel like eating straight after Shabbath, one can wait until later, but

c. one should not engage in any activity which absorbs one's attention for any length of time, until one has eaten one's *m^e^laveh malkah* meal.

d. It is preferable to perform the mitzva before the end of the first third of the night.

e. At any rate, one should certainly not delay until after midnight.

6. *a.* Somebody whose third Shabbath meal is prolonged until after nightfall need not have a *m^e^laveh malkah* meal. *extended third meal*

b. Nonetheless, there is an opinion that, even in such a case, the *m^e^laveh malkah* meal should be eaten.

7. *a.* Even a person who is still full from the Shabbath meals should make an effort to keep the mitzva of eating the *m^e^laveh malkah* meal. *importance*

b. Still, eating the *m^e^laveh malkah* meal is not an obligation to the same degree as eating the three Shabbath meals.

8. *a.* If one can, one ought to *what to eat*

1) have this meal too with bread, like the other Shabbath meals, and
2) dignify the meal with a warm dish of some kind.

b. If one is unable to eat bread, for example because one is full from the Shabbath meals, one should eat

1) baked or cooked food made from wheat, barley, rye, oats or spelt, or, at least,
2) some cooked dish, even if it is only stewed fruit.

c. In circumstances of difficulty, one can discharge one's duty by just having a hot drink, such as tea or coffee.

9. It is good to prepare a dish specially for this meal, and not eat merely the leftovers from the Shabbath meals. *preparing specially*

10. There is a difference of opinion among the authorities as to whether one may eat meat left over on a Shabbath occurring during the first nine days of the month of Av, at the *m^e^laveh malkah* meal one has after that Shabbath. *Nine Days* *lights and z^e^miroth*

11. Some have the custom, at this meal,
a. to put on more lights and
b. to recite the special hymns which are intended to be said after the expiry of Shabbath.

folding tallith

12. It is a laudable practice, straight after the end of Shabbath, to fold up the *tallith* in which one wrapped oneself during prayer on Shabbath, so as to begin the new week with a mitzva. (See Chapter 15, paragraphs 44 to 46, with respect to folding clothes on Shabbath.)

working after Shabbath

13. *a.* 1) There are places where women have the custom not to perform certain workaday activities during the whole of the night following the expiration of Shabbath.
2) Some are accustomed to abstain only when the activity is done for money.
3) Others refrain from those activities which demand close attention for any length of time, such as sewing or knitting.

b. At all events, there is no reason whatever to forbid an activity which is for the purpose of a mitzva, such as sewing a cover for a *sefer Torah*.

c. Moreover, there are authorities who negate the whole custom and state that all workaday activities become permissible immediately after *havdala* is made.

"omens" for the coming week

14. *a.* One should beware of being apprehensive about "omens" on the expiry of Shabbath.

b. For instance, if somebody is asked to pay a debt, or to give money to charity, on the evening after Shabbath has ended, he should not reject the request with the argument that it does not augur well for the coming week to begin it by paying out money.

c. To do this would be to transgress the biblical prohibition, "You shall not practice divination nor soothsaying" (Leviticus 19:26).

d. Instead, one should comply with the precept in Deuteronomy 18:13, "Be wholehearted with the Lord your God."

e. Rashi's comment on this latter verse is, "Walk with Him wholeheartedly and place your hope in Him. Do not probe into the future, but accept wholeheartedly whatever comes upon you. Then will you be with Him and become His."

Chapter 64

Attending to the Dead, and the Laws of Mourning on Shabbath and Yom Tov, Up to the Burial

ACTIONS REQUIRED AS A RESULT OF A DEATH ON SHABBATH AND YOM TOV, UP TO THE BURIAL

the dying

1. *a.* One must violate the Shabbath to prolong, even if only for a brief while, the life of a person who is dying. (See Chapter 32, paragraph 2.)

b. 1) One should say the Confession before Death with a person who is on the point of dying, even if it is Shabbath or Yom Tov.

2) a) The Confession is said even in a place in which it is not fit to pray, due to the presence, for example, of uncovered excrement.

b) In such a place, however, the Confession should be recited without pronouncing the Name of God.

tearing garments on Shabbath or Yom Tov

2. *a.* 1) Neither those present at a death, nor the close relatives of the deceased, should tear their garments in mourning on Shabbath or Yom Tov (as they would do on an ordinary weekday).

2) This applies

a) even on *yom tov sheini shel galuyoth* and

b) even if the burial takes place on Yom Tov (as explained in paragraph 16 below).

blessing on death on Shabbath and Yom Tov

b. 1) On the other hand, the blessing:

בָּרוּךְ אַתָּה יהוה אֱלֹהֵינוּ מֶלֶךְ הָעוֹלָם דַּיַּן הָאֱמֶת

("Blessed art Thou, O Lord our God, King of the universe, the true Judge")

is recited on Shabbath and Yom Tov,* and

2) it should not be repeated at the time when the garments are torn in mourning after Shabbath or Yom Tov.

3) Should the blessing not have been recited at the time of the decease, then it should indeed be pronounced later, when the clothes are torn in mourning, or at the funeral.**

4) In the event that the blessing was not pronounced at the funeral either, it should be pronounced subsequently, but

   a) the blessing should be said in full only during the first three days, starting with the day of the burial, whereas,

   b) afterwards, the Name and kingly attributes of the Almighty should be omitted and the blessing abbreviated to, בָּרוּךְ דַּיַּן הָאֱמֶת (*"Baruch Dayan ha-emeth* — Blessed is the true Judge").

tearing garments on chol ha-mo'ed or after Yom Tov

3. *a.* 1) Somebody who is present at a death on Shabbath or Yom Tov, and so cannot then tear his clothes in mourning, does not have to tear them after Shabbath or Yom Tov either (unless he is one of the close relatives mentioned immediately below).

2) The sons, daughters, father, mother, brothers, sisters and husband or wife of the deceased are obliged to tear their clothes in mourning when Shabbath or Yom Tov ends, except that,

3) if their relative (even a father or mother)

   a) passed away during the first days of Pesach or

---

* *a.* The blessing is recited in full on the decease of a relative for whom one is obliged to mourn (as in paragraph 3 below), of a great Torah scholar or of a rabbi who taught one most of what one knows.

b. On the decease of some other good Jew over whose death one grieves, the custom is to say the blessing in its abbreviated form, omitting the Name and kingly attributes of the Almighty.

** There is in fact a widespread practice not to tear the garments or recite the blessing until the funeral cortege is about to leave.

Sukkoth and

b) was buried on Yom Tov (on the first day of Yom Tov by a non-Jew, or on *yom tov sheini shel galuyoth* by a Jew, as explained in paragraph 16 below),

they should not tear their clothes when Yom Tov terminates, that is to say, on *chol ha-mo'ed*, but only after the whole Festival has ended.

b. 1) According to some authorities, a person who is present at a death on *chol ha-mo'ed* should tear his clothes in mourning, whereas

2) others hold the custom to be that even a person who is present at a death does not tear his clothes in mourning on *chol ha-mo'ed** (except on the death of a parent or, in accordance with the view mentioned in *c*2)b) below, a close relative).

c. 1) A person whose father or mother has passed away should tear his clothes when present at the death or at the funeral on *chol ha-mo'ed*.

2) a) The custom is not to tear the clothes on *chol ha-mo'ed* in mourning for other close relatives (except at the death, according to the view mentioned in *b*1) above), but only after the termination of the whole Festival.**

b) There are, however, those who do tear their clothes on *chol ha-mo'ed* for other close relatives too.

d. At all events, the shoes should not be removed in mourn-

---

* *a.* At any rate, the blessing, "*Dayan ha-emeth*", should not be postponed until the clothes are torn, but should be recited on *chol ha-mo'ed*, at the time of the death, or the burial, as the case may be.

b. As in paragraph 2 above, the blessing should not be pronounced again when the clothes are torn, or the days of mourning begin, after the Festival ends.

** *a.* At any rate, the blessing "*Dayan ha-emeth*" should not be postponed until the clothes are torn, but should be recited on *chol ha-mo'ed*, at the time of the death, or the burial, as the case may be.

b. As in paragraph 2 above, the blessing should not be pronounced again when the clothes are torn, or the days of mourning begin, after the Festival ends.

ing on *chol ha-mo'ed*, nor should those laws which are openly indicative of mourning be observed, as elucidated in Chapter 65, paragraph 38.

e. 1) It is forbidden to eulogize a deceased on Shabbath or Yom Tov, even at a burial which is taking place on Yom Tov in accordance with what is stated in paragraph 16 below,

2) nor does one deliver a eulogy on *chol ha-mo'ed*, even over a Torah sage at his funeral.

f. 1) See Chapter 65, paragraphs 51 to 53, with regard to the receipt on Shabbath or Yom Tov of the news of a death.

2) See Chapter 65, paragraphs 54, with regard to the receipt on *chol ha-mo'ed* of the news of a death.

4. *a.* In most cases, the performance of autopsies is considered an unjustifiable desecration of the dead. *autopsies*

b. Nonetheless, it is forbidden, on Shabbath or Yom Tov, to sign a form of objection to a postmortem, since writing is a transgression of a Torah prohibition.

c. One may, however, violate a Rabbinical prohibition in order to save a deceased from having his body desecrated, as in paragraph 13 below.*

5. *a.* There is room for taking a lenient view and kindling a light in honor of a deceased on Yom Tov, provided one does not make a "new" light, but kindles it from a flame which is already burning. (See Chapter 13, paragraphs 2 and 3.) *lights*

b. It is well to kindle the light in the synagogue, and not in the room where one eats, or in a room where one spends one's time the whole day, since this could lead one to mourn on Yom Tov.

c. 1) In difficult circumstances, there are grounds for al-

---

* From paragraph 29 below, it can be seen that one may request a non-Jewish doctor to write out and sign a death certificate, in order to avoid a postmortem examination.

lowing the light to be kindled, not in the synagogue, but in the room where the body is.

2) Still, it is better not to kindle the light oneself, but to request a non-Jew to do so.

d. In any event, it is customary, on Yom Tov, not to follow the practice of kindling lights round the body, even through the agency of a non-Jew.

kohanim

6. *a.* Generally speaking, although a *kohen* is forbidden to come into contact with, or be under the same roof as, a corpse, he may do so if it is that of a close relative (as defined in paragraph 3 above), provided the body is whole and has no part missing.

b. Nevertheless, it is proper for a *kohen* to act strictly and refrain from this on Shabbath, unless it is necessary in order to save the deceased from indignity.*

c. The same applies on Yom Tov, except when the burial is taking place that day (as detailed in paragraph 16 below).

pouring out water

7. *a.* 1) Despite the fact that there is a custom to pour away water contained in vessels in a house where there is a corpse, and in neighboring houses, this is not done on Shabbath.

2) The practice is not to pour away such water on Yom Tov either.

b. Furthermore, this water is also not poured away at the end of Shabbath or Yom Tov.

c. Moreover, it is customary not to pour away (even before Shabbath) hot water prepared in honor of Shabbath.

ATTENDING TO THE BODY OF A DECEASED ON SHABBATH OR YOM TOV

prohibition on moving corpse

8. *a.* On Shabbath and Yom Tov, a corpse is *muktzeh* and may not be moved (except as mentioned below).

---

* This might be the case where, for instance, one is afraid that, if the body is left alone, rodents might nibble at it.

b. 1) Consequently, one should not close the eyes of a person who has died, or straighten his limbs.

2) a) Nevertheless, there are those who are accustomed to be lenient in this respect, and, in such case, one should raise no objection, but,

b) if possible, they should perform these activities with the aid of a non-*muktzeh* object which they hold, so that their hands should not come into direct contact with the dead body.

c. One may tie a bandage round the head of the corpse, to prevent the jaw from opening wider, but

1) one should not tighten the bandage in such a way as to close the already open mouth and

2) one should beware not to tie a double knot, but should either

a) tie a bow over a single knot or

b) tuck in the end of the bandage to secure it.

9. *a.* It is permitted to extract infusion needles and tubes from the body of the deceased (but one should not move him in order to do this). *cleaning corpse*

b. 1) One may also wipe off dirt, blood and so forth, whose presence detracts from the dignity due to a human corpse, but, in so doing, one should refrain from squeezing out any liquid.

2) Therefore, one

a) should not use absorbent cotton (cotton wool), an absorbent cloth or a sponge for the purpose, but

b) should wipe it off with one's hands, wearing rubber or nylon gloves.

10. *a.* The custom is to remove the clothes of the deceased. *taking clothes off corpse*

b. One should pull them off the body without lifting the corpse or the limbs (so as not to transgress the laws relating to *muktzeh*).

c. One should also try not to move each limb as one draws the clothes off over it.

taking corpse off bed

11. *a.* It is also the custom to take the body off the bed and lay it on the floor.

b. It is proper to move the corpse, on Shabbath or Yom Tov, only together with a non-*muktzeh* object which one has placed by its side, or on top of it.

c. In pressing circumstances, it is possible to be more lenient and take the deceased off the bed without the accompaniment of a non-*muktzeh* object, provided he is wearing clothes which will be taken off him later.

d. If death took place near the end of the day, one should leave the body where it is and not take it off the bed until after Shabbath or Yom Tov.

preference for attendance by Jew

12. *a.* Out of respect to the dead, a Jew should attend to the deceased's needs (such as closing his eyes, cleaning him, taking off his clothes or lowering him from the bed to the floor), even if a non-Jew is available, but

b. he should do so within the limits set out in paragraphs 8 to 11 above.

moving corpse to avoid degradation

13. *a.* 1) One may move a dead person on Shabbath or Yom Tov,

a) after placing an object which is not *muktzeh* on him, or by his side, as explained in paragraph 11 above,

b) for the purposes of the deceased himself, that is to say, in order that he should not be left in a degrading situation.

2) In the event that one has no such object, one may move him without it (to save him from degradation).

b. If one does so to save him from a postmortem operation, one may take him out even into a place where it is forbidden to carry things about, so long as it is not a *r^e^shuth ha-rabbim* in the strict sense (as defined in Chapter 17, paragraph 3).

c. 1) Should one indeed take a dead person out into such a place (where it is forbidden to carry), one should also put a non-*muktzeh* article on him or by him, as above in paragraph 11.

2) The reason is that carrying the non-*muktzeh* article and the *muktzeh* corpse together make the fact that one is moving the *muktzeh* corpse less blatant.

3) This is deemed to be a more important consideration than that by doing so one will be carrying into a forbidden place more than one has to, since, after all, both the article and the corpse are being taken out in one and the same action.

moving corpse because of kohen

14. *a.* As stated in paragraph 6 above, it is generally forbidden for *kohanim* to be under the same roof as a corpse.

b. To save *kohanim* in the house from transgressing this prohibition, one may have the corpse removed by a non-Jew on Shabbath or Yom Tov (subject to the reservation in *d* below).

c. The body may be removed by a Jew (subject to the reservation in *d* below)

1) only for the purposes of a *kohen* who is ill, and so cannot leave the house himself, and

2) only together with a non-*muktzeh* object placed on top of it or by its side, as in paragraph 13 above.

d. In either of the above cases, the body may be taken out even into a place where one may not carry things about, as long as it is not a *reshuth ha-rabbim* in the strict sense.

watching over corpse

15. *a.* 1) It is a mitzva to watch over a deceased from the time of death to the time of burial,

a) out of respect for him and

b) to protect him from harm or indignity.

2) a) One is allowed to receive remuneration for watching over a corpse, but

b) the authorities differ as to whether the prohibition against receiving remuneration for work done on Shabbath or Yom Tov applies where the work is a mitzva, as here. (See Chapter 28, paragraph 66.)

b. 1) One may sprinkle vinegar and the like on the deceased's clothes, or on the sheet covering him, on Shabbath or Yom Tov, to prevent an unpleasant odor and so make it easier to perform the traditional purification later.
2) One may also put ice over him for the same purpose.

burial

16. *a.* It is forbidden to carry out a burial on Shabbath, even through the agency of a non-Jew.
b. The same applies on Yom Kippur.
c. 1) So far as Yom Tov is concerned, a distinction must be made between
a) the first day, when a burial may be performed through the agency of a non-Jew, and
b) the second day (either the second day of Rosh Hashana or *yom tov sheini shel galuyoth*), when the burial may be performed by a Jew.
2) In any event, a qualified halachic authority should be consulted as to if and how a burial should be performed on Yom Tov.
d. When a funeral does take place on Yom Tov,
1) one must not follow the custom of pulling up growing grass after the burial and
2) one must not wash one's hands over sown ground, or over ground which is going to be ploughed or sown. (See Chapter 26, paragraph 5.)

MOURNING ON SHABBATH AND YOM TOV UP TO THE BURIAL

meaning of onein

17. *a.* A person is obliged to mourn upon the death of a close relative, as defined in paragraph 3 above.
b. From the time of the death to the burial he is known as an *onein*.
c. One does not prevent an *onein* from weeping over his dead on Shabbath or Yom Tov.

laws relating to onein in outline

18. *a.* 1) On an ordinary day of the week, an *onein* is free from all positive commandments,* whether imposed by the Torah or by the Rabbis, including the mitzvoth
a) to read the *Sh^{e}ma*,
b) to recite the daily prayers and
c) to put on *t^{e}fillin*.

2) He does not
a) pronounce blessings,
b) respond with "Amen" to blessings he hears, nor
c) count towards the quorum needed for *birkath ha-zimun* or to make up a *minyan*.

3) He is forbidden to
a) study Torah,
b) eat meat,
c) drink wine,
d) wash any part of his body with warm water, or the whole of his body even with cold water,
e) apply oil to his skin,
f) have his hair cut,
g) rejoice,
h) exchange greetings with other people,
i) work,
j) trade or
k) engage in marital relations.

b. However, during any period when he is unable to make arrangements for the funeral, as on Shabbath, and often on Yom Tov, the laws normally relating to an *onein* apply only to a very restricted extent, as will be seen below.

---

* *a.* An *onein* may certainly not violate any prohibition, even if it relates only to a usage introduced by the Rabbis.

b. Thus, if he wishes to eat bread,
1) he should first wash his hands, but
2) he should not say the blessing on washing hands, nor the blessing before eating bread, nor *birkath ha-mazon*.

c. 1) Similarly, when he rises from bed in the morning, he should pour water over each hand alternately three times, as he always does, but without reciting the blessing.
2) Likewise, after relieving himself, he should wash his hands, but not pronounce the usual blessing.

kaddish

19. *a.* A son who becomes an *onein* upon the death of his father or mother may go to the synagogue to say *kaddish*, provided there is someone else available to watch over the deceased. (See also paragraph 20 below.)

b. However, other mourners have precedence over him (in those synagogues where the custom is that only one person at a time says *kaddish*) until the burial takes place.

mitzvoth

20. *a.* On the following days and occasions, an *onein* is obliged to perform all mitzvoth and to pronounce all blessings:

1) on Shabbath,
2) on the first day of Yom Tov, if the burial is not taking place that day (through the agency of a non-Jew),
3) on the second day of Yom Tov (whether of Rosh Hashana or *yom tov sheini shel galuyoth*), if for some reason the burial is not taking place that day, and
4) in the situations described at the end of paragraph 23 below.

b. A person who is an *onein* in such circumstances

1) a) may go to the synagogue to pray and
   b) is counted towards the ten congregants required for a *minyan*, but
2) should not lead prayers if someone else who can do so is present.

c. 1) He does not change his place in the synagogue in accordance with the custom detailed in Chapter 65, paragraph 24,
2) nor does he refrain from wearing his Shabbath or Yom Tov clothes, even if his custom is not to wear them at all in the year of mourning, as mentioned in Chapter 65, paragraph 7.

d. He

1) a) may study Torah and
   b) may, of course, go over the weekly portion from the Torah (twice) with its *Targum*, but
2) should try and avoid being called up to the reading of the Torah.

e. 1) In the event that he is a *kohen*, he should not pronounce the priestly benedictions (when the person leading prayers repeats the final blessing of the *Amidah*).

2) Indeed, he would do well to go out of the synagogue before the person leading prayers starts saying the blessing of the *Amidah* commencing *Retzei*.

f. 1) On the other hand, he is bound, as on a weekday, by those laws applying to an *onein* whose observance is not evidenced by any outward indication of mourning.

2) Thus, he should not wash (within the parameters outlined in paragraph 18 above) or engage in marital relations.

meat and wine

21. *a.* On Shabbath, the *onein* should sit down at the Shabbath table, and eat meat and drink wine, as on any other Shabbath.

b. 1) On Yom Tov, provided the burial is not taking place that day (as amplified in paragraph 20 above), he is bound by the mitzva to rejoice, by drinking wine and eating meat.

2) He is not allowed to take upon himself a more restrictive course of conduct.

death just before Shabbath or Yom Tov

22. *a.* Another situation in which the laws applicable to an *onein* do not take effect immediately is where the death takes place late on Friday, or late on the day before Yom Tov, so that there is no time to perform the burial before Shabbath or the Festival start.

b. 1) The deceased's relatives

a) are obliged to recite the weekday afternoon prayer, as usual,

b) should put on their Shabbath clothes (as in paragraph 20 above), and

c) kindle lights, with the appropriate blessing, as on the commencement of any other Shabbath or Yom Tov, but

2) they should not wash in honor of Shabbath or Yom Tov.

c. In fact, the laws relating to an *onein* come fully into force only after Shabbath or Yom Tov expire.

when funeral on Yom Tov

23. *a.* If the funeral is to be held on Yom Tov, as in paragraph 16 above, all of the laws relating to an *onein* (outlined in paragraph 18 above) must be observed by him until after the burial (subject to what is mentioned below).

b. Since he is free from the observance of all positive commandments during this period,

1) he does not make *kiddush*,
2) on Rosh Hashana, he does not have to hear the *shofar* blown and,
3) on Sukkoth, he is not obliged to take the *lulav* or eat in the *sukka*.

c. 1) On the night of Yom Tov, however, the laws relating to an *onein* do not apply, because it is not customary to hold a funeral then (but to wait until the morrow).*

2) Therefore, the rules set out in paragraph 20 above apply and the *onein* has an obligation
   a) to recite prayers,
   b) to make *kiddush*,
   c) to say blessings before and after eating,
   d) on Pesach, to eat matza and fulfill the other mitzvoth of the evening and,
   e) on Sukkoth, to eat a *ka-zayith* of bread in the *sukka*.

d. The next morning too, if he wants to hold the funeral but the members of the burial society refuse to deal with it before the Festival prayers are over, the laws relating to an *onein* still do not apply to him, until the time they leave the synagogue.

---

* Within the walled city of Jerusalem, the laws relating to an *onein* apply also in the night, as it is forbidden to leave a corpse overnight, even for reasons of respect to the deceased, and one has to bury him that evening.

24. On *chol ha-mo'ed*, all of the laws relating to an *onein* (summarized in paragraph 18 above) apply, as on a weekday. *chol ha-mo'ed*

25. *a.* If the funeral is due to take place after Shabbath or Yom Tov, *making Havdalah*

1) the *onein* should recite the three paragraphs of the *Shema* towards evening, but
2) he should not
   a) pronounce the blessings normally said before and after the *Shema*, nor
   b) recite the evening prayer, nor
   c) make *Havdalah* over a cup,

   until after the burial.

b. 1) An *onein* in this position should not listen to *Havdalah* recited by someone else either, with the intention of thereby discharging his own obligation in that respect.

2) If he does, his obligation is not discharged, and he will still have to make *Havdalah* after the burial.*

c. 1) If the funeral took place after Shabbath, he should make *Havdalah* as soon thereafter as he can,** but in any case before the sun sets on Tuesday.

2) If the funeral took place after Yom Tov or Yom Kippur, he only has until sunset on the following day to make *Havdalah*.

3) However, he can pronounce the blessings on the spices and on the light only when making *Havdalah* on the night Shabbath or Yom Kippur, as the case may be, expires, and not if he recites *Havdalah* on the following day (or later).

4) See further, Chapter 58, paragraph 20.

d. 1) a) When he makes *Havdalah* after the funeral, he should, if possible, not use his own wine. (See

---

* There is a contrary opinion, to the effect that, after the event, the obligation of the *onein* is discharged if he has made or heard *Havdalah*, and he must not repeat it again later.

** He should not eat after the burial until he has made *Havdalah* over a cup.

Chapter 65, paragraph 1.)

b) His neighbors should provide him with the wine for *Havdalah*.

2) In accordance with the rule mentioned in Chapter 60, paragraph 23, and Chapter 65, paragraph 35, he

a) does not say the preliminary verses commencing, "*Hinei Keil yeshuathi ...*," but

b) begins *Havdalah* directly with the blessing on wine.

eating and performing forbidden activities before Havdalah

26. *a.* An *onein* who is waiting for the funeral to take place after Shabbath or Yom Tov may eat without making *Havdalah*.

b. 1) He may also, after the expiration of Shabbath or Yom Tov, perform, for the purposes of the deceased, activities which are prohibited on Shabbath or Yom Tov, even though he has not made *Havdalah*.

2) Nevertheless, he would do well, before performing such an activity,

a) to say, "*Baruch Ha-Mavdil bein kodesh le-chol*," or

b) to listen to somebody else saying it, with the intention of discharging for him whatever liability he may have to make *Havdalah*.

c. 1) If the funeral takes place on the night Shabbath or Yom Tov expired, he should recite the evening prayer after the burial, with the insertion of "*Atah chonantanu*," but,

2) if it does not take place until the next morning, he should recite the morning prayer after the burial, but without inserting "*Atah chonantanu*" in the *Shemoneh Esrei*.

TEFILLIN, MOURNERS ABROAD, DEATH CERTIFICATES, CHOL HA-MO'ED AND PRELIMINARY PREPARATIONS

tefillin

27. *a.* The general rule is that a mourner for a close relative (as defined in paragraph 3 above) does not put on *tefillin* on the day of the burial.

b. If the burial takes place on the evening Shabbath or Yom Tov expires, he should not put on *tefillin* on the morrow,

1) even if the death occurred on Shabbath or Yom Tov, or
2) even if it occurred the day before Shabbath or Yom Tov, but there was insufficient time to arrange the burial for the same day.

c. 1) a) When a burial takes place on Yom Tov (through the agency of a non-Jew, as mentioned in paragraph 16 above,) in Eretz Yisrael, where only one day of Yom Tov is observed, the mourners should not put on *tefillin* the next day.

b) Nonetheless, there are those who hold that, in this situation, the mourners should put on *tefillin* the next day.

2) All the authorities are, however, agreed that, when a burial takes place

a) outside Eretz Yisrael, either on the first day of Yom Tov or on *yom tov sheini shel galuyoth*, or
b) on either day of Rosh Hashana, whether inside or outside Eretz Yisrael,

the mourners should put on *tefillin* the day after the Festival, pronouncing the usual blessings.

d. 1) In places where it is customary to put on *tefillin* on *chol ha-mo'ed*, the mourners should also put them on,

a) whether the funeral took place on Yom Tov (as in paragraph 16 above), or
b) whether the funeral took place on the expiry of Yom Tov (that is to say, on the first evening of *chol ha-mo'ed*), or
c) even when the deceased died on *chol ha-mo'ed* and was buried on that same day,

but, if it is the day of the funeral (including the morrow after the evening of the funeral), without pronouncing the usual blessings.

2) After *chol ha-mo'ed* and the last day of the Festival,

they should put on *t^efillin*, with the usual blessings, even on their first day of open mourning.

mourners abroad

28. *a.* When a resident of Eretz Yisrael (who intends to return home) is outside Eretz Yisrael, and a close relative of his (as defined in paragraph 3 above) dies there on *yom tov sheini shel galuyoth*,

1) he does not tear his clothes in mourning on that day, but
2) all of the laws which apply to an *onein* apply to him, even if he has no possibility of arranging the funeral for the same day; however,
3) this latter rule is not universally accepted, and there is a view that the laws relating to an *onein* do not apply to him if he has no possibility of arranging the funeral for that day.

b. In the parallel situation of somebody from outside Eretz Yisrael who happens to be in Eretz Yisrael (but intends to return home) when a close relative dies on *yom tov sheini shel galuyoth*, the situation is as follows:

1) He does not tear his clothes in mourning on *yom tov sheini shel galuyoth*.
2) If it is possible for him to arrange the burial for that day, all the laws of an *onein* apply to him, as outlined in paragraphs 18 and 23 above.
3) If not, the rules set out in paragraph 20 above apply.
4) a) He may participate in the funeral of his relative (or of anyone else for that matter), on *yom tov sheini shel galuyoth* and
   b) he may even help carry the bier, but
   c) he should not be present if the deceased is eulogized, since it is, after all, Yom Tov for him.
   d) Nevertheless, there are those who hold that he may attend the eulogy of his deceased relative or of a Torah sage delivered at the funeral.

death certificate

29. *a.* One may not ask for a death certificate to be written out on Shabbath or Yom Tov, unless the absence of a certificate would make it impossible to perform the burial on the expiry of Shabbath or Yom Tov, or would otherwise result in indignity to the deceased.*

b. In such case,

1) if the doctor is not Jewish, one may ask him to write out and sign the certificate, and,

2) if he is Jewish, one may request him to tell a non-Jew to do the writing and signing.

c. 1) There is generally no justification for the Jew to write or sign the death certificate, although

2) there is room for permitting him to do so on *yom tov sheini shel galuyoth*, or on the second day of Rosh Hashana, provided this will enable the interment to take place that day.

30. It is forbidden to eulogize a deceased on *chol ha-mo'ed*, and the custom is not to do so even at the funeral of a deceased Torah sage. *eulogies*

31. *a.* One may do whatever is needed for a deceased on *chol ha-mo'ed*, even work which one performs in a professional (as distinct from an amateurish) manner. *chol ha-mo'ed*

b. Nonetheless, one should not pull up grass, as some are accustomed to do after the interment of the body. (See Chapter 67, paragraph 43.)

c. One may wash one's hands after leaving the cemetery, even if the water spills on to sown ground. (See Chapter 68, paragraph 31.)

d. After the burial,

1) the mourners do not remove their shoes, since open mourning is prohibited on *chol ha-mo'ed*, but

2) those who attended the funeral line up (where this is the custom) and comfort the mourners who pass before them.

---

* See also paragraph 4 above.

waiting for a bus

32. *a.* 1) A person may, towards the end of Shabbath or Yom Tov, walk to a bus station and wait there, so that, as soon as Shabbath or Yom Tov expires, he can board a bus,* with the object, for example, of going

a) to obtain a burial licence or

b) to have obituary notices printed.

2) This is not an infringement of the prohibition (based on Isaiah, Chapter 58, verse 13), against "pursuing your business" on Shabbath, since he is engaged in doing a mitzva, which is the business of Heaven. (See Chapter 29, paragraph 12.)

making arrangements verbally

b. 1) He may also speak

a) with the representatives of the burial society, so that they should come straight after Shabbath or Yom Tov to make arrangements for the funeral, and

b) with the printers, so that they should print the notices straight after Shabbath or Yom Tov.

2) a) He should not, however, discuss the amount of their remuneration with them.

b) What he can do is promise to pay them the next day whatever is the standard price for the work, or whatever they will agree between them.

---

* He must make suitable arrangements to travel, since he is not permitted to take fare money or a ticket with him.

Chapter 65

Laws of Mourning on Shabbath and Yom Tov in General

THE FIRST MEAL AFTER THE BURIAL

1. *a.* 1) A mourner (for a close relative, as defined in Chapter 64, paragraph 3) is not allowed to eat the first meal after the burial from his own food. *the mitzva*

2) The same applies to the first meal after receiving news that a close relative has passed away within the preceding thirty days.

b. It is a mitzva for the neighbors to bring him their food.*

c. The meal should include

1) bread or cake and

2) a shelled, hard-boiled egg.

d. 1) There are those who permit the mourner also to eat some of his own food, other than bread (and cake), at the first meal.

2) According to other opinions, even what he drinks should not be his own.

2. *a.* If the burial takes place close to the commencement of Shabbath or Yom Tov, it is as well *burial close to Shabbath or Yom Tov*

1) for the neighbors not to bring food for the first meal, and

2) for the mourners not to eat their own food until they have their Shabbath or Yom Tov meal in the evening. (See Chapter 42, paragraphs 25, 28 and 31.)

b. A mourner who does not eat a meal from other people's food on Friday or on the day before Yom Tov has no obligation to do so subsequently, neither on Shabbath or Yom Tov nor afterwards.

---

* If nobody brings him food, he does not have to fast, and may eat his own food.

c. 1) If the burial takes place on the evening Shabbath or Yom Tov expires, the mourners should not eat their first meal from their own food even if they only want to have it the next morning.

2) With respect to the wine for *Havdalah*, see Chapter 64, paragraph 25.

burial on Yom Tov

3. When the burial is performed on Yom Tov (on the first day through the agency of a non-Jew, and on the second day by a Jew, as explained in Chapter 64, paragraph 16), the mourners do not have to eat a meal from other people's food at all, neither on that day, nor after Yom Tov.

burial on chol ha-mo'ed

4. *a.* 1) When the burial takes place on *chol ha-mo'ed*, the next meal which the mourners eat that day should be from other people's food.

2) Should it be one of the intermediate days of Sukkoth, they have to eat the meal in the *sukka*.

b. 1) The custom in Jerusalem on *chol ha-mo'ed* is to bring food for the first meal after the funeral only to those who are mourning for their father or their mother.

2) According to this custom, food is not brought for other mourners, unless they are present when it is being brought to the son or daughter of the deceased.

c. 1) When food is brought to mourners for their first meal after the burial on *chol ha-mo'ed*, it can comprise bread, cake and so forth, but should not include eggs, as it would do on other days of the year.

2) The mourners should sit at the table in the normal way, and not on the floor.

COUNTING SHABBATH AND YOM TOV AS DAYS OF MOURNING

burial just before Shabbath or Yom Tov

5. *a.* If a burial took place shortly before the commencement of Shabbath, so that, in practice, the mourners did not start observing the laws of mourning at all before Shabbath, Friday is, nevertheless, counted as the first of the Seven

Days of Mourning.

b. 1) However, if a burial took place shortly before the commencement of a Festival, and the mourners did not observe the laws of mourning at all before Yom Tov, not even for a short while ,

a) the day before Yom Tov is not counted as one of the days of mourning and

b) the laws of mourning will have to be observed at the end of the Festival.

2) The rules concerning the reckoning of the Seven Days of Mourning are the same as those set out in paragraphs 38 and 51 below.

6. *a.* Shabbath does not interrupt the reckoning of the days of mourning, but is counted as one of the Seven Days. *curtailing days of mourning*

b. Yom Tov, on the other hand, can bring the mourning to a premature close, as explained in paragraph 37 below.

PREPARING FOR SHABBATH AND YOM TOV

7. *a.* 1) All the laws of mourning apply on Friday, or on the day before Yom Tov, until close to the commencement of Shabbath or of the Festival (and see further paragraph 45 below, with particular reference to Yom Tov). *how the mourner should prepare*

2) There are, however, authorities who take a more lenient view, and hold that, on these days, a mourner should not conduct himself in accordance with the laws of mourning from the time of *p^elag ha-minchah* onwards.

b. 1) Thus the mourner may put on his shoes in honor of Shabbath (shortly before Shabbath, according to the former, stricter view, and from the time of *p^elag ha-minchah* onwards, according to the latter, more lenient view), and may sit on a chair.

2) a) He may also wash his face, hands and feet, but not the whole of his body, in cold water (as indeed he may on an ordinary weekday).

b) He may not immerse himself in a *mikveh*, even if the water is cold, and even if he is in the habit of immersing himself in a *mikveh* every Friday.

3) He would do well to recite the afternoon prayer before making his preparations in anticipation of Shabbath or Yom Tov.

c. Whether one takes the stricter view (as in *a*1) above) or the more lenient view (as in *a*2) above), a mourner may, towards the beginning of Shabbath or a Festival, spread laundered cloths on the tables in his house, as usual before Shabbath or a Festival.

d. 1) The custom in Eretz Yisrael, following the opinion of the Vilna Gaon, is for the mourner to put on his Shabbath and Yom Tov clothes in honor of Shabbath and Yom Tov.*

2) a) Nonetheless, there are those whose custom is for the mourner not to wear Shabbath or Yom Tov clothes during the whole period of mourning (twelve months on the decease of a father or mother and thirty days for other relatives).

b) At all events, he should not wear torn clothes on Shabbath or Yom Tov.

e. The mourner may do housework, such as sweeping, or washing the floor, so there is nothing wrong with his cleaning the house in honor of Shabbath.

mirrors

8. *a.* The practice is to cover the mirrors in the house of mourning, but,

b. on Friday afternoon, prior to the kindling of the Shabbath lights, the covers should be removed for the duration of the Shabbath.

memorial light

9. *a.* The custom is for a light to be left burning in the place where the deceased expired, from the time of the death until the end of the Seven Days of Mourning.

---

* The mourner may change his underwear and socks even on a weekday, if he does so owing to perspiration.

b. In the event that the light was not lit before Shabbath, due to forgetfulness, or if the light went out, it is permitted, during *bein ha-sh^emashoth*, to tell a non-Jew to kindle it.

c. Once the stars have come out, however, on Shabbath eve, it is forbidden to tell a non-Jew to put on the light.

d. Indeed, even if the non-Jew comes of his own accord to kindle the light after the stars have come out, the Jew must protest.

e. So far as concerns kindling a light in honor of a deceased on Yom Tov, see Chapter 64, paragraph 5.

OBSERVING THE LAWS OF MOURNING ON SHABBATH

10. *a.* 1) On Shabbath, certain of the laws which apply during the Seven Days of Mourning are observed, while others are not. *the principle*

2) a) Those laws which are generally observed in privacy, or whose observance is not an obvious indication of mourning, apply on Shabbath.

b) Those which are an open demonstration of a state of mourning are not kept on Shabbath.

b. The following are forbidden under the head of "private" mourning, and are consequently prohibited on Shabbath too:

1) washing the whole of the body, even in cold water;
2) washing even parts of the body in warm water;
3) marital intercourse;
4) studying Torah (even in silent meditation). (See further paragraph 11 below.)

c. The following laws openly demonstrate a state of mourning, and should not be kept on Shabbath:

1) not wearing leather shoes;
2) wearing a torn garment;*
3) sitting on the floor (or on a very low seat).

---

* With regard to the clothes to be worn on Shabbath, see paragraph 7 above.

d. 1) When the seventh day of mourning occurs on Shabbath, the laws relating to "private" mourning should be observed until after prayers on Shabbath morning.

2) Subsequently, all activities which are prohibited only during the first Seven Days of Mourning, including those which are forbidden under the head of "private" mourning, are permitted.

the weekly portion of the Torah

11. Even though a mourner may not study Torah during the whole of the Seven Days of Mourning, including Shabbath (as mentioned in paragraph 10 above), he may, on Shabbath, read the weekly portion of the Torah (twice), with its *Targum*,* but

a. he should not study it with the commentary of Rashi and,

b. if the seventh day of mourning falls on Shabbath, he would do well to delay reading the portion and its *Targum* until after prayers in the synagogue on Shabbath morning.

greetings

12. *a.* A mourner may greet other people on a Shabbath which falls within the Seven Days of Mourning.

b. 1) So far as concerns other people's greeting him, this is dependent on the local custom.

2) In some places, a lenient attitude is taken; in others, the approach is strict.

c. In places where they are strict, one should try not to meet the mourner on Shabbath, so that one should not have to greet him, in order to avoid giving the appearance of an open show of mourning on Shabbath.

Friday night prayers

13. *a.* A mourner does not say

1) the psalms which it is customary to recite towards the commencement of Shabbath (up to *Mizmor shir l^e^-yom ha-Shabbath*) nor

2) the second Chapter of the Mishnayoth, Tractate

* See Chapter 42, paragraph 57.

Shabbath ("*Ba-meh madlikin*"), which it is the practice to say during the Friday night service.

b. 1) However, mourners who do say these psalms and "*Ba-meh madlikin*" have authorities on whom they can rely.

2) Furthermore, according to these latter authorities, a person who customarily recites the Song of Songs between the end of the psalms with which one receives Shabbath and the beginning of the evening prayer can do so also when he is in mourning.

c. All the authorities are agreed that a mourner says *Mizmor shir le-yom ha-Shabbath* and thereby receives the Shabbath, in the usual way.

"seven-in-one" blessing

14. If prayers are said with a *minyan* in the mourner's house on Friday night, the "seven-in-one" blessing* is not recited (since it is said only in a fixed place of prayer).

Shabbath hymns

15. *a.* 1) During the first Seven Days of Mourning a mourner may sing the usual Shabbath hymns at home, including the hymn, "*Shalom aleichem,*" on Friday night, although

2) there are those who hold that he should not say "*Shalom aleichem.*"

she-hecheyanu

b. A mourner may recite the *she-hecheyanu* blessing over new season's fruit.

"Tzidkathcha tzedek"

16. When the Shabbath *minchah* prayer is said in the house of a mourner, the verses commencing "*Tzidkathcha tzedek*" are recited as usual.

Avoth

17. A mourner during his first Seven Days of Mourning does not say

a. the Mishnayoth from Tractate Avoth which it is customary to say after the Shabbath *minchah* prayer in the summer, nor

---

* See Glossary.

"Bar^e^chi nafshi"

b. the psalms beginning "*Bar^e^chi nafshi*" which it is customary to say in the winter.

psalms after service

18. When praying in the house of a mourner on Shabbath, one does not add any of the special psalms which it is usual to recite in the house of a mourner after prayers on a weekday.

visiting mourners

19. *a.* 1) The Talmud (*Shabbath* 12b) recounts us that the Rabbis only reluctantly permitted the visiting of mourners on Shabbath for the purpose of comforting them, because they were afraid that the visitors themselves would grieve with the mourners on Shabbath.

2) Therefore, the conduct of those who come to visit mourners only on Shabbath is to be deprecated.

3) However, someone who is so busy during the week that he cannot find the time to come and comfort a mourner may come on Shabbath.

4) The form of words to be addressed to the mourner on Shabbath is, "One may not comfort on Shabbath, but comfort is near at hand."

b. At all events, it is not the custom nowadays to go to a mourner to comfort him on Shabbath.

preparing for mikveh

20. *a.* According to one widely accepted view, a married woman who is due to immerse herself in the *mikveh* on the expiry of Shabbath should wash her hair in preparation before Shabbath commences.

b. Nevertheless, in the event that she is a mourner, and her seventh day of mourning falls on that Shabbath, she should, if possible, postpone washing her hair until after Shabbath.

c. If this is not possible,

1) she should wash her hair prior to Shabbath, in the same way as she would on any other day of the week, in warm water, but

2) she should not cut her fingernails until after Shabbath.

21. *a.* It is customary for certain relations of the deceased who are not among the close relatives listed in Chapter 64, paragraph 3, also to keep some of the laws of mourning. *more distant relatives*

b. Examples of such relations are
1) a grandson (or granddaughter) on the death of his grandfather (or grandmother) and
2) a son-in-law (or daughter-in-law) on the death of his father-in-law (or mother-in-law).

c. They follow this custom
1) whether or not they are in the presence of the obligatory mourners (the close relatives), but
2) only until the end of the first Shabbath after the burial.

d. They do not
1) wash themselves in warm water, nor
2) have their hair cut or shave, nor
3) cut their nails, nor
4) attend social dinners, even if the meal is a mitzva, nor
5) wear their Shabbath clothes on an ordinary day of the week (or even on Shabbath in a place where ordinary mourners do not wear them on Shabbath).*

e. Still, the practice is for them to be lenient
1) regarding washing themselves a little in honor of Shabbath, and
2) regarding cutting their hair in honor of Shabbath, if it has grown long (and shaving, if they are used to shaving every day).

f. Furthermore, if the seventh day of mourning occurs on Shabbath, these more distant relations may do whatever is required in honor of Shabbath.

---

* See paragraph 7*d* above.

THE MOURNER IN THE SYNAGOGUE ON SHABBATH AND YOM TOV

general custom on Friday night

22. *a.* 1) The custom is for the mourner to go to the synagogue on the Shabbath which occurs during the first seven days of mourning.

2) On Friday evening, when he comes to the synagogue, close to the commencement of Shabbath, he should wait at the entrance until the congregation is about to receive Shabbath, and then,

3) just before *Mizmor shir le-yom ha-Shabbath* is said, the entry of the mourner is announced, senior members of the community go out to meet him and invite him in, and the congregation comforts him as he enters.

4) See paragraph 24 below, regarding the mourner's changing his seat.

b. 1) One does not go out to meet the mourner on a Friday evening which occurs

a) during a Festival, or even

b) immediately on the expiry of a Festival,

if the mourner did not begin observing the laws of mourning before the Festival commenced.*

2) This could be the case where the burial took place

a) only shortly before the Festival began, as in paragraph 5*b* above,

b) on the first day of a Festival, through the agency of a non-Jew, or on the second day (whether the second day of Rosh Hashana or *yom tov sheini shel galuyoth*), through the agency of a Jew, as explained in Chapter 64, paragraph 16, or

c) on *chol ha-mo'ed*.

c. 1) On the first Friday night after a Festival, one goes out to meet the mourner (subject to *b* above), but only if seven days, starting with the day of the burial, have not yet passed.

---

* One should behave as in paragraph 23 below.

2) See further paragraph 38 below.

late arrival on Friday night

23. *a.* One does not go out to meet a mourner who comes to the synagogue after the congregation has already received Shabbath (for instance, by reciting *Bo'i ve-shalom* or *Mizmor shir le-yom ha-Shabbath*).

b. He should enter the synagogue unannounced, and individuals may come up to him and comfort him. (See paragraph 19 above.)

changing seat

24. *a.* 1) The prevalent custom among Ashkenazi Jews is for a mourner to change his seat in the synagogue, even on Shabbath.

2) a) Nevertheless, the Rabbi of the city and specially important personnages should not change their places in the usual manner on Shabbath, since this could be considered an affront to the honor of the community, at whose head they stand.

b) They would, however, do well to make the change unobtrusively, by moving to another seat close to their own.

b. 1) The custom is practiced

a) during the twelve-month mourning period for a father or mother and

b) during the thirty-day mourning period, commencing with the day of the burial, for other relatives.

2) Some authorities hold that a mourner for a father or mother may also take a more lenient course on Shabbath, and sit in his usual place after the expiry of thirty days beginning with the day of the burial.

c. 1) According to one view, a mourner who, during his first seven days of mourning, comes to the synagogue,

a) on Friday night, after Shabbath has been received, or

b) on Shabbath, during the day,

should not change his seat.

2) According to another view, he should change his seat even then.

d. 1) If the death took place on Yom Tov or *chol ha-mo'ed*, the mourner should not change his seat until the end of the Festival, since it is only then that he begins to observe those laws which openly demonstrate a state of mourning.

2) See also paragraph 39 below.

kaddish: general rule

25. *a.* 1) In some places, it is the custom for only one person at a time to recite the mourner's *kaddish*, and there are rules for deciding which of those who are obliged to say the *kaddish* has precedence.

2) Where this is the custom, if someone mourning for his father or mother comes to the synagogue on Shabbath during the Seven Days of Mourning, he has precedence in saying the *kaddish* after *Aleinu* at the end of each of the prayers during the day,

a) even if he does not regularly attend that synagogue, but is a visitor, and

b) even if there is also present a person who needs to say *kaddish* because he has *yahrzeit* for one of his parents that same day.

b. When the mourner is a minor (under thirteen years of age), he nonetheless has the same rights to say *kaddish* as an adult, subject to the following reservations:

1) A person who has *yahrzeit* for his parents takes precedence over the minor in saying *kaddish* after *Aleinu* at the end of **one** of the services during the course of the Shabbath.

2) a) In the event that more than one person who has *yahrzeit* that day for his father or mother is present, **each** one of them takes precedence over the minor in saying *kaddish* after *Aleinu* at **one** of the services.

b) This is so, even if, as a result, there will be no such *kaddish* at all left for the minor to say.

c. As to *kaddish* said during other parts of the service, for example after the psalm specifically allotted to each day of the week, the mourner within the Seven Days of

Mourning has no precedence over other mourners.

26. *a.* 1) As explained in paragraph 37 below, if a mourner starts observing the laws of mourning before the commencement of a Festival, for however short a time, the festival cuts short his Seven Days of Mourning. *kaddish: effect of Yom Tov*

2) So far as concerns saying *kaddish* throughout the seven days beginning with the day of the burial, a mourner in this situation has the same rights as a minor (regarding which, see paragraph 25*b* above).

b. 1) The position with regard to *kaddish* of a mourner who did not start observing the laws of mourning at all before the Festival (for example because the burial took place on Yom Tov, as in Chapter 64, paragraph 16) is similar.

2) That is to say, he has the same rights, throughout the first seven days commencing with the day of the burial, as the minor in paragraph 25*b* above.

3) It should be noted, however, that, when these seven days are over, he has the same rights as any other mourner within the thirty-day period of mourning, even if he is observing Seven Days of Mourning after the Festival, as in paragraph 38 below.

c. These customs are, of course, relevant solely in a place where only one person at a time recites *kaddish*, and not in a place where all the mourners say *kaddish* together.

27. *a.* 1) The custom is that, with the exceptions mentioned below, a mourner does not lead prayers before the congregation on Shabbath or Yom Tov, or even on *chol ha-mo'ed*. *leading prayers*

2) This applies

a) to someone in mourning for his father or mother, during the twelve-month period of mourning, and

b) to someone in mourning for other relatives, until the end of thirty days from the day of the burial.

3) He should not lead prayers even for the introductory hymns forming the earlier part of the morning

service.

b. A mourner may lead prayers on Shabbath, Yom Tov or *chol ha-mo'ed*, even during the first seven days of mourning, if
1) he is the regular prayer leader in that synagogue, or
2) there is nobody else present who is as fit to lead prayers as he is.

c. After the first seven days of mourning, a mourner may lead prayers on the *yahrzeit* of his father or mother which falls on Shabbath, Yom Tov or *chol ha-mo'ed*.

blowing shofar

28. *a.* One should not appoint a mourner to blow the *shofar* on Rosh Hashana, unless
1) he regularly blows the *shofar* in that synagogue or
2) there is nobody else there who is as fit to blow the *shofar* as he is.

b. This applies both to
1) a mourner for his father or mother during the twelve-month mourning period and
2) a mourner for other relatives during the thirty-day mourning period.

reading Torah

29. *a.* 1) It is better for a mourner within the first seven days of mourning not to go, on Shabbath, to a synagogue where he usually reads to the congregation from the *sefer Torah*.
2) He may, however, go to that synagogue, and read from the *sefer Torah*, if there is no other synagogue to which he could go.
3) He may also read from the *sefer Torah* in a synagogue where nobody else knows how to do so.

b. The rules with regard to reading from the *sefer Torah* in the twelve months of mourning for a parent, or during the thirty days of mourning for other relations, are the same as those with regard to leading prayers. (See paragraph 27*a* and *b* above).

30. *a.* 1) It is forbidden (except as mentioned below) to call up a mourner within his Seven Days of Mourning to the reading of the Torah, even on Shabbath. *being called up to Torah*

2) If his seventh day of mourning falls on Shabbath, it is better not to call him up during the morning service, but only at *minchah*.

b. In the following cases, a mourner may go up to the reading of the Torah on the Shabbath which occurs during the Seven Days of Mourning:

1) after the event, if he has been called up;

2) if the practice is to call him up to the Torah every Shabbath, so that failure to call him up on this Shabbath will amount to an open demonstration of mourning;

3) if

a) the mourner is a *kohen* or a Levite and

b) there is no other *kohen* or Levite* in the synagogue to be called up to the reading of the first and second sections respectively of the portion for the week.

c. There are those who take a lenient approach and also call up to the Torah mourners who are considered to have an obligation to be called up, for instance

1) a mourner whose son is being circumcised that Shabbath, or

2) a mourner who has *yahrzeit* for one of his parents on that Shabbath, or during the course of the ensuing week (and whom it is customary to call up for the reading of *maftir*).

d. None the less, if a mourner anticipates that one of the situations listed in *b* or in *c* above may arise, it is preferable for him to avoid being in the synagogue during the reading of the Torah, so that they should not come to call him up.

e. There is a custom for a mourner, after the Seven Days

---

* A Levite has to be called up to the reading of the second section only if a *kohen* has been called up to the reading of the first.

of Mourning, to be called up for *maftir* during the whole twelve-month period of mourning for his father or mother.

priestly blessings

31. *a.* 1) A *kohen* who is within the Seven Days of Mourning ought not to go up to pronounce the priestly blessings before the congregation,
a) even on Shabbath, and
b) even when there is no other *kohen* in the synagogue.

2) If he can, he should go out of the synagogue before the person leading prayers starts to say aloud the blessing in the *Shemoneh Esrei* commencing, "*Retzei.*"

3) In the event that he
a) did not leave the synagogue, and
b) was requested to go up to pronounce the blessings,
he should go up, because, in those circumstances, he would otherwise be violating three positive obligations to bless the people.

b. 1) There are those who hold that, in general, a mourner for a parent should not go up to pronounce the priestly blessing for the whole twelve-month mourning period, and a mourner for other relations during the whole thirty-day mourning period.

2) They make an exception where there are not two other *kohanim* in the synagogue, in which case he should go up.

c. 1) Notwithstanding the above, there is a custom that a mourner does go up to say the priestly blessings, even during the Seven Days of Mourning.

2) This is especially so if there is no other *kohen*, and, in that case, the mourner should go up, since, if he leaves the synagogue, the mitzva of blessing the congregation will not be performed at all.

3) a) He should likewise go up to bless when there is only one other *kohen*, apart from himself,

in the synagogue.

b) The grounds for this are an opinion to the effect that the Torah (as distinct from the Rabbinical) obligation is fulfilled only when the mitzva is performed by at least two *kohanim* blessing the congregation.

32. *a.* The custom is that *Hallel* is not said in the house of mourning on *rosh chodesh* or Chanuka, either by the mourner or by the others praying there* (except as mentioned immediately below). *Hallel*

b. 1) If, however, the mourner comes to the synagogue on a Shabbath which is *rosh chodesh* or Chanuka, or if prayers are said then in his house, *Hallel* is recited.

2) According to some, even the mourner himself is then permitted to recite *Hallel*.

c. When the burial took place on Yom Tov (as in Chapter 64, paragraph 16), or on *chol ha-mo'ed*, and the mourner comes to the synagogue on Yom Tov or *chol ha-mo'ed*, he says *Hallel* as usual with the rest of the congregation.

THE LAWS OF MOURNING ON THE TERMINATION OF SHABBATH

33. *a.* On the termination of Shabbath, the mourner should remove his shoes after the intonation of *Bar^{e}chu*, except that, *changing shoes and clothes*

b. if he is going to lead prayers, he should say, "*Baruch Ha-Mavdil bein kodesh l^{e}-chol*" and take off his shoes before intoning *Bar^{e}chu*.

c. When he takes off his shoes, he should also change out of his clothes and put on his torn mourning clothes.

34. *a.* 1) There are places where a mourner *omissions in evening service*

a) does not say the verse commencing "*Vi-y^{e}hi no'am*" after the *Sh^{e}moneh Esrei* at the evening

---

* On Chanuka (as distinct from *rosh chodesh*), the others should recite *Hallel* later, when they go home.

prayer on the expiration of Shabbath, but

b) goes straight on to "*Yosheiv b^e^-seither*" (Psalm 91).

2) In other places, the custom is that he should say "*Vi-y^e^hi no'am*" too, since it forms part of the normal order of the service.

b. 1) Similarly, some have the custom that a mourner should not say the passages beginning "*V^e^-yithen l^e^cha*" at the end of the evening service on the expiration of Shabbath, whereas

2) others have the custom that he should say it, since it forms part of the normal order of the service at the end of Shabbath.

Havdalah

35. *a.* 1) A mourner may himself make *Havdalah* over a cup, but

2) he does not say the verses which normally precede the blessing on the wine.

b. As to the blessing on the spices, some have the custom that a mourner does not say it, while others have the custom that he does.

sanctifying new moon

36. *a.* A mourner in his first seven says of mourning is permitted to sanctify the new moon, if the time for its sanctification will pass before the end of the seven days.

b. He may even go outside his house for this purpose.

c. Yet, one should not address to him the greeting, "*Shalom aleichem*," which is customary on this occasion, nor should he greet others in this way.

d. Indeed, he should not say more than the blessing on the sanctification of the new moon, and not the usual psalms and other additions.

LAWS OF MOURNING ON FESTIVALS

curtailing days of mourning

37. *a.* Yom Tov brings the Seven Days of Mourning to a premature end, if the mourner started at least partially, to observe the laws of mourning before Yom Tov began.

(See also paragraph 5 above.)

b. Since there are many details regarding the counting of the days of mourning and their interruption, both as to the seven-day period and the thirty-day period, it is well to consult a rabbi who is an expert on these laws.

38. *a.* 1) The usual laws of mourning do not apply until after the last day of the Festival, if the burial takes place *burial during Festival*

a) on the first day of Yom Tov (through the agency of a non-Jew),

b) on the second day of Rosh Hashana or on *yom tov sheini shel galuyoth* (through the agency of a Jew), or

c) on *chol ha-mo'ed.**

2) Nevertheless, in these cases, the mourner should, during the Festival, observe those laws which are not an open indication of mourning, that is to say

a) he should not wash even parts of his body in warm water,

b) he should not wash the whole of his body even in cold water,

c) he should not engage in marital intercourse and

d) he should not study Torah.

3) There are, however, those who are lenient with regard to the study of Torah.

b. A mourner in this situation ought not to be called up to the reading of the Torah, except on Simchath Torah, when the custom is to call up all the members of the congregation.

c. 1) A mourner should not carry on his work, including business or trade, during the Seven Days of Mourning.

2) Thus, a mourner of the type under discussion (that is to say where the burial took place during the Festival, as above) should not himself open his store

---

* For another case where the observance of the usual laws of mourning does not commence until after the Festival, see paragraph 5 above.

on *chol ha-mo'ed.*

3) This is so, even if he sells items which it is permitted to sell on *chol ha-mo'ed* (as explained in Chapter 67, paragraph 27 below).
4) Still, he may put someone else into his store, to sell his merchandise for him.
5) Moreover, if
   a) he has nobody to take his place in the store and
   b) he is accustomed to opening his store every *chol ha-mo'ed*,

   he can rely on the opinion of certain authorities who permit him to sell his goods himself, otherwise he might appear to be giving a public demonstration of mourning.

d. 1) One comforts the mourner during the whole seven-day period commencing with the burial, including on *chol ha-mo'ed*, or even on Yom Tov itself.
2) At the end of the seven days, there is no longer any need to comfort him, even though he is still observing the laws relating to the first seven days of mourning.
3) See further, paragraph 22 above.

e. 1) The mourner in these circumstances (where the burial took place during the Festival, as above) starts to count the Seven Days of Mourning immediately after
   a) the seventh day of Pesach,
   b) the first day of Shavuoth,
   c) Shemini Atzereth or
   d) the first day of Rosh Hashana.
2) a) The second day of Rosh Hashana is counted as the first day of mourning, even though it is Yom Tov, so that only the laws relating to "private" mourning can be observed.
   b) The same is true of the eighth day of Pesach, the second day of Shavuoth and Simchath Torah, outside the Land of Israel, where it is still Yom Tov.
   c) Shabbath occurring on the morrow of the Fes-

tival is also counted as one of the Seven Days of Mourning (despite the fact that only "private" mourning will have been observed for the first two of the Seven Days of Mourning).

3) See further paragraphs 22 and 26 above.

f. The days of the Festival from the day of the burial and onwards are counted towards the thirty-day mourning period, since "private" mourning has to be observed, as in *a* above.

39. *a.* If the burial took place on Yom Tov or *chol ha-mo'ed*, the mourners do not change their places in the synagogue during the Festival, since they will not yet have started openly to observe the laws of mourning.* *changing place*

b. According to one view, even a mourner who began openly to observe the laws of mourning before Yom Tov does not change his place in the synagogue during the Festival.

40. *a.* 1) A mourner for his father or mother, during the twelve-month mourning period, and a mourner for other relatives, during the thirty-day mourning period, is allowed to wear a *kitel* on Yom Kippur, although *wearing kitel*

2) there are places where it is the custom for mourners not to wear it.

b. 1) On Pesach too, differing customs exist with respect to wearing a *kitel* on the seder night.

2) a) Some have the custom that a mourner should not wear it, whereas,

b) in the view of others, if a mourner puts on a *kitel* on the seder night, one should not raise any objection.

41. *a.* 1) There are various customs as to whether a mourner (for a parent, in the twelve-month mourning pe- *Sukkoth*

---

* A mourner in this situation should, nevertheless, not leave his house, except to go to the synagogue.

riod, and, for other relatives, during the thirty-day mourning period,) should join the procession around the synagogue with his *lulav* on Sukkoth.

2) According to one opinion, he should refrain from doing so, but, to avoid giving an open indication of mourning, he
   a) should not just stand still with his *lulav*, but should give it to someone who wishes to join the procession, or
   b) should try to be chosen as the person who takes the *sefer Torah* out of the ark and holds it while the others walk around with their *lulavim*.
3) Others have the custom that a mourner walks around with his *lulav* on the Yom Tov of Sukkoth, and on Hoshanah Rabbah, but not on the other days of *chol ha-mo'ed*.
4) Yet another authority writes that a mourner loses nothing by walking round with his *lulav* on all the days of the Festival (including *chol ha-mo'ed*) and indeed performs a mitzva for which he will be rewarded.

Simchath Torah

b. 1) There are also varying customs concerning walking around the synagogue with a *sefer Torah* on Simchath Torah.
2) At all events, a mourner should not join in the dancing.

THE DAY PRECEDING SHABBATH OR YOM TOV

The following paragraphs explain how, when it comes to the relaxation of the laws of mourning, the Rabbis have drawn distinctions between

A. Shabbath and Yom Tov,
B. the day preceding Pesach and the day preceding other Festivals,
C. the seven-day period of mourning and the thirty-day period of mourning, and
D. the different restrictions on washing oneself, cutting nails,

laundering one's clothing and cutting one's hair or beard.

cutting hair and washing within thirty days

42. *a.* 1) A mourner for a relation other than a parent is not allowed to cut his hair or beard, even in honor of Shabbath, for a period of thirty days.

2) In the case of a mourner for a father or mother, the prohibition lasts until his friends rebuke him because of the length of his hair, so long as at least thirty days have elapsed.

b. 1) For as long as he observes the thirty-day mourning period, a mourner should not wash his body in warm water,

a) not even just his face, hands or feet, and

b) not even in honor of Shabbath.

2) a) The custom is to be strict also about washing the whole body (as distinct from just parts of the body), even in cold water, but

b) there is room, once he has finished observing the seven-day mourning period, for the mourner to be lenient about washing even the whole of his body in cold water, in honor of Shabbath.

thirtieth day on Shabbath

43. *a.* When the thirtieth day, commencing with the day of the burial, falls on Shabbath, the mourner may wash himself on Friday with hot water, in honor of Shabbath.

b. 1) There are those who permit a mourner, other than a mourner for a father or mother, also to cut his hair or beard on the Friday in these circumstances, but

2) some authorities take a stricter view, and do not allow him to cut his hair or beard on the Friday, since it is not yet the thirtieth day.

cutting nails

44. *a.* 1) A mourner is forbidden to cut his fingernails or toenails for thirty days, but,

2) if his nails are very long, he may cut them in honor of Shabbath.

b. If the thirtieth day falls on Shabbath, there are those who permit the nails to be cut in any event on the Friday, whereas others prohibit it.

day before Yom Tov in first six days of mourning

45. *a.* 1) If one of the Seven Days of Mourning (other than the seventh, as to which see paragraph 47 below) occurs on the day preceding Yom Tov, it is customary for the mourners to be lenient and wash (even the whole body) in hot water shortly before Yom Tov, but

a) they should take care that they do not come to violate Yom Tov and

b) they should be particular to recite the *mincha* prayer first.

2) One should not object if a mourner acts in this way, in spite of the fact that, according to a stricter view, he may do no more than wash his face, hands and feet in cold water, as on a Friday in the Seven Days of Mourning. (See paragraph 7 above.)

b. 1) At any rate, on the day preceding Yom Kippur, the mourner may, even according to those who take the stricter view, wash in hot water, and immerse himself in a *mikveh*, an hour or two before sunset, provided he has said the *mincha* prayer.

2) This is because the immersion (and preparing for it) is a mitzva.

c. On the day preceding Yom Tov, he may also wash* his clothes for the Festival, but

1) he would do well not to wash them until after midday,

2) he must be careful that he does not come to violate Yom Tov and

3) he should not put the clothes on until nightfall.

d. 1) Other laws of mourning, that is to say

a) not wearing leather shoes and

b) not sitting on an ordinary chair,

are observed until the Festival commences. (See paragraph 7*a*1) above.)

2) This is in addition to the observance of "private"

---

* He should also dry them before Yom Tov, to avoid the prohibition detailed in Chapter 15, paragraph 15.

mourning, defined in paragraph 10 above (except for washing).

3) Cutting his hair or beard also remains prohibited, for as long as he continues to observe the laws applicable in the Thirty Days of Mourning.

e. If the day before Yom Tov is Shabbath, then the mourner may already wash himself, (according to those who take the more lenient approach, as above), and may also launder his clothes, on Friday, shortly before Shabbath begins, but

1) he should be careful that he does not come to violate Shabbath and

2) he should not wear the clothes he has washed until the Festival.

f. 1) There is a difference of opinion as to how the mourner should eat the final meal before the commencement of the fast of Yom Kippur.

a) Those who adopt the stricter view hold that a mourner should not sit on an ordinary chair at this meal either, whereas

b) according to a more lenient view, he does sit on a chair.

g. 1) After midday on the day preceding Pesach, the mourner may

a) put on leather shoes and

b) sit on an ordinary chair, although

2) there are authorities who take a stricter view, and hold that he should not do so.

3) a) Consequently, if the burial took place after midday on the day preceding Pesach, the mourner will not openly demonstrate his mourning at all, according to the more lenient view, and will wear his leather shoes, and sit on a chair, as usual.

b) Nonetheless, even those who hold this opinion agree that the onset of the Festival abrogates the obligation of the mourner to observe the laws applicable during the Seven Days of Mourning, since he has observed "private" mourning.

h. Even in the view of those who permit washing and laundering just before Yom Tov begins, as above, the restrictions apply again after the Festival, for as long as the mourner has to continue observing the laws relating to the thirty-day period of mourning.

seventh day on Shabbath

46. *a.* 1) If the last of the Seven Days of Mourning falls on a Shabbath which is the day before a Festival, a mourner for a relative other than a parent may cut his hair or beard on the day following the Festival.

2) This is because, in these circumstances,* the Festival abrogates the obligation to observe the laws relating to the thirty-day mourning period.

3) Indeed, the mourner, in this particular case, may even cut his hair or beard on *chol ha-mo'ed*, although this is normally prohibited, since he had no opportunity of doing so previously.

b. 1) With regard to washing in hot water, and laundering clothes, on the Friday, in honor of the Festival, see paragraph 45 above.

2) The mourner should not launder his clothes on *chol ha-mo'ed*.

Yom Tov on or after eighth day of mourning

47. *a.* If

1) the burial took place at least seven days prior to the Festival, and

2) the mourner observed the laws applicable to the Seven Days of Mourning,

the Festival abrogates his obligation to observe the laws normally applicable to the thirty-day period (with the exception as to hair-cutting mentioned immediately below).

b. 1) Therefore, the mourner (with the exception of a mourner for his father or mother) may cut his hair or beard on the day preceding Yom Tov.

2) Furthermore, any mourner, including a mourner for

* See paragraph 47 below.

his father or mother, may wash on that day in hot water and cut his nails.

3) a) The mourner should do these things after saying the *mincha* prayer, just before the commencement of Yom Tov, and

b) he should take care that he does not come to violate Yom Tov.

4) He may also wash his clothes, and put them on close to the beginning of the Festival.

c. It should be noted that the above applies even to a mourner whose seventh day of mourning occurs on the day preceding Yom Tov.

d. When the day before Pesach occurs during the thirty-day mourning period,

1) a mourner for relatives other than his parents may cut his hair or beard, but he should do so before midday, whereas

2) washing in hot water is permitted to all mourners, including those mourning the decease of a parent, immediately after midday.

e. A mourner who does not cut his hair or his beard, or wash his clothes, before Yom Tov, in circumstances where this is permitted,

1) may not do so on *chol ha-mo'ed* (due to the rabbinical injunction against cutting hair and laundering on *chol ha-mo'ed*), but

2) should wait until after the Festival.

eighth day on Shabbath before Yom Tov

48. *a.* If the eighth day of mourning falls on a Shabbath which is the day prior to Yom Tov, a mourner for a relative other than a parent may cut his hair or beard on Friday, and

b. even a mourner for a parent may wash himself and launder his clothes on that Friday.

c. Should he not cut his hair or his beard, or wash his clothes, on the Friday, he must not do so on *chol ha-mo'ed* but should wait until after the Festival.

HEARING OF A DEATH ON SHABBATH OR A FESTIVAL

From the following paragraphs, it will be seen that, when news of a close relative's* death is received on Shabbath or a Festival, the rules which the Rabbis applied vary, depending on

A. whether the news is of a recent or not-so-recent death, and,

B. if the death is recent, whether the news is heard on Shabbath or on a Festival.

on ordinary Shabbath within thirty days

49. *a.* If
1) the news is received on Shabbath, and
2) it is still within the thirty-day** period commencing with the day of the decease,

the person receiving the news should act as set out below.

b. He should, on Shabbath,
1) recite the blessing, "*Dayan ha-emeth*," and
2) observe "private" mourning, as detailed in paragraph 10 above, namely the restrictions on
    a) washing,
    b) marital intercourse and
    c) studying Torah.

c. It is the custom not to bring him a meal from other people's food (in accordance with the practice described in paragraph 1 above), either on Shabbath or on its expiration.

d. On the termination of Shabbath, he should tear his clothes in mourning.

e. Shabbath counts as the first of the Seven Days of Mourning,*** and he has to count a further six days.

50. *a.* If
1) the news is received on a Shabbath which is the day before Yom Tov, and

* This is as defined in Chapter 64, paragraph 3.

** When the news is received on the thirtieth day itself, the rules are somewhat different, as explained in paragraph 52 below.

*** On the morning of the morrow (Sunday), he should put on *t^e^fillin*.

on Shabbath preceding Yom Tov within thirty days

2) it is still within the thirty-day period commencing with the day of the decease,

the person receiving the news should act as set out below.

b. He should, on Shabbath,

1) recite the blessing, "*Dayan ha-emeth*," and

2) observe "private" mourning for the duration of Shabbath, as detailed in paragraph 10 above.

c. He does not eat his first meal from other people's food (as in paragraph 49 above).

d. The onset of the Festival abrogates his obligation to observe the laws relating to the Seven Days of Mourning.

e. 1) A mourner for his father or mother should tear his clothes on the expiry of Yom Tov, provided it is not *chol ha-mo'ed*.

2) When it is *chol ha-mo'ed* on the expiry of Yom Tov, he should tear them only after the Festival ends since clothes should not be torn in mourning on *chol ha-mo'ed* if the news was not received that day.

3) A mourner for a relative other than a father or mother does not tear his clothes at all in the situation described in this paragraph.

f. With respect to news received on *chol ha-mo'ed*, see paragraph 54 below.

on Yom Tov within thirty days

51. *a.* If

1) the news is received on Yom Tov, and

2) it is still within the thirty-day period commencing with the day of the decease,

the person receiving the news should act as set out below.

b. He should, on that day of Yom Tov,

1) recite the blessing, "*Dayan ha-emeth*," and

2) observe "private" mourning, as detailed in paragraph 10 above.

c. He does not eat the customary meal from other people's food, neither on Yom Tov nor afterwards, as in the comparable case in paragraph 3 above.

d. 1) Whether he is in mourning for his father or mother

or for another* relative, he should tear his clothes on the expiry of Yom Tov, provided it is neither Shabbath nor *chol ha-mo'ed.*

2) When it is *chol ha-mo'ed* on the expiry of Yom Tov, he should tear them only after the Festival ends, (provided it is not Shabbath), since clothes should not be torn in mourning on *chol ha-mo'ed*, if the news was not received that day.

3) If it is Shabbath on the termination of the Festival, he should wait until after Shabbath.

e. Regardless of when during the Festival he heard the news, he begins to count his Seven Days of Mourning** (as in the situation described in paragraph 38 above) only immediately after

1) the seventh day of Pesach,
2) the first day of Shavuoth,
3) Sh^emini Atzereth or
4) the first day of Rosh Hashana.

f. The days of the Festival, beginning with the day he heard the news, are counted towards the thirty-day mourning period.

g. With respect to news received on *chol ha-mo'ed*, see paragraph 54 below.

on thirtieth day

52. *a.* If

1) the news is received on Shabbath or Yom Tov, and
2) it is the thirtieth day, counting from (and including) the day of the decease,***

the person receiving the news should act as set out below.

b. He should, on that day,

---

* It should be noted that a mourner for a relative other than a father or mother does not tear his clothes, even after the Festival, if the thirty-day period has ended by the time he is permitted to tear (or, it seems, if seven days have elapsed since he heard the news).

** The mourner in these circumstances does not put on *t^efillin* on the day after the Festival, although there are authorities who hold that he should do so.

*** For the significance of the passing of the thirtieth day, see paragraph 53 below.

1) recite the blessing, "*Dayan ha-emeth*," and
2) observe "private" mourning, as detailed in paragraph 10 above.

c. He does not eat the customary meal from other people's food (as in paragraph 49 above).

d. 1) A mourner for a parent should tear his clothes after Shabbath or Yom Tov, as detailed in paragraph 50 above.
2) A mourner for other relations does not tear his clothes at all in the situation described in this paragraph.

e. 1) After Shabbath or Yom Tov, the mourner should, for a short while, conduct himself in a way which demonstrates that he is in mourning.
2) It is sufficient if, for instance, he
a) takes off his shoes or
b) sits on the ground.

after thirty days

53. *a.* If
1) the news is received on Shabbath or Yom Tov, and
2) more than thirty days, counting from (and including) the day of the decease, have passed,

the person receiving the news should act as set out below.

b. On that day,
1) he should recite the blessing, "*Dayan ha-emeth*," but
2) he should not observe any mourning, not even "private" mourning.

c. 1) He does not eat the customary meal from other people's food.
2) Indeed, someone who hears of a death after more than thirty days does not eat the meal, even if he receives the news on a weekday.

d. 1) A mourner for a parent should tear his clothes after Shabbath or Yom Tov, as detailed in paragraph 50 above.
2) A mourner for other relations does not tear his clothes at all in the situation described in this paragraph.

e. After Shabbath or Yom Tov, the mourner should, for a short while, conduct himself in a way which demonstrates that he is in mourning, as elaborated in paragraph 52 above.

on chol ha-mo'ed

54. *a.* 1) If
- a) the news is received on *chol ha-mo'ed*, and
- b) it is still within the thirty-day period commencing with the day of the decease,

the person receiving the news should act as set out below.

2) He should, on that day,
- a) recite the blessing, "*Dayan ha-emeth*,"
- b) tear his garments, if he is mourning a parent, and
- c) observe "private" mourning, as detailed in paragraph 10 above.

3) When he is mourning a relative other than a parent, the custom is for him not to tear his clothes on *chol ha-mo'ed*, but only after the Festival, as detailed in Chapter 64, paragraph 3.*

4) The mourner (whether for a parent or for another relation) starts to count his Seven Days of Mourning at the end of the Festival, as set out in paragraph 51 above.

5) The days of *chol ha-mo'ed* and Yom Tov, including the day he heard the news, count towards the thirty-day mourning period.

6) So far as the meal which a mourner customarily eats from other people's food is concerned, the rules are parallel to those set out in paragraph 4 above.

b. 1) If
- a) the news is received on *chol ha-mo'ed*, and
- b) more than thirty days, counting from (and including) the day of the decease, have passed,

---

* See also note * to paragraph 51 above.

the person receiving the news should act as set out below.

2) On that day,
   a) he should recite the blessing, "*Dayan ha-emeth*," but
   b) he should not tear his clothes, even if he is mourning his father or mother, and
   c) he should not observe any mourning.

3) a) A mourner for a parent should tear his clothes after the Festival, as detailed in paragraph 50 above.
   b) A mourner for other relations does not tear his clothes at all in the situation described in this subparagraph.

4) After Yom Tov, the mourner should, for a short while, conduct himself in a way which demonstrates that he is in mourning, as elaborated in paragraph 52 above.

55. There are additional laws relating to hearing news of a death on Shabbath and Yom Tov, and it is advisable to consult an authority who is well versed in these laws. *consulting expert*

A MISCELLANY, INCLUDING INFORMING OF A DEATH, SEEING GRAVES, COMMEMORATIONS, EULOGIES AND FASTING

56. *a.* One should not say anything on Shabbath or Yom Tov which will cause grief to the hearer. *informing on Shabbath or Yom Tov*

b. Consequently, one should not tell a person, on Shabbath or Yom Tov, that a relative of his has died.

c. This would, however, be permitted if his intention is
   1) that a son should say *kaddish* for his father or mother that day, or
   2) that the son should be ready, as soon as Shabbath or Yom Tov ends, to do whatever is needed for the deceased.

seeing graves

57. The blessing recited upon seeing graves for the first time in thirty days, "*Asher yatzar ethchem ba-din*," should be said even on Shabbath or Yom Tov.

praying for the dead on Shabbath

58. *a.* One prays for the souls of the departed and says the "*Keil malei rachamim*" prayer (subject to what is stated below) on the Shabbath before the *Yahrzeit*, after the reading of the Torah in the morning.

b. 1) One does not, however, pray for the dead, at the morning service,

a) on the Shabbath when the new moon is blessed,

b) when there is a new bridegroom or a circumcision in the synagogue, and also

c) on the four Shabbathoth (mostly in the month of Adar) when one reads *Parashath Shekalim*, *Parashath Zachor*, *Parashath Para* or *Parashath Ha-chodesh*.

2) What one can do, on these occasions, is to say the prayer after the reading of the Torah at the *mincha* service.

c. One does not pray for the dead, even at the *mincha* service, on a Shabbath on which one does not say the verses commencing "*Tzidkathcha tzedek*," for example

1) during the month of Nissan,

2) on *rosh chodesh*,

3) on Purim or

4) during Chanuka.

d. Nevertheless, even a person who recites the "*Keil malei rachamim*" prayer on any of the above days has authority to support him.

memorial lights on Yom Tov

59. *a.* With respect to kindling lights which will burn when memorial prayers are said on Yom Tov for the departed, that is to say on the last day of Pesach, on Shavuoth and on Shemini Atzereth, see Chapter 13, paragraph 6.

b. See there also for the kindling of a memorial light when a *Yahrzeit* occurs on Yom Tov.

c. When Yom Tov falls on Friday, and the *Yahrzeit* is on

that Shabbath, one should, if possible, not kindle the memorial light oneself, but should request a non-Jew to do so.

60. *a.* A mourner during the twelve-month mourning period participates when the members of the congregation recite the memorial prayers for the dead on the Yamim Tovim mentioned in the preceding paragraph, as well as on Yom Kippur. *Yizkor*

b. However, there are those whose custom is not to say these prayers during that period, so as not to provoke tears and arouse grief, since Yom Tov is given to us for pleasure and joy.

61. *a.* During the thirty days which precede Pesach, Sukkoth or Shavuoth, *eulogies within thirty days before Yom Tov*

1) one may not eulogize a deceased who died before that period (except in the case mentioned below in this paragraph), but
2) one may, even on the day before Yom Tov, eulogize a deceased who died within that period.

b. Even if it so happens that one is in any case eulogizing a deceased who died within that period, one should not at the same time eulogize a deceased who died before it.

c. An exception occurs, and one may eulogize, even within the thirty days preceding the Festival, a deceased who died outside that period, if

1) the deceased was a great man
2) there was no earlier opportunity to eulogize him and
3) his relatives are not present.

62. *a.* 1) It is a custom to fast on a *Yahrzeit*, that is to say on the anniversary of the day on which one's father or mother died, but *Yahrzeit on Shabbath*

2) one should not fast if the *Yahrzeit* occurs on a Shabbath or on any other day on which the *Tachanun* prayer is not said.

b. 1) As to visiting the grave if the anniversary of the

death occurs Shabbath,
   a) the practice is to bring the visit forward to Friday, although
   b) there are those who postpone it to Sunday.
2) Still, if the Friday is *rosh chodesh* or Purim, even those who generally hold that the visit should be brought forward agree that it should be put off till Sunday.

Yahrzeit on Friday

63. *a.* Even when the *Yahrzeit* falls on Friday, one should complete one's fast; in other words one should not make *kiddush* until after the stars come out, although,
b. in places where Shabbath is received early, as detailed in Chapter 47, paragraphs 22 and 23, and the evening prayer is recited when it is still daylight, one
   1) need not wait until after nightfall, if one finds the fast difficult, but
   2) may make *kiddush* and eat straight after the evening prayer.

EATING OUT

scope of prohibition

64. *a.* 1) A mourner for a parent in the twelve-month mourning period, and for other relations in the thirty-day mourning period, should not participate in any meal, outside his home, other than an ordinary meal, of the kind eaten on a weekday.
   2) In this connection, it makes no difference
      a) if the meal is a mitzva, or
      b) whether the meal is eaten on a weekday or on Shabbath or Yom Tov.
b. Notwithstanding the above,
c. 1) there are those who allow the mourner to eat meals in honor of Shabbath at a friend's house.
   2) When eating the third Shabbath meal at a friend's house, he need not be concerned if the meal continues until after nightfall.

65. *a.* In accordance with what is stated in the first part of the previous paragraph, the mourner should not leave his home to attend *shalom zachar, circumcisions, Simchath Torah*

1) a *shalom-zachar* on Shabbath eve in the house of a baby boy who was born that week, or

2) a meal in celebration of a circumcision.

b. However, the authorities referred to at the end of the previous paragraph permit a mourner, after the seven-day mourning period, to go on Shabbath to a meal which does not involve too much rejoicing, such as a *shalom-zachar* or a meal to celebrate a circumcision.

c. The mourner may also attend a meal on Simchath Torah in honor of the *Chathan Torah* and the *Chathan Bereshith*.

d. A mourner, after the seven-day mourning period, who is in the synagogue on Shabbath may take part in the third Shabbath meal which is eaten there, despite the fact that it lasts on into the night.

66. *a.* Some authorities permit mourners who are related to the bride or the groom to participate in *sheva b*e*rachoth* on Shabbath, even outside their (the mourners') home, but this is not the custom. *sheva b*e*rachoth*

b. 1) In practice, the only mourners who take part and eat the *sheva b*e*rachoth* meal on Shabbath outside their (the mourners') home, are the parents of the bride or the groom, to the exclusion of other relatives, although

2) there are those who also allow the grandparents to participate in *sheva b*e*rachoth* outside their (the grandparents') home, like the parents.

67. *a.* 1) Right up to the end of the last day of the twelve-month mourning period, a mourner for a father or mother should not participate in any meal, other than an ordinary weekday meal, outside his home (as above), even on Shabbath. *end of prohibition*

2) It is customary to extend the prohibition to cover

also the day of the *Yahrzeit* which follows the twelve-month mourning period.

b. A mourner for other relations, on the other hand, may participate in any meal, even outside his home, after sunrise on the last day of the thirty-day mourning period.

"...AND HE WHO IS OF GOOD HEART SEES EVERY MEAL AS A FEAST."
(*Proverbs* 15:15)

"...to teach you that a person should rejoice in his lot."
(Rashi's commentary on that verse)

Chapter 66

Chol Ha-Mo'ed: Its Sanctity, the Needs of the Festival, Body Care and Laundering

THE SANCTITY OF CHOL HA-MO'ED AND ITS NATURE

joy and respect

1. *a.* "The days between the first* and the seventh days of Pesach and between the first* and the eighth days of the Festival of Sukkoth...are those which are called 'the weekdays of the Festival,' and [so] they, [also] are called 'Festival' and... one is obliged to rejoice on them and forbidden...to fast...." (Maimonides, *Mishneh Torah, Hilchoth Yom Tov* 6:22.)

b. "'And on the first day there shall be a convocation to sanctity...' (Exodus 12:16). Sanctify it with food and with drink and with clean clothing. Only the first and last days of Yom Tov are called a convocation to sanctity [in the verse]. How do I know that *chol ha-mo'ed* is too? I learn it from, 'These are the appointed times [a term including *chol ha-mo'ed*] of the Lord which you shall call convocations to sanctity...' [Leviticus 23:37]." (*Mechilta*, Exodus 12:16)

c. "And there is this about *chol ha-mo'ed*...,that all the seven days of Pesach and eight days of the Festival [of Sukkoth]...a person is obliged to be joyful and of good heart, he, his children, his wife, the members of his household and all his dependents. This joy is a positive commandment of the Torah, as stated [in Deuteronomy 16:14], 'And you shall rejoice on your Festival, you and your son and your daughter, etc.'" (*Shulchan Aruch Ha-Rav, Orach Chaim*, Chapter 529, paragraph 6.)

d. "We find that *chol ha-mo'ed* is called by the name 'Yom Tov,' but one does not apply this name to these days, so as

* The second, outside Eretz Yisrael.

not to disparage the actual Yom Tov, since their sanctity is not on the same level." (Commentary of Rashba — attributed to Ritva — on Tractate *Sukka* 38a)

e. "One is obliged to honor *chol ha-mo'ed* with food, with drink and with clean clothing, not just as on an ordinary weekday, and...it is a mitzva to eat a meal with bread, once in the evening and once in the morning." (*Mishnah Berurah, Shulchan Aruch, Orach Chaim*, Chapter 530, comment 1)

f. "The custom is that the cloth should be spread on the table all the days of *chol ha-mo'ed*, as on the days of Yom Tov." (*Aruch Ha-Shulchan, Orach Chaim*, Chapter 530, paragraph 4)

g. At the termination of the first days of Yom Tov (when *chol ha-mo'ed* commences), the custom is to address each other with the greeting, "*Mo'adim le-simchah*," and not "*Shavua tov*."

partial rest

2. *a.* "*Chol ha-mo'ed* is not termed a day of rest, but, since it is called a convocation to sanctity and is the time for [bringing] the festive offering in the Temple, [certain] activities are forbidden on it, so that it should not be like other days of the week, which have no sanctity at all.... Not every activity of labor is prohibited on it, as on Yom Tov, because the ultimate purpose of the prohibitions on it is so that it should not be altogether like a weekday. Therefore, there are activities which are prohibited on it and activities which are permitted on it." (Maimonides, *Mishneh Torah, Hilchoth Yom Tov* 7:1)

b. The Sifra on Leviticus 23:37 tells us, in the name of Rabbi Akiva, "What is taught us by [the verse], 'These are the appointed times of the Lord, which you shall call convocations to sanctity' [Leviticus 23:37]?... These are the days of *chol ha-mo'ed*, on which [certain] activities are forbidden. You may think all activities of labor are forbidden on them [as on Yom Tov]. We are taught [in Leviticus 23:36], 'It is an Assembly.' On it [Yom Tov] all activity of labor is forbidden, but all activity of labor is not forbidden on the days of *chol ha-mo'ed.'"*

3. *a.* Our Sages were given the power to permit on *chol ha-mo'ed*, according as they saw the need, activities which are forbidden on Shabbath or Yom Tov. *categories of forbidden activities*

b. Most of the activities which they permitted fall within one of five categories (defined and illustrated in detail in this and the following two chapters),

1) those required in the preparation of food,
2) those whose omission would result in a loss,
3) those required for other purposes of the Festival, so long as they are performed in a nonprofessional manner,
4) those required for the benefit of the public and
5) those done in employing somebody who does not have anything to eat.

c. Certain activities were not permitted, even though they are needed for the Festival, for instance shaving and washing clothes (which are discussed later in this Chapter).

d. 1) Some activities were permitted or forbidden without any reference to the above five categories.

2) Examples can be found in Chapter 68, paragraphs 24 to 31.

4. *a.* It must be borne in mind that, although there are principles for what is prohibited and permitted on *chol ha-mo'ed*, they are not hard-and-fast rules, since the individual laws are independent and cannot be extrapolated one from the other. *basis of prohibitions*

b. Sometimes, the Rabbis allowed a seemingly onerous activity in one context, and forbade a seemingly insignificant one in another.

c. This is not to be wondered at, as the Torah left the details of what is prohibited and what is allowed on *chol ha-mo'ed* entirely within their discretion.

d. 1) There are cases where the Rabbis have consented to a person's performing an activity, because failure to perform it would result in financial loss to another individual, for example his employer.

2) Similarly, they permitted an employer or a customer to have work (which he himself does not urgently require) done by an employee or craftsman who would not otherwise have what to eat.

e. The rule to be adopted in relation to allowing work and other activities on *chol ha-mo'ed* is that one should go to great lengths to avoid permitting anything which makes light of the sanctity of *chol ha-mo'ed.*

f. The Talmud tells us (in Tractate *Mo'ed Katan* 10b) how Ravina, who passed over an opportunity to sell his goods on *chol ha-mo'ed*, out of respect for its sanctity, was blessed by Heaven after *chol ha-mo'ed* and sold them for double the price.

purpose of chol ha-mo'ed

5. The *Mishnah B^erurah (Shulchan Aruch, Orach Chaim,* Chapter 530, comment 2) quotes the Jerusalem Talmud and the *Kol Bo*, who respectively describe the purpose of *chol ha-mo'ed*, with its prohibition on work and other activities, as being to enable one

a. "to eat and drink and devote all one's energy to studying Torah" and

b. "to become attached to the Almighty in fear and love, and to occupy oneself with His perfect Torah."

PREPARING FOOD

the principle

6. One may deal with food on *chol ha-mo'ed* in any way necessary to prepare it for consumption

a. on *chol ha-mo'ed*,

b. on Yom Tov (including *yom tov sheini shel galuyoth*), or

c. on Shabbath immediately following Yom Tov.

permitted activities

7. *a.* Under this heading are permitted not only cooking and baking, but any activity performed on the actual substance from which one is going to benefit, and which is needed in the preparation of the food, such as

1) reaping,
2) grinding,
3) trapping,
4) slaughtering and
5) lighting a flame.

b. It is also permissible to separate *t^erumoth* and *ma'asroth*. (See Chapter 68, paragraph 26, below.)

8. *a.* One may perform the activities involved in the preparation of food, *scope of permitted activities*

1) even if one does so in a professional way,
2) even if they entail a great deal of bother and
3) even without making any change from the manner in which one performs them on an ordinary day of the week.

b. 1) When undertaking such an activity for others, one is permitted to receive remuneration for one's work.

2) Nevertheless, a person who is inspired by a fear of Heaven and takes particular care in the performance of mitzvoth would do well not to accept payment for the work involved in preparing food on *chol ha-mo'ed*.

c. One may also (subject to the limitations set out in paragraph 13 below) prepare food on *chol ha-mo'ed* for sale, if one's intention is that the purchaser should be able to use it on *chol ha-mo'ed* (or Yom Tov).

9. One is permitted to plan one's work in advance in such a way that one leaves the preparation of food (as above) to be done on *chol ha-mo'ed*. *purposely waiting till chol ha-mo'ed*

10. *a.* 1) As long as one's intention is to prepare food for *chol ha-mo'ed* (or Yom Tov), one does not have to minimize and work out the exact amounts one requires, but *doing more than necessary*

2) one can prepare liberal quantities, and, if some is left over, so be it.

3) In this connection, reference should also be made to paragraph 12 below.

4) One must not, of course, purposely prepare more than one needs for *chol ha-mo'ed*, with the express object of leaving it for after the Festival.

b. 1) Where one requires paid assistance to prepare food, one may give the assistant more work to do than one needs for *chol ha-mo'ed* (or Yom Tov), if
   a) one cannot find anyone who is willing to do only the amount of work needed to prepare the food one requires for *chol ha-mo'ed*, or
   b) one has to pay the same remuneration for work done for *chol ha-mo'ed* alone as one has to pay for that work together with work not required for *chol ha-mo'ed*.

2) See further Chapter 67, paragraph 12.

c. 1) Likewise, a person may hire a car to transport food from one place to another for the purpose of *chol ha-mo'ed* and,

2) if it is possible at the same time to save expense by transporting a load which is not needed for *chol ha-mo'ed*, one may add it and fill up the car.

3) It is as well, in these matters, to ask the opinion of a recognized halachic authority on the facts of each individual case.

when there is food already available

11. *a.* 1) One may do an act which would otherwise be forbidden on *chol ha-mo'ed* in order to prepare food oneself, even though one could
   a) buy the same food ready-made, or
   b) borrow it from a friend, or
   c) eat canned or bottled food that one has in the house.

2) Thus, one
   a) may pick growing fruit, and does not have to buy it instead in the market, and
   b) may travel elsewhere to pick and bring back fresh produce.

b. However, one may not do such acts, even to prepare food one will use on *chol ha-mo'ed*, if one has the same food ready at home, unless the new food is superior to what one already has, in quality or in taste, as illustrated in paragraph 12 below. *writing when buying food*

c. 1) Somebody who is going to buy provisions for the Festival may draw up a list, so that he remembers what he has to buy, notwithstanding the general prohibition on writing during *chol ha-mo'ed*.

2) If he does not pay by cash, he may also write out a check in payment for the goods he purchased.

12. In each of the following sets of circumstances, one may prepare food in the same way as one does on an ordinary weekday, and need not make just the minimum amount one requires: *preparing more food than necessary*

a. 1) where the preparation of a larger quantity than is essential does not indeed involve more trouble,

2) for example, when one bakes a large loaf of bread, while one needs only a small one;

b. 1) where the preparation of a larger quantity is essential to improve the taste of the dish one is going to eat on the Festival,

2) for example, when one cooks a large quantity of meat so as to improve the soup, despite the fact that one intends to eat only a little meat;

c. 1) where one only possesses food which is inferior or not tasty and prepares something better,

2) for example, when one only has stale bread and bakes fresh;

d. 1) where one repeats the same process several times, in order to have a selection from which to choose the best for the Festival,

2) for example, when one picks several apples off the tree, with the object of choosing the best of them (it being hard to make the choice while they are still on the tree).

food for sale

13. *a.* 1) a) It is permissible to make all the arrangements and prepare food on *chol ha-mo'ed,* if one wishes to sell it for use during the Festival, as stated in paragraph 8 above, but

b) one may do so openly only when it is obvious, from what one is doing, that it is for the Festival, and then

c) it is permissible even if one is a professional.

2) On the other hand, when it is not obvious from what one is doing that it is for the Festival, one may do it, but not openly.

b. 1) Thus, one may openly operate a bread bakery (including the office which deals with the day-to-day work of the plant), since everyone knows that the baking is taking place there for the purpose of the Festival.

2) a) On the other hand, a chocolate factory should not be operated openly, even if one intends that the chocolate produced should be marketed during *chol ha-mo'ed,* since it is usual to manufacture chocolate for a long time in advance.

b) If indeed the chocolate produced is intended to be marketed only after the Festival, there is no justification for manufacturing it on *chol ha-mo'ed* at all.

c. With regard to trading on *chol ha-mo'ed,* see further Chapter 67, paragraph 27.

d. With regard to ordering a gas cylinder on *chol ha-mo'ed,* to replace one which has been exhausted, see Chapter 67, paragraph 25.

APPLIANCES AND OTHER IMPLEMENTS FOR PREPARING FOOD

the principle

14. *a.* Not only acts done directly with the food are allowed on *chol ha-mo'ed,* but also activities designed to make fit for use implements needed to prepare food for the Festival.

b. By way of example, one may (subject to the contents of

the succeeding paragraphs)
1) sharpen a knife or
2) repair
   a) a cooking stove,
   b) a kitchen water tap,
   c) a refrigerator or
   d) a food-mixer.

15. *a.* 1) A person may perform all of the activities involved in making fit for use appliances or tools needed to prepare food for the Festival, *scope of principle*
   a) even if he does so in a professional way,
   b) even if he takes a great deal of trouble and
   c) even without making any change from the manner in which he performs those activities on an ordinary day of the week.

2) a) A workman is allowed to receive remuneration in return for his work on *chol ha-mo'ed* on such instruments.
   b) Still, someone who is inspired by a fear of Heaven and takes particular care in the performance of mitzvoth would do well not to accept payment for his work on *chol ha-mo'ed* on such implements.
   c) If one could find a non-Jewish workman to do the work, for payment, that would be preferable.

b. 1) It is forbidden to do work for payment on *chol ha-mo'ed*, if that work is not required for the Festival.
2) This is so, even if the remuneration will be used to purchase food for the Festival.
3) For exceptions concerning workmen who have nothing to eat, see Chapter 68, paragraphs 19 to 23.

16. *a.* A person may, on *chol ha-mo'ed* (subject to the contents of paragraph 17 below), repair or make an implement he needs in order to prepare food for the Festival, *repairing when another implement is available*
1) even if he could
   a) buy another one, in working order, or
   b) borrow one from a friend,

2) but not if he himself has another one which he could use.

b. Thus, he may, even in a professional manner,

1) sharpen a blunt knife and
2) repair a knife which breaks on *chol ha-mo'ed*, provided he does not have another he could use, as might be the case, for instance, where he only has one bread knife.

preparing before the Festival

17. *a.* 1) One should, before the Festival, prepare all the instruments and equipment one will need to make food.

2) One should not, for example, leave any faulty appliances to be repaired on *chol ha-mo'ed*.

3) Furthermore, when one can use something as it is, without doing anything more to it, it is proper to refrain from working on it on *chol ha-mo'ed*.

b. 1) Thus, if one has a wood-burning stove, one should prepare chopped wood for burning in it before the Festival, and,

2) if the logs are big, but it is, nonetheless, possible to burn them in the stove, it is proper not to chop them up into smaller pieces on *chol ha-mo'ed*.

c. In the event that one intentionally left work on implements for preparing food to be done on *chol ha-mo'ed*,

1) one should perform the work in a nonprofessional manner, that is to say, like a person who is not skilled in that particular work, or,
2) if one performs the work like a professional, one should make some recognizable change in the manner in which it is done.* (See paragraph 37 below.)

d. 1) Someone who is accustomed to immersing new metal vessels in boiling water prior to use (so that they should exude any forbidden substance they may have absorbed in the polishing process at the factory) should do this before the Festival.

---

* A further possibility is to have the work carried out by a non-Jew.

2) If he did not immerse them in boiling water before the Festival, he may do so on *chol ha-mo'ed* (but one must not so immerse, on the *chol ha-mo'ed* of Pesach, vessels impregnated with *chametz*).

18. Somebody whose practice is to wash the pots and dishes straight after he has used them may do so also on *chol ha-mo'ed*, even if he is not going to use them for the rest of the Festival. *washing dishes*

19. *a.* The Rabbis differentiated between *two categories of implements*

1) repairing, or otherwise working on, implements which are themselves used to prepare the food for eating (or to preserve it), and
2) repairing, or otherwise working on, implements which are indeed needed in connection with the food, but are not themselves used to prepare it for eating (or to preserve it).

b. 1) The rules applicable in the case of the former are those outlined in paragraphs 14 to 18 above.

2) The rules applicable in the case of the latter are the same as those applicable to the needs of the Festival not connected with food, and outlined in paragraphs 34 to 45 below.

c. 1) An example of the former is the repair of a cooking stove.

2) Examples of the latter are

a) the repair of a defective ladder which is required in order to reach the food, but whose actual repair does not produce any direct change in the state of the food,
b) the repair of a broken dining table which, although it is not used to prepare the food, does give one something at which to sit and eat the food, and
c) the repair of a motor car which one needs to bring

oneself* food products from the farm, but whose actual repair has no direct effect whatsoever on the state of the food.

d. 1) a) In accordance with the above, a person may himself repair a refrigerator which has broken down on *chol ha-mo'ed*, or which broke down before the Festival and which he could not then repair, as amplified in paragraph 39 below.

b) He may also call in a repairman to do the work.**

c) It is permitted to repair the refrigerator even if there is a possibility of storing the food at a neighbor's.

2) On the other hand, he may not repair the draining board (counter) or the working surface in the kitchen in a professional manner, even if they broke on *chol ha-mo'ed*, since he does not prepare the food for consumption with them, but only on them.

e. 1) Even if one's refrigerator broke down before the Festival, but the repairman could not come earlier, one may let him effect the necessary repair on *chol ha-mo'ed*.

2) If, however, the repairman could have come before the Festival, but one put him off for one's own reasons,*** then (where he is a Jew) one may let him do the repair only when he can, and does, introduce some change, as explained in paragraph 17 above.

BODY CARE IN GENERAL

the principle

20. *a.* The Rabbis permitted one to perform on *chol ha-mo'ed*, not only activities involved in the preparation of food,

---

* If the car will be used to transport food for the use of the public, see Chapter 68, paragraph 8.

** See paragraph 40 below for the employment of another person on *chol ha-mo'ed*.

*** One may have had a reason which justified putting off the repairman before the Festival, even though one knew he would now come on *chol ha-mo'ed*, and, in this connection, one should consult the opinion of a qualified halachic authority.

but also those required in attending to the human body (with the exceptions mentioned in paragraph 21 below).

b. 1) The rules governing attention to the body on *chol ha-mo'ed* are the same as those governing the preparation of food.

2) The rules governing the preparation of instruments and appliances required for attending to the body are the same as those governing the preparation of appliances and other implements required for making food.

c. Consequently, one may do everything for the purpose of treating a person who is ill,

1) even if he is not dangerously ill, and
2) even if he has no more than a minor ailment.

(See also paragraph 28 below.)

d. 1) One may do what is necessary to preserve one's health, and

2) one may also take vitamins or fish-oil to fortify one's constitution.

21. *a.* The following are illustrations of activities permitted in attending to the body on *chol ha-mo'ed*: *illustrations*

1) heating water with which to wash oneself, even if one wishes to bathe one's whole body;
2) cleaning one's teeth;
3) washing with soap, whether a bar of soap or liquid soap;
4) combing one's hair;
5) plaiting one's hair;
6) putting on lipstick;
7) tearing toilet paper.

b. All of the above activities may be done in the same way as they are done on an ordinary day of the week.

c. By way of exception to the general rule, the Rabbis placed restrictions on cutting hair, shaving and trimming nails on *chol ha-mo'ed*, as detailed in paragraphs 22 to 33 below.

d. One may, on *chol ha-mo'ed*, repair a window pane which broke during the Festival, in one's house or apartment, if it is cold outside, as explained in paragraph 54 below.

e. As to sanitary works on *chol ha-mo'ed*, see paragraph 58 below and Chapter 68, paragraph 14.

CUTTING THE HAIR, TRIMMING THE BEARD, SHAVING AND CUTTING THE NAILS

before the Festival

22. It is a mitzva to cut one's hair and trim one's beard or shave* (according to one's custom), before the Festival, and also to cut one's nails.

general prohibition on cutting hair

23. *a.* In order to encourage one to carry out this mitzva, the Rabbis laid it down that one must not cut one's hair, trim one's beard or shave on *chol ha-mo'ed* (subject to certain exceptions, some of which are set out in paragraphs 25 to 31 below).

b. The prohibition applies

1) even on the last day of *chol ha-mo'ed*, before the concluding day (or days outside Eretz Yisrael) of Yom Tov,
2) even if one did cut one's hair, trim one's beard or shave on the day preceding the Festival,
3) even if the barber is
   a) a non-Jew or
   b) a Jew whom one is employing because he has nothing to eat,
4) both to the hair of the head and to hair on other parts of the body and
5) equally to men and to women (in so far as relevant).

when hair not cut before the Festival

24. One is not allowed to cut one's hair, trim one's beard or shave on *chol ha-mo'ed*, even if one could not do so before the Festival due to no fault of one's own, for example where one had to continue working for one's employer until just before the Festival began.

---

* It goes without saying that shaving may only be done in a manner permitted by the Halacha.

25. However, the Rabbis made an exception in the case of a person who is released from prison (including a Jewish prison),* *after release from prison*

a. on *chol ha-mo'ed*, or

b. on the day before the Festival, close to sunset, so that he could not manage to cut his hair, trim his beard or shave in time, prior to the commencement of the Festival.

26. *a.* The Rabbis made a further exception in the case of a traveler on a long journey who *travelers*

1) a) arrives at his destination on *chol ha-mo'ed* **and**,

b) was not in an inhabited region** on the day preceding the Festival,

or

2) arrives so close to sunset on the day preceding the Festival that he has no time left to cut his hair, trim his beard or shave before its commencement.

b. 1) The exception does not include a tourist who leaves Eretz Yisrael for the purpose purely of sightseeing, since this is not a reason which justifies leaving Eretz Yisrael in the first place.

2) He is not permitted to cut his hair, trim his beard or shave on *chol ha-mo'ed*, even if he was not in an inhabited region on the day before the Festival.

c. Someone who traveled by air on the day before the Festival may not cut his hair, trim his beard or shave on *chol ha-mo'ed*, since he could have done so on the day before the Festival.

---

* The Rabbis took into account that, even if the prison authorities permit shaving and so forth, a prisoner's depressed state of mind might bring him to neglect himself in captivity, but it is an open question whether this applies where the prison regimen compels prisoners to shave daily.

** It is a matter of opinion whether a person who did indeed travel through an uninhabited region, but had available all the necessary facilities, as where he traveled on board a ship, may cut his hair, trim his beard or shave on *chol ha-mo'ed*.

how to do it when permitted

27. *a.* Whoever is permitted to cut his hair, trim his beard or shave on *chol ha-mo'ed* should do so privately, and not in a barber's shop, as he might do on another day of the year.

b. This is because people who see him might not know that his case is exceptional, and would come to make light of the prohibition upon haircutting and shaving on *chol ha-mo'ed.*

c. Nevertheless, a person who is allowed to cut his hair and so forth on *chol ha-mo'ed* may have it done by a Jew (in private), and may pay him for his trouble.*

hair around a wound

28. Somebody who receives an injury on *chol ha-mo'ed* may cut away, from around the wound, hair which is liable to hinder the healing process.

married women

29. The Rabbis also permitted a married woman to cut or shave as much of her hair as

a. protrudes from beneath her head scarf or wig and

b. cannot be covered,

in order to avoid an immodest display.

children

30. *a.* One may cut a child's hair if it has grown in such profusion that it causes him discomfort.

b. One may even have it cut in public, so long as the child does not look big enough to be mistaken for a thirteen-year-old (or a twelve-year-old, if a girl), in which event it should not be cut, except in private.

c. In this case too, one may employ, and pay, a Jewish barber.**

mourners

31. *a.* A mourner whose days of mourning terminate on *chol ha-mo'ed* should consult a qualified halachic authority regarding the cutting of his hair or the removal of his beard on *chol ha-mo'ed.*

---

* But see Chapter 67, paragraph 4.

** See previous note.

b. See also Chapter 65, paragraphs 46 and 48.

32. *a.* 1) One may comb one's hair on *chol ha-mo'ed*. (See paragraph 21 above.) *combing*

2) A woman is allowed to plait her hair.

b. 1) A woman may smooth down, or even comb, the hair of her wig.

2) However, if she wishes it to receive more professional attention, she should ask authoritative advice from a rabbi as to whether this is permitted.

33. *a.* The custom is not to trim the nails on *chol ha-mo'ed*, unless *nails*

1) they were trimmed on the day before the Festival or
2) they need to be cut for the purposes of a mitzva, for instance in the case of
   a) a *mohel* who has to trim his fingernail before a circumcision, or
   b) a woman before her immersion in the *mikveh*.

b. 1) Nonetheless, someone who trims his nails every Friday should not depart from his practice when Friday occurs during *chol ha-mo'ed*.

2) He may trim either his fingernails or his toenails, even with scissors, in the same way as he does every Friday.

OTHER NEEDS OF THE FESTIVAL

34. *a.* Subject to the conditions contained in the succeeding paragraphs, a person may perform any activity which is needed for *chol ha-mo'ed* or for Yom Tov, even if it has nothing to do with the preparation of food. *general rule*

b. Even if it seems no more than likely to him that a particular activity will be needed for *chol ha-mo'ed* or Yom Tov, he may perform it.

35. As will be apparent from the principles set out in the following six paragraphs, the Rabbis distinguished, in this *distinctions made* connection,

a. between work done in a nonprofessional way and work done in a professional way,

b. between performing an activity for oneself and performing it for another, and

c. between doing something for payment and doing it for nothing.

amateurs

36. If the person in question is an amateur, that is to say he is not trained and skilled in that particular activity, he may do it in the usual way.

professionals

37. *a.* If he is a professional, that is to say trained and skilled in that activity, he must do it in a nonprofessional way, namely, by making some change, recognizable in the finished product, from the way he is used to doing it on an ordinary day of the week.

b. He may not do it in his usual way, without such a change, even for the purposes of a mitzva (except for a mitzva one cannot perform after the Festival, as to which see Chapter 67, paragraph 37),

c. nor may one have the work done through the agency of a non-Jewish professional, unless it has to be done on *chol ha-mo'ed* for the purposes of a mitzva. (See further Chapter 68, paragraph 35.)

d. 1) When sickness is feared, a professional may do what is needed, even in a professional way, without a change, since, in such circumstances, it is deemed to be required for the purposes of attending to the human body. (See paragraphs 20 and 21 above.)

2) For examples, see paragraph 54 below.

simple activities

38. *a.* An activity which

1) involves no trouble,

2) is required for the Festival and

3) does not need any expertise or skill

may be performed on *chol ha-mo'ed*, even without varying the usual manner of performance.

b. Illustrations are

1) squeezing out a mop or a wet floor-cloth, as in paragraph 47 below, and
2) polishing shoes, as in paragraph 48 below.

purposely leaving work for chol ha-mo'ed

39. *a.* A person must not purposely plan to perform the activity on *chol ha-mo'ed* because he will then be free from his normal work.

b. If he does, he is forbidden

1) to perform it, albeit in a nonprofessional manner, or
2) even to ask a non-Jew to perform it in a nonprofessional manner.

c. Where somebody does purposely leave work to be done on *chol ha-mo'ed*, a Rabbinical court which has the appropriate powers can penalize him, by depriving him of the results of his labors.

d. All of the above applies even to someone who purposely left his work to be done on *chol ha-mo'ed*, because he mistakenly thought it was permissible to do so.

e. It does not apply to the following persons, and they may perform on *chol ha-mo'ed* activities, necessary for the Festival, which they have left to be done on *chol ha-mo'ed*, since their failure to act was not deliberate:

1) somebody who had no possibility of performing the activity before the Festival;
2) somebody who, through no fault of his own, did not perform it before the Festival;
3) somebody who forgot to perform it before the Festival;
4) somebody who thought the work would not be necessary on *chol ha-mo'ed*, and is now seen to have been wrong;
5) somebody who, through his idleness, caused the matter to drag on until *chol ha-mo'ed*;
6) somebody who left it because he thought he would still have time to do it before the Festival, and then forgot.

who may perform the activity

40. *a.* Whenever one requires an activity to be performed on *chol ha-mo'ed* for the purposes of the Festival, in a permitted way (as defined in paragraphs 36 to 38 above),
1) one should do it oneself or, if this is not practicable,
2) one
   a) may have it done by somebody who will take no remuneration, or
   b) should try and find a non-Jew to do it (even for reward).

b. A Jewish workman may also be employed, if one does not give him a fixed remuneration, but simply invites him to eat with one.

c. A Jew may be employed to do the work for a fixed remuneration only if
1) none of the above possibilities exist or
2) the Jewish workman has nothing to eat (as to which see Chapter 68, paragraphs 19 to 23).

d. 1) It is perfectly in order to accept remuneration for work* over a particular period which includes *chol ha-mo'ed*, as where the employment and payment is on a monthly basis. (See Chapter 28, paragraph 58, for the same rule applied on Shabbath.)
2) It makes no difference if one month of the employment finishes, and another begins, in the middle of the Festival.

e. One may pay for any service one receives on *chol ha-mo'ed*, if the payment also includes expenses of the person providing the service, for food, heating or the like, as illustrated in Chapter 28, paragraphs 62 and 64 (in connection with Shabbath).

benefitting from forbidden activity

41. *a.* There may be restrictions on the derivation of a benefit from an activity performed on *chol ha-mo'ed* in a forbidden manner, or in forbidden circumstances, just as there are on the derivation of a benefit from the performance

---

* Of course, one may only do work in the various permitted circumstances enumerated in this and the next two chapters.

of a forbidden activity on Shabbath.

b. This could occur if, for example,

1) one did something in a professional manner, albeit for the purposes of the Festival, but in a case where one is only permitted to do it in a nonprofessional manner, or
2) one did something indeed in a nonprofessional manner, or with a variation from the usual manner, but not for the purposes of the Festival.

c. The restrictions are imposed only if the activity was performed in the knowledge that it was wrong and, in that event,

1) the person who performed it is never allowed to benefit from it, whereas
2) others are allowed to benefit from it, but only after the Festival.

activities not needed for the Festival

42. An activity is not permitted as being for the purpose of the Festival, and may not be performed on *chol ha-mo'ed*, even in a nonprofessional manner, if

a. one does not in fact intend to use the product of that activity for the purpose of the Festival, or

b. one can do without it, and yet still have all one needs for the Festival.

acts required to maintain dignity

43. *a.* An activity which is required to be done to maintain a person's dignity on the Festival, although not in order to satisfy any material need he has, is regarded as a need of the Festival.

b. It may be performed on *chol ha-mo'ed*, in a nonprofessional manner,

1) if indeed its results will be used on the Festival, or even
2) if its results might be used on the Festival.

c. For an illustration, see paragraph 52, below.

needs of yom tov sheini shel galuyoth and Shabbath

44. *a.* 1) An activity done on *chol ha-mo'ed* for the purposes of *yom tov sheini shel galuyoth*, by a Jew residing outside Eretz Yisrael, is considered to be for the purpose of the Festival.

2) This is because the observance of *yom tov sheini shel galuyoth*, having the force of a tradition handed down from generation to generation, is, in nearly all cases, treated just like the other days of the Festival.

b. Furthermore, one may perform an activity on *chol ha-mo'ed* for the purposes of Shabbath occurring on the day immediately following Yom Tov, in the same circumstances as one may perform it for the purposes of the Festival.

c. Notwithstanding the above, a resident of Eretz Yisrael who is abroad may not perform a forbidden activity on *chol ha-mo'ed* for the purpose of *yom tov sheini shel galuyoth*, even for a local resident.

preparing utensils

45. Insofar as the Rabbis allowed the performance in general of activities required for the Festival, they also allowed one to prepare instruments or utensils to be used in those activities, provided their preparation did not involve a great deal of bother.

laundering

46. By way of exception to the overall rule, the Rabbis did not permit laundering on *chol ha-mo'ed*, even for the purposes of the Festival. (See paragraphs 63 to 68 below.)

cleaning the floor

47. *a.* 1) It is permitted

a) to wash the floor,

b) to squeeze out the mop or wet rag afterwards and

c) to pour the dirty water away onto the ground, even if it falls on plants which one is not allowed to water on *chol ha-mo'ed*. (See Chapter 68, paragraph 31.)

2) It is forbidden to shine the floor with polish and the like. (See paragraph 50 below.)

b. 1) One may clean a carpet with an electrically operated

vacuum cleaner, but
2) one must not vigorously shake the dust out of a carpet.

48. *a.* One may polish shoes, but only if one is going to wear them on the Festival, and *polishing shoes*
b. there is a view that one should not polish shoes at all on *chol ha-mo'ed.*

49. One is allowed to kill insects which cause distress to human beings. *killing insects*

50. *a.* A home help who is dependent on her wages to buy food for herself and her family daily may be paid as usual. (See also Chapter 68, paragraphs 19 to 23.) *home help*
b. If the situation is otherwise, as when she has no family and receives her food in the house where she works,
1) one should try and persuade her not to receive payment separately for *chol ha-mo'ed*, but only together with what is due to her from before the Festival, or for after the Festival, and,
2) only in the event that she does not agree, may one pay her as usual. (See paragraph 40 above.)

51. *a.* 1) The Rabbis permitted one *repairing clothes: the rule*
a) to repair a garment which has torn or
b) to sew on a button which has come off,
provided that one needs to wear the garment during the Festival.
2) It does not matter whether the garment tore, or the button came off, during the Festival itself or beforehand (but see paragraph 39 above).
b. 1) a) Since the woman of the house is practiced in sewing, her work is considered professional.
b) Consequently, she must vary her usual method of sewing, in such a way that the change will be apparent in the results of her work.
2) a) The man of the house, on the other hand, is not

practiced in sewing, and may, therefore, sew in the same way as he would on an ordinary day of the week.

b) This notwithstanding, he too ought to behave more strictly, and vary his usual method of sewing.

repairing children's clothes

52. One may also repair a child's garment, or sew back a button (with a variation, as in paragraph 51 above), even if the child could wear the garment unrepaired, but his father or mother would be ashamed to take him out with a torn garment.

repairing shoes

53. *a.* One must not give torn shoes even to a non-Jewish shoemaker on *chol ha-mo'ed* for repair, because to have them repaired in a professional manner on *chol ha-mo'ed* is prohibited.

b. However, one may perform a light repair which does not call for professional expertise, for instance by extracting a nail that makes it uncomfortable to wear the shoes on *chol ha-mo'ed*.

c. Where

1) the shoes will tear altogether if one wears them without repairing them now and
2) one needs to wear them on the Festival, as one has no others which are suitable,

one might be permitted to repair them to avoid the loss. (For details see Chapter 67, paragraphs 13 and 17.)

repairing window

54. *a.* One is allowed to repair a broken windowpane on *chol ha-mo'ed*, even in a professional manner, if

1) a) it broke during the Festival or
   b) it broke before the Festival, but one could not, or did not, repair it before Yom Tov, for any of the reasons listed in paragraph 39*e* above,

and

2) there is a risk of harm to human health should the repair not be carried out.

b. For the same reason, one may repair a heater, or have it repaired by an expert, if *repairing heater*

1) one is indeed going to use it on the Festival

and

2) a) the climate is cool and one is bothered by the cold

or

b) there are in the house small children who are naturally sensitive to the cold.

55. *a.* 1) a) One may write a social letter on *chol ha-mo'ed*, as long as one does not deliberately leave it to be written on *chol ha-mo'ed*, and, *writing*

b) all the more so, may one reply to a social letter one has received.

2) The custom is to write the first line at a slant, so as to introduce a variation into the normal manner of writing.

3) One may write even if the letter will reach its destination only after the Festival.

b. 1) Somebody who is used to writing his letters with a typewriter or a word processor is permitted to do so on *chol ha-mo'ed* too.

2) It is also allowed to impress a document with a rubber stamp.

3) Neither of these two activities is regarded as writing in a professional manner, and they are, thus, permitted for the purposes of the Festival (which include writing a social letter).

c. 1) One is allowed to write in a non-permanent way on *chol ha-mo'ed* (even if it is not for the purpose of the Festival), for instance by

a) writing letters or making patterns on a misted windowpane,

b) writing with chalk on a blackboard or

c) writing with, or in, sand or dust.

2) One may likewise make computations on a pocket calculator, where the writing that appears is not going to last, but only if the digits or letters are

not printed onto paper. (See, however, Chapter 67, paragraph 33.)*

folding and ironing

56. *a.* It is permitted to fold an article of clothing, a tablecloth or the like into its previous creases.

b. 1) One may likewise iron it along its usual creases, if
   a) one is ironing for the purpose of the Festival and
   b) one has not purposely left the ironing to be done on *chol ha-mo'ed*,

   but

   2) one may not iron new creases into it, since that requires attention of a more professional kind.

watering and picking plants

57. *a.* One may water plants which are usually watered at frequent intervals, since they will die otherwise, and one will thus be caused a loss.

b. 1) One may also pick plants, so long as one intends to use them for the Festival, but,
   2) if it is not required for the Festival, one is not allowed to pick even one leaf.

repairing plumbing

58. *a.* It is forbidden to repair the plumbing of the bathtub (except as mentioned below),
   1) even in a nonprofessional way and
   2) even in order to have a bath in honor of the Festival,

although

b. 1) it is of course permissible to carry out even a professional repair, if water will otherwise go to waste (in accordance with the rule set out in Chapter 67, paragraph 17), and
   2) one may also do so if, for example, a sewage pipe is leaking, and failure to effect an immediate repair will result in water or smells entering one's home.

c. 1) Notwithstanding the above, there are those who per-

---

* Recording information onto a computer disk or a diskette is forbidden on *chol ha-mo'ed* (except where permissible for the purposes of the Festival or to avoid a loss).

mit the repair of the bathtub plumbing, provided that

a) it is not done in a professional manner,

b) the defect came to light during the Festival, or the defect came to light before the Festival, but one did not purposely leave the repair to be done on *chol ha-mo'ed* (as particularized in paragraph 39 above),

c) the purpose of the repair is to enable one to have a bath on *chol ha-mo'ed* **and**

d) there is no other possibility for one to have a bath in one's home (since there is no other bathroom).

2) In a case where

a) one suffers discomfort if one is unable to bathe on *chol ha-mo'ed*,

b) it is not possible to carry out the repair in a nonprofessional manner **and**

c) the work does not involve an especially large amount of bother (such as breaking walls and tiles),

there is room for allowing it to be done even in a professional manner.

3) In these situations, one should always consult the judgement of a qualified rabbi, who will base his view on the facts as he sees them in the individual instance.

4) The rules which apply to the bathtub plumbing apply also to the plumbing of the toilet, and one may even install a new one, if

a) it became defective during the Festival, or it was defective before the Festival, but one did not deliberately leave the repair for *chol ha-mo'ed*, and

b) that is the only toilet one has in the house.

(See also Chapter 68, paragraph 14.)

d. One may unblock a drainage pipe with the aid of a rubber plunger, in accordance with the rule contained in paragraph 38 above.

outings

59. *a.* One is allowed to go on an outing* on *chol ha-mo'ed,*** whether on foot or with a vehicle.

car care

b. 1) One may drive a car, even if one could go by foot, and

2) one may fill up with fuel, clean the car and so forth (provided one does not deliberately leave this for *chol ha-mo'ed*).

c. One must not, however, have the car repaired by a mechanic (since he would do the repair in a professional manner), unless

1) one is stranded en route (in a place where the vehicle will be a prey to thieves or vandals if abandoned) or

2) one needs it on *chol ha-mo'ed* for an important, permissible purpose, and would otherwise have to spend money to rent a car.

electrical repairs

60. *a.* 1) It is allowed to repair an electrical fuse, or to effect simple repairs to the electricity system, but

2) it is forbidden to call in an electrician to change or replace the wiring, even for the purpose of the Festival, since this requires him to exercise his professional expertise.***

telephone repairs

b. 1) Likewise, if one's telephone is out of order, one should not require the company to repair it on *chol ha-mo'ed*, even if it became faulty on *chol ha-mo'ed* and one needs the line (except in cases similar to those mentioned below),

---

* Still, one should not go on too many outings on *chol ha-mo'ed*, but should use that time as intended by God, to come closer to Him, in fear and love, and occupy ourselves with His Torah. (See paragraph 5 above.)

** The mitzva of eating in a *sukka* should be observed on an outing, as the exemption granted to travelers does not apply in such a situation.

*** One would, when necessary, be allowed to call in a professional on *chol ha-mo'ed* to repair an electrical system which has broken down during the Festival, if this were permissible by the general rules applicable to *chol ha-mo'ed*, as

a. where it is too dark to eat,

b. where one needs the current to cook the food,

c. where the food in the refrigerator will spoil, or perhaps even

d. where one needs light to study Torah in the house and has no other convenient place to study.

2) nor should one ask the company, on *chol ha-mo'ed*, to repair the telephone after the Festival, since the staff on duty will write down one's name and particulars.*

3) One may notify the telephone company, and request that the repair be made as soon as possible,
   a) if the telephone serves the needs of someone who is ill (pursuant to the rule stated in paragraph 20 above), or
   b) if it is in a shop, where it is used to take orders from the public at large for food and other items needed for the Festival. (See Chapter 68, paragraphs 1 to 4.)**

61. *a.* 1) One may play a musical instrument on *chol ha-mo'ed* at a gathering in celebration of the Festival, and, *musical instruments*

2) if the instrument develops a fault, one may effect a simple repair, but should not have it repaired by an expert.

b. One may also record talks or songs on a tape recorder, if one *tape recorder*

1) does so for the purposes of the Festival, or
2) fears that the opportunity to do so will not be repeated after the Festival.

LAUNDERING AND CLEANING CLOTHES

62. It is a mitzva to wash one's clothes before the Festival, since part of the duty to honor the Festival is wearing clean clothes. *before the Festival*

63. *a.* It is forbidden to launder on *chol ha-mo'ed* (except in the cases mentioned in the following paragraphs), *the prohibition*

1) even for the purpose of the Yom Tov at the end of the Festival,

---

* This would be allowed outside Israel where the staff is not Jewish.

** In all cases similar to those mentioned in this paragraph, a competent halachic authority should be consulted, and he will have to take into account the specific considerations in each instance.

2) even if the garment one wishes to wash is the only one of its kind one has, and one washed it before the Festival, but it became dirty since,
3) even through the agency of someone who has nothing to eat, or of a non-Jew,
4) even if it would be done without charge,
5) whether by hand or with a washing machine, and
6) even if one was unable to do the laundry before the Festival through no fault of one's own, as where one had to keep working for one's employer until just before the Festival began.

b. However, the Rabbis did allow those whom they permitted to cut their hair on *chol ha-mo'ed* (as to which see paragraphs 25 and 26 above) to wash their clothes, if they do not indeed have clean clothes for the Festival.

c. Concerning ironing on *chol ha-mo'ed*, see paragraph 56 above.

baby clothes

64. *a.* 1) One may wash baby clothes (both diapers and other articles of clothing), since they are constantly being made dirty.
2) One may wash several such items of clothing at the same time, even though one does not immediately need them all.

b. Whatever one is permitted to wash, one may wash even in a washing machine, and in the same way as one would wash on an ordinary day of the week.

c. 1) Somebody who, throughout the year, is accustomed to using cloth diapers, and washing them when dirty, may also wash them on *chol ha-moed* even if he has the possibility of using disposable diapers (which it would cost him money to buy), but
2) somebody who is accustomed to using disposable diapers throughout the year should not wash diapers on *chol ha-mo'ed*.

d. 1) At all events, it is not permitted to leave dirty baby clothes from before the Festival, in order to wash them on *chol ha-mo'ed*.

2) This is forbidden, even if the intention is to wash them on *chol ha-mo'ed* together with other baby clothes which will become soiled during the course of the Festival.

65. *a.* One may also wash the clothes of small children who can no longer be termed babies, since they too are constantly soiling what they wear. *children's clothes*

b. Their clothes should only be washed as and when needed.

66. *a.* Kitchen towels, handkerchiefs, socks and nylon stockings may all be washed during *chol ha-mo'ed*, as and when needed, if *towels, handkerchiefs and socks*

1) the way one normally uses them calls for them to be changed several times during the Festival and

2) one indeed does not have enough for the Festival.

b. When the only thing one has to wear is a garment made from synthetic material (which is easy to wash), one may wash it on *chol ha-mo'ed*, so that one can wear it on the Festival. *synthetic material*

c. One is also allowed to wash the clothing of a person who is ill with an infectious disease, so as to prevent infection. *avoiding infection*

67. It is also permitted to wash towels which are washed after each use, as in a public *mikveh*, if one in fact estimates that there might not be enough for all those who will require them during the course of the Festival. *towels washed after each use*

68. *a.* Whenever it is permissible to do the laundry, one may also have it done by a laundress and, *employing laundress*

b. if she requires to be remunerated for her work, one may pay her.

c. See further, paragraphs 40 and 50 above.

69. *a.* Laundry which one is allowed to wash on *chol ha-mo'ed* may also be hung up to dry in the sun, since it comes out better that way. *drying laundry* *b.* It follows that wash which dries equally well in a drier should preferably be dried there discreetly on *chol ha-mo'ed*, rather than by being hung up openly in the sun.

wet clothes

70. *a.* Clothes which have become wet may be squeezed out and spread out to dry in the sun.

b. One need not be afraid that people will think one has offended against the prohibition upon washing clothes on *chol ha-mo'ed*. (Contrast the stricter attitude adopted on Shabbath, as reflected in Chapter 15, paragraphs 9 to 13.)

c. Nevertheless, see paragraph 69*b* above.

repairing washing machine

71. *a.* One must not call in an expert technician to repair the washing machine on *chol ha-mo'ed*, even if

1) it broke down on *chol ha-mo'ed* and
2) one needs it for washing articles which one is allowed to wash on *chol ha-mo'ed*.

b. One may, however, on *chol ha-mo'ed*, fix a date with him to come and repair the machine after the Festival, provided (if he is Jewish) that he does not make a note of it in his appointments book.

stains

72. *a.* Cleaning a stain out of a garment is also included within the injunction against laundering on *chol ha-mo'ed*.

b. Thus, if

1) the garment became stained before the Festival and
2) one deliberately left it to be cleaned on *chol ha-mo'ed*,

it is forbidden to clean the stain out on *chol ha-mo'ed*.

c. If

1) a) one did not deliberately leave the cleaning for *chol ha-mo'ed* or
   b) the garment became stained only during the Festival,

and

2) one has no other suitable garment,

one is allowed to take the stain out with a stain remover or other suitable cleaning agent, but one must not have the whole garment cleaned.

d. Where the garment is stained on *chol ha-mo'ed* in such a way that, if it does not receive immediate treatment, the stain will not be able to be removed,

1) one may soak it in water or, if that is not sufficient, may remove the stain (even if one does not need to wear the garment during the Festival), to avoid the loss one would otherwise be caused, but
2) one must not wash it on *chol ha-mo'ed*, unless there is no other way of taking out the stain.

73. *a.* For polishing shoes, see paragraph 48 above. *polishing shoes and ironing*

b. For ironing clothes, see paragraph 56 above.

74. One is permitted to brush the dust off a hat or other articles of clothing on *chol ha-mo'ed*. *brushing off dust*

Chapter 67

Chol Ha-Mo'ed: Avoiding a Loss, Commerce and Activities in Furtherance of a Mitzva

AVOIDING A LOSS

extent of loss

1. *a.* One may (subject to the contents of the following paragraphs) perform, on *chol ha-mo'ed*, any activity whose omission would result in a considerable loss.

b. The Rabbis permitted the performance of the activity, not only where there will certainly be a loss, but even where there is a reasonable fear of loss.

c. A loss, for these purposes, is what people in general, who found themselves in similar circumstances, would consider a loss, and which they would go to trouble to avoid.

d. See further paragraphs 16 to 18 below.

how to perform act

2. *a.* It is permissible (subject to what is stated below, in this paragraph and in paragraph 18) to perform, in a professional manner, an activity for the avoidance of loss, in the same way as one would on an ordinary day of the week, even if one could easily

1) do it in a nonprofessional manner or
2) make a recognizable change in the usual manner of performance.

b. 1) At all events, one should reduce to a minimum the amount of trouble one takes.

2) See also paragraph 16 below.

c. Notwithstanding the above, if the loss involved is not so significant, one may carry out the activity only in a nonprofessional way, or with some change which will be apparent in the finished product.

kind of loss

3. A person may perform an activity designed to avoid loss, *a.* even if it is not in any way for the purposes of the Festival, and

b. even if the loss would not be his.

4. *a.* When one has to have work done on *chol ha-mo'ed* to avoid loss, it is right to try and find *employing workman*

1) a workman who has nothing to eat, as explained in Chapter 68, paragraph 19, or

2) a non-Jewish workman who will work for a fixed remuneration, or

3) a Jewish workman who will work without receiving any remuneration.

b. In the event that none of these is a possibility, one may employ a Jewish workman and pay him his full remuneration.

5. *a.* An otherwise prohibited activity may be performed to avoid a loss, only if one did not purposely leave it to be done on *chol ha-mo'ed* (as this concept is defined in Chapter 66, paragraph 39). *purposely leaving work for chol ha-mo'ed*

b. Should one have purposely left it for *chol ha-mo'ed*, one is forbidden to do it then,

1) even if it involves no excessive bother and

2) even through the agency of a non-Jew.

c. One is not deemed to have purposely left the activity to be performed on *chol ha-mo'ed*, and may perform it then,

1) if one thought one could leave it to be done after the Festival without suffering loss, but now turns out to have been wrong, or

2) if one started doing it, but, due to force of circumstances, was unable to complete it before the Festival.

6. *a.* One may perform an activity on *chol ha-mo'ed* for the purposes of the Festival, or to avoid loss, even if, **as a result**, one may, to avoid losing one's capital, have to do an act which is normally forbidden on *chol ha-mo'ed* and involves bother. *Torah prohibitions*

b. 1) Consequently,

a) one may (in accordance with the rules set out in paragraphs 19 to 21 below), buy grapes on *chol ha-mo'ed* because one will not have the opportunity to buy them so cheaply after the Festival, and,

b) if it transpires that they cannot be kept until after the Festival without going bad, one may also press them on *chol ha-mo'ed* to make wine.

2) However, one may not buy grapes on *chol ha-mo'ed* **with the object** of pressing them on *chol ha-mo'ed*, even if one will not find the opportunity of buying them so cheaply after the Festival.*

c. A shopkeeper who is permitted to sell his merchandise on *chol ha-mo'ed* in honor of the Festival (as detailed in paragraphs 27 to 29 below) is also allowed to record particulars of the credit he gives, in case he forgets them.

loss resulting from act done before Festival

7. *a.* A person may do something before the Festival, right up to its commencement, even if he knows that he will, as a consequence, have to perform an otherwise forbidden activity on *chol ha-mo'ed*, in order to prevent loss.

b. 1) Thus, he may sow prior to the Festival, and water the sown area, even though he knows that the seeds will sprout and it will be necessary to water them again on *chol ha-mo'ed*.

2) He is in fact allowed to water them on *chol ha-mo'ed* only if he watered them prior to the Festival, but not if he sowed seeds in dry ground without watering them.

3) See also paragraph 17*d* below.

c. He may also pour cement on the day preceding the Festival, despite the fact that it will be necessary to

---

* This case must be distinguished from the preceding one, in 1) above, since,
a. in this case, one's whole intention is directed to the forbidden activity which involves bother, namely pressing the grapes, whereas,
b. in the preceding case, one merely intended to buy the grapes, and the pressing resulted from that.

water the concrete during *chol ha-mo'ed*, so as to prevent it from cracking and to strengthen it. (See, however, Chapter 23, paragraph 43.)

d. 1) One may pay for merchandise on the day before the Festival, even though one knows it will only be available on *chol ha-mo'ed*, and one will then have the task of transporting it home.

2) One should not collect the merchandise on *chol ha-mo'ed*, if

a) it is not going to be used during the Festival and

b) one can leave it where it is, and collect it only after the Festival, without suffering loss (as where there are no storage charges).

8. *a.* In so far as one is able to perform an act designed to avoid loss discreetly, one is obliged to do so. *discreetness*

b. Only if it is impossible to do it discreetly may one do it openly.

9. One may do an act on *chol ha-mo'ed* to avoid loss, even if the loss prevented is not immediate, but would occur only subsequent to the Festival. *loss which will occur later*

10. *a.* Having started performing an activity in order to prevent a loss, one may complete it, even if one will be doing more than is required for that purpose.* *continuing activity after loss prevented*

b. Yet, once the activity is completed, one may not commence another, if there is no need for it in order to prevent the loss.

11. *a.* When the Rabbis permitted one to work on *chol ha-mo'ed* in order to avoid a loss, they included in this the avoidance of a consequential loss not directly related to the work in hand. *consequential loss*

---

* Thus, if one starts irrigating a field because the crop would otherwise be lost, one may complete the task in the usual way, even after sufficient water has been used to prevent the loss.

b. 1) a) Therefore, a salaried employee who is liable to lose his employment (and not just his pay for the days he is absent), if he does not present himself for work on *chol ha-mo'ed*, may work on *chol ha-mo'ed*.

b) If, however, his employer lets him take all or some of the days of *chol ha-mo'ed* as a vacation (either without pay or at the expense of his annual entitlement to vacation), he must not work on those days (but see *c* below).

c) Indeed, as mentioned in paragraph 14 below, an employee must make an effort to obtain leave for *chol ha-mo'ed*, even without pay, or at the expense of his annual entitlement to vacation leave (subject to *c* below).

d) An employee who cannot obtain leave for *chol ha-mo'ed*, and fears that he will lose his employment, may work on *chol ha-mo'ed* even if the subject matter of his work would itself not suffer any loss by his failure to do so.

e) It goes without saying that someone who is accustomed to working overtime, just in order to boost his salary, must not do so on *chol ha-mo'ed*.

2) On his part, a Jewish employer may certainly not refuse his employees leave on *chol ha-mo'ed*, since he must not give them work in the first place on *chol ha-mo'ed*, unless this is halachically justified, as where they have nothing to eat (as in Chapter 68, paragraph 19).

c. 1) Somebody who

a) has no money with which to pay his debts that fall due on *chol ha-mo'ed*, and

b) will suffer a loss in the event that he does not pay on time,

may work on *chol ha-mo'ed*, so that he will be able to settle his obligations and avoid financial loss.

2) A person in such a situation would do well to consult an experienced halachic authority, to make sure that

his own (subjective) view of the position is correct.

d. 1) One may also pay bills for such things as electricity, water and city taxes,
   a) which fall due on *chol ha-mo'ed*, and
   b) whose nonpayment on time will result in additional impositions,

   provided one does not deliberately leave them to be paid on *chol ha-mo'ed*.

2) It is even permissible to write out checks for the purpose of such payments.

3) See further paragraph 17*i* below.

keeping business open

12. *a.* 1) The owner of an undertaking which employs a permanent work-force, receiving a regular wage, may keep it open and let them work on *chol ha-mo'ed*, to avoid the substantial loss which would be caused to him in either of the following circumstances:
   a) where he would have to pay the employees their full wages, even if he closed for *chol ha-mo'ed*, because they do not agree to these days being set off against their entitlement to annual vacation leave;
   b) where the nature of the business does not permit it to be completely closed on *chol ha-mo'ed*, as in the case of a supermarket. (Regarding the opening of stores, see also paragraphs 27 to 29 below.)

2) Nonetheless, it is prudent to ask the opinion of a qualified halachic authority, as there is a view which prohibits the opening of a business on *chol ha-mo'ed* in such situations.

paying for more work than needed

b. 1) The position is similar where
   a) one needs to employ workmen to do half a day's work, in order to avoid a loss, or for some purpose which is permitted on *chol ha-mo'ed*, but
   b) will in any case have to pay them for a full day's work.

2) So that one should not pay out money for nothing,

one may give them a full day's work to do, even if the additional work in itself is not directed to avoiding a loss, and is in no way required for the Festival.

3) See also Chapter 66, paragraph 10.

alternative ways of avoiding loss

13. *a.* 1) One is not permitted to perform an otherwise forbidden activity on *chol ha-mo'ed* in order to avoid a loss, unless there is no practicable way of avoiding the loss without performing the activity.

2) Should there be an alternative course of action, one is not allowed to perform the forbidden activity, even through the agency of a non-Jew.

b. 1) As a result, someone whose shoes are torn to such an extent that they will become irreparably ruined by further wear in their existing condition (as to which see paragraph 17*b* below) is not allowed to have them repaired on *chol ha-mo'ed*,

a) if he has other suitable shoes he could wear or

b) if he could easily buy new shoes on *chol ha-mo'ed.**

2) Similarly, it is prohibited to darn socks on *chol ha-mo'ed*, even when they would be irreparably ruined by further wear in their present state, if one can easily buy others on *chol ha-mo'ed*.

advance arrangements to avoid working

14. *a.* A person who is self-employed must try to arrange his affairs in advance in such a way that he does not have to work on *chol ha-mo'ed*.

b. 1) Someone who is in the employ of others, and has leave entitlement, must also try to arrange his vacations in such a way that he does not work on *chol ha-mo'ed*.

2) a) It is the practice in many factories and offices in Israel to work shorter hours on *chol ha-mo'ed*, but

b) an employee must not take into account that he

---

* However, if he cannot afford to buy an additional pair, he may have the old ones mended.

will lose the benefit of these shorter hours if he takes his vacation then, since this is not a loss which justifies working on *chol ha-mo'ed*.

3) a) However, the loss of whole days is considered such a loss.

b) Therefore, he does not have to take his vacation on *chol ha-mo'ed* if his employer makes this conditional on his giving up two days of vacation for every one day that he does not work on *chol ha-mo'ed*.

15. From the following paragraphs it will be seen that, although the Rabbis permitted the performance of an otherwise forbidden activity on *chol ha-mo'ed* in order to avoid loss, the extent of that permission is not the same in all cases. *variability of rule*

16. *a.* It is an important principle that one may not perform such an activity on *chol ha-mo'ed* in order to avoid loss, if one is **certain** it will involve a great deal of trouble, unless *activities involving trouble*

1) there is a risk of serious physical injury to a human being or
2) one fears that the loss may be particularly large.

b. What is termed a great deal of trouble and what is called a particularly large loss is dependent on circumstances of place and time, and must be decided by the halachic authority whose opinion is consulted, in accordance with the facts of each individual case.

17. *a.* If failure to perform an activity is liable to result in a loss of one's property (whether material or incorporeal, as explained below), either in whole or in part, one may perform that activity on *chol ha-mo'ed*, *preventing loss of property*

1) even when it involves bother and would normally be prohibited on *chol ha-mo'ed*, and
2) even when one performs it in a professional manner, provided one has not deliberately left it to be done on

chol ha-mo'ed.

repairing shoes

b. Consequently, one may have shoes repaired on *chol ha-mo'ed* in the following circumstances:

1) a) One's shoes became torn on *chol ha-mo'ed* or

b) they became torn before the Festival, but one did not know they were torn, or one did not know that one would have to wear them on the Festival (or in any one of the other situations listed in Chapter 66, paragraph 39*e*),

and

2) one needs to wear them during the Festival, **and**

3) if one wears them unrepaired, they will become irreparably ruined.

(See also paragraph 13 above.)

taking fruit off trees

c. One may take the fruit off one's trees to avoid its rotting there or being stolen, even if one does not eat it during the Festival.

irrigation

d. 1) a) It is permitted to water a field (or a vegetable patch) which depends on artificial irrigation, even when one does not intend to eat any of the crop during the Festival, if one is afraid that failure to irrigate on *chol ha-mo'ed* might result in loss.

b) This could be the case were one to discontinue watering a field which one has already watered at least once before the Festival.

2) Whether or not artificial irrigation is allowed must be determined with reference to the type of crop, local conditions and the weather.

3) a) A field which is watered only to improve the crop, and where the only damage caused by failure to water will be the loss of this improvement, must not be irrigated on *chol ha-mo'ed.*

b) This is forbidden, even if the sprinklers are already in position and all one has to do is turn on the taps.

attending to animals

e. 1) One is permitted to milk an animal in the normal way on *chol ha-mo'ed*, even if the milk will not be drunk during the Festival.

2) Furthermore, one should not withhold medical attention from an animal on *chol ha-mo'ed*, even if it involves an activity which would otherwise be forbidden on *chol ha-mo'ed*.

f. 1) One may repair a defective door lock on *chol ha-mo'ed*, for fear of a burglary. *burglar protection*

2) One may even buy and install a new lock in replacement.

3) It is also allowed to repair an automatic alarm system.

g. At a time of rampant inflation, one may invest one's money on *chol ha-mo'ed* in stocks, shares and the like, to stop its value being eroded, unless one could have done so before the Festival, but purposely left it for *chol ha-mo'ed*. *investment loss*

h. Somebody who has to borrow money on *chol ha-mo'ed* from a lender who insists that he first sign a promissory note or an IOU may complete and sign the note, and the surety may also sign a bond or guarantee, if *borrowing money*

1) the borrower is in need of the money now or

2) he will not find anyone to lend him the money after the Festival.

i. 1) One may pay accounts on *chol ha-mo'ed* for such things as city taxes, if one can obtain a reduction only by paying now (but one must not deliberately leave the payment to be made on *chol ha-mo'ed*). *paying bills*

2) This could happen where, for example, one has only just received one's salary and did not previously have any money with which to pay.

3) One may even write a check for the purpose.

4) See further paragraph 11 above.

j. 1) a) One may write down on *chol ha-mo'ed* thoughts one has had, or which one has heard from others, on Torah study, since one is liable to forget them otherwise. *notes on Torah subjects*

b) The logic of this is that, if one may perform forbidden activities on *chol ha-mo'ed* to avoid the loss of money, one should all the more be allowed to do so to avoid the loss of priceless pearls of wisdom from our precious Torah.

c) Indeed, one will be rewarded from Heaven for writing them down.

2) For the same reason, one may take a photostat of a page in a book that one needs for one's studies, if one will not be able to obtain the book after the Festival.

3) However, someone who has written notes on Torah subjects, but wishes to rearrange them in a different order, must not rewrite them on *chol ha-mo'ed.*

4) It is also prohibited to fasten together loose pages, if one binds them in a professional manner.

halachic responsa

k. 1) It is permitted to write responsa to halachic questions on *chol ha-mo'ed,*

a) if those asking need to have the answer (in writing) during the Festival, or

b) if it is necessary in order to prevent a person infringing a prohibition, or,

c) even when the answer is not required for the Festival, if there is a danger of its arriving too late in the event that one despatches it only after the Festival.

2) In all of these cases, one may make a copy of the responsa for retention, before sending them off, on *chol ha-mo'ed.*

correcting printing errors

1) If one discovers a straightforward printing error in a book on *chol ha-mo'ed*, one should make a mark by its side, and correct it after the Festival, but,

2) where the mistake is discoverable only upon close study, and one is afraid that, if one waits until after the Festival to correct it, one may forget the train of thought which led one to the right version, one may correct it on *chol ha-mo'ed.*

lost property

m. 1) a) Someone who finds lost property on *chol ha-mo'ed* may write out a notice and put it up in the synagogue, or in some other public place.

b) This is because of the possibility that the owner will be in the district only for the duration of the

Festival, so that he would not see a notice put up after the Festival, and would, thus, be precluded from recovering his property.

2) The owner of lost property may also put up a notice, so that the finder should know to whom to return it.

n. A person who is permitted to write on *chol ha-mo'ed* in order to avoid a loss does not have to restrict himself to writing only the essentials, but may write whatever he would on an ordinary day of the week.

18. *a.* If failure to perform an activity is not liable to result in the loss of one's property, but its quality is liable to deteriorate to some extent, one may not perform that activity on *chol ha-mo'ed*, unless all three of the following factors are present: *preventing deterioration of property*

1) a) the activity cannot be postponed till after the Festival without risk of damage, or

b) one needs the property in question for the purposes of the Festival;

2) one

a) performs the activity in a nonprofessional manner, or

b) makes an alteration, recognizable in the finished product, from the normal way in which it is done;

3) one has not deliberately left it to be done on *chol ha-mo'ed*.

b. Consequently, shoes which have torn, and will tear further if one wears them without repairing them on *chol ha-mo'ed*, but not to the extent that they will be irreparably damaged, may not be given for repair on *chol ha-mo'ed*, even to a non-Jewish shoemaker.

c. 1) If there is a breach in one's garden fence, one may repair it, to prevent strangers from trespassing, even if they would not cause much damage, but,

a) when there is no fear that they would come to steal, one may effect the repair only in a nonprofessional manner, (or with some alteration as in *a.*2)b) above) whereas

b) when there is a fear that they might come to steal one's property, one may carry out the repair even in a professional way. (Compare paragraph 17*f* above, regarding a door lock.)

2) Where one has no fear of theft or substantial damage, there is no justification for constructing a new fence, even in a nonprofessional way.

3) It is advisable, in these cases, to consult an experienced halachic authority as to what may and may not be done. (See paragraph 16 above.)

d. 1) a) One may exterminate mice which have invaded a field, since they destroy the crop (and do not merely cause a deterioration in its quality).

b) It is permitted to use the same means as on an ordinary day of the week, such as poisoned bait or sprays.

c) It is also allowed to set mousetraps in the house.

2) Similarly, one may destroy ants' nests, if there is a risk that the ants may spoil food.

3) In all of these cases, one is permitted to act only where one could not have done so before the Festival, or at any rate did not purposely leave the matter for *chol ha-mo'ed* (as in the circumstances enumerated in Chapter 66, paragraph 39*e*).

e. 1) It is forbidden to spray plants with pesticide merely as a matter of routine, where there is no fear that a single omission to spray on *chol ha-mo'ed* would result in damage to them.

2) However, if one sees

a) that the plants are being damaged by pests which have already invaded the field, or

b) that destructive pests are liable to spread into the field,

one may spray on *chol ha-mo'ed* to avoid the threatened loss of one's crop, so long as one has not purposely left the spraying for *chol ha-mo'ed*.

19. *a.* 1) If failure to perform an activity on *chol ha-mo'ed* is not liable to cause loss, or even deterioration, of one's property, but will result in a small to moderate* loss of profits,** of a saving,*** or of an opportunity which will not occur again (as in *c.* below), *moderate loss of profits*

a) one is permitted (subject to the limitations set out below) to perform an activity which would normally be prohibited on *chol ha-mo'ed*, provided that it does not involve what the Rabbis would regard as bother,**** but,

b) where the prohibited activity **does** involve bother, it may **not** be performed, even if the resultant loss of profits is considerable.

2) A prohibited activity (not involving bother) may be performed to avoid a small or moderate loss of profits only if one

a) spends part of the profits on the enjoyment of Yom Tov and *chol ha-mo'ed* and

b) would not have been in a position to spend so much money for this purpose without those profits.

3) When permitted, the activity may be performed even if

a) only a small amount of profit is to be earned and

b) one does it in public, and not in private.

4) In circumstances where it is merely doubtful whether a loss of profits would result from a failure to act, one must not perform even forbidden activities which involve no bother.

b. 1) Consequently, one may sell merchandise on *chol ha-mo'ed*,

a) even when it is not for use for the purposes of the Festival, and

---

* For loss of a large profit, see paragraph 20 below.

** For the loss of an opportunity for profit which is not always readily available after the Festival, see paragraph 21 below.

*** For an example, see paragraph 30 below.

**** See Chapter 66, paragraph 4, and Chapter 68, paragraphs 24 and 26.

b) even in public,
if, as a result, one will have in hand sufficient money to be able to spend part of it on enjoying the Festival.

2) However, this does not permit trading on *chol ha-mo'ed* by somebody who has all the money he needs to spend on enjoying the Festival, even if the loss of the *chol ha-mo'ed* profit will cause him to cut down on his expenditure for that purpose.

3) See paragraphs 22 to 31 for trading on *chol ha-mo'ed.*

c. 1) Relatives or friends who meet on *chol ha-mo'ed* may be photographed, if the opportunity will not arise again after the Festival.

2) The same applies if one makes a trip during *chol ha-mo'ed* and wishes to photograph the sights one sees. (See Chapter 66, paragraph 59, with respect to making trips on *chol ha-mo'ed.*)

3) Nevertheless, it is forbidden to develop the film on *chol ha-mo'ed*, since nothing will be lost by developing it after the Festival.

d. One must not pick the fruit off an ownerless tree, when one does not need it for the Festival, even though one can assume that, if one does not pick the fruit now, there will be none left after the Festival.

e. A person may order a travel ticket on *chol ha-mo'ed* for a journey he will be making on the day after the Festival, if he will indeed have to leave immediately, and will not have time to obtain the ticket then.

loss of special opportunity for large profit

20. *a.* If failure to perform an activity on *chol ha-mo'ed* is not liable to cause loss, or even deterioration, of one's property, but will prevent the receipt of a large profit, which, while not unusual, has arisen outside the ambit of one's day-to-day business,* then

1) one is permitted to perform an activity which would normally be prohibited on *chol ha-mo'ed*, provided

---

* For the loss of an opportunity for profit which is not always readily available after the Festival, see paragraph 21 below.

that

a) it does not involve what the Rabbis would regard as bother,*

b) one does it discreetly and

c) one spends part of the profit on the enjoyment of the Festival,** but

2) one is indeed **not** permitted to perform a prohibited activity which **does** involve bother.

b. Consequently, one may discreetly perform a transaction that has come one's way for the sale or purchase of goods and which is likely to bring in a large profit, but should spend part of the profit on the enjoyment of the Festival.

loss of profit which is not always available

21. *a.* 1) If failure to perform an activity on *chol ha-mo'ed*

a) is not liable to cause loss, or even deterioration, of one's property, but

b) will result in the loss of an opportunity to make a profit which is not always readily available after the Festival,

one may perform an activity which is normally forbidden on *chol ha-mo'ed*, but does not involve what the Rabbis would regard as bother,*** even if one does not spend any part of the profit on the enjoyment of the Festival.

2) The reasoning behind this is that it is in the nature of a business (and, therefore, one's livelihood) to be dependent on the making of profits of this kind too.

3) See also paragraph 29*c* below.

b. 1) Consequently, one may visit a trade fair which takes place on *chol ha-mo'ed*, and do business there,

a) provided that one would otherwise irrevocably lose the opportunity it affords to make a profit,

b) even if the date of the fair was specially fixed

---

* See Chapter 66, paragraph 4, and Chapter 68, paragraphs 24 and 26.

** It does not matter that, even without the additional large profit, one would have enough money to spend on the Festival.

*** See Chapter 66, paragraph 4, and Chapter 68, paragraphs 24 and 26.

for *chol ha-mo'ed* by unobservant Jews, on the pretext that people are free from their work then and have time to come and buy.

2) On *chol ha-mo'ed*, a person may also buy all kinds of goods for his use,
   a) if there is a fear of the market price going up after the Festival,
   b) as long as he did not purposely leave the purchase to be made on *chol ha-mo'ed*.

3) See further paragraph 30 below.

TRADING ON CHOL HA-MO'ED

general prohibition

22. *a.* Buying and selling is, as a general rule, prohibited on *chol ha-mo'ed*.

b. Details of the laws, and of defined cases in which the rule does not apply, are contained in the following paragraphs.

c. When trading is prohibited, it is forbidden even through the medium of a non-Jew. (See Chapter 68, paragraph 34.)

avoiding loss of profit

23. *a.* In certain defined cases, and subject to specified limitations, one may buy or sell in order to benefit from particularly advantageous terms, or to avoid the loss of a profit.

b. For details, see paragraphs 29 to 31 below and paragraphs 19 to 21 above.

when money urgently needed

24. *a.* 1) Whilst commerce which is not for the purpose of the Festival is, in general, forbidden on *chol ha-mo'ed*, if one wishes to trade
   a) because one does not have enough money for the Festival, or even
   b) in order to generate some income for a workman (such as a porter) who does not have what to eat,

one may do so, provided that is indeed one's true purpose, and not merely a pretext for carrying on business during *chol ha-mo'ed.*

2) See also Chapter 68, paragraph 23.

b. It is also permitted to engage in commerce, when one fears that one may lose customers if one does not sell to them on *chol ha-mo'ed.* *to avoid loss of customers*

c. Since the halachic view in these matters varies according to the situation, one ought to consult the opinion of a recognized Rabbinical authority in each individual case.

25. In the event that one of a pair of gas cylinders runs out, one is not allowed to order a replacement cylinder on *chol ha-mo'ed*, if the gas in the remaining cylinder will suffice for one's needs during *chol ha-mo'ed* and Yom Tov (and for the period after Yom Tov until one can order and receive a new cylinder).* *replacing gas cylinder*

26. *a.* A person may buy on *chol ha-mo'ed* utensils which he requires for the purpose of the Festival. *what may be bought*

b. Nevertheless, he should try to buy before the Festival items which are not obviously being bought for the purpose of the Festival.

27. *a.* Foodstuffs which are obviously intended for the purpose of the Festival, such as *foodstuffs*

1) vegetables and fish, or

2) matzoth on the intermediate days of Pesach,

may be sold on *chol ha-mo'ed* in the same way as on an ordinary day of the week.

b. They may be sold on *chol ha-mo'ed*, even for use on *yom tov sheini shel galuyoth*, or for use on a Shabbath which immediately follows the last day of the Festival.

c. 1) If a non-Jew comes to buy, one may sell to him too on *chol ha-mo'ed*, but

2) one may not open one's store and sell one's mer-

---

* Outside Israel, where the employees are non-Jewish, one can place orders on *chol ha-mo'ed*, even for delivery after Yom Tov of items not needed for the Festival.

chandise in a town where all of the customers are non-Jews (except in the circumstances described in paragraph 29 below).

d. One may perform otherwise forbidden activities for the purpose of preparing food, even if one intends to sell it (for use during the Festival), but see Chapter 66, paragraph 13.

e. 1) When buying foodstuffs, one may buy liberal quantities, and does not have to be exact in estimating the precise amount one requires for the Festival.

2) Furthermore, one may buy more of a foodstuff than one needs for the Festival, even if one has in mind to leave part of it for use after Yom Tov.

3) See also paragraph 30 below.

f. 1) One must not, however, sell even foodstuffs, if one in fact knows that the purchaser

a) intends to use them only after the Festival and

b) has no justification for buying them on *chol ha-mo'ed* (as in the circumstances mentioned in paragraph 30 below).

2) Nonetheless, one need not ask the buyer what his purpose in making the purchase is.

selling discreetly

28. *a.* Goods may not be sold, in other than a discreet manner, in shops whose merchandise is not obviously for use during the Festival, even if the sale is for the purpose of the Festival.

b. For instance, if the shop has two doors, only one should be opened.

c. Examples of such shops are those selling clothing, footwear, hardware or jewellery.

d. See also paragraph 29 below.

e. 1) A shopkeeper must not open his shop on *chol ha-mo'ed* on the off-chance that somebody might want to buy something for the Festival, but

2) he may open his shop upon receiving a request to buy something for the Festival (or if he regularly has such customers), as above.

29. *a.* 1) One should not open one's shop on *chol ha-mo'ed* to sell articles which are not needed for the Festival (subject to what is stated below), even if *opening shop*

a) one can assume that people will be free from their work on *chol ha-mo'ed*, and will come shopping, and

b) keeping the shop closed on *chol ha-mo'ed* will result in the loss of a good opportunity to make large profits.

2) The situation in paragraph 20 above should be distinguished from this one, since there the loss is of a special opportunity outside the ambit of the normal day-to-day business.

3) Articles which might be used for the purpose of the Festival may be sold on *chol ha-mo'ed* in the normal way when the prospective loss of profits is large, but, otherwise, subject to the contents of paragraph 28 above.

b. If

1) the buyers in the town are non-Jews and

2) one will lose a good opportunity to make large profits in the event that one does not open the shop,

one may open, and sell even items which are not for the purpose of the Festival.

c. 1) a) Where a trade fair has been fixed for *chol ha-mo'ed*, one may open one's shop, on *chol ha-mo'ed*, to avoid the loss one would be caused if only one's competitors' shops were open.

b) This is so, even if the date of the fair was specially fixed for the Festival by unobservant Jews, on the pretext that people are free from their work then and can come and buy.

2) Similar considerations apply in the case of end-of-season sales fixed for *chol ha-mo'ed*.

d. As it is difficult to define these matters with any exactitude, it is best to ask the opinion of an authority on the halacha in each case.

when buying for after Yom Tov is allowed

30. *a.* One may buy goods on *chol ha-mo'ed*, even for sale after the Festival (unless one could have made the purchase before the Festival, but purposely left it for *chol ha-mo'ed*), if one is genuinely afraid
1) that one will not be able to find such goods after the Festival or
2) that their price will go up after the Festival, causing one financial damage.

b. See also paragraphs 5 and 6 above.

c. At all events, it is advisable to consult an expert on the halacha, so that one should not come to regard *chol ha-mo'ed* as an ordinary weekday, and carry on business as usual.

real estate

31. *a.* It is not permitted to deal in buildings or land on *chol ha-mo'ed*, unless
1) the purchaser actually wishes to use them during the Festival, or
2) it will be difficult for him to find a comparable property after the Festival, or
3) either the purchaser or the vendor will lose an unrepeatable opportunity to buy or sell at a good price.

b. One should not open one's office for the purpose of such trading, except if requested to do so (as in the parallel situation in paragraph 28 above), and, even then, business should be carried on in a discreet manner.

banks

32. In connection with the opening of banks on *chol ha-mo'ed*, for the purpose of the various transactions carried out there, see Chapter 68, paragraph 2.

writing when buying or selling

33. *a.* In all of the instances mentioned above where a tradesman is allowed to do business on *chol ha-mo'ed*, he may also record the amounts of credit which he gives, lest he forget them. (See also paragraph 6 above.)

b. In places where the law obliges one to write the price on each article for sale, or to record all income and outgoings on a cash register, one may do so on *chol ha-mo'ed* too (when one is allowed to sell on *chol ha-mo'ed*).

c. It is also permissible for a purchaser to write a check in payment for goods he buys on *chol ha-mo'ed*,
1) if indeed he has no cash, or
2) if delivery of the check to the vendor serves him as a receipt for the payment.

34. Likewise, if one needs to write for the purposes of one's business, because one will suffer a loss if one does not do so, one may write in the usual way. *writing for business purposes*

35. *a.* A person may collect his debts on *chol ha-mo'ed*, but *collecting debts*
b. he should not file a legal claim for a debt (since this will involve him in writing), unless he is afraid that he will lose his money if he holds up the filing of the claim.

ACTIVITIES PERFORMED IN FURTHERANCE OF A MITZVA

36. The following paragraphs explain the various categories of activities performed in furtherance of a mitzva, and the extent to which they are permitted on *chol ha-mo'ed*. *introductory*

37. *a.* There are mitzvoth which are transitory — that is to say, if they are not fulfilled at the due time, they cannot be subsequently fulfilled at all. *transitory mitzvoth*
b. One may perform an activity on *chol ha-mo'ed* to enable the fulfillment of such a transitory mitzva,
1) even if one has purposely (albeit wrongfully) left the activity to be done on *chol ha-mo'ed*,
2) not only where the mitzva is to be fulfilled by oneself, but also where it is to be fulfilled by other individuals, and
3) even when one performs the activity in a professional manner.

c. A distinction must, however, be made between a mitzva one is going to fulfill oneself and one which is to be fulfilled by other persons.
d. If the mitzva is one's own, one may, on *chol ha-mo'ed*,

perform the activity required to enable its fulfillment, even if the mitzva is not to be fulfilled until after the Festival.

e. If it is somebody else's mitzva, then,

1) in the event that it is to be fulfilled on the Festival, one may perform the activity on *chol ha-mo'ed*, either

a) for remuneration, but only when this will permit one to spend more money on enjoying the Festival,

or

b) free of charge,

whereas,

2) in the event that the mitzva is not to be fulfilled during the Festival, the preparatory activity may be performed on *chol ha-mo'ed* only by a workman who has nothing to eat (as in Chapter 68, paragraph 19).*

tefillin and mezuzoth

38. *a.* It follows from the contents of the preceding paragraph that a person may, on *chol ha-mo'ed*, write *tefillin* and *mezuzoth* which are required during the Festival**

1) for his own use or

2) for the use of another, provided that

a) he writes them without charge or

b) his remuneration will furnish him with the wherewithal for spending more on the enjoyment of Yom Tov.

b. He may, on *chol ha-mo'ed*, write *tefillin* and *mezuzoth* which are not required until after the Festival, but only if

1) a) they are for his own use and

b) he is afraid that he may not manage to write them after the Festival, in time to perform the mitzva when the obligation arises,

---

* See paragraph 45 below, for cases where the circumstances are such that it is possible to do the preparatory work in a nonprofessional manner.

** This would be applicable, so far as concerns *tefillin*, in the case of those who follow the opinion of the Rema, as expressed in the Shulchan Aruch, and put on *tefillin* during *chol ha-mo'ed*.

or

2) he does not have anything to eat (as in Chapter 68, paragraph 19), and is being paid to write them.

c. Someone who does have what to eat may not write *tefillin* and *mezuzoth* on *chol ha-mo'ed* for others to use after the Festival, even if he writes them

1) free of charge or
2) in order to be able to spend what he earns on the enjoyment of Yom Tov.

d. Subject to the above principles, one may, on *chol ha-mo'ed*, also correct a *mezuzah* (where this is halachically permissible), even when it is to be affixed at an entrance which only doubtfully requires a *mezuzah*.

39. *a.* One must not correct an error, albeit in just one letter, even in one's own *sefer Torah*, on *chol ha-mo'ed*, unless *sefer Torah*

1) it is necessary to read from it during the Festival, and
2) the conditions outlined in Chapter 68, paragraph 10, exist.

b. The reason for this is that, although

1) it is a mitzva for a person to write a *sefer Torah* during his lifetime and
2) the mitzva is not kept so long as the error in the *sefer Torah* remains uncorrected,

one can fulfill the mitzva by making the correction after the Festival too.

40. *a.* A person may build a *sukka* on *chol ha-mo'ed*, whether it be *building sukka*

1) for himself or
2) for somebody else

(as in paragraph 37 above).

b. He may do so even if he already has a *sukka*, but wants a more spacious one.

41. *a.* It is proper, and in keeping with the honor due to the mitzva, to take new *aravoth* with one's *lulav* on each *cutting aravoth* day of the Festival of Sukkoth to replace those of the previous day which no longer look so fresh.

b. Consequently, one may cut them from the tree on *chol ha-mo'ed*, for this purpose (or for Hoshanah Rabbah), even in order to sell them to others who wish to perform the mitzva.

fencing roof

42. *a.* One may make a fence or rail round the edge of one's roof on *chol ha-mo'ed*, where it is a mitzva to do so.

b. This is permitted, even if one could have done it before the Festival, because every moment that the fence or rail remains unconstructed one is transgressing

1) the injunction, "You shall not make your house the cause for spilling blood," and
2) the positive command, "You shall make a fence round your roof"

(both contained in Deuteronomy 22:8).

c. Nonetheless, if it is possible to close off the entrance to the roof, so that nobody should be able to reach it, one should not construct a fence or rail, except in a nonprofessional manner.

needs of deceased

43. *a.* One may do whatever is needed for a deceased on *chol ha-mo'ed*, including work which one performs in a professional manner.

b. However, one should not pull up grass in the cemetery, as some are accustomed to do after the interment of the body.

se'udath mitzva after Festival

44. If a meal which is a mitzva (such as a meal in celebration of a circumcision) is timed to take place shortly after the Festival, and one will not have the possibility of preparing it on the expiry of the Festival, one may prepare what one needs on *chol ha-mo'ed*.

non-professional activities

45. *a.* 1) It is permitted to perform an activity in a nonprofessional manner on *chol ha-mo'ed*, for the purposes of a mitzva,

a) even if the mitzva is to be fulfilled by another person and
b) even if it is not to be fulfilled until after the Festival,

provided one will not have the opportunity to perform the activity in time after the Festival.

2) One may receive payment for the work, if one will thereby have more money to spend on enjoying the Festival.

b. As a result,

1) one may tie *tzitzith*, not only on to one's own *tallith*, but also onto someone else's (even if he is not going to wear it until after the Festival),
2) one may insert the parchment scrolls into *tefillin* and sew the *tefillin* shut, and
3) one may cut the *tefillin* straps and attach them to the *tefillin*, but
4) one may not make the *tefillin* themselves (that is to say, the actual phylactery cases) on *chol ha-mo'ed*, for someone else to use after the Festival, since this can only be done in a professional way. (See paragraphs 37 and 38 above.)

46. *a.* 1) It is forbidden to build a synagogue on *chol ha-mo'ed*, even if construction commenced before the Festival and it only needs the final touch, for example, painting. *works in synagogue*

2) It is also prohibited to paint the Holy Ark, containing the *sifrei Torah*.
3) The reason, in both cases, is that the work has to be done in a professional manner.

b. For the same reason, one may not sew clothes for a bride and groom, even if one started sewing before the Festival and the wedding is due to take place immediately after the Festival. *sewing for wedding*

47. *a.* One may, on *chol ha-mo'ed*, *engagements, weddings*

1) become engaged to be married and may also

2) write out the agreement containing the terms upon which the marriage is to take place.

b. The Rabbis did indeed forbid the holding of marriages during a Festival, but only so that the joy of the Festival should not be forgotten in the joy of the marriage.

c. It is allowed to dance at the celebration of an engagement.

d. See further, Chapter 68, paragraphs 27 and 29.

leaving work for chol ha-mo'ed

48. It should be noted that an otherwise forbidden activity may be performed for the purposes of a mitzva, as set out in the preceding paragraphs, even if one has (albeit wrongfully) left it on purpose to be done on *chol ha-mo'ed*.

Chapter 68

Chol Ha-Mo'ed: Public Needs, Impoverished Workmen, a Miscellany Including Activities Involving Trouble, and Using the Services of a Non-Jew

ACTIVITIES FOR THE BENEFIT OF THE PUBLIC

1. *a.* One may attend to all public needs on *chol ha-mo'ed*, within the limits set out in the following paragraphs. *why permitted*

b. 1) The principle reason why this is permitted is because public affairs tend to be dealt with only when people are free from their normal business and can meet together in order to take care of them.

2) If one is not allowed to work on these matters then, they will be neglected, and will not be attended to at all.

3) Taking this into consideration, the permission to work on public affairs during *chol ha-mo'ed* is similar to the permission to work in order to avoid a loss. (See Chapter 67, paragraphs 1 to 21.)

4) It also has an affinity to working for the purposes of a mitzva, which is permitted too. (See Chapter 67, paragraphs 36 to 48.)

c. One may deal with public affairs on *chol ha-mo'ed*, even if a great deal of trouble is entailed.

2. *a.* 1) Anything used by the public is considered to be a public need, including those public services on which the regular conduct of daily life depends, even if the service in question caters, in each specific case, for the needs of individuals. *scope*

2) It is in the public interest to keep these services running, so that they can be used to the extent permitted on *chol ha-mo'ed*.

b. Thus, one may repair a public thoroughfare, so that passersby should not meet with an accident.

c. On similar grounds, Rabbinical courts of law may do whatever is required for them to continue functioning, such as writing out the pleadings of the parties. (See paragraph 18 below.)

d. An additional illustration is the banking service, which can be used on *chol ha-mo'ed*, for example
   1) by somebody who is forced to borrow or exchange money for the purposes of the Festival, or
   2) to deposit money in one's account,
      a) so that it should not be stolen from one's house, or
      b) in order to cover a check one has drawn, or
      c) in the form of a check one has received, and which one wishes to have collected immediately, in case the drawer will not have the funds to cover it in his account after the Festival.

e. Due to the difficulties of definition and the danger of widespread, unjustified violations of the sanctity of *chol ha-mo'ed*, it is right to ask a recognized halachic authority for his opinion on the facts of each individual case.

distinctions

3. As will be explained below, the Rabbis made distinctions, with respect to activities carried out for the needs of the public,

a. between those done in a professional manner and those done in a nonprofessional manner and

b. between those done for the purposes of the Festival and those not done for the purposes of the Festival.

how to do them

4. *a.* Work may be carried out for public purposes in a normal professional manner on *chol ha-mo'ed* only if
   1) it serves a physical, human requirement (that is to say, the physical welfare or physical convenience of the public) **and**
   2) it is needed for the Festival.

b. It may be carried out
1) in a nonprofessional manner, or
2) in a professional manner, but with a variation which will be apparent in the finished product,

even if it neither serves a physical, human requirement, nor is needed for the Festival.

c. The work may not be done in a normal professional manner, even when one's intention is to perform a mitzva,
1) if it does not serve a physical, human requirement, **or**
2) if it is not needed for the Festival

(except in the case of a transitory mitzva, as to which see Chapter 67, paragraph 37).

planned for chol ha-mo'ed

5. *a.* In the event that one is unable to find suitable workmen on an ordinary day of the week, one may deliberately arrange to carry out work for public purposes on *chol ha-mo'ed.*

b. What is more, the workmen may receive remuneration for their work, even if it is executed openly and with a great deal of trouble.

public and private purposes compared

6. Upon examination, it will be apparent that the differences between performing on *chol ha-mo'ed* an activity which is forbidden on Yom Tov for public purposes and performing it for private purposes are those which follow.

a. 1) Activities for the benefit of the public, needed for the Festival, may be performed even in a professional manner, so long as they serve a physical, human requirement.

2) Activities for the benefit of an individual, needed for the Festival, may not be performed in a professional manner, even if they serve a physical, human requirement, except as set out in Chapter 66, paragraphs 8, 21 and 37.

b. 1) Activities for the benefit of the public, needed for the Festival, may be performed even if one deliberately left them to be done on *chol ha-mo'ed.*

2) Activities for the benefit of an individual, needed for the Festival, may not be performed if one deliberately left them for *chol ha-mo'ed*, except that one may leave the preparation of food for *chol ha-mo'ed*. (See Chapter 66, paragraph 9.)

c. 1) Activities for the benefit of the public, not needed for the Festival, may be performed
   a) in a nonprofessional manner or
   b) in a professional manner, but with a variation which will be noticeable in the finished product.

2) Activities for the benefit of an individual, not needed for the Festival (as defined in Chapter 66, paragraph 34), must not be performed at all, except in the circumstances referred to in Chapter 67, paragraphs 2 and 3. (See Chapter 66, paragraph 42.)

d. 1) The receipt of remuneration in return for work performed for the public is permitted.

2) The receipt of remuneration in return for work performed for an individual is prohibited, except
   a) by a workman who has nothing to eat (as to which see paragraphs 19 to 23 below), or
   b) in the other circumstances set out in Chapter 66, paragraph 40.

roads, mikva'oth, electricity and transport

7. *a.* 1) It follows that it is permitted
   a) to repair pathways and roads and to remove obstructions, so that people should not stumble over them, and in order to prevent accidents happening,
   b) to build and repair *mikva'oth*,
   c) to install water taps in the synagogue, so that congregants can wash their hands before prayers, and
   d) to repair the electricity network on a public or communal staircase, if there is a risk that people might stumble in the dark or fall down the stairs.

2) All of these things are permitted only provided the work is finished on *chol ha-mo'ed*, so that it will still

be possible to benefit from it during the Festival.

b. Public transport is allowed on *chol ha-mo'ed*.

8. *a.* A mechanic may make any repairs required to a vehicle which is used for public transport on *chol ha-mo'ed*. *vehicle repairs*

b. This includes repairs to trucks designated for the transport of foodstuffs for the Festival.

c. In all such cases, one is allowed to receive remuneration for one's work.

d. Here too, work is permitted only if it is completed on *chol ha-mo'ed*, so that a benefit can be derived from it during the Festival.

9. *a.* A carpenter may make new seats, or repair broken seats, for a synagogue on *chol ha-mo'ed*, since arguments may be caused if there are not enough seats for the Festival prayers. *synagogues*

b. One may also call in a professional electrician to repair the electricity network, if there would otherwise be no light in the synagogue, so that one could not see to pray there.

c. Nevertheless, in cases such as these, one ought to consult the opinion of a Torah sage, because people may not take *chol ha-mo'ed* seriously if they see work continuing as usual.

d. It is forbidden to build a synagogue on *chol ha-mo'ed*, or to whitewash it, or to paint the Holy Ark containing the *sifrei Torah*, as none of these things serves a physical, human need.

10. *a.* 1) If a *sefer Torah* is found to be halachically unfit for use, even in the middle of the reading, it should not be corrected on *chol ha-mo'ed* (except in the instances mentioned below), but a second one should be taken out. *correcting sefer Torah*

2) This is so, even if the second *sefer Torah* is the only one there fit to be used, so that the congregation will be kept waiting while it is rolled to the right place

for the reading of *maftir* on Yom Tov.

b. 1) Should there be no other *sefer Torah* at all there which is fit for reading during the Festival, one may correct the defective *sefer Torah* on *chol ha-mo'ed.*

2) The reason is that the inability to read the appropriate portions on each day of the Festival is considered a loss which one may take steps to avoid on *chol ha-mo'ed.*

3) The *sefer Torah* may be corrected in these circumstances, even if it would be possible to bring another *sefer Torah* from elsewhere.

c. In the following cases, the type of correction needed requires no professional expertise and may, consequently, be made on *chol ha-mo'ed*, even if there is another *sefer Torah* in the synagogue which could quite easily be taken out and used:

1) where nothing has to be done other than to separate letters which are touching;

2) where one just has to erase a superfluous letter, and will not have to extend adjoining letters to fill the gap created by the erasure;

3) where a letter has been rubbed out, but its impression is still recognizable, so that all one has to do to make the *sefer Torah* fit for use is to retrace the existing marks with the quill.

finishing sefer Torah

11. *a.* If a scribe finished writing a *sefer Torah* before the Festival, but left the last few words with just the outside contours of the letters marked, one may ink them in on *chol ha-mo'ed.*

b. This is because filling in the already marked outlines does not require professional expertise.

c. None the less, it is proper to finish writing the *sefer Torah* altogether before the Festival.

scribe's quill and ink

12. In all those cases mentioned above where it is permissible to correct a *sefer Torah* on *chol ha-mo'ed*, it is also allowed to sharpen the quill and prepare ink for the writing one has to do.

13. *a.* 1) Those who take a lenient view and publish a religious newspaper on *chol ha-mo'ed* have authority on which they can rely, and one should not raise any objection to their action. *newspapers*

2) In the first place, the printing of the newspaper could be considered a public necessity, since

a) people are used to reading the press, in order to inform themselves of the world news, so that,

b) if they do not find religious papers, they will go and read other papers, and

c) there is a strong risk of their being infected by the heretical views appearing in those other papers.

3) Secondly, there is cause to believe that, if the newspaper does not appear on *chol ha-mo'ed*, it will result in a loss of the kind one may take steps to avoid on *chol ha-mo'ed*, as explained in Chapter 67, paragraph 12.

b. One may publish all kinds of advertisements in a religious newspaper which appears on *chol ha-mo'ed*, even if their subject matter is not required for the purposes of the Festival.

c. 1) One may certainly not, however, write and print articles on *chol ha-mo'ed*, with the object of having them ready for the days following the Festival (except in circumstances like those set out in Chapter 67, paragraph 12).

2) Thus, one must not write in advance, on *chol ha-mo'ed*, articles for supplements which will be sold with the newspaper after the Festival, as they are in no way needed for the Festival.

14. *a.* 1) One is permitted to carry out public, sanitary works on *chol ha-mo'ed*. *sanitation*

2) Therefore, one may unblock a clogged sewage system.

b. 1) As detailed in Chapter 66, paragraph 58, there are also circumstances in which such works may be carried out for an individual.

2) For example, if the toilet breaks on *chol ha-mo'ed*, it may be replaced (at least according to one view mentioned there), even in a professional manner.
3) On the other hand, it is prohibited to install an additional washbasin in a private home, if one could manage without.

handling public affairs

15. *a.* There is a practice of settling public matters during *chol ha-mo'ed*.
b. Illustrations are
1) the appointment of individuals to lead the community and manage its affairs and
2) the calculation of charitable finances.
c. One may even write for these purposes, but one should use a normal script, which does not require any professional expertise.
d. It is also allowed for a fund-raiser to write a receipt for a charitable contribution, if the donor so requests.

appointing rabbi or cantor

16. *a.* One may write and send a letter to a rabbi or a cantor on *chol ha-mo'ed*, inviting him to accept a position with the congregation.
b. It should be written in a script which does not demand any professional expertise.

writing k^e^thubah

17. *a.* One may write a *k^e^thubah* on *chol ha-mo'ed* for a married woman who does not have one.
b. However, one should not write it in the script in which *sifrei Torah* or *m^e^zuzoth* are written, but in an ordinary script which does not require any professional expertise.

Rabbinical courts

18. *a.* Hearings may take place in the Rabbinical courts of law on *chol ha-mo'ed*.
b. One may also write down the particulars of the pleadings and the judgments.
c. The reason is that these matters are considered to be a public need.

IMPOVERISHED WORKMEN

19. *a.* One may give any kind of work on *chol ha-mo'ed* to a workman who does not have anything to eat, so that he should be able to earn something. *the principle*

b. Such a workman may also work for a non-Jew on *chol ha-mo'ed*, in order to earn some money.

c. The relevant laws applicable fall into two categories, as will be explained below.

20. *a.* A workman who does not have enough to buy the basic daily food for himself and the members of his family is not obliged to sell his household goods so as to avoid the necessity for working on *chol ha-mo'ed*. *earning enough to eat*

b. He

1) may take on even work which is required
   a) neither for the purpose of the Festival,
   b) nor in order to avoid a loss, and
2) may work in a professional manner, even without making any change from the usual way in which the work is done.

c. Furthermore, even if he purposely (and impermissibly) scheduled the performance of the work in advance for *chol ha-mo'ed*, one does not penalize him for doing so, and he is allowed to earn enough to support himself and the members of his household.

d. 1) He is indeed obliged to do the work discreetly, insofar as possible, since not everyone knows that he is permitted to work on account of his penury, but,
2) where the work cannot be performed discreetly, he may do it openly.

e. 1) Nonetheless, even a workman who has reached such a level of poverty is not permitted, on *chol ha-mo'ed*,
   a) to cut the hair, or trim or shave the beard, of a Jew, or
   b) to launder a Jew's clothes, although
2) he may carry out these services for a non-Jew.

earning more than minimum needed for food

21. *a.* A workman who is as penurious as described in the preceding paragraph, and is permitted to work on *chol ha-mo'ed* to earn a living, may finish the work he has started, even though he will thereby earn more than he needs to support his family.

b. He may even initially take on such work, although he knows that it will bring him in more than the minimum that he needs.

c. Once he has finished this work, however, he must not take on any additional work.

earning Festival needs

22. *a.* 1) Someone who has food for his basic, daily requirements, but cannot afford to buy what he needs for the Festival, may work on *chol ha-mo'ed*, even in a professional manner, but only for the purposes of a mitzva to be performed during the Festival.

2) See Chapter 67, paragraph 37.

b. 1) If he does the work in a nonprofessional manner, he may perform it even for the purposes of a mitzva to be fulfilled after the Festival, since the remuneration he receives in return will make it easier for him to expend money on enjoying Yom Tov.

2) For details, see Chapter 67, paragraph 45.

trading to earn Festival needs

23. Such a person, who has enough food for his daily requirements, but not sufficient for the other needs of the Festival, may engage in commerce, so long as he spends part of his profits on enjoying the Festival. (See Chapter 67, paragraph 19.)

ACTIVITIES INVOLVING TROUBLE, AND WORKADAY ACTIVITIES WHICH ARE PERMITTED

activities forbidden due to bother: the rule

24. *a.* 1) There are activities which, if performed on Yom Tov, would not contravene any prohibition, but which the Rabbis forbade on *chol ha-mo'ed*, because they involve a great deal of trouble.

2) There are also activities which involve only a small

amount of trouble, but which the Rabbis forbade, because they were afraid that doing them would impair a person's enjoyment of the Festival.

3) See also Chapter 67, paragraph 16.

b. 1) It is, consequently, forbidden to move house on *chol ha-mo'ed*, except in special circumstances, as where one is moving

a) from a rented apartment to one's own, or

b) from a shared apartment to an apartment of which one will have exclusive occupation.

2) A duly recognized halachic authority should be consulted to ensure that one's own specific circumstances justify moving on *chol ha-mo'ed*.

c. It is also prohibited, because of the trouble involved, to move heavy articles from one place to another, if indeed they are safe where they are now.

d. 1) One may not, generally speaking, trade in merchandise which is not required for the purpose of the Festival.

2) See, in this connection, Chapter 67, paragraphs 24 to 31.

e. One must not bring articles, even through the medium of non-Jewish porters, from the workshop where they have been completed or repaired, unless they are required for the purpose of the Festival.

f. 1) One is allowed to order a refrigerator and have it brought home on *chol ha-mo'ed*, if one will still make use of it during the Festival, but

2) one is forbidden to order a washing machine, since one does not wash clothes on *chol ha-mo'ed*, as explained in Chapter 66, paragraph 63.*

---

* In those cases in which one may wash clothes on *chol ha-mo'ed* (as to which see Chapter 66, paragraphs 64 to 67), it may indeed be permitted to order a washing machine, if one will still be able to use it on *chol ha-mo'ed*.

veterinary treatment

25. One may give veterinary treatment to animals on *chol ha-mo'ed*, even by a method involving activities that would otherwise be prohibited on *chol ha-mo'ed*.

examples of forbidden and permitted activities

26. *a.* 1) It is not always clear whether a particular activity which is forbidden on Yom Tov is forbidden or permitted on *chol ha-mo'ed*, if not needed for the purpose of the Festival.

2) a) There is, however, a general rule, in addition to what is contained in this, and the preceding two, chapters, which should be used as a guide.

b) Whatever the Rabbis, **as they saw it**, considered to involve excessive bother they forbade on *chol ha-mo'ed*, because it could inhibit one's enjoyment of the Festival.

b. For instance, the Rabbis forbade the following activities, where they are not being performed for the Festival:

1) painting;
2) tying and untying knots;
3) cutting materials into small pieces.

c. 1) On the other hand, we find that the following activities were not in themselves prohibited on *chol ha-mo'ed*:

a) transferring objects from one place to another, even without any need;
b) moving things which would be *muktzeh* on Yom Tov;
c) asking somebody to do later what is forbidden now (as to which see Chapter 29, paragraph 51);
d) separating *t^erumoth*, *ma'asroth* and *challa*, even if one does not need the item of food in question on the Festival;
e) immersing vessels in a *mikveh*, even if one has no need for them during the Festival;
f) walking to any distance;
g) kindling a fire.

2) a) There is also room for being lenient, to a large extent, with regard to the performance of an activity

forbidden on Yom Tov, by an animal belonging to, or led by, a Jew (as to which see Chapter 27, paragraphs 1 to 16).

b) The animal may perform the activity on *chol ha-mo'ed*, even without any need, provided it is not an activity which is forbidden to the Jew himself on Yom Tov by virtue of a Torah (as distinct from a Rabbinical) prohibition.

c) Thus, one may allow an animal to go out, with a burden on its back, into a place which does not strictly fulfill the criteria of a *r^eshuth ha-rabbim*, as defined in Chapter 17, paragraph 3.*

music and dancing

27. *a.* The general prohibitions on producing a sound on Shabbath or Yom Tov by means of a musical instrument, and on dancing and clapping hands, as explained in Chapter 28, paragraphs 32, 36 and 38, are not applicable on *chol ha-mo'ed*.

b. See also Chapter 66, paragraph 61.

release of vows

28. Although the release of vows is forbidden on Shabbath or Yom Tov, except when it is required for Shabbath or the Festival, or for the purpose of a mitzva, as stated in Chapter 29, paragraph 58, it is permitted in all cases on *chol ha-mo'ed*.

marriages and other celebrations

29. *a.* 1) Weddings should not be held on *chol ha-mo'ed*.

2) It is also the custom not to marry on the day before a Festival, except in case of great need, as where it is not possible to postpone the marriage.

3) When a marriage took place before a Festival, one may have *sheva b^erachoth* on Yom Tov and *chol ha-mo'ed*.**

---

* It will be seen, from Chapter 19, paragraphs 2 and 7, that transfers from one place to another may be forbidden on Yom Tov if they serve no purpose.

** When one has *sheva b^erachoth* on the Festival of Sukkoth, one should eat in the *sukka*, but neither the groom nor the guests should pronounce the blessing on being in the *sukka* (since it may well be that they have no obligation to eat there).

b. 1) It is permitted, on *chol ha-mo'ed*, to become engaged to be married, and to write out the customary agreement containing the terms upon which the marriage is to take place.

2) There is likewise nothing wrong with the practice of eating cakes and confectionery at the time of writing the agreement.

3) Nonetheless, one should not at that time serve a full-scale meal, since celebrating the joy of a private occasion to such an extent tends to dilute the joy one ought to feel on account of the Festival.

c. See also Chapter 67, paragraph 47.

d. 1) The joy engendered by other celebrations is not considered to be on the same level as that at weddings and engagements, and so does not detract from the joy of the Festival.

2) Therefore, one may serve a proper meal

a) at a circumcision or

b) at the redemption of a firstborn son

(regardless of whether they are taking place on time or whether they have been delayed).

3) Similarly, one may serve a proper meal at a housewarming.

tape recordings

30. One may record a speech or a song on a tape recorder on *chol ha-mo'ed*,

a. if one is indeed doing it for the purpose of the Festival, or

b. if one is afraid that the opportunity to do so will not be repeated after the Festival.

incidental performance of forbidden activity

31. *a.* It is in order to perform an activity which is usually forbidden on *chol ha-mo'ed*, if it is merely incidental to a permissible activity, as long as

1) one's intention is in fact to do only the permissible, and not the forbidden, activity and

2) it is plain from one's actions that one's intention is directed solely to the permissible activity.

b. Chapter 66, paragraph 47, contains an illustration of this principle, and others follow below.

c. By way of further example, one may cut growing branches to put on one's *sukka*, provided one cuts them all from one side of the tree, so that one should not seem to be pruning the tree on *chol ha-mo'ed*.

d. 1) One is permitted to eat in a garden, even though it is extremely likely that some drink will be spilled there.

2) One may also wash one's hands from a tap which is in the garden.

3) There is no room to prohibit these activities on the grounds that the water will irrigate plants which it is forbidden to irrigate on *chol ha-mo'ed* (as to which see Chapter 67, paragraph 17*d*).

e. 1) It is permissible to clean the yard for the Festival,

a) even with a broom made of straws, twigs or reeds,

b) even if some of the straw, twigs or reeds will break in the process and

c) even if one will come to level out depressions in the floor of the yard.

2) It is, however, forbidden to clear the accumulated refuse out of the yard, unless it increases inordinately in quantity.

32. *a.* For tearing one's clothes in mourning for a deceased on *chol ha-mo'ed*, see Chapter 64, paragraph 3, and Chapter 65, paragraph 54. *mourning*

b. For laws relating to an *onein* on *chol ha-mo'ed*, see Chapter 64, paragraph 24.

c. 1) It is prohibited to eulogize a deceased on *chol ha-mo'ed*, except in the case of a Torah sage, at his funeral.

2) Still, the custom is not to eulogize even a deceased Torah sage at his funeral.

d. Concerning burial, attending to other needs of a deceased on *chol ha-mo'ed* and the custom of pulling up grass after the burial, see Chapter 67, paragraph 43.

e. Regarding the first meal following the burial, which mourners eat from other people's food, see Chapter 65, paragraph 4.

f. With respect to mourning on *chol ha-mo'ed*, see Chapter 65, paragraphs 32, 38, 39, 46 and 48.

ACTIVITIES PERFORMED ON CHOL HA-MO'ED BY, OR FOR, NON-JEWS

general prohibition on acting through non-Jew

33. *a.* Whatever a Jew is forbidden to do on *chol ha-mo'ed*, he may not tell a non-Jew to do for him.

b. The following types of situation are among those falling within this prohibition:

1) where a loss will indeed be caused by failure to act, but the Jew deliberately arranged in advance to take the required action on *chol ha-mo'ed*;

2) where
   a) although failure to act will not actually cause a loss of one's property,
   b) it is liable to deteriorate to a certain extent, but
   c) not all of the conditions listed in Chapter 67, paragraph 1801a are fulfilled;

3) where something has to be done for the purpose of the Festival, but
   a) the Jew deliberately arranged in advance to take the required action on *chol ha-mo'ed*, or
   b) he wishes to have it carried out in a professional manner;

4) where something which might otherwise be permitted is forbidden due to the excessive bother involved;

5) trading which is not for the purpose of the Festival.

c. The prohibition on employing a non-Jew applies even if one has the opportunity of hiring him to work on *chol ha-mo'ed* at a cheaper rate than usual.

buying through non-Jew

34. *a.* 1) A Jew must not ask a non-Jew to buy something for him on *chol ha-mo'ed*, if the Jew himself is forbidden to make the purchase because of the sanctity of *chol ha-mo'ed*. (See Chapter 67, paragraph 24.)

2) This is prohibited, even if the Jew tells him before the Festival to make the purchase on *chol ha-mo'ed*.

b. 1) He may, however, tell the non-Jew to buy something for himself, and promise to buy it from him after the Festival.

2) He is even allowed to lend him money for this purpose. (Compare Chapter 30, paragraph 34, and Chapter 31, paragraph 16.)

35. *a.* 1) One may request a non-Jew to do on *chol ha-mo'ed* anything which is for the purpose of a mitzva to be performed during the Festival. *for a mitzva*

2) Thus, one may ask a non-Jew to paint the synagogue, provided he finishes before the end of *chol ha-mo'ed*, so that it will still be possible to pray there during the Festival.

b. 1) One may also engage a non-Jew to work on a communal project on *chol ha-mo'ed*, if a mitzva which it is intended to perform straight after the Festival could not otherwise be performed.

2) Thus, one may let him carry out repairs in a school, if halting the work would leave the building unfit to be used immediately after the Festival, for such activities as public Torah study, which would, therefore, be cancelled.

36. Regarding *work ordered, or done, on chol ha-mo'ed*

a. the delivery of work to a non-Jew before the Festival, to be done on *chol ha-mo'ed*, or

b. the delivery of work to a non-Jew on *chol ha-mo'ed*, to be done after the Festival,

one should consult the opinion of an expert in the Halacha, since there are many fine distinctions in the rules applicable.

37. *a.* 1) A Jew must not perform any workaday activity for a non-Jew on *chol ha-mo'ed*, as long as he is not compelled to do so by the unavoidable force of cir- *working for non-Jew* cumstances.

2) This is so, even if the activity is one which he would be allowed to perform for himself or for another Jew, for instance
   a) in preparing food or
   b) for the purposes of that day, with a change in the way it is done, or in a nonprofessional manner.

selling to non-Jew

b. 1) Nonetheless, if one's shop is permissibly open on *chol ha-mo'ed*, as in the cases described in Chapter 67, paragraph 27, one may sell to a non-Jew who comes to buy one's merchandise.

2) Furthermore, one may perform those ancillary acts which are required by law when one effects a sale, such as
   a) writing him a receipt or
   b) printing one out on a cash register.

benefitting from work done on chol ha-mo'ed

38. If a non-Jew does perform a forbidden activity for a Jew on *chol ha-mo'ed*, the Jew is, nevertheless, permitted to benefit from that activity, even during the Festival.

Glossary

Comprehensive index to Volumes I, II, and III appears in a separate volume.

Glossary

(Please note: This Glossary is not intended to give an exhaustive and precise definition of each expression which it contains. It is designed merely to help the reader obtain a *general* idea of the meaning of unfamiliar words he may find in the text. Its use for any other purpose may well be misleading.)

afikoman: The piece of matza eaten at the end of the meal on seder night.

Aleinu: Prayer recited towards the end of each of the daily services.

al ha-michya: The blessing recited (in most cases) after eating cake or cookies (biscuits).

al ha-nissim: An additional prayer inserted into *birkath ha-mazon* and *Shemoneh Esrei* on Chanuka and Purim.

al ha-peiroth: The blessing recited after eating grapes, figs, pomegranates, olives or dates.

"al kein beirach": The words with which the Shabbath morning *kiddush* is begun (literally, "therefore, blessed...") according to the custom of some.

"al teshiveinu": Words in the sixteenth blessing of *Shemoneh Esrei* (literally, "do not turn us away") after which miscellaneous supplications may be added.

"al yechassreinu": Concluding words of the fourth blessing of *birkath ha-mazon* (literally, "may He not deprive us").

amah (plural ***amoth***): A measure of length, 22.7 inches (57.6 centimeters) by one halachic view, 18.9 inches (48 centimeters) by another. In any given instance involving this measure, that view is followed which makes for greater stringency.

Amidah: *Shemoneh Esrei.*

aravoth: Willow twigs, one of the *arba'a minim* used on Sukkoth.

arba kanfoth: A four-cornered garment with a prescribed tassel (*tzitzith*) at each corner, worn to fulfill the biblical injunction to wear fringes on the corners of one's garment.

arba'a minim: Collective name for *ethrog, lulav, hadassim* and *aravoth.*

Asher yatzar ethchem ba-din: The blessing recited upon seeing graves.

"Atah chonantanu": Opening words of a passage added in *Sh^{e}moneh Esrei* at the end of Shabbath or Yom Tov, when followed by an ordinary weekday (including *chol ha-mo'ed*). Literally, "You have graced us."

"Atah chonein": Opening words of the fourth blessing of *Shemoneh Esrei*. Literally, "You grace."

"Atah v^{e}chartanu": Opening words of the fourth blessing of the *Amidah* on Yom Tov. Literally, "You have chosen us."

Av: The month of the Jewish calendar in which the Temple was destroyed.

"Ba-meh madlikin": The second chapter of Mishnayoth, Tractate Shabbath, customarily recited on Friday night. Literally, "With what does one kindle."

"Bar^{e}chi nafshi": Commencement of the first of a number of psalms customarily recited on Shabbath afternoon in the winter. Literally, "Bless, O my soul."

Bar^{e}chu: The first word (literally, "Bless") of the phrase calling upon the congregation to bless God.

"Baruch atah Ha-shem Ha-Mavdil bein kodesh l^{e}-chol": "Blessed art Thou, O Lord, Who divides between the holy and the profane."Conclusion of the blessing of *havdala* after Yom Tov, or when it is an ordinary week-day after Shabbath.

"Baruch atah Ha-shem Ha-Mavdil bein kodesh l^{e}-kodesh": "Blessed art Thou, O Lord, Who divides between one holiness and another." Conclusion of the blessing of *havdala* when it is Yom Tov at the end of Shabbath.

"Baruch Dayan ha-emeth": "Blessed is the true Judge." Abbreviated form of the blessing recited on receiving bad news.

"Baruch Ha-Mavdil bein kodesh l^{e}-chol": "Blessed is He Who divides between the holy and the profane." Pronouncement made to mark the end of Shabbath or Yom Tov.

"Baruch Ha-Mavdil bein kodesh l^{e}-kodesh": "Blessed is He Who divides between one holiness and another." Pronouncement made to mark the end of Shabbath when it is Yom Tov on Sunday.

"Baruch Hu u-varuch sh^{e}mo": "Blessed be He and blessed be

His name," the customary response on hearing the name of the Almighty mentioned in a blessing.

basis la-davar ha-assur: An article which the Halacha subjects to the same restrictions on handling as a *muktzeh* object that has been placed or hung on it.

bein ha-shemashoth: The period between sunset and when the stars come out.

"be-Yom Ha-kippurim ha-zeh": Literally, "on this Day of Atonement." Inserted into *Ya'aleh Ve-yavo* of *birkath ha-mazon* if one has to eat on Yom Kippur.

birchoth ha-Torah: Blessings recited before the study or reading of the Torah.

"Bi-reshuth rabbothai": "With the permission of my masters...," the words pronounced before a blessing, requesting permission to commence from the others for whom it is also being said.

birkath ha-mazon: The blessing recited after eating bread or a meal including bread (Grace after Meals).

birkath ha-zimun: The form of introduction to, and commencement of, *birkath ha-mazon* used when three or more people have eaten together.

"Bo'i ve-shalom": The last verse of *Lecha dodi. Literally, "Come in peace."*

"bonei berachamav Yerushalayim amen": Concluding words of the third blessing of *birkath ha-mazon*. Literally, "Who rebuilds Jerusalem in His mercy. Amen."

"borei atzei besamim": End of the blessing on sweet-smelling woods. Literally, "Who creates sweet-smelling woods."

"borei issuei bessamim": End of the blessing on sweet-smelling herbs. Literally, "Who creates sweet-smelling herbs."

"borei me'orei ha-eish": End of the blessing on light after Shabbath. Literally, "Who creates the lights of the fire."

"borei minei besamim": End of the blessing on spices after Shabbath. Literally, "Who creates varieties of spices."

carmelith: An area which is not *reshuth ha-rabbim*, but to which the Rabbis applied rules similar to those applying to *reshuth ha-rabbim*.

challa: A portion of the dough which has to be removed once it is kneaded and which, in Temple times, was given to a *kohen.*

chametz: Food which is made from, or contains, flour and which is leavened. It may not be eaten or kept on Pesach.

Chanuka: The Feast of Lights.

charoseth: A mixture of nuts, wine, cinnamon and apples eaten on Passover night.

Chathan B^e^reishith: The person honored to be called up to the reading of the opening paragraphs of the Torah on Simchath Torah.

Chathan Torah: The person honored to be called up to the reading of the concluding verses of the Torah on Simchath Torah.

cholent: A stew, normally containing meat, potatoes, barley and beans, put on the fire before the commencement of Shabbath and left there all night, so that one should be able to have a hot meal during the day.

chol ha-mo'ed: The intermediate days of Pesach and Sukkoth, between the first and last days of Yom Tov.

Chumash: The Pentateuch.

day: Unless otherwise indicated, or inconsistent with the context, a day, for the purposes of the Halacha, is regarded as commencing and terminating at what can colloquially be called nightfall.

"Dayan ha-emeth": Conclusion of the blessing recited upon receiving bad news. Literally, "the true Judge."

"D^e^vy haseir": Opening words of the customary introduction to *birkath ha-zimun* at *sheva berachoth*. Literally, "Remove distress."

dreidel: A spinning-top used for playing a Chanuka game.

eiruv: An abbreviation for *eiruv tavshilin* or for *eiruv chatzeiroth*; often used as a general term including both *eiruv chatzeiroth* and *shitufei m^e^vo'oth.*

eiruv chatzeiroth: The arrangement for permitting the transfer of objects on Shabbath from one *reshuth ha-yachid* to another, or within a *reshuth ha-yachid* which belongs to two or more adjoining occupiers in common. The expression is often used as a general term including also *shitufei m^e^vo'oth.*

eiruv tavshilin: The arrangement whereby one is permitted on

Yom Tov to make preparations for Shabbath occurring on the following day; also, the food set aside before Yom Tov for this purpose.

Eretz Yisrael: The geographical area of the Land of Israel within the boundaries defined by the Halacha. In case of doubt, a competent halachic authority should be consulted.

ethrog (plural ***ethrogim***): Citron, one of the *arba'a minim* used on Sukkoth.

"ga'al Yisrael": Termination of the blessing in the *haggada* said after the first part and before eating. Literally, "Who redeemed Israel."

hadass (plural ***hadassim***): Myrtle twig, used on Sukkoth.

haggada: Traditional recital, on seder night, of praises and narrative concerning the Exodus from Egypt.

Halacha (adjective: halachic): Jewish religious law.

Hallel: Psalms of praise, recited on Festivals, *rosh chodesh* and Chanuka.

Ha-mavdil: The blessing of the *havdala*.

"ha-Rachaman": Opening word of supplications added at the end of *birkath ha-mazon*. Literally, "The merciful One."

"Hashiveinu": First word of the fifth blessing of *Sh^emoneh Esrei*. Literally, "Bring us back."

Havdalah: The blessings recited at the termination of Shabbath or Yom Tov.

"Hinei Keil y^eshuathi": First words of the introductory verses to *havdala* (literally, "Behold, God is my salvation...") when recited at home after Shabbath.

Hoshanah Rabbah: Seventh day of Sukkoth.

"Im tashiv mi-Shabbath raglecha": Words commencing Isaiah 58:13 (literally, "If you draw back your foot because of Shabbath...") with which some begin Shabbath morning *kiddush*.

Iyar: The only month the whole of which falls within the counting of the *omer*.

ka-beitzah: A measure of volume twice the size of a *ka-zayith*.

kaddish: A prayer in sanctification of God's name recited after certain other prayers or after studying Torah when ten or more male adults are present.

kasher: To make meat or liver fit for a Jew to eat, by extracing the blood in accordance with the Halacha.

kosher: See *kasher*.

kashruth: State of fitness of food etc. in compliance with the Halacha.

kav: A measure of volume four times the size of a *log*.

ka-zayith: A measure of volume, concerning whose size there is considerable controversy. The two most commonly accepted views equate it to 49.8 cubic centimeters and 28.8 cubic centimeters. In practice, the size attributed to the *ka-zayith* varies with the purpose for which it is required, and a competent halachic authority should be consulted when the quantity involved is between these two figures.

k^edusha: A sanctification of God's name recited by the congregation, in conjunction with the person leading prayers, when the latter repeats the *Sh^emoneh Esrei*.

"Keil malei rachamim": Prayer for the souls of the departed. Literally, "God, full of mercy."

k^eli rishon: The pot or other vessel in which food has been cooked, so long as it retains a temperature of 45 degrees centigrade (113 degrees Fahrenheit) or more, even if it is no longer on the fire.

k^eli sheini: A pot or other vessel into which food is transferred from the vessel in which it was cooked.

k^eli shelishi: A pot or other vessel into which food is transferred from a *k^eli sheini*.

k^eli she-melachto le-issur: (plural ***keilim she-melachtam le-issur***): An object which is *muktzeh* because it is used for performing an activity that is forbidden on Shabbath.

k^ethuba: Contract which regulates the obligations of the husband on marriage.

kiddush: The blessings recited in sanctification of Shabbath and Yom Tov; often colloquially used for a snack which follows.

kil'ei kerem: Produce which grows from seeds sown within a given distance of vines; the grapes which subsequently grow on those vines.

ki-m^elo logmav: Amount of liquid which would fill one side of one's mouth when one's cheeks are puffed out.

kitel: White overgown worn on Yom Kippur and Rosh Hashana, and by some on seder night.

kohen (plural ***kohanim***): A priestly descendant of Aaron, the High Priest.

Kol Nidrei: Opening prayer at the Yom Kippur eve service.

Lag Ba-omer: Thirty-third day of the *omer*, when cutting the hair is permitted.

"lamdeini chukecha": Last two words of Psalms 119:12. Literally, "teach me Your statutes."

"Lecha dodi": Hymn welcoming the Shabbath, intoned on Friday evening. Literally, "Come, my friend."

"le-chayim": Literally, "for life." Part of the supplications contained in *Ya'aleh Ve-yavo.*

lechem mishneh: Two whole loaves with which one begins each Shabbath meal.

"le-tova": Literally, "for good." Part of the supplications contained in *Ya'aleh Ve-yavo.*

"li-vracha": Literally, "for blessing." Part of the supplications contained in *Ya'aleh ve-yavo.*

log: A measure of volume, containing four *revi'ioth.*

lulav (plural ***lulavim***): Palm branch, one of the *arba'a minim* used on Sukkoth.

ma'aser sheini: The Second Tithe removed from food grown in Eretz Yisrael. At the time when the Temple stood, it was eaten in Jerusalem; today, one must redeem it in the prescribed manner and may then eat it anywhere.

ma'asroth: The various tithes removed from food grown in what the Halacha regards as Eretz Yisrael.

maftir: Final portion read from the Torah on Shabbath and Yom Tov.

matza: (plural ***matzoth***): Unleavened bread.

matza shemura: Matza required for seder night, baked from wheat especially supervised, usually from the time of its harvesting.

mekom petur: An area which is neither *reshuth ha-rabbim*, nor *reshuth ha-yachid*, nor *carmelith.*

melaveh malkah: Meal eaten in honor of Shabbath after its termination.

mezuza (plural ***mezuzoth***): Parchment scrolls inscribed with extracts from the Pentateuch, in accordance with halachic requirements, and affixed to the doorposts.

mikveh (plural ***mikva'oth***): A ritual bath complying stricly with the requirements of Jewish religious law.

mincha: Afternoon prayer.

minyan: Quorum of ten for prayers.

mitzva (plural ***mitzvoth***): A religious obligation or duty.

"Mizmor shir l^{e}-yom ha-Shabbath: Hymn recited on Friday evening in honor of the Shabbath, after *Lecha dodi.*

"Mo'adim l^{e}-simcha": Greeting used on *chol ha-mo'ed* (literally, "Appointed times for joy").

mohel: A person who performs circumcision in accordance with the Halacha.

muktzeh: A term describing objects whose handling is subject to restrictions of various kinds on Shabbath and Yom Tov.

muktzeh mei-chamath chesron kis: Denotes an object, having an appreciable value, which is *muktzeh* because its owner is particular not to use it for other than its intended purpose, lest it be damaged. In most cases, the object's intended use is one that is forbidden on Shabbath.

muktzeh mei-chamath gufo: Denotes an object which is *muktzeh* because it is neither designed nor designated for any use, and is not fit for either human or animal consumption.

muktzeh mei-chamath mitzva: An object which has been set aside for use in the performance of a mitzva, and from which it is forbidden, as a result, to derive a benefit.

mussaf: Additional Amidah prayer recited on Shabbath, Festivals and *rosh chodesh.*

niddah: The state of menstruation, as defined by the Halacha; a woman who is in such a state.

"Nodeh l^{e}-shimcha": Opening words of customary introduction to *birkath ha-zimun* after circumcision, and sometimes at *sheva b^{e}rachoth.*

omer: The period of forty-nine days which is counted between the first day of Passover and Shavuoth.

onein: A mourner from the time of the death to the burial.

orla: Fruit which grows on a tree in the first three years after planting.

Parashath Ha-chodesh: Special portion read from the Torah on the Shabbath which falls on, or closest before, the *rosh chodesh* of Nissan, the month in which Pesach occurs.

Parashath Para: Special portion read from the Torah on the Shabbath before that on which *Pareshath Ha-chodesh* is read.

Parashath Shekalim: Special portion read from the Torah on the Shabbath which falls on, or closest before, the *rosh chodesh* of Adar, the month in which Purim occurs.

Parashath Zachor: Special portion read from the Torah on the Shabbath before Purim.

parsa (plural ***parsaoth***): A measure of length, comprising 8,000 *amoth*.

parve: Refers to food which contains neither meat nor dairy products; also, to a utensil which is used exclusively for food which is neither meat nor dairy.

pelag ha-mincha: One and a quarter hours before sunset, where one hour is defined as one-twelfth of the time between sunrise and sunset on the day in question.

Pesach: Passover.

Purim: The day on which one celebrates the deliverance of the Jews, some 2,500 years ago, from death and destruction, as described in the Book of Esther.

reshuth (plural ***reshuyoth***): A term used to denote one of the four categories of place: *reshuth ha-yachid, reshuth ha-rabbim, carmelith* and *mekom petur.*

reshuth ha-rabbim: A public thoroughfare meeting criteria laid down by the Halacha; such an area is subject to restrictions with regard to the moving of objects into, out of, or within it.

reshuth ha-yachid (plural ***reshuyoth ha-yachid***): A place which is enclosed in a manner complying with the Halacha, and within which one may carry, but which is subject to restrictions with regard to the moving of objects into and out of it.

Retzei: (1) An additional prayer inserted into *birkath ha-mazon* on Shabbath. (2) First of the final three blessings of the *Shemoneh Esrei.*

revi'ith (plural ***revi'ioth***): A liquid measure equivalent, according to three prevalent views, to 86 cubic centimeters, 137 cubic centimeters or 150 cubic centimeters.

rosh chodesh (plural ***rashei chodashim***): The first day of the Hebrew month (and also the previous day when the preceding month has thirty days).

Rosh Hashana: The New Year.

sandak: Person honored to hold the baby while it is circumcised.

s^e^chach: The roofing material of a *sukka.*

seder night: The first night of Pesach.

sefer Torah (plural ***sifrei Torah***): A scroll containing the Pentateuch.

"seven-in-one" blessing: Summarized version of the Friday night *Amidah*, repeated by the person leading prayers.

sha'atnez: A combination of wool and linen.

Shabbath Shira: The Shabbath on which the regular weekly portion read from the Torah includes the song sung by Moses and the Children of Israel at the crossing of the Red Sea.

"Shalom aleichem": First two words of the hymn customarily recited after arriving home from the synagogue on Friday night.

"Shavua tov": Greeting used after the conclusion of Shabbath or Yom Tov.

Shavuoth: The Festival of Weeks.

she-assa nissim: Blessing recited on Purim and Chanuka.

she-hecheyanu: Blessing recited in gratitude to the Almighty for enabling us to reach a particular occasion, such as a Festival, or eating the new season's fruit or wearing new clothes.

Sh^e^ma: Extracts from the Pentateuch whose recital is obligatory twice every day and commences with an acceptance of the sole sovereignty of God.

Sh^e^mini Atzereth: The Eighth Day of Solemn Assembly.

Sh^e^moneh Esrei: The principal of the prayers, recited in a standing position at least three times every day (with variations on Shabbath and other special days).

sheva b^e^rachoth: Blessings pronounced at a marriage and after the celebratory meals held on the ensuing days, in honor of the bride and groom.

shitufei m^e^vo'oth: The arrangement by which it becomes permissible to transfer objects in, to or from the street on Shabbath.

shi'urim: Prescribed quantities forming the limit of what may be eaten over short periods of time on Yom Kippur by a person whose life would otherwise be in danger (and who is not in need of more).

shofar: Horn blown on Rosh Hashanah.

Simchath Torah: The Festival of the Rejoicing of the Law.

Sivan: Month of the Hebrew calendar which occurs after Iyar, and in which Shavuoth falls.

siyata di-Shmaya: Help from Heaven.

sukka: The booth in which one resides during Sukkoth.

Sukkoth: The Festival of Tabernacles.

Tachanun: Prayer usually recited after the *Amidah* on weekday mornings and afternoons.

tachshit (plural ***tachshitim***): An ornament, or an object which is not an article of clothing but is worn for the purposes of the body.

tallith (plural ***tallitoth***): A prayer shawl.

Tamuz: Month of the Hebrew calendar which occurs after Sivan and before Av.

taref: Halachically unfit for consumption, or for use with food.

Targum: Literally, "translation." Used especially of the Aramaic translation of the Torah by Onkelos.

tefach (plural ***tefachim***): A measure of length, 3.8 inches (9.6 centimeters) by one halachic view, 3.15 inches (8 centimeters) by another. In any given instance involving this measure, that view is followed which makes for greater stringency.

tefillin: Phylacteries.

teruma (plural ***terumoth***): That part which is initially removed from food grown in what the Halacha regards as Eretz Yisrael, and which, in Temple times, was given to a *kohen*. The plural form, *terumoth*, is often used to denote *teruma* and *terumath ma'aser.*

terumath ma'aser: A tenth part which is removed for the tithe designated for the Levite out of food grown in what the Halacha regards as Eretz Yisrael, and which, in Temple times, was given to a *kohen.*

Teveth: Winter month of the Hebrew calendar, containing the Fast of the Tenth of Teveth.

"three-in-one" blessing: Short form of Grace after Meals, recited after cake, cookies, certain fruits and cooked cereals and wine.

Tik'u va-chodesh: Words with which the Rosh Hashanah morning *kiddush* is customarily commenced.

Torah: The Pentateuch; the whole body of Jewish law and learning; a *sefer Torah.*

tosefeth: Time which must be added at the beginning and end of Shabbath, Yom Tov and Yom Ha-kippurim.

"Tzidkathcha tzedek": Verses usually recited after the Shabbath *mincha* prayer.

tzitzith: Fringes which the Halacha requires to be worn on the four corners of a garment.

"u-medubakim be-yir'atecha": Last words of "*Atah chonantanu.*" Literally, "and attached to fear of You."

"U-venei Yerushalayim": Commencing words of the last part of the third blessing of *birkath ha-mazon*. Literally, "And rebuild Jerusalem."

Va-todi'einu: Additional prayer inserted into the evening *Amidah* when it is Yom Tov on the expiry of Shabbath.

Va-yechulu: Verses from Genesis 2:1-3, recited during and after the Friday night *Amidah* and at the beginning of the Friday night *kiddush*.

"Va-yedaber Moshe": Words with which the morning *kiddush* is customarily commenced on Festivals.

"Va-yehi erev va-yehi voker": Phrase prefaced by some to the Friday night *kiddush.*

"Ve-atah kadosh": Opening words of Psalm 22, verse 4, introducing the prayer said after the *Amidah* on the expiry of Shabbath.

Ve-shameru: Verses from Exodus 31:16-17, customarily prefaced to the Shabbath morning *kiddush.*

"Ve-yithen lecha": Opening words of a series of passages recited after the service at the end of Shabbath.

"Vi-yehi no'am": Opening words of Psalm 90, verse 17, usually recited after the *Amidah* on the expiry of Shabbath.

Ya'aleh Ve-yavo: An additional prayer inserted into *birkath ha-mazon* or *Shemoneh Esrei* on special days such as Yom Tov.

yahrzeit: Anniversary of death (often used specifically with relation to parents).

"Yiheyu le-ratzon": Sentence marking the end of *Shemoneh Esrei*. Literally, "May they find favor."

Yom Ha-kippurim: Yom Kippur.

"Yom ha-shishi. Va-yechulu ha-shamayim": First words said aloud when making Friday night *kiddush*.

Yom Kippur: Day of Atonement.

Yom Tov (plural ***Yamim Tovim***): The first and last days of Pesach and Sukkoth (that is to say, including Shemini Atzereth and Simchath Torah), Shavuoth and the two days of Rosh Hashana. The rules which apply to Yom Kippur are by and large those which apply to Shabbath and not those which apply to Yom Tov.

yom tov sheini shel galuyoth: The second and eighth days of Pesach, the second day of Sukkoth, the day after Shemini Atzereth (known as Simchath Torah) and the second day of Shavuoth, which have to be observed as Yom Tov by Jews living outside the boundaries of Eretz Yisrael.

"Yosheiv be-seither": Opening words of Psalm 91.

Zachor: Verses from Exodus 20:8-11, customarily included in the introduction to the Shabbath morning *kiddush*.

בית מדרש הלכה — מוריה ירושלים תובב"א

עם הספר

הצלחתו המופלאה של הספר "שמירת שבת כהלכתה" במהדורתו הראשונה, אשר הגיע כמעט לכל בית מישראל בכל קצוות תבל, עוררה את הצורך לעיון מחודש בכל ההלכות שהובאו בו במגמה להוציאו לאור מחדש, מוגה ומורחב, שיהא בו כדי למלא את יעודו ולהקל על הלימוד וההתמצאות בהלכות שבת, וכך נתבקשנו ע"י גדולי ירושלים וע"י המחבר הרב הגאון ר' יהושע י. נויבירט שליט"א, לעמוד לימינו ולהיות לו לעזר במשימה קדושה זו. הקדשנו לעבודה זו עמל מבורך של כמה שנים, שפרנו והרחבנו, והיום הזה זכינו בסייעתא דשמיא לברך על המוגמר ולהגיש את הספר מתוקן ומורחב לבית ישראל.

"בית מדרש הלכה—מוריה" נוסד בזמנו במגמה לפעול להפצת דבר ההלכה בעם, בארץ ובתפוצות. במסגרת תכניותיו להוציא לאור סדרת ספרי הלכה לעם במתכונת ספר זה, אשר תקיף את מרבית ההלכות אשר להן נצרך כל אדם מישראל.

ובפתחו של ספר זה נציב דבר תודה וברכה מעומקא דליבא לכל ידידינו העומדים לימיננו במסירות ובנאמנות, ישלם להם ה' כפועלם מאוצרו הטוב. ותודה מיוחדת למרן הגאון רבי שלמה זלמן אויערבאך שליט"א, שהנחה אותנו והאיר לנו לאורך כל הדרך, והיה לנו לעינים.

והננו תפילה לשוכן מרומים לראות ברכה בעמלנו, לבל תצא תקלה מתחת ידינו. וזכות שמירת השבת תעמוד לנו ולכל המסייעים בידינו לטוב להם ולנו כל הימים, ונזכה לראות במהרה בנחמת ציון וירושלים ובבנין בית מקדשנו ותפארתנו.

כסלו תשל"ט | **יעקב ווייל** | **אשר זלצמן**

The Distributors' Foreword to the second Hebrew edition

Beit Midrash Halachah—Moriah/Jerusalem

Upon Publication

The wonderful success of the book *Sh^{e}mirath Shabbath K^{e}hilchathah* in its first edition, which has reached almost every Jewish home in all corners of the globe, has aroused the need for a new examination of the *halachoth* it contains, with the aim of re-publishing it, checked and expanded, so that it should be able to fulfill its object and facilitate the learning of, and familiarity with, *hilchoth Shabbath*. Consequently, we have been requested by the great Torah scholars of Jerusalem and by the author, Harav Hagaon Rabbi Yehoshua Y. Neuwirth, long may he live, to stand at his right hand and be of assistance to him in this holy task. We have devoted to this work the blessed toil of several years, we have improved and expanded, and today we have been privileged, with the help of Heaven, to see completion of the labor and to present the book, corrected and expanded, to the House of Israel.

"Beit Midrash Halachah—Moriah" was originally founded with the object of working for the spread of the word of the Halachah among the people, in Israel and in the Diaspora. Within the framework of its program is the publication of a series of popular books on Halachah, along the lines of this book, which will comprehend most of the *halachoth* that are necessary for every Jewish individual.

At the beginning of this book we state our gratitude and blessings, from the bottom of our hearts, to all our friends who stand at our side with devotion and faithfulness. May Hashem pay them according to their deeds from His goodly treasure-house. Special thanks are due to Maran Hagaon Rabbi Shlomo Zalman Auerbach, long may he live, who has guided us and lit our way and has been our "eyes."

We pray to Him Who resides on high that we may see blessings from our toil and that no faults may result from our work. May the merit of the observance of the Shabbath always stand us and all those who help us in good stead and may we deserve soon to see the consolation of Zion and Jerusalem and the building of our Temple of holiness and glory.

Kislev 5739 | *Yaakov Weil* | *Asher Saltzman*

Translation of the Distributors' Foreword to the second Hebrew edition